CONGRATULAZIONI, SIGNOR BARZINI

Molte grazie for your spectacular full-length portrait of Italy. Where above all the show's the thing. Where even clocks and speedometers are made to lie for one's happiness. And *grazie, grazie, grazie* for that wicked analysis of the fatal charm that intoxicates 20,000,000 tourists a year. And finally, *grazie* for revealing a thousand intimate things about the dark forces at work behind the seductive face and body the whole world loves. *Che magnifico libro!*

THE ITALIANS
by Luigi Barzini

"A literary triumph . . . In all the centuries that writers have sought to explain the Italian people, none up to now really has succeeded."

NEWSWEEK

Turn page for more rave reviews.

D0828135

"THE
MOST ILLUMINATING
BOOK ABOUT
THE ITALIANS
I HAVE
YET ENCOUNTERED."

HARPER'S

"Brilliant . . . Should be bought and read by everyone who is making a trip to Italy; and for everyone who is permanently homesick for that charming and exasperating land, it is a solace. It covers an enormous and delightful variety of topics."

BOOK-OF-THE-MONTH CLUB NEWS

"The most illuminating book about the Italians I have yet encountered; it explains things about the Italian character and behavior which have been puzzling and infuriating me for the last twenty years, and does it all with the wit, brio and charm which distinguish everything Barzini writes."

HARPER'S

"Altogether wonderfully readable. Luigi Barzini paints a full-length portrait of his countrymen that is at once grave and witty, cynical and compassionate, somber and glittering, scholarly and stimulating."

CHICAGO TRIBUNE

"One of the truest, most perceptive, most revealing national portraits to appear in years . . . I am convinced that Luigi Barzini's book is destined to remain the standard work on his countrymen for years to come."

SATURDAY REVIEW SYNDICATE

The Italians

LUIGI BARZINI

BANTAM BOOKS
TORONTO · NEW YORK · LONDON

*This low-priced Bantam Book
has been completely reset in a type face
designed for easy reading, and was printed
from new plates. It contains the complete
text of the original hard-cover edition.*
NOT ONE WORD HAS BEEN OMITTED

THE ITALIANS

*A Bantam Book / published by arrangement with
Atheneum Publishers*

ACKNOWLEDGMENTS

PERMISSION *to quote is gratefully acknowledged to the following:*
Faber and Faber Ltd., *for J. R. Hale's* England and the Italian
Renaissance; *MacGibbon and Kee Ltd. and Monthly Review
Press, for Danilo Dolci's* Waste; *Laurence Pollinger Ltd., the
Estate of the late Mrs. Frieda Lawrence, and The Viking Press,
Inc., for* The Collected Letters of D. H. Lawrence; *Martin Secker
and Warburg Ltd., for Norman Douglas'* Siren Land; *and
Thames and Hudson Ltd., for Paolo Monelli's* Mussolini.

The maps on pages 362–367 were drawn by Joan Emerson.

PRINTING HISTORY
Atheneum edition published August 1964

2nd printing..September 1964	6th printing....October 1964
3rd printing..September 1964	7th printing....October 1964
4th printing....October 1964	8th printing..November 1964
5th printing....October 1964	9th printing..November 1964

10th printing...January 1965
One chapter published in HARPER'S *August 1964*
Book-of-the-Month Club edition published February 1965
Bantam edition published September 1965

All rights reserved.
Copyright © 1964 by Luigi Barzini.
*No part of this book may be reproduced in any
form, by mimeograph or any other means, without permission
in writing from the publisher. For information address:*
Atheneum Publishers, 162 East 38th Street, New York, N.Y. 10016.

Published simultaneously in the United States and Canada.

*Bantam Books are published by Bantam Books, Inc, a subsidiary
of Grosset & Dunlap, Inc. Its trade-mark, consisting of the words
"Bantam Books" and the portrayal of a bantam, is registered in the
United States Patent Office and in other countries. Marca Registrada.
Bantam Books, Inc., 271 Madison Avenue, New York, N. Y. 10016.*

PRINTED IN THE UNITED STATES OF AMERICA

Contents

Foreword

*Past things shed light on future ones; the world was
always of a kind; what is and will be was at some
other time; the same things come back, but under
different names and colours; not everybody recognizes them, but only he who is wise and considers
them diligently.*

FRANCESCO GUICCIARDINI

*Is there any other country in Europe where the
character of the people seems to have been so little
affected by political and technological change?*

W. H. AUDEN
(in the introduction to Goethe's *Italian Journey*)

THIS BOOK does not pretend to be a scientific treatise.
It is no more ambitious nor accurate than the opening chapters of a leisurely nineteenth-century novel in
which the author described at length the country in
which his story would unfold, the historical moment, and
the people themselves. The reader of this book, having
read, can go to Italy and supply his own novel, with
whatever live characters he meets on the spot. He will
have learned more or less what to expect. Italy is still a
country of limitless opportunities. It offers stage settings
for all kinds of adventures, licit or illicit loves, the study
of art, the experience of pathos, the weaving of intrigues.
It can be gay, tragic, mad, pastoral, archaic, modern, or
simply *dolce*.

I have tried to set down only the most distinguishing
features, following the technique of the honest portrait
painter, who puts on canvas those traits which make the
sitter the person he is and not another. The sitter happens
to be my country, and I have felt at times like the man
who does that most exacting of all things, the 'Portrait of
the Artist's Mother.' The Mother, in this case, is notoriously distinguished. Her past is glorious, her achievements
are dazzling, her traditions noble, her fame awe-inspiring,

ix

and her charm irresistible. I have known her and admired her for a long time. I love her dearly.

As I grew older, however (like many sons of famous mothers), I became disenchanted with some of her habits, shocked by some of her secret vices, repelled by her corruption, depravity and shamelessness and hurt when I discovered that she was not, after all, the shining paragon I believed her to be when I was young. Still, I could have no other mother. I could not stop loving her. When I was writing this book, I did not want to hurt her feelings, I did not want to be unnecessarily cruel, I did not want to forget her good points; but, at the same time, I tried hard not to flatter her, not to be seduced by her magical charms or misled by my own sentiments. I was determined to do the most honest job of portraiture I possibly could.

*

This book was difficult to compile. It is notoriously easier to write about things and people one does not really know very well. One has fewer doubts. But to write about one's own country was a tortured enterprise. I knew too much. I saw too many trees. I sometimes could prove one thing or its contrary, with equal ease. I was embarrassed by the exceptions. I questioned every idea and watched every word. In my younger days sentimental patriotism was the fashion. In my anxiety to correct such prejudices, was I too eager to demolish sound and durable notions? I was afraid to be too conservative and, at almost the same time, too ready to follow new intellectual fashions, the rage among contemporary intelligentsia, to embrace seductive new theories which might be obsolete before the book appeared in print.

One of the sources of confusion was the absurd discrepancy between the quantity and dazzling array of the inhabitants' achievements through many centuries and the mediocre quality of their national history. Italians have impressively filled Europe and most of the world with the fame of their larger-than-life-size famous men. Italian architects and masons built part of the Kremlin in Moscow and the Winter Palace in Leningrad; Italian artists have embellished the Capitol in Washington. They have strewn churches, princely palaces, and stately villas all over Catholic Europe, especially in Vienna, Madrid, Prague, and Warsaw; their influence on architecture was felt almost everywhere else, exterior architecture, to be sure, designed to impress and please the onlooker more than to serve strictly practical purposes. They have filled South America with ornate and rhetorical monuments to the local heroes.

Italy's smaller contributions to everyday life are so numerous as to go unnoticed. There would be no pistols but for the city of Pistoia; no *savon* in France but for the city of Savona; no faience anywhere but for the city of Faenza; no millinery but for the city of Milan; no blue jeans but for the city of Genoa, *Gênes,* where the blue cotton cloth was first produced, and no Genoa jibs; no Neapolitan ice cream, no Roman candles, no Venetian blinds, no Bologna sausages, no Parmesan cheese, no Leghorn hens. Italians have discovered America for the Americans; taught poetry, statesmanship, and the ruses of trade to the English; military art to the Germans; cuisine to the French; acting and ballet dancing to the Russians; and music to everybody. If some day this world of ours should be turned into a cloud of radioactive dust in space, it will be by nuclear contrivances developed with the decisive aid of Italian scientists.[1]

[1] The list of the famous Italians is awe-inspiring. It is well to record them here, as they will scarcely be mentioned in the rest of the book written with the presumption that the reader is well acquainted with them. Here are some of the main ones: the saints: Saint Francis, Santa Catarina da Siena, San Bernardino da Siena, San Luigi Gonzaga, Saint Thomas of Aquino. The sinners: the Borgia family (Spanish but acclimatized), Cellini, Caravaggio, Cagliostro, Casanova. The political thinkers: Dante Alighieri, King Frederick of Hohenstaufen of the two Sicilies (born in Italy, the inventor of the modern state, the 'state as a work of art'), Lorenzo de Medici (inventor of the 'balance of power'), Machiavelli, Guicciardini, Mazzini, Cavour. The military leaders: Giovanni dalle Bande Nere, Raimondo Montecuccoli (who led Austrian armies), Napoleon, Garibaldi. The admirals: Andrea Doria, Mocenigo, Morosini, Bragadin, Caracciolo. The scientists: Galileo Galilei, Leonardo da Vinci, Volta, Marconi, Fermi. The navigators: Columbus, Vespucci, the Cabots. The thinkers: Saint Thomas of Aquino, Campanella, Croce, Vico. The poets: Dante Alighieri, Boccaccio, Petrarch, Leopardi, Manzoni. The sculptors: Verrocchio, Donatello, Ghiberti, della Robbia, Cellini, Michelangelo, Bernini. The painters: Giotto, Botticelli, Fra Angelico, Leonardo da Vinci, Piero de la Francesca, Perugino, Michelangelo, Raphael, Titian, Tintoretto, Tiepolo, Modigliani. The musicians: Palestrina, Pergolesi, Monteverdi, Vivaldi, Rossini, Verdi, Bellini, Donizetti, Puccini, Toscanini. These are, of course, the names of first magnitude. The second and third category could easily fill a small city's telephone book.

There is no denying that all her geniuses made Italy great, one Italy, at least, the spiritual country, the land of culture, art, and ideas, of which only her best sons can be considered full citizens, as well as the distinguished foreigners who at all times felt themselves at home in it. Oddly enough, these great men did not make another Italy great, the concrete country to be found in almanacs and history books, the real Italy of past wars, invasions, treaties, political upheavals. In fact, it can be stated that many of these mental giants exercised little or no influence whatever.

Italians always loved a good entertainer who could stir their emotions and divert them from themselves; they were always delighted by a talented painter, musician, sculptor, architect, actor, dancer, as long as he did not engage their higher faculties. They respected and admired great scientists, especially if their discoveries and theories were abstract and incomprehensible. They endured and feared a forceful leader, but they always thoroughly enjoyed his fall. As a rule, however, most of them ignored, neglected, opposed, or derided disarmed prophets, philosophers, political and religious reformers, preachers, revolutionary scientists who proposed new and upsetting theories, men of outstanding stature in all fields.

It is true that in other countries great men have also occasionally been persecuted and put to death. Nowhere else, however, has this happened with the same discrimination, regularity, and determination. The majority of heroes in other civilized countries were allowed to live and flourish, to contribute to the power, prestige, and greatness of their native lands. They were, as a rule, not considered crackpots, deviations from the norm, but shining examples, impersonations of the national ideal, average men magnified, who indicated the path to follow. Italy instinctively neutralized all the men who tried to foist moral greatness on their countrymen. Nicolò Machiavelli was kept away from important affairs; Giambatista Vico, the father of modern thought, lived in a garret in extreme poverty; Galileo Galilei was persecuted for his ideas; Dante Alighieri, Giuseppe Mazzini, and many others went into exile. Some, like Tomaso Campanella, spent most of their lives in dungeons. A few of the worthiest were killed amidst the rejoicing of the populace, burned at the stake like Giordano Bruno and Savonarola, hanged like the patriots of the Neapolitan Republic in 1799, stabbed and stoned by the crowd like Cola di Rienzo.

✻

The coexistence of these two Italies presents some perplexing problems. Why did Italy, a land notoriously teeming with vigorous, wide-awake, and intelligent people, always behave so feebly? Why was she at all times so prone to catastrophes? She has been invaded, ravaged, sacked, humiliated in every century, and yet failed to do the simple things necessary to defend herself. This is not because the people shrank from fighting and dying. They have fought as many bloody wars as their more glorious neighbours, often under the foreigners' colours, and died in even greater numbers, the civilians massacred by foreign soldiery, the soldiers usually overwhelmed by superior enemies. A few wars they won, to be sure, but then mostly against other Italians and the Austrians. Perhaps the most difficult and deadly of all wars, a three and a half years' struggle in the snows of the Alps, they fought gallantly and, in spite of the Caporetto setback, finally won against not only the Austrians but the tougher Germans too. But most other wars they lost. It is absurd to think this is because the people are effete, cowardly, and too civilized. They are notoriously lively, brave, energetic. They can at times endure more and dare more than others.

Winning wars, after all, is the ultimate test not of the quality of single men but of their capacity to work together and accept common sacrifices. This is why the riddle which fascinated Machiavelli four hundred years ago is still endlessly debated among us: why did we not achieve national unity and a centralized government when other European nations did? Why did we not create a political régime of our own? It is possible to trace constant trends, too constant to be merely the result of coincidence, which have prevented Italians from coagulating into one nation: the rapid and enthusiastic acceptance of changing political fashions and of foreign conquerors which made all revolutions irresistible but superficial and all new régimes unstable; the art of living as if all laws were obnoxious obstacles to be overcome somehow, an art which made the best of laws ridiculously ineffective; the habit of treating whatever ruler was in command, local or foreign, as if he were corruptible, which soon transformed the most scrupulous and liberal ruler into a corrupt one; the certainty that the most inflexible government could, in the long run, be corroded from the inside. Most of the national governments we achieved at one time or another were therefore feeble, arbitrary, and inefficient, including our late totalitarian dictatorship, which was defined as a 'tyranny tempered by the complete disobedience of all laws.' Why were we so late in developing modern industries and free institutions? Why did we set about conquering colonies when all other imperial powers were on the point of losing theirs?

The qualities and defects which made us what we are fascinated foreigners, even though some of our characteristic habits were far from admirable. Travellers did not hide their contempt for us, since the end of the Quattrocento, to be exact. Yet they never stopped coming to Italy. Many begin to admire us today, listen to us, imitate us, and even envy us. Why? We are, of course, still great in the things which always came easy to us. We have improved, to be sure, in many fields, but not perceptibly in those which made us the object of foreigners' scorn in the past. We are not more honest, reliable, and lawabiding than we were, we are badly organized and badly governed. Our love life is still highly uncontrolled. Could it be that foreigners are no longer certain that their virtues are best? Or could it be that our vices have turned out to be desirable advantages in the modern world, qualities essential for survival? Did we or did the rest of the world change? And what exactly are the Italians' virtues and defects?

*

I know of no sure way to ascertain the Italian national character. There are no questionnaires for the dead. There are no authors to rely on. Descriptions of Italian habits and customs by Italian writers are very rare and seldom explicit. Few of them are trustworthy. Each writer had his own axe to grind, thesis to prove, course of action to propose, or spite to vent. Each wrote from his particular vantage point, the bias imposed by his century, class, province, education, political views, and luck in life.

There are, however, three or four small exceptions. There is an essay by Giacomo Leopardi, the nineteenth-century poet, a remarkable man who managed to be objective in spite of the fact that he was an aristocrat, a man of genius, and a hunchback, and lived in a dreary provincial town; there are also revealing passages in Nicolò Machiavelli and Francesco Guicciardini; a few essays on Italian literature as a key to national character by Francesco de Sanctis, a professor at the Zurich Polytechnic one hundred years ago, and little more. Leopardi himself had to admit: 'Italians do not write or think about their customs, as if they thought such studies were not useful to them.' There are, of course, thousands of books by foreigners, but, among them, there is only one real authority, Stendhal. John Addington Symonds is, in my opinion, the next best, although blinded at times by his stern moral views and his hatred for Popery. All others, for some reason, either love us or hate us too much. Their best books on Italy often contain brilliant flashes of intuition and some revealing truths, in a clutter of clichés, superficial appraisals, supine acceptance of preconceived notions, wrong information, and misspelled Italian words.

I have been helped, however, by the fact that, though Italians do not write about their national virtues and vices, they talk about them incessantly. The debate goes on in railway compartments, sidewalk cafés and newspaper offices, on the most fascinating subject of all, why are we the way we are? I have participated in such endless discussions all my life. I heard infinite theories and no conclusive answers. I discovered, however, that we all instinctively agree that some habits, traits, tendencies, and practices are unmistakably our own. We call them *cose all'italiana*. The words are sometimes pronounced proudly, sometimes with affection, irony, compassion, amusement, or resignation, very often with rage and contempt, but always with underlying sadness.

What exactly are these *cose all'italiana?* They are things in which we reflect ourselves as if in mirrors: a gratuitous *beau geste*, a shabby subterfuge, an ingenious deception, a brilliant improvisation, an intricate stratagem, a particular act of bravery or villainy, a spectacular performance. . . . Such *cose* may not be statistically prominent, but they can happen only in Italy. They should not be taken lightly. They are clues. By looking for them, following them, adding them together carefully, the good and the bad, I slowly began to see a pattern. They prove that there are things that come easy to us and others that are impossible. They clearly determined the course of past events. They will surely determine the future. Perhaps there is no escape for us. And it is this feeling of being trapped within the inflexible limits of national inclinations which gives Italian life, under the brilliant and vivacious surface, its fundamentally bitter, disenchanted, melancholic quality.

CHAPTER ONE

The Peaceful Invasion

ITALIANS are pleased and perplexed. Every year since the end of the war they have seen the number of foreign visitors to their country increase at an incredibly rapid rate. The phenomenon has now reached unprecedented, practically inexplicable, and almost alarming proportions. In the 1950s the tourists numbered eight, ten, twelve million yearly. A little later, only yesterday, they were fifteen, seventeen, nineteen million. They have now passed the twenty million mark, a proportion of more than one tourist to every two and a half Italians, and the total is still growing. It appears that, if circumstances remain favourable, the travellers will reach thirty million within a decade, and will eventually match and even surpass the number of native inhabitants in the peninsula. Nothing daunts foreigners. Nothing frightens them. Nothing stops them. They arrive in a steady stream, by all forms of transport and even on foot, by day and night, from the sea or via the Alps. What is but a small trickle in the winter months grows in the spring to the size of a stream, and, in April, May, and June, turns into a monsoon flood, breaking all dikes, covering everything in sight. It begins to recede in September. It never completely dries up.

People come from all parts of the five known continents, from the old established nations of Europe and America and from the newly founded ones in Africa and Asia. The largest number come from the north, the vast, democratic, bourgeois, industrial north of Europe and America. Some now also come from Russia, in some ways the most northerly of all countries, organized parties of sightseers, behaving like military units traversing a dangerous territory inhabited by treacherous natives, as diffident and self-contained as Xenophon's Greeks marching across Asia Minor. Russian tourists all wear the same box-like clothes, as new as those of provincial newly-weds, and ankle-length raincoats. They look well-fed, self-satisfied, and well-behaved. They appear . eager to acquire as much culture, in all its forms, as rapidly and cheaply as possible. They have a disturbing resemblance to the diligent German tourists at the beginning of the century, the solid subjects of William II.

There are many travellers who, in order to obey the urge that drives them south, abandon their own countries, whose delights and tourist attractions are being advertised and celebrated all over the world. What do they seek that is better than what they left behind? Not many Italians willingly travel abroad in any direction, north, south, east or west. They always feel more or less exiled and unhappy in alien lands, and honestly believe the attractions of their homeland to be most satisfying. They are the first victims of the famous charm of Italy, never satiated with her sights, climate, food, music and life. Familiarity never breeds contempt in them. Neapolitans, for instance, after many thousand years, still gaze with the same rapture on their native landscape, eat *spaghetti alle vongole* as if they had never tasted them before, and compose endless songs dedicated to the immortal beauty of their women and their bay. Those Italians who travel abroad are, as a rule, the privileged—Milanese industrialists and Roman princes who have adopted foreign ways, cabinet ministers, diplomats, newly-weds—and the disinherited who go looking for work. They are usually all equally homesick abroad; the rich and the poor look for *caffè espresso*, a good Italian restaurant, wherever they go, and sigh for the day of their return.

At the high tide of the tourist season, from early June till late September, visitors fill every empty space available in Italy. Trains, buses, boats, restaurants, churches, museums, Greek and Roman ruins, chapels, concert halls, historic landmarks, and famous belvederes, whence romantic landscapes (two stars in the guide books) can be admired, are packed to capacity with foreigners. One literally finds them everywhere, often at one's table, unknown friends of friends, sometimes even in one's bathroom and bed. They also fill a couple of universities, Perugia and Urbino, set aside for them, where they study the language, imbibe the Latin sun-drenched culture, make love, go swimming, and feed themselves cheaply on pasta, olive oil, tomatoes, and garlic. American universities sometimes hold summer sessions, in art appreciation, history of civilization, and related subjects, in some ancient villa on a hilltop near Florence with a view over the whole city, or a *palazzo* on the Grand Canal. Swedish and Norwegian workers' clubs have purchased wooded strips of deserted Italian coastline, where they have built their own club-houses and recreation centres.

There are sultry days in July and August when the cities, emptied by the natives, are almost completely taken over by the swarms of dusty and perspiring foreigners. During the siesta hour, when even the carriage horses sleep under their straw hats, the relentless tourists finally slow down. They bivouac everywhere. They recline on park benches, kerbstones, the stone brims of fountains, or ancient ruins. They place their heads over their crossed arms on café tables for a siesta among the empty bottles, the dirty napkins, and the recently purchased souvenirs. They then really look like a tired and bedraggled army after a fatiguing battle, who have occupied a city abandoned by their fleeing enemy. They have conquered. The place is theirs.

I am not talking here of the minority, the experienced foreigners who know why they come to Italy and what Italy is. Many have come here before and know their way about, others have never been here but somehow know what to do and what they want. They all avoid the heat and the dust, seldom visit the obvious places but, when they have to (the obvious places are often the most desirable), they go at convenient hours, when the crowd is away and the air is cool. They wear ordinary clothes, the same as everybody else. Some are in love with nature, others with art, culture, archaeology, or music. Some like meeting people and making friends, others discover little-known beaches or unexplored islands. There are those who make lengthy detours, to see some little-known masterpiece, and those who like food and wine and know the *trattorie* which only few natives and no foreigners have yet discovered. There are many who speak the language well. These easily disappear in the background. They do not interest me here.

There is nothing peculiar about them. I am talking of the vast majority of tourists, the millions driven by some unknown urge.

They are so punctual and numerous that their mass arrival, in the eyes of ordinary Italians, appears as irresistible as a natural event, as ineluctable as the seasonal return of migratory birds, swallows, quails, or partridges, driven by instinct; or as an anthropological phenomenon like the migration of nomadic tribes seeking green pastures for their herds. The impression is heightened by the fact that many of these travellers look somewhat alike to Italian eyes. They dress in garishly-coloured clothes, much as the members of the ancient barbaric hordes once did and as the Gipsies and Berbers still do. A great number of Germans, Scandinavians, Britons, and Dutch have pink skins, which the sun seldom succeeds in tanning a decent brown but reddens to the tender colour of *prosciutto* or covers with freckles. They perspire freely in the heat, under their nylon shirts. They wear barbaric sandals. They have dark glasses over their eyes and their heads are bare or covered with cheap straw hats on whose brims are printed or embroidered the names of cities, sanctuaries, beaches, islands, or other famous landmarks.

There is something mysteriously significant about the behaviour of many of them. A mild frenzy takes most of them and transforms them once across the Italian border. It resembles the irresistible excitement which captures some living organisms and makes them forget themselves and everything else, when, like salmon going upstream, they obey some deep and secret impulse of Nature; or the intoxication, the gentle and sweet delirium, which makes all honeymooners quietly mad everywhere in the world and honeymooners in Italy doubly so, both because they are on their honeymoon and they are in Italy. Like all newly-weds, in fact, many ordinary travellers seem deliciously drunk with new illusions and hopes. The sedate professional man, the sober shopkeeper, the loyal employee, the rigorous scientist, the stern educator, the tidy housewife, the bespectacled spinster, the innocent maiden, the virtuous wife, the resigned husband, all behave as they probably never dared to behave before and as they probably would not behave publicly in their native habitat.

More exactly, they behave as if they had shed the rôles assigned to them and the personalities bestowed on them by Nature, because such rôles and personalities had suddenly become repugnant and alien to them; or as if all the rules of the game of life had been changed or suspended. Some seem strangely deprived of all, or part of, their customary discernment, of their powers of control and discrimination, and of the scepticism, diffidence, prudence, suspicion, and fear necessary for survival in most countries. They get into all sorts of scrapes. They make friends with all sorts of people. They look at all things with indulgent and dewy eyes, apparently ready to love, admire, understand, or, at least, excuse and forgive almost everything, the good, the bad, the indifferent, the repugnant. They are often easily swindled, but many do not always mind if they are.

Most of these visitors from Northern Europe drink vast and indiscriminate quantities of wine. They drink, with equal good-natured enthusiasm, anything at all: costly vintages from famous vineyards, raw wines still smelling of sulphur and wooden staves, sweet and syrupy wines made for people who know little about such things. It is, for some curious reason, the first thing Germans and Austrians do, as soon as they cross the Brenner pass on their southward trip. They stop the car at one of the many wineshops which line both sides of the valley road, just beyond the border, as frequent as the petrol stations. Each *osteria* has a wrought-iron hanging sign, a terrace in the quivering shadow of a leafy pergola, checked tablecloths, waitresses in *dirndl*, everything designed in a tasteful fairy-story style, a style which is a mixture suited to the geographical and psychological spot, half German and half Italian, half Walt-Disney-Tyrolean and half *Il Trovatore or* Palio-di-Siena-Medieval. On the Brenner road, German and Austrian tourists behave as the Americans did under prohibition, when they rushed for the first bar across the Canadian border. There is no obvious explanation for this phenomenon. There is no scarcity of cheap wines, local or imported, in Germany and Austria. Perhaps these people are trying to quench not a physiological but a psychological thirst. This may be an unconscious magic rite; they drink wine as if it were a potion necessary to acquire a new personality, or they drink it as one drinks champagne on New Year's eve, on the stroke of midnight, to celebrate the crossing of a spiritual border and to inaugurate new hopes and a new life.

With equal indulgent enthusiasm, these summer visitors indiscriminately enjoy all kinds of doubtful attractions, things they probably shunned at home. They listen with the same breathless rapture and delighted smiles to the best opera singing in the world at Rome, Milan, or Spoleto, and to wheezy village bands, to impeccable Vivaldi quartets and to tinny dance orchestras. They eat the dainty food of famous chefs with the same pleasure with which they devour gross peasant dishes, mostly composed of garlic and tomatoes, or fisherman's octopus and shrimps, fried in heavily scented olive oil on a little deserted beach. They buy vast quantities of souvenirs to take home, smart things they cannot find elsewhere, cheap trinkets made in Japan, costly masterpieces, tawdry imitations.

Many try to speak Italian. A few creditably manage this in a short time. Others think they do. Things seem, of course, more significant and enjoyable when expressed in the native language. A spade is only a spade, a *Shaufel* but a *Shaufel*, but a *badile* cannot help being a pagan, Mediterranean, intoxicating *badile*. Some study lists of words phonetically spelled in handbooks. Some pick them up in random conversations. They also try hard to gesticulate wildly as they speak. They usually manage it in the style of amateur comedians playing an Italian character. They laugh loudly and converse with everybody, the people at the next table, travelling companions in the trains, the waiters, the beggars, the street singers, the cicerones, anybody in sight, with the same good-natured lack of discrimination with which dog lovers pet any dog.

The men, many men at least, those of all ages who have a natural bent for that sort of thing, admire and pursue Italian girls. It must be said that the Italian girls and young women, for reasons nobody knows for sure, are now more disturbingly beautiful than they have ever been in men's memory and perhaps in history, certainly more attractive and desirable than the models of the most famous statues and paintings in the past; Botticelli's

'Venus', Titian's 'Sacred Love', and Raphael's 'Fornarina' would not make anybody turn around in the streets. Italian girls are more attractive, and approachable, not only than in the past but also than in many other countries today. Feminine beauty, before the war, like prosperity, seemed to be a privilege reserved to rare local cases, but widespread among many foreigners, especially Americans. Smart Italian young men of the time anxiously awaited the disembarking of the American girls in the spring, well-shaped, well-washed, well-dressed, and incredibly long-legged, who always looked as if they really arrived from another and younger world. They were healthy, witty, free, and unafraid. Now our women, too, have somehow surprisingly acquired long and shapely legs; they have lovely and pert faces, overbearing breasts, thin waists, and harmonious behinds like double mandolins. But, more than this, they have simple, unembarrassed, friendly manners: they can say tender words with heart-breaking candour or, at times, prettily pronounce unprintable ones.

Foreign men, it is true, have always pursued women in Italy. The courtesans of Venice and Rome during the Renaissance were much appreciated. The Carnival season in Rome and Venice was for centuries merely an excuse to chase masked girls through the streets. Now the hunt has acquired a more determined, almost desperate, character. Many visitors are fascinated by the girls to the point that they often lose all powers of coherent speech and judgment: they are bewitched by the girls' sinuous and provocative walk, their inviting and hospitable ways, their smart clothes which often look as if they are sewn on them, or, more especially, their tiny two-piece bathing suits. Foreign men sometimes follow some specially provocative specimens in the street like hungry dogs following butcher boys delivering meat. Striking up an acquaintance is not always difficult, in a *caffè* or on the beach. Many men easily, too easily perhaps, find their way to some girl's bedroom. Some of these always fall deeply in love. They earnestly want to get married. They want to bring back a living souvenir of the land of sunshine and amiable ways to their gloomy countries. At the end of every summer, there are men who threaten suicide (a few kill themselves), for the love of a beautiful woman,

7

with whom they can scarcely talk, and who would possibly discredit them and make them unhappy if she became their wife.

Many foreign women think Italians are irresistible. The men too have a long-established reputation. Some are indeed irresistible. Their charm, skill, lack of scruples, and boldness are proverbial. Most of them always feel free as birds, even the married ones, or those who are deeply in love or engaged. Many are disposed to make love at the drop of a hat, anywhere, in a car, on a beach, behind a bush, on mountain summits, under water, or even in a bed, during the day or at night. They are not too difficult to please, young or mature men, fat or lean, peasants or city playboys with Maserati cars. They seldom waste time. All that a woman has to do in many cases is throw a meaningful glance across a café table, smile cryptically to herself, wave a hand, or put an unlighted cigarette in her mouth and look vainly for matches in her handbag. The better men take just a little more effort to attract. Naturally, some women, the ugly ducklings with flat chests, the middle-aged who still feel young at heart, the lonely and well-preserved grandmothers, all come to Italy with the hope of enriching their lives with the souvenir of an Italian love affair, a pagan romance under the stars, by the sea, accompanied by guitar music. There are even inexpensive camps, collections of straw huts on lonely beaches in Southern Italy and on the islands, founded by foreign institutions, dedicated to the meeting of neglected and impecunious foreign women and eager Italian men, whatever men the primitive surroundings provide, fishermen, sailors, soldiers, and unemployed farm-hands, with brilliantine in their curly hair and flashing smiles.

*

Many foreigners come back the next year. Some come back more and more often. Some stay a little longer, every time, and decide to live in Italy for a spell. A few eventually discover to their dismay they can no longer leave. They cannot help feeling there is something cowardly in the decision to live here for ever. Their sensations have been well described long ago by Nathaniel Hawthorne, a tourist in Rome, who watched himself gradually turning into an expatriate: 'The years, after all, have a kind of emptiness,' he wrote, 'when we spend too many of them on a foreign shore. We defer the reality of life, in such cases, until a future moment, when we shall again breathe our native air; but, by and by, there are no future moments; or, if we do return, we find that the native air has lost its invigorating quality, and that life has shifted its reality to the spot where we have deemed ourselves only temporary residents. Thus, between two countries, we have none at all, or only that little space of either in which we finally lay down our discontented bones.'

How many of these transplanted foreigners are there in Italy today? A few hundred thousand? One million? Nobody knows. Some are inconspicuous. They are the *Italianizanten*, in love with the place, those who have always been here and who know why they are here. A special mental disposition, an elective affinity makes them honorary Italians. A few of them are more Italian than the Italians themselves: they know more about the country, its literature, its manners, its past history, its hidden treasures, and its possibilities than many natives. Those who interest me are the others. The most conspicuous are naturally the rich, the millionaires from turbulent South American countries afraid of revolutions, the successful artists, the Hollywood actors, the dilettanti rentiers, the world-weary aesthetes with Swiss bank accounts.

They spend a season, a few years, or a lifetime in a house in Florence or in some stately Medicean villa over-looking the town, among priceless paintings and frescoed walls (like Queen Victoria, the Brownings, Mark Twain, Bernard Berenson, Aldous Huxley). They rent a *palazzo* on the Canal Grande, complete with gilded gondolas and liveried gondoliers (like Lord Byron, de Musset, Ruskin, Wagner, Barbara Hutton, and Cole Porter). Or, like a character out of a Henry James novel, they settle in the *piano nobile*, the noble first floor with the high-ceilinged rooms, in some Roman *palazzo*. Some prefer to inhabit quaint and dramatic houses, perched on hilltops, over-looking the sea or a lake (like Shelley at Lerici; Axel Munthe, Norman Douglas and Krupp von Bohlen in Capri; Gorki in Sorrento).

The rich come because, understandably, they want to

avoid paying heavy income tax at home, or have their fortunes riddled by death duties. Others want to go on living opulently, surrounded by servants, as the rich have always done, and as it will be possible to do in Italy for but a few years more. The *nouveaux riches* crave the reassurance of noble surroundings. All of them want a maximum of visible splendour with the minimum possible outlay of money. But there is something more. Many clearly want to withdraw from the rude turmoil of active life, to preserve and cherish a romantic illusion about themselves, their excellent taste, genius, beauty, and rank, which could be shattered by unkind confrontations in their own country. They pathetically want not to be contradicted by facts.

Then there are the poor expatriates. They greatly outnumber the rich, and they increase yearly. Many of them, as they were in past centuries, are artists, some are good artists, others are the struggling young, the old failures and the young hopefuls, the successful and those who will never amount to anything; they know it, and do not care. Italy suits them, a country in which one may work, decant one's own and other people's ideas, experiment, meet stimulating people and generally develop latent possibilities. There are all kinds: writers, painters, dancers, musicians, actors, sculptors, poets, or followers of new and as yet unnamed arts. Some are mere dabblers, dilettanti, people whose love for art is much greater than their modest capacities and talents, who somehow eke out a living in artistic surroundings, on the margin of the art world. For all these, Italy is the world's timeless refuge, the river bank on which to withdraw from the rapidly rushing stream.

The inartistic impecunious are perhaps more numerous than the artists. They are of all sorts. There are German war widows, decrepit French courtesans who live on the prizes of love games of a forgotten era, Indian Army colonels, pensioned Scandinavian school teachers, American grandparents who dislike Southern California, misfits, *déclassés*, divorcees of all nations, and all kinds of beachcombers. Many live in the big cities, where they often rent tiny furnished flats in decrepit houses or artists' studios. They avoid the busy industrial centres and the brazenly new and anonymous blocks of flats. They prefer Italy picturesque, poor, and decrepit. There is comfort in decay. Many also prefer the historic hill-towns, the villages perched on mountain tops, the tiny fishing ports along the coast, the rocky islands. Some of the delightful spots impecunious foreigners discovered in past generations, like Capri, Ischia, Ravello, Taormina, or Bordighera (where Edward Lear lived his last years and wrote his last limericks), have now become very famous, expensive, noisy, and overcrowded. But there are always others, new unspoiled ones.

The impecunious wear shabby but picturesque clothes, sometimes cook their own meals, sometimes board with peasants or fishermen, or eat in a cheap *pizzeria* or wine-shop for a few lire. Ordinary food is as good as in provincial France or as it once was in China. Most of these poor foreigners say they came to Italy mainly because the climate is milder and the money goes further than anywhere else. What they like, of course, is not only low prices and sunshine but a place where indigence looks like modest affluence by contrast with the surrounding poverty, where poverty can be worn with dignity, as it is not noticeable or embarrassing. Lack of wealth, in fact, is seldom the object of pity or contempt among ordinary Italians. It is considered the natural condition of man. Poverty is a private matter, like religion, politics, or other qualities, habits, and vices, not to be questioned. What these people look for, in other words, is the Italians' traditional indifference to other people's personal appearance and idiosyncrasies, poverty among them, and indifference which verges on indulgence and sometimes on encouragement.

The Italy of these foreigners, both rich and poor, is mainly an imaginary country, not entirely corresponding to the Italy of the Italians. The expatriates often do not really pay attention to, see clearly, or like the Italy of the Italians. Many know too few natives, to begin with, and see them too fuzzily to understand them and their problems. The poor foreigners mostly meet servants, hotel concierges, waiters, shopkeepers, an artisan or two, the postman, and sundry hangers-on. The rich also meet bright members of the local café society, the Italians who speak foreign languages, have travelled abroad, sometimes have foreign relatives, and drink whisky. Few ever know the great mass of the people. These foreigners treat natives kindly enough: many mistake the amused and indulgent manners with which the Italians treat them, which sometimes approach the condescension with which one treats children, for courtesy and sympathy.

The problems of contemporary Italy are too disturbing and too difficult to understand; local political events have always seemed mysterious and negligible. Before the war, many who disliked the Fascist régime nevertheless thought it was a harmless and picturesque buffoonery, 'good enough for the natives'. After the war, there were some who believed that a little Communism 'would do the Italians good'. Ezra Pound's ideas about Mussolini and his government, before and during the war, are perhaps the most illustrious example of this kind of utter but honest confusion. There is also a minority who heartily dislike the Italians. These think that the beautiful scenery, which is the stage setting of their own dream life, is incongruously cluttered up by millions of extras, men, women, boisterous children, and ruined by *vespas*, fluorescent lighting, noise, modern constructions, pretensions and complications of all kinds. The country most of these foreigners really inhabit is the tiny Italy of the expatriates, made up of a few celebrated quarters of the ancient cities, some towns, villages, famous landscapes, three or four islands, where they consort mostly with people like themselves.

Many find, at one point, like Hawthorne, that they can no longer leave this practically non-existent country. They can no longer face the harsher world where they came from, where they see things perhaps too clearly, and where every word in their familiar language has a precise meaning. They have become hopelessly addicted to the amiable and mild ways of Italy. Many also have nobody left to go back to. They cling to their little lair, the view of the sea from the hill, the view of the Coliseum from the window if you turn your neck far enough to the right, the view of the Grand Canal, the roofs of Florence, the decayed villas of Rapallo, a clutter of antiques they picked up during the years, and their set habits. Italy is filled with people growing old, who can no longer think of leaving, living alone, comforted by a cat or a dog, waited on by a servant, an honest person at times but often enough an unscrupulous maid who feeds her family with what she steals. A day comes when these old people grow ill and helpless, far from the familiar sights and sounds of their youth, self-exiled for reasons which have become dim in their memories, in an alien place which they never really saw as it is and quite understood. At the end, they wait for death, some of them still dressed in gaudy and youthful resort clothes, surrounded by foreign sights and people who have somehow become the necessary props and conventional supporting characters of the imaginary drama of their lives. Many die every year and are buried hurriedly in the corner of an Italian cemetery reserved for heathens or heretics; some bodies are shipped home to practically unknown and indifferent relatives. Many die without having really discovered why they chose to live the last years of their lives in Italy, of all places.

*

Many idle expatriates are not old but young. They do not seek a princely life of splendour at reduced rates, modest and easy comfort, or the slightly cowardly peace without competition and adverse criticism which Italy can afford. They do not want to nourish illusions about themselves, pursue unusual inclinations, or prepare themselves for a future of glory. Many of them are not weak and desperate but vigorous, hopeful, lively, and healthy. On late summer afternoons in Rome, when the sea breeze, or *ponentino*, cools the leaden air, these young foreigners of both sexes, uncombed, sun-burned, wearing crumpled cotton clothes and dusty sandals, the men sometimes looking strangely feminine and the girls strangely masculine, crowd the stairway of Trinità dei Monti on the Piazza di Spagna.

They lean against the old travertine stone balustrade, sit or lie on the steps, and wait. For what or for whom do they wait? Without knowing it, they occupy one of the spots where, in past times, one hundred years or so ago, other youths met, lazy artists' models waiting for a job. There, on the Spanish steps, sat holy monks with white beards, brigands, pilgrims with their scallop shells, and beautiful *contadine* in their costumes, prepared to pray at some painter's wayside shrine, off-duty bandits with conical hats and bushy beards, Holy Families appropriately grouped. There were theatrical assassins, Judases, Bacchuses, young Saint Johns, shepherds in cloaks of goatskin or buffalo hide, looking like antique satyrs, white-bearded Eternal Fathers, and fierce-eyed peasants from the hills. Without knowing it, these young foreigners also occupy one of the spots where, before the artists' models, thieves, murderers, and other desperate people, pursued by the Papal gendarmes, once found inviolable asylum. According to an ancient privilege, they could not be arrested as long as they did not stray from there.

The contemporary youths have an improbable appearance of make-believe like the models of old, and look, in their shabby and crumpled clothes, as if they, too, had run away from home and were seeking some sort of asylum. They also are left alone by the Italian authorities, to do and dress as they please, as if they were protected by some ancient privilege. From what unnamed and unknown modern crimes and horrors are these young foreigners fleeing? What mysterious emptiness in their souls is filled by merely standing on Italian soil?

CHAPTER TWO

The Eternal Pilgrimage

A<small>LL THIS IS</small>, of course, very old, so old it could be considered part of the very nature of things. Its beginnings go back to the dawn of time, to the days when Saturn, the father of all the gods, after being deposed and humiliated by his son Jupiter, fled from Olympus. He is said to have found refuge in Latium, the territory embracing the yet unfounded city of Rome, where he became king and ruled in the golden age. He, too, was a disillusioned refugee trying to forget misunderstanding, ingratitude, and defeat. Italy is still known in poetical jargon as *Saturnia tellus*, Saturn's land. *Saturnalia*, the week in December dedicated by the Romans to the expatriate god, the first of all their foreign guests, was, significantly enough, the feast when everything was permitted, all laws could be violated, and the world was turned upside down. Schools were closed, no war was declared or battles fought, poor men gave orders to the rich, slaves insulted their masters, thieves could not be molested, and the timid seduced haughty women.

Immortal and mortal foreigners, armed and unarmed, alone and in vast numbers, have sought a Saturnian interlude in Italy as far back as men can remember. The Barbarians came, in the declining days of the Roman empire, in great hordes, apparently driven by a desire for peace, stability, rich plunder, new pasture-lands, and, above all, by the pathetic and provincial hope of somehow acquiring the graces, accomplishments and respectability of decadent and effete Roman citizens, and to be taken for Romans. Northern travellers came to the Holy City even before being baptized, like the fair English youths Pope Gregory the Great once met in the forum, when he was still a simple priest. *Angeli non Angli*—they are Angels and not Angles—is the famous pun he made on that occasion.

Through the obscure centuries of the remote Middle Ages, pious travellers never stopped coming, following each other like ants along the decaying imperial roads, the Aurelian, Cassian, and Flaminian ways, on foot, on horse, on mule-back. All roads at that time truly led to Rome. Kings, lords, commoners, clerics, bishops, monks, saints, vagabonds, adventurers, bandits, knights, merchants, scholars, were all pilgrims to Rome. They all wanted, before they died, to behold the seat of the Universal Church and be blessed by the Pope himself, Christ's vicar on earth. Language was no barrier then. All Christians spoke Latin. They devotedly thronged famous basilicas and miraculous shrines, attended Pontifical functions, listened to world-renowned preachers, prayed to venerated images and sacred relics. They were not yet interested in the memory of ancient times, and no one bothered to gaze on the awe-inspiring ruins of imperial Rome. In fact, the more devout were horrified by what they believed to be the remnants of the works of Satan himself or the handicraft of damned souls. Were not the heathen gods but the disguises of the Devil?

Through the later Middle Ages German emperors and military leaders often came down at the head of their iron-clad armies. They came only incidentally to pray; above all they wanted to impress the Popes and the Italians with their power, to plunder and raze rebel Italian city-states, reward their loyal friends and allies, the Ghibellines, and destroy their enemies, the Guelphs. They could as easily have gone somewhere else. They could, for instance, have picked a quarrel with the Sultans of Turkey or the Grand Dukes of Muscovy, they could have pursued the Teutonic Knights into the Baltic, or followed Alexander's itinerary to the Indies, thus changing the whole history of Europe and the face of the world. Most of the time they preferred travelling south, as if attracted by a magnet, over the snowclad Alps, down the narrow and rocky peninsula, among treacherous and unpredictable people, who did not understand and like them, where the plunder was slim at best, because they, like all Germans, were fascinated by the name of Rome and all it still evoked, so fascinated that they called themselves 'Roman', not 'German' Emperors, and their emperor

Caesar, Kaiser. They felt that they could not legitimately rule unless crowned, like Charlemagne, by the Pope himself, in Saint Peter's, and in the name of a ghostly empire which had disappeared centuries before.

The emperors were also fascinated by other things, of which they were scarcely aware and which they seldom mentioned. Being solid northerners, they were attracted and repelled by all that which was to attract and repel so many northerners in future centuries; they liked the mild climate but feared it, as they liked but feared at the same time the Italians' elegant life, easy pleasures, adaptable morals, intricate reasoning, wines, women, the harmonious landscapes, the feeling of being immersed in history and ennobled by it. They were thrilled by one of the pleasurable sensations Italy always gives visitors from the north, that of feeling morally superior to the natives. The emperors carried away all kinds of souvenirs, the clever workmanship of the contemptible Italians. All conquerors did that down the centuries. Napoleon stole the bronze horses from Saint Mark's which the Venetians themselves had taken from Constantinople; Hitler and Goering filled railway trains with the best *objets d'art* they could find.

The crusaders, too, travelled through Italy on their way to the Holy Land. It was the shortest route. On their way back, Richard Coeur de Lion spent an uncomfortable winter in Messina; Guy de Montfort hacked the young Henry of Cornwall to pieces as he clung to the altar in the cathedral of Viterbo. Traders later came to buy the goods which arrived from the Orient, spices, precious stones, silks, and Arab stallions. Others, still later, during the Renaissance, came to learn the newest arts of bankers and merchants, how to handle and multiply money, keep books, exchange and speculate on merchandise and gold. Chaucer came twice on business as a diplomatic representative for his king, and went perhaps as far as Padua, on his own, to meet Petrarch. Bishops came to confer with the Pope; theologians, jurists and scholars to study with famous masters at Bologna; horsemen to perfect the art of schooling horses. Knights drifted south in search of adventure. Sir John Hawkwood is perhaps the most illustrious of them all, the early prototype of a different kind of nordic expatriate, who flourished in Italy through the centuries and is still flourishing, the professional man or businessman who makes a fortune because he is reputed by the Italians to be duller and more honest than his local competitors, their own compatriots.

Sir John Hawkwood arrived in 1360. When the peace of Bretigny interrupted the King of England's hundred years war against the French, he found himself unemployed. He had been at Crécy; had gained the favour of the Black Prince; had enjoyed the luxury of inhabiting splendid castles commandeered with all their inhabitants, servants, kitchen and cellar; had known the love of beautiful and accomplished continental ladies. Like all wartime temporary gentlemen, he was reluctant to put on civilian clothes; he disliked the prospect of returning to his native Essex and his trade as a tanner. He felt somehow attracted by Italy. He crossed the Alps over the Mont Cenis Pass, at the head of a group of mounted men who called themselves the White Company. They were quickly snapped up by local princes to fight their little wars. From this unimportant beginning, the White Company went on to fight for wealthier and more powerful patrons. Their leader was celebrated as Giovanni Acuto, by no means because of his mental sharpness, but because the word *acuto* was the nearest the Italians could come to the original pronunciation of his name.

He was tall, ruddy-faced, blue-eyed, slow of movement, taciturn and brave. He was believed to be a sound man, not too expensive, who tried to carry the day as best he could, without unnecessarily losing too many of his own soldiers, but reckless with the lives of his enemies, a man who never betrayed his masters, one of the few reliable and reasonably honest *condottieri* of his times. The Pope gratefully made him Signore de Bagnacavallo, or Lord Horsebath, a good title for an English cavalry man. He successfully ended his career as permanent commander-in-chief of the army of the Republic of Florence, a solid and enviable position.

Accurate descriptions of some of his battles have come down to us. They are well conceived and diligently executed military operations. His English soldiers served him well. They fought better than their opponents, also because they fought with a youthful desire to win which was then considered unusual and dangerous. The White Company were the first well-drilled, uniformly armed, disciplined, spit-and-polish troops ever seen in Italy. Contemporary astonishment is described by Filippo Villani, the chronicler:

'They were all young men and therefore hot and impetuous, quick with weapons, careless of safety. In the ranks they were quick and obedient to their superiors, yet in camp, by reason of their unrestrained dash and boldness, they sometimes lay scattered about in disorderly and incautious fashion. . . . Each had one or two pages and some had more. When they took off their armour, the pages set to polishing them, so that when they appeared in battle their arms seemed like mirrors and were therefore so much more terrible . . . Bound and compact, with lowered lances, they marched with slow steps towards the enemy, making a terrible outcry, and their ranks could hardly be pried apart.' Villani concluded sadly: 'They succeeded rather by the cowardice of our people than because of their own valour.'

The Florentines, Machiavelli pointed out, trusted Sir John and did not fear he would enslave them, as many *condottieri* had enslaved other free cities, because they did not believe the Englishman was astute enough to do it. He lost in the end. He had stipulated with the Republic that after his death an equestrian statue should be erected to him in the Duomo. He died in 1394. The expensive statue was reduced to a cheap fresco, very high over the door, and so badly done that Paolo Uccello had to repaint it years later.

⁜

Travel to Italy, in the old days, was, for the solitary private man, always risky and adventurous. Many found their unmarked graves at the side of the road. Death, however, when met on a pilgrimage to Rome, was recognized as meritorious by the Church, sufficiently so to alleviate a lengthy punishment in Purgatory. The mortal dangers began on the Alps. The paths were often erased by sudden snow storms or avalanches. Even the guides lost their way at such times. Some of them were unreliable rascals, who robbed and killed their clients. Dead bodies of travellers always cropped up in the spring, as soon as the high snow had thawed. Avalanches were the next great menace. To find and restore their buried victims, hospices were built along the main passes by religious orders. The monks kept stores of wood and food, good beds, warm blankets, brandy, and sturdy dogs, who could sniff out a live body several feet under the snow. Avalanches were so much part of the necessary emotions of the trip that until just before the Alps were finally pierced by railway tunnels sporting Englishmen would stop in suitable spots and fire pistols at the mountains, in order to disturb the still air and cause the snow to slide down from the high peaks. A mountain crossing without avalanches was thought to be as insipid as a sea crossing without sighting a whale or meeting a hurricane. Bold travellers were sometimes buried alive with their luggage and companions as the result of their own successful scientific experiments.

Bandits awaited travellers along the roads in the plains. Those who were not ambushed, robbed and killed on the way, were sometimes murdered in their beds by greedy innkeepers. It was prudent therefore to appear as poor as possible, in order to avoid arousing the rapacity of all sorts of people, including travelling companions. All kinds of subterfuges were employed. Vespasiano da Bisticci, the Florentine Renaissance bookseller, relates one of them: 'William Gray (later Bishop of Ely) was a student in Cologne. . . . When the time came for him to leave for Italy it was necessary to order his departure with the greatest caution, because he was reputed to be a very rich man, and one who might pay a high ransom; moreover, there were many in Cologne who were on the watch for his leaving, designing to attack him somewhere on the road. Also the road was full of minor barons, and travel was dangerous. From the reports which were brought to him he decided on a plan by which he might travel in safety. It seemed best to him that he should feign illness, and should call the physician to visit him every day and then unknown, with a single companion, should steal away in the garb of Irish pilgrims. Meantime he arranged that the physician for the next seven or eight days should visit his apartment regularly.'

Then there were local wars to avoid. Travellers always tried to gather information about who was fighting whom on the road ahead. It was a tricky business. News was seldom available and not very reliable when it was. Italian politics were always puzzling to foreigners, as they still are today. Wars broke out unexpectedly. Fronts shifted without warning. Allies became enemies overnight and vice versa. Travellers often found themselves suddenly in the middle of a battle and disappeared without leaving a trace, dead among the dead. Others met a victorious army rejoicing, the soldiers drunk with looted wines, or met a defeated army mourning its losses, the soldiers just as drunk on looted wines. Both were equally dangerous. The lucky or obstinate foreigners who did not die or disappear on their way sometimes met their doom when peacefully resting and enjoying the sights and pleasures of some Italian city. Large numbers of them, down the centuries, were murdered by ruffians, killed in duels by gallant gentlemen they had picked a quarrel with in an inn, or died of some unknown disease. At best they were jailed for being without means of support after being robbed.

A sea voyage was often even more dangerous than the overland trip. At times, storms wrecked the ships, or crews mutinied in order to loot the cargo and to rob the passengers. Not infrequently the ship was boarded by Muslim pirates and all hands were taken prisoner. It is impossible to say how many good Christians on their way to Rome spent the rest of their lives as oarsmen on Turkish galleys or obscure slaves in North Africa and the Orient. Their families never knew they were still alive and prayed for their souls. Only a few, now and again, managed to send word of their survival and be ransomed. They sometimes returned to freedom and their families as broken old men, unwanted by wives who had forgotten them and found other consolations. As late as 1805, sailing from Genoa to Sicily, the ship on which Washington Irving was travelling was seized by a privateer and boarded by a crew of desperadoes with rusty cutlasses, pistols and stilettoes. This incident understandably predisposed the American author to see bandits everywhere when he set foot on Italian soil. The pirates released him after seeing the letters of introduction to distinguished people the young traveller bore on his person. Pirates were not snobs, easily impressed by high rank and famous names, but rightly feared the revenge of the well-connected more than that of the unknown poor.

Travellers who chanced on an uneventful journey had other troubles to worry about. Beds were rare, in Italy, as everywhere else in Europe. They were usually stinking and crawling with insects. Bed sheets and blankets were dirty with the sweat and grime of all the people who had slept in them for months or years. Guests of both sexes and of all ages and degrees of cleanliness were usually forced to share the few beds available. There were no glass panes in the windows until late in the seventeenth century. (Montaigne continually grumbled in his diary about the cold draughts in his rooms, which the wooden shutters were usually inadequate to keep out.) The food was bad, often nauseating. As late as the eighteenth century, Smollet still complained that 'the inns are enough to turn the stomach of a muleteer' and 'the victuals . . . cooked in such a manner to fill a Hottentot with loathing'.

There was as yet no way to heat houses in the winter except for an occasional fireplace and brazier. Murray's *Guide for Southern Italy*, in its 1858 edition, still found no great improvement in the little provincial inns since the Middle Ages. It says: 'In the remote districts the *osterie* are as bad and comfortless as they were in the time of Montaigne, except that the wooden shutters have mostly been replaced by glazed panels. The traveller . . . who can make his own omelette, and instruct the *padrona* how to cook a dish of ham and eggs, will find these commodities in the highland villages, where even milk and butter are rarely to be met with.' Local cookery must indeed have been repulsive, if English amateur efforts were to be preferred to it.

To hire a horse, a carriage, a servant, a guide or a room was a tricky, difficult and sometimes even dangerous business. This continued to be true until very recently. Murray's 1858 Guide still advised travellers to make 'their bargains with the landlords on their first arrival. All foreigners make it a rule to adopt this precaution, and for this reason they not only pay about a third less than

English travellers, but escape the annoyances and delays of disputed bills.' Another nineteenth-century guide-book for northern travellers warned: 'Whenever you engage your place [on a coach], always stipulate for a front seat, and by all means reduce your bargain to writing, and then have it witnessed by a public notary.' Recourse to local police, in remote as well as more recent times, was a risky business. Often the policeman preferred to help the dishonest countryman with whom he had to live the rest of his life, rather than the guileless foreign traveller, whom he would never see again.

Nevertheless travellers never stopped coming. In spite of inconveniences and contretemps, draughty windows, cold rooms, rutted roads, verminous beds, poisoned food, robbers, bandits, and murderers, braving tornadoes, avalanches, earthquakes, wars, marauding armies, Muslim pirates and obscure diseases, more people certainly undertook the trip to Italy during the Middle Ages than to any other country. Religion was undoubtedly the strongest single moving force. Pilgrims came to Rome at all times and seasons but they especially thronged the Eternal City during holy years, at fifty-year intervals, when blessings and indulgences were particularly plentiful. An average of two hundred thousand of them were present every day during the first holy year of all, when the practice was inaugurated, in 1300. During the second holy year, in 1350, Matteo Villani, the chronicler, estimated that a total of one million two hundred thousand people entered the city's gates. Those are impressive figures, even if inaccurate. Many were probably Italians from nearby provinces, but a substantial number arrived from farther afield and from abroad.

Rome offered unique advantages to the believer. And yet the journey was not strictly necessary. There were other ways to gain Paradise, cheaper, quicker, and safer ways to wash away sins and achieve a state of grace. One could travel to a nearby sanctuary, anywhere in Europe, pray to the same God, obtain the same or almost the same indulgences and be back safe and sound in a matter of days. Or one could do even better: one could lead a godly life, practise the principal virtues, and achieve sanctity without leaving one's village. The trip to Rome was, if not superfluous, not indispensable from a religious point of view.

The quest for eternal salvation, indeed, gradually ceased to be the only justification for the trip. Visits to shrines, sanctuaries, miraculous images; attendance on Pontifical ceremonies and rare festivals; the absolution of specially grievous sins, or the liberation from sacred ties, the privileges which could only be obtained in Rome, never ceased to be among the principal reasons for many people leaving home. They still are. But their paramount importance slowly faded as the years advanced. More and more holy buildings began to be visited not only for the reverence and edification they inspired but also for their profane new elegance, the wealth and perfection of the decorations and the works of art adorning them. Pictures of the Madonna were increasingly admired not only for the renown of their supernatural powers but also for the excellence of their workmanship, the fame of their painters and the beauty of the models.

For the first time in centuries art became something to be appreciated for itself. In fact, religious art was only partially dedicated to the praise of God and His Saints. It was also dedicated to the praise of man, woman, beauty, the pleasures of life on earth, colours, sunshine and hard work. Behind the shoulders of the Virgin or some bearded Father of the Church, the Italian painter joyfully depicted a miniature town or a well-cultivated landscape, so small that only from a very short distance could all the details be discerned, the walls, towers, churches, streets, the artisans at work, the ships in the river, the ladies on the balcony, the children, the barking dogs, the gaily coloured clothes drying in the sun, the ploughman and the hunter. Many nordic travellers who lagged behind the times apprehensively thought they detected a slight odour of sulphur and brimstone about art and life in Italy, the 'odour of unsanctity'. They still detect it today. The country was in fact slowly acquiring that pagan, slightly irreverent, sacrilegious reputation which it was never to lose. The reputation did not repel visitors. In fact, the danger of losing their souls attracted as many of them as the hope of gaining everlasting salvation.

*

It is not surprising that more people came during the impious Renaissance than during the pious and severe Middle Ages. Italy had become the richest, most dazzling, cultured, irreverent, and intelligent nation of Christendom. Italians had transformed the universe, or, at least, man's ideas about the universe and his place in it. They had started a revolution which was to transform Europe during the following centuries. Humanism, or the study of man's achievements, involved the acceptance of man's immense capacities for good and evil, his virtues, foibles, his nature split between the animal and the angelic. Within a few years, amazing new inventions, discoveries, and techniques were made or adopted. New activities produced incalculable and unimaginable wealth, which, in a chain-reaction, sparked off other new activities, producing yet more wealth; geographic discoveries, daring scientific experiments, ingenious commercial and banking devices, and intellectual speculations all managed to multiply the available financial resources. Wealth also encouraged the refinement of manners, supported schools and academies, made life easy for poets, painters, sculptors and scholars.

There was a thrilling darker side, too. John Addington Symonds wrote: 'Beneath the surface of brilliant social culture, lurked gross appetites and savage passions, unrestrained by medieval piety, untutored by modern experience. Italian society exhibited an almost unexampled spectacle of literary, artistic, and courtly refinements, crossed by brutalities of lust, treason, poisonings, assassinations, violence. . . . Steeped in pagan learning, emulous of the manners of the ancients, used to think and feel in harmony with Ovid and Theocritus, and at the same time rendered cynical by corruption, the educated classes lost their grasp upon morality. Political honesty ceased almost to have a name in Italy. The Christian virtues were scorned by the foremost authors and the ablest thinkers of the time, while the antique virtues were themes for rhetoric rather than moving-springs of conduct.' Symonds knew the matter well. He was rich, in bad health, and was ordered by his doctors to spend a long time in Italy where he studied the Renaissance in order to write his monumental work. His private life was a struggle between the principles of the Anglican Church and his own 'gross appetites and savage passions', above all his inclination for the love of effeminate young men. He died in Rome, alone, in a hotel room, and was buried in the Cimitero degli Inglesi, not far from Keats. Few people were at his funeral. Among them, his young Swiss valet was seen weeping copiously.

Nothing of any importance could be undertaken anywhere in Europe at the time without first travelling to see what the Italians had lately been up to and what they had recently discovered or invented. Painters, architects, sculptors, as well as shipwrights, doctors, theologians, engineers, astronomers, jurists, mathematicians, scientists, and scholars arrived uninterruptedly from abroad. English literati came to learn how to write poetry in their own tongue and to copy new models of composition. Merchants plied back and forth among market towns, leading caravans of loaded mules on better and slightly safer roads than before. Note was taken of all the novelties seen, of the new fashions. Thomas Coryat wrote, in 1611, describing to his uncouth countrymen one of the things that had dazzled foreigners for more than a century: 'I observed a custom . . . that is not used in any other country that I saw in my travels. The Italians and also most strangers that are commorant in Italy do always at their meals use a little fork when they cut the meat. . . . The forks are for the most part made of iron or steel, and some of silver, but those are used only by gentlemen. The reason for this is that the Italian cannot by any means endure to have his dish touched with fingers, seeing all men's fingers are not alike clean.'

A few inns had by then become more hospitable. The best was in Urbino, built by the duke, perhaps the first comfortable hotel of the modern age. An anonymous Frenchman described it in 1578: 'It is the best and most extensive in Italy. There are forty bed rooms, all on the same floor, and all opening on the same long gallery. There are also five or six dining rooms, which are very beautifully decorated as if the building were a nobleman's castle.' Everybody came, who was anybody. The universities were filled with foreign young men. Some studied hard, and all had a rollicking time. Wealthy and powerful northern fathers sent their sons to Italy to acquire some knowledge of Italian, which was the language suited for diplomacy, court life, love, and intrigue; they were following the Emperor Charles V's maxim: 'I speak Spanish to God, Italian to women, French to men, and German to my horse.'

Young men were sent to learn one thing above all, how to become perfect gentlemen. The model had been invented and perfected by the Italians of the time, and it was widely copied. 'To be a gentleman,' wrote Symonds, who was one, 'meant to be a man acquainted with the rudiments at least of scholarship, refined in diction, capable of corresponding or of speaking in choice phrases, open to the beauty of the arts, intelligently interested in archaeology, taking for his models of conduct the great men of antiquity rather than the saints of the Church. He was also expected to prove himself adept in physical exercises and in the courteous observances which survived from chivalry. To this point the awakened intelligence of the Renaissance, instructed by humanism, polished by the fine arts, expanding in genial conditions of diffused wealth, had brought the Italians at a period when the rest of Europe was comparatively barbarous.'

*

Even after the Reformation had swallowed many great countries in the north of Europe, travellers did not stop coming. They found Italy once more transformed. Within a few fateful decades, at the end of the fifteenth century and the beginning of the sixteenth, ruin, defeat, and ignominy had followed pride and splendour. Foreign armies had fought on her territory, the proudest cities had been occupied and sacked. The Catholics still came to be comforted and strengthened by the old faith. Many still came to study. Most foreigners no longer expected to be edified and instructed, and to bask in the brilliance of a flourishing civilization. They came to look upon things in Italy with amusement, condescension, or contempt, to gape with horror at the abyss in which the country had sunk. She was for many of them the devil's own country. As J. R. Hale, the English historian, puts it:

'Enforced by geographers' opinion of the effect of the climate on character, the idea that the quick, crafty Meridional peoples were milking the slower stolid Septentrionals had become a plaintive obsession. Machiavelli was judged by an age that expected to find subtlety and cunning in the hot South. And it became a fixed idea, in spite of travellers' accounts of the general sobriety of Italian customs, that the Italians did not even turn the money they cozened out of the Northerners to good use, but squandered it on fantastic dress and curious vice. The *Inglese Italianato* mocked God in foreign-bought ribbons that led straight from the tailor to the bawdy house and the pit. The traveller who had mastered the arts of dressing and making a bow would probably bring back as well the arts of atheism, whoring, poisoning, and sodomy.'

A great part of Roger Ascham's famous treatise *The Schoolmaster,* published in London in 1570, was dedicated to warning guileless youth against the irresistible seductions of Italy. If a young English gentleman incautiously went there without a prudent tutor, he pointed out, he would inevitably fall into 'popery and filthy living'. 'Some Circes shall make him, of a plain English man, a right Italian.' Thomas Palmer, writing in 1606 an essay on foreign travel, pointed out that, as far as Italy was concerned, it was safest not to go there at all. Italians would teach the honest northerner such arts as stiletto stabbing, poisoning, intriguing, and treason. In John Webster's two plays, Italian characters poison their victims in four ways: by the leaves of a book, the lips of a portrait, the pommel of a saddle, and an anointed helmet. The number of Italian traitors, cheats, pimps, spies, and murderers in nordic literature becomes practically endless from that time on. The parade starts with the many cowardly and crafty killers in the Elizabethan theatre, continues in the Gothic novels, nineteenth-century historical romances and the more recent inventions of Baron Corvo, and practically reaches our days with the Mediterranean murderers and Sicilian gangsters of contemporary detective stories and films.

Nevertheless such sinister warnings did not discourage many travellers. Either they wanted to witness or experience such debased debauchery personally, in order to develop the proper horror for it, or they thought that Italy, even in her degenerate condition, could still enrich their culture and exercise their intelligence. Young Englishmen dared everything to follow Richard Lassels' advice, 'to season their minds with the gravity of that nation which has civilized the whole world and taught mankind what it is to be a man'. Italy was irresistible. Milton himself was troubled by doubts on the real reasons why he had undertaken the trip to a country a virtuous and religious man should have carefully shunned. 'Why Italy?' he asked himself. 'Was it that, like another Saturn, I might find a hiding place in Latium?' He answered his own questions a little defiantly, as if afraid of not being believed: 'No. It was because I well knew, and have since experienced, that Italy, instead of being, as you suppose, the general receptacle of vice, was the seat of civilization and the hospitable domicile of every species of erudition.'

*

The eighteenth century saw no diminution in the number of travellers. Their justification, however, for making the journey was a novel one: they wanted to improve themselves and thought that nothing could beat a trip to Italy for that purpose. A lengthy visit to Venice, Florence, Rome, and Naples was believed to be an indispensable part of a man's education, the necessary completion to his studies, a real *voyage philosophique*. After the Holy Italy of the Middle Ages, the Unholy Italy of the Renaissance, the Italy of Ostentation, Corruption, and Superstition, we had the Italy Propaedeutic, or the World's Finishing School. It was also, in a way, a status symbol. Doctor Johnson, for instance, believed that 'A man who has not been in Italy is always conscious of an inferiority, for his not having seen what is expected a man to see.' Like most other people at the time, the Doctor thought that a man acquired moral stature and authority if he saw not what he liked or what interested him but what public opinion commanded him to look at.

The man who stayed at home might not have been inferior to the returned traveller, but nevertheless felt so in himself and was thought so by others. To be rid of this inferiority, he had only to transport himself and his things many miles, follow a recommended itinerary, roughly equivalent to the one which pilgrims to Rome had followed from time immemorial, post letters home with well-known post marks, fill a diary with wonderful experiences, strange encounters, natural catastrophes and, like Boswell, the description of the comely women who had consented to sleep with him. Many felt so superior on their return that they were practically unrecognizable. Italy had gone to their heads. They affected Italian mannerisms, carelessly dropped Italian words in their conversation, sang arias from the operas, wore ornate clothes, and sighed for the only country where they could be happy.

The best results could be obtained by following the routine, as prescribed by the guide-books, and omitting none of the sights indicated. Those were always the same. The century spurned all the products of the Middle Ages and the early Renaissance as ugly and worthless. It liked only a limited number of relatively recent *palazzi*, statues, churches, and paintings. The style of the late sixteenth century was considered supreme. Raphael and Guido Reni, the 'divine Guido', were the greatest painters who ever lived. Together with art, the traveller was not to miss the natural beauties, the famous Italian views described by poets and painters: the snowclad Alps, the lakes, the fever-infested Campagna, the gulf of Naples. 'Of all the countries in the world,' enthusiastically wrote an English author at the time, 'Italy is the most adorned by the arts. Of all the countries in the world, she has the least need of them.'

After Art and Nature, a traveller had to dedicate his devoted attention to the remnants of ancient buildings, those very ruins which were ignored by all until a few years before. Education, Self-Improvement and Culture could be imbibed only by direct contact with what was left of the monuments of Roman antiquity, the historical landmarks and the scenes of mighty events. Some of these spots were of doubtful authenticity, to be sure, some of the sights mere tourists' traps, such as the alleged ruins of Cicero's villa at Formia, Virgil's tomb at Naples, or Nero's tomb on the Cassian way near Rome. Still, they obtained their effect on people who thought they were genuine. Many were undoubtedly authentic. The traveller would stand watching the celebrated landscapes, the shores of Lake Trasimeno and the plains of Cannae (where the

Carthaginians defeated the Romans), the Appian way or Mount Soracte (described by Horace), the beach near Gaeta (where Cicero was knifed to death), Capri (where Tiberius spent his abominable last years), and fill them with the ghosts of his imagination. People stood in silence, their heads bared, on the spot in the Forum where Caesar had been slain, or in the Coliseum where so many Christians had been devoured by lions.

The concentration on art, nature, and the remnants of Roman antiquity was perhaps one of the reasons why the rest of the Italian scene seemed to interest travellers so little. They watched the contemporary life of the people with the absent-minded detachment with which Egyptologists consider the mores of fellahin in Egyptian villages. The people crowding the streets in their colourful costumes were seldom described and then only as if they were not really alive, but quaint wooden puppets in a vast *Presepio*. Stendhal shrewdly noted the Englishman's unawareness of contemporary Italians: 'Many English people,' he wrote, 'limit themselves to reading, in every spot, the descriptions left by Latin poets, and go away cursing the Italian manners, which they only know from mixing with the lowest classes.' Most of them concentrated on the masonry. In a letter written to his mother, Gray wrote from Rome as if the city was deserted: 'As high as my expectation was raised, I confess the magnificence of this city infinitely surpassed it. You cannot pass along a street but you have views of some palace, or church, or square, or fountain, the most picturesque and noble one can imagine.' Only the memory of antiquity could add interest to a contemporary scene. A traveller wrote: 'See where that wretch is strumming his mandoline. It is perhaps the place where a virtuous father killed his child rather than see her handmaid to an Emperor's lust!'

Guide-books provided scanty information on contemporary Italy but furnished many ready-made extracts from Greek and Latin authors, in the original texts, suitable for each historical spot. Translations of the Greek fragments were provided in footnotes but not of the Latin quotations. Gentlemen were supposed to read fifty or sixty hexameters or a massive chunk of archaic prose without help. Diaries and letters home, to north Europe,

England, the Russias and America, were filled with ample quotations cribbed from the guide-books and great thoughts, some of them original, which the sights of Italy always inspired in pensive travellers. The stones and walls, overgrown with wild figs and fennel, made them meditate on the frailty of human greatness and inspired some to higher achievements. 'It was at Rome, on the 15th of October, 1764, as I sat musing amidst the ruins of the Capitol,' remembered Gibbon, 'while the barefooted friars were singing vespers in the Temple of Jupiter, that the idea of writing the decline and fall of the city first started to my mind.' Only dead Italians were deemed worthy of attention, the longer dead the more worthy.

The eighteenth-century Italy of foreigners' desires, the country of dead languages, dead Italians, and mute stones, was never so dissimilar from the Italians' Italy. Of course, travellers could not help also seeing the gay, profane and corrupt reality, which was all around them. It did not disturb them. It shocked a few. It seduced many. They enjoyed it. They had a wonderful time. But few would admit they had come principally for the fun of mingling with such contemptible people. Theirs was an earnest quest for knowledge, only rarely interrupted by inevitable interludes of immorality. It is interesting to note that this fictitious Italy, the Pedagogic Museum, was perhaps the invention of one man more than any other. It was he who authoritatively closed visitors' eyes to what was really going on around them and concentrated their attention exclusively on the worthy things which would inspire them with great thoughts. He was, naturally enough, an antiquarian, a Puritan, a converted Protestant, born in Prussia. He worked in Rome all his life, busy with his intellectual construction; he never confessed even to himself that he lived there also because life was enchanting, morals laxer, the wine cheap and people paid little attention to the private weaknesses of solitary erudite gentlemen. It is instructive to review his life, as he is the prototype of many expatriates who followed in his footsteps.

His name was Johann Joachim Winckelmann. He came to Rome as a young man in 1735, was converted to the Catholic faith, was befriended and encouraged in his artistic studies and his religious zeal by friendly high prelates.

He was quickly promoted to the rank of abate. An abate wore priestly clothes, which made him inconspicuous in Rome, but was not technically a priest. Cardinal Alessandro Albani, a wealthy amateur who filled one of Rome's most sumptuous villas with priceless masterpieces, became his patron. As the cardinal was practically blind, he especially needed the young Prussian's help for the purchase of paintings; statuary he could touch. The Villa Albani is still intact today as the cardinal and the abate furnished it.

Winckelmann felt a profound repulsion for the southern sensuality which was rampant everywhere and tainted everything. He preferred the frigid chastity of Roman statuary, the harmonious but cold lines of classical architecture. To test his powers of resistance to earthly temptations, he used to lie in bed for hours with Margherita Guazzi, the shapely Italian wife and model of his friend and countryman, the painter Raphael Mengs. The abate and the lady, naked in the heat of the Roman summer, carried on elevated conversations on cultural subjects. The experiment, while meritorious, was not as difficult as it sounds. Winckelmann preferred, to the knobby and often unharmonious prettiness of women, the smooth beauty of adolescent boys, so much nearer to the perfection of his beloved Greek statuary. This preference of his only rarely made his life difficult. It usually went unnoticed. Once, though, his tender friendship with a winsome *castrato*, the popular singer of *soprano* rôles in operas, provoked a scandal. The Vatican, where Winckelmann was employed as librarian, disapproved. His patrons were jealous. The liaison had to be dropped.

The Prussian abate was the first man to have seen, measured, studied, caressed, catalogued, and classified so many statues from Greek to Roman times, practically all those to be found in Italy, which were then almost all that existed. He was among the first to travel as far south as Paestum to visit the ruins of the Greek temples, facing the sea on the lonely beach, amidst wild roses and herds of water buffaloes, where no man dared to linger after nightfall for fear of the marsh fever. He was also a constant visitor to Pompeii, which had been discovered a few years before and was still mostly concealed under its

blanket of ashes; and to Herculaneum, which was then a
dark underground city, to be reached through tunnels
dug under the houses of Portici, and to be seen by torch-
light.

His theories about beauty and art were finally com-
pressed in his *Geschichte der Kunst des Altertums,* which
marked a revolutionary break from past ways of thinking.
It was the birth of a new discipline, the history of art.
Either his enthusiasm and scholarly pursuits mysteriously
changed the taste of his contemporaries, or Providence
had put him on this earth with his own unique preferences
and novel ideas at the proper time. The fact is that he
originated the Neo-Classic style. Greek sculptors, according to him, had reached ultimate perfection, beyond which
man could not go. They had observed and reproduced
idealized human forms at their best, Praxiteles by meas-
uring his many exquisite concubines, Pheidias by visiting
the gymnasium daily, where he studied naked athletes at
their games. In the art of painting, curiously enough, the
abate, like most of his contemporaries, thought only
Raphael had approached the Greek sculptors' perfection.
Of all later painters, only one German could be compared
to the Italian master, his friend Mengs. (Mengs was, of
course, not very good: just a diligent and scrupulous
eclectic, who, as he himself explained, mixed 'the expression of Raphael, the colour of Titian, and Correggio's
wonderful harmony of light and shade'. Winckelmann
compared him to the bee, who 'culled various sweets from
different flowers and made its honey sweeter'.)

Perfection, for the Prussian abate, was stately and harmonious form, almost anonymous in its regularity, un-
marred by individual traits, frigid, devoid of emotions and
showing no explicit sexual characteristics. The fact that
human beings in the streets of Rome often happened to
be more beautiful than the insipid Greek models or
Raphael's vapid Madonnas did not disturb him. He believed living people's beauty to be only apparent. They
were beautiful in a wrong and meaningless way, therefore not beautiful at all, only agreeable, pleasing, pretty.
Nobody knows how far his revolution towards Greek
canons in art and love would have gone had he lived
longer. He died, a victim of his proclivities, at the rela-

tively early age of fifty-one in a dingy hotel in Trieste, on his way back from Vienna, where he had been received with great honours by the Empress Maria Theresa and his friend and patron, Prince Kaunitz, the Imperial Chancellor. He was murdered by a scullery boy of eighteen, whom he had invited to his rooms to show some ancient medals of rare design. The boy was later found roaming the countryside with the medals in his pockets. He was tried and hanged.

What Winckelmann had done in the realm of visible art, another man probably did in literature, a good friend of his and Mengs', Johann Wolfgang von Goethe. The poet liked pretty girls all his life. At seventy-three he complained to his friend Chancellor Müller: 'I don't feel well perhaps because I am at present in love with nobody and nobody is in love with me.' In his Italian journey he left no petticoat unturned. He arrived in Rome in 1786, when thirty-seven years of age. Winckelmann's books were his guide through classical Rome, taught him to overlook all the Baroque and contemporary buildings, illustrated the principal statues in private and public collections and fanned in him an ardent love for ancient ideals.

All Winckelmann's teachings strengthened Goethe's vague conceptions, which he had come to Italy to perfect. The trip had been on his mind for years. He had dreamed of it as a break from his past, a symbol of revolt against the nordic romanticism of *Sturm und Drang*. Once in Rome he translated the calm, passionless, Olympic aesthetics of the converted abate into literary, poetical, philosophical, and moral rules. The contact with the unruly country somehow taught him that everything in art and life was to be the result of control, a show of man's mastery over accident, excesses, storms of passion and chaos. 'Certainly,' he wrote, 'people out of Rome have no idea how one is schooled here. One has to be born again, so to speak, and one learns to look back upon one's old ideas as upon the shores of childhood.' Everything, he discovered, must have a law and a form. *Gestalt* (Form) and *Gesetz* (Law) were to curb Nature. *Gesetzlichkeit*, or the essence of legality, was to reign supreme. All forms of disorder, whether created by God, Michelangelo, or Shakespeare, were equally to be deplored and avoided.

All this Pheidian harmony, frigidity, restraint, and immobility, all this nordic love for legality, all this contempt for disorderly passion and the untrammelled expression of human weakness and instincts, Goethe and many other foreigners after him sought in Italy, of all places, the very same country where the natives obeyed exactly opposite rules; they gave themselves to the unconfined sway of passions, the uncurbed expression of instincts, *joie de vivre*, freedom from dull duties and stupid laws, indulgence for all human frailties. Which was Italy? Goethe himself must have had doubts. In one of his first days in the country he asked an innkeeper at Torbole, near Venice, where the bathroom or *cabinet d'aisance* was. The man vaguely pointed to the courtyard. Where exactly in the courtyard, the German poet insisted. The answer was, '*Ma da per tutto, dove vuole.*' ('Wherever you wish, anywhere.') This was no *Gesetzlichkeit;* this was scarcely an example of man's mastery over the disorder of Nature.

We now suspect that travellers of the late eighteenth century and early nineteenth century unconsciously came to enjoy the interludes of fun among the live Italians more than the lessons of ancient history among the dead Italians. Few foreigners would admit it to themselves. Very few tried to analyse the nature of the particular pleasures they found in watching the Italians live their noisy lives, mingling with them, and accepting their lax rules and indulgent habits. This sense of liberation which they experienced was, first of all, a distinct physical sensation they felt the moment they passed the frontier, a muted excitement, a quickening of the senses. What its cause was nobody dared explore.

Stendhal thought it was principally due to the climate. He describes the feeling: 'It is certain that the climate alone produces a nervous and inexplicable effect on arriving foreigners. When the army corps commanded by Marbot, after having crossed Germany, in 1806, arrived in the Venetian Friuli, a new spirit seemed to overtake those fifteen thousand Frenchmen; the harshest characters appeared to have become sweet; everybody was happy; in everybody's soul spring had taken the place of winter.' It is to be noted that the climate of Friuli, the northernmost part of the Venetian provinces, differs but little from the climate of the southernmost German provinces across the border, which the French soldiers of Marbot had just left.

Shelly more or less agreed. Meteorology was his explanation too. 'No sooner had we arrived in Italy,' he wrote, a few days after crossing the Alps, 'than the loveliness of the earth and the serenity of the sky made the greatest difference in my sensations.' He later confirmed his first impression in the preface to *Prometheus Unbound*: 'The bright blue sky of Rome and the effect of the vigorous awakening Spring in that divinest climate and the new life with which it drenches the spirit even to intoxication were the inspiration of this drama.' It was perhaps natural that visitors from the gloomy north should be more impressed by sunshine and (as Goethe put it) 'moonlight brighter than daylight' and more easily inclined to think that the light and climate prepared the mind for the enjoyment of many other enchantments. Heinrich Heine once in Italy reminded himself: 'Our German summers are but winters painted green. . . . The very sun wears a flannel coat. . . . In this yellow flannel sunshine fruits do not ripen. . . . Confidentially speaking, the only ripe fruits we have at home are cooked apples.' Russian poets thought of little else. Apollon Nicolayevich Maykov wrote enthusiastically: 'Under that fiery sun, in the roar of a waterfall, inebriated you said to me: "Here we can die together, the two of us".' Gogol noted: 'Who has been in Italy can forget all other regions. Who has been in Heaven does not desire the Earth. Europe compared to Italy is like a gloomy day compared to a day of sunshine.' 'I was born here,' he proclaimed to his friend the poet Zhukovsky. 'Russia, Saint Petersburg, the snows, the nasty people . . . all this has been but a bad dream.'

Germans and Scandinavians naturally dedicated to the sunshine and warm weather of Italy a flood of second-rate poems and a few of their best. But it is curious to note that travellers from milder climates, the French, for instance, who were certainly not starved for a sight of the sun, were also impressed. Chateaubriand wrote to his friend de Fontanes, in a famous letter: 'You have undoubtedly admired, in Claude Lorrain's paintings, that light which seems ideal and more beautiful than in nature?

Well, it is the light of Rome!' Alfred de Musset wrote of the 'enchanted sky, so pure that a sigh rises to God more freely than in any other place on earth.'

Whether caused by the sun, the climate, the sky, the light, or by anything else, the sensation was a powerful, almost an overwhelming one, often strong enough to change a man's life. Macaulay incredulously recorded: 'I had no idea that an excitement so powerful and agreeable still untried by me was to be found in the world.' Henry Adams remembered later: 'Italy was mostly an emotion and the emotion naturally centred in Rome. Rome, before 1870, was seductive beyond resistance. The month of May 1860 was divine. . . . The shadows breathed and glowed, full of soft forms felt by lost senses.' 'Rome is beautiful, wonderful, magical,' Ibsen wrote in 1866, 'I feel an extraordinary capacity for work and the strength of a giant-killer. I kept struggling with my poem, "Brand", for a whole year, before it took shape clearly. Then one day I strolled into Saint Peter's and there I suddenly saw in strong and clear outlines the form for what I had to say.' On his first day in Rome, in 1869, Henry James confided to his diary: 'At last, for the first time, I live.'

Under the influence of this sensation, Italy did not seem to many a land like all others, created by the same God, but a masterpiece made by Him in a moment of special felicity, each mountain shaped, each lake designed, each tree planted, and each shoreline etched in the exact way to achieve some particular poetic or pictorial effect. Anatole France suspected the existence of another God, a better artist. 'But look, darling,' he wrote in *Le Lys Rouge,* 'look again. What you see is unique.' (What the characters were seeing was Florence from the Fiesole heights.) 'Nowhere else is Nature so subtle, elegant and fine. The God who made the hills of Florence was an artist. How could it be possible that this violet hill of San Miniato, so purely and firmly designed, be by the author of the Mont Blanc?'

There was also in many voyagers the Proustian temptation to compare everything to a figment of the artistic imagination. They sought to attribute every landscape to the appropriate painter, every real person to the writer who could have invented him, every sensation of the soul to the poet best suited to express it. This was more than a literary trick. Faced with the Italian scene many experienced in the past and still experience today the heightened emotions which only great art usually imparts. It is as if Italy were not only the home of Art but an immense and elaborate *objet d'art* herself. 'Thou art the garden of the world,' wrote Byron, signifying by 'garden' something planned and carefully laid out by an artist with the precise intention of delighting and amusing human beings.

'There is only one country in Europe,' noted Alexander Herzen, the Russian revolutionary millionaire, 'which can give you a feeling of peace, which can make you shed tears not of disgust and disillusionment but of delight, and that country is Italy.' The words are obviously more suited to describe the impression produced by great music, tragedies or immortal poetry than those produced by a foreign country. The 'feeling of peace' and the shedding of delighted tears are among the unmistakable signs of Aristotle's catharsis at work. Many were tempted to think that the translation of everyday scenes into durable masterpieces was far easier in Italy, where the distance between nature and art was shorter, and more easily bridged than in less picturesque and more familiar parts of the world. Wordsworth regretted having discovered this quarry of practically ready-made poems too late for profit: 'My mind has been enriched by innumerable images,' he deplored, 'which I could have turned to account in verse and vivified by feelings; earlier in life they would have answered noble purposes in a way that now are little likely to do.'

The delusion that art and nature were one in Italy irritated Byron, who had been one of the principal victims of it, when he sensed it in others. Thomas Moore tells this revealing story of his meeting his great friend in Venice after a long separation. 'We stood out on the balcony, in order that, before daylight had quite gone, I might have some glimpse of the scene which the Grand Canal presented. Happening to remark, in looking at the clouds, which were still bright in the west, that "what had struck me in Italian sunsets was that peculiar rosy hue"—I had hardly pronounced the word "rosy" when

Lord Byron, clapping his hand on my mouth, said with a laugh, "Come, damn it, Tom, don't be poetical".'

✻

The rapture and delight were not pure. They were often mingled with other sensations, different, disturbing and alarming. There was, for example, the bitter pleasure of pitying and despising the Italians. They were oppressed by corrupt, inept, and avaricious tyrannies. Still, one could not help thinking that they deserved them. They seemed to lack all the virtues which had made other people great. They were dirty. Their clothes, houses, and streets were dirty. They were incredibly noisy. They were deceitful. They were improvident. Their misfortunes seemed to be the natural result of their lack of virtue and their lack of virtue, in turn, the inevitable consequence of their misfortunes. There was no easy way to break the vicious circle. Ruskin, who loved Italy with more passion than he loved his wife, wrote to his father in 1845: 'Take them all in all, I detest the Italians beyond measure. . . . They are Yorick's skull with the worms in it, nothing of humanity left but the smell.' In *Mornings in Florence,* he complained: 'In the streets . . . you never hear a word uttered but in rage, either just ready to burst, or for the most part explosive instantly: everybody—man, woman, or child—roaring out their incontinent, foolish, infinitely contemptible opinions and wills, on every smallest occasion, with flashing eyes, hoarsely shrieking and wasted voices—insane hope to drag by vociferation whatever they would have, out of man and God. . . . Look at the talkers in the streets of Florence, being essentially unable to talk, they try to make lips of their fingers. How they poke, wave, flourish, point, jerk, shake fingers and fist at their antagonist . . . impersuasive and ineffectual as the shaking of tree branches in the wind.'

Walter Savage Landor, who spent long years in Florence, wanted little to do with the same Florentines. 'I visit none of them,' he declared firmly. 'I admit none of them within my doors. I never go to the gaming house, to the coffee house, to the theatre, to the palace, to the church.' The natives so irritated him, in fact, that he sometimes kicked and punched labourers who worked in his house and garden, and once threw out his landlord, who had come to his rooms with his hat on. D. H. Lawrence, many years later, felt an overwhelming repugnance for 'city' Italians, the bourgeoisie. 'Then I got to beastly Milan,' he wrote to Lady Cynthia Asquith, on October 23, 1913, 'with its imitation hedgehog of a cathedral and its hateful city Italians, all socks and purple cravats and hats over the ear.' A few days later he added: 'I loathe and detest the Italians. They never argue, they just get hold of parrot phrases, shove up their shoulders and put their heads to one side, and flap their hands. And what is an honest man to do with them?'

And many asked themselves whether Italy was really as beautiful and pleasant as one's misled senses led them to believe, or whether it was a mirage. Was one the victim of some devilish trick done with emotional mirrors? The puzzled defencelessness of a moral gentleman from the north was eloquently described by Hawthorne:

'When we have once known Rome, and left her where she lies, like a long decaying corpse, retaining a trace of the noble shape it was, but with accumulated dust and fungous growth overspreading all its more admirable features—left her in utter weariness, no doubt, of her narrow, crooked intricate streets so uncomfortably paved with little squares of lava that to tread over them is a penitential pilgrimage, so indescribably ugly, moreover, so alley-like, into which the sun never falls, and where a chill wind forces its deadly breath into our lungs—left her, tired of the sight of those immense seven-storied, yellow-washed hovels, or call them palaces, where all that is dreary in domestic life seems magnified and multiplied, and weary of climbing those staircases, which ascend from a ground floor of cookshops, cobblers' stalls, stables, and regiments of cavalry, to a middle region of princes, cardinals, and ambassadors, and an upper tier of artists, just beneath the unattainable sky—left her, worn out with shivering at the cheerless and smoking fireside by day, and feasting with our own substance the ravenous little populace of a Roman bed at night—left her, sick at heart of Italian trickery which has uprooted whatever faith in man's integrity had endured till now, and sick at stomach of sour bread, sour wine, rancid butter, and bad cookery, needlessly bestowed on evil meats—left her, disgusted with the pretence of holiness and the reality of nastiness, each equally omnipresent—left her, half lifeless from the languid atmosphere, the vital principle of which has been used up long ago, or corrupted by myriads of slaughters—left her, crushed down in spirit with the desolation of her ruin, and the hopelessness of her future—left her, in short, hating her with all our might, and adding our individual curse to the infinite anathema which her old crimes have unmistakably brought down—when we have left Rome in such a mood as this we are astonished by the discovery, by and by, that our heart strings have mysteriously attached themselves to the Eternal City and are drawing us thitherward again, as if it were more familiar, more intimately our home, than even the spot where we were born.'

That Italy possessed a magic power to weaken foreigners' resistance to temptation was discovered by many, who were also shocked to realize, like Hawthorne, that the process did not displease them or fill them with remorse, but gave them a feeling of resignation, acceptance, and repose. Bulwer Lytton, for instance, wrote: 'Clime that yet enervates with a soft Circean spell, that moulds us insensibly, mysteriously, into harmony with itself. . . . Whoever visits thee seems to leave earth and its harsh cares behind—to enter the Ivory Gate into the Land of Dreams.' Art, too, the ennobling pursuit of the more earnest visitors, the main purpose of the pilgrimage for many of them, inevitably also came under suspicion. Was it not sometimes merely an excuse for profligacy and loose living? Hawthorne was tortured by this doubt. 'Every young sculptor,' he wrote in *The Marble Faun*, 'seems to think that he must give the world some specimen of indecorous womanhood, and call it Eve, Venus, a Nymph, or any name that may apologize for a lack of decent clothing. I am weary even more than I am ashamed of seeing such things. Nowadays people are as good as born in their clothes and there is practically not a nude human being in existence. An artist, therefore, cannot sculpture nudity with a pure heart, if only he is compelled to steal guilty glimpses at hired models. The marble inevitably loses its chastity under such circumstances.'

CHAPTER THREE

The Fatal Charm of Italy

W HAT THEN is this fatal spell of Italy? Sometimes it seems almost possible to measure it exactly—just as the scientist measures the refraction of light in water by observing the angle at which a stick appears bent in it—by comparing the difference between a traveller's enraptured recollection of his personal experiences and more sober and objective accounts of the same events. Take, for instance, Lord Byron's letters home on his first stay in Venice. What wonderful women he described, all young, all in love with him, all incredibly beautiful, some *ragazze* from humble families, some proud *contesse*. They all visited his famous apartment in the Palazzo Mocenigo or his special *garçonnière* at Santa Maria Zobenigo, in an endless cortège, sometimes fighting with each other for his attentions.

He wrote to his friends in London:

'I have fallen in love . . . fathomless love. My goddess in only the wife of a Merchant of Venice, but then she is pretty as an antelope, is but two and twenty years old, has the large, black Oriental eyes, with the Italian countenance, and dark glossy hair. . . . Then she has the voice of a lute and the song of a Seraph (though not quite so sacred), besides a long postscript of graces, virtues, and accomplishments. . . . But her great merit is finding out mine: there is nothing so amiable as discernment.'

'A Venetian girl, with large black eyes, a face like Faustina's and the figure of a Juno—tall and energetic like a Pythoness, with eyes flashing, and her dark hair streaming in the moonlight—one of those women who may be made anything. . . . I am sure if I put a poniard into the hands of this one, she would plunge it where I told her—and into me if I offended her. . . .'

Then take Shelley's sober description of Lord Byron's same love life in Venice:

43

'The fact is that the first Italian women with whom he associates are perhaps the most contemptible of all who exist under the moon, the most ignorant, the most disgusting, the most bigoted. Countless smell so strongly of garlic that an ordinary Englishman cannot approach them. Well, Lord Byron is familiar with the lowest sort of these women, the people his gondolieri pick up in the streets. He associates with wretches who seem almost to avow practices which are not only not named, but I believe seldom even conceived in England. He says he disapproves, but he endures.'

What then is this fatal spell? What dulled Byron's sense of discrimination? It made a severe, dutiful, middle-class naval hero, Horatio Nelson, forget his virtuous wife, the honour due to his uniform, the respect due to His Majesty's Minister to the Court of Naples, and fall in love with the worthless and fascinating Lady Hamilton. It gave middle-aged and resigned people the sensation of being, if not young again, at least daring and pleasing to others, and the illusion that they could still bite the fruits of life with their false teeth. At the same time, the spell drove a few sinners to an existence of prayer and penitence. It made and still makes unwanted people feel wanted, unimportant people feel important, and purposeless people believe that the real way to live intelligently is to have no earnest purpose in life. This fatal spell is very old. It can be traced back to the most remote antiquity. It is still one of the forces to be reckoned with in the modern world, a force that somehow helps to shape the lives of multitudes. It is easy today to show that it was the search for this unique quality in Italian life, for a sensation which gave strength and urgency to all others, which enticed people here, rather than all other motives, because millions now come for all the reasons which attracted them in the past, reasons so contradictory as to exclude and cancel each other.

Many, of course, are still in quest of holiness or the reassurance of religion. Not all of them are Catholics. There are Protestants, Jews, Buddhists, and Moslems, not to speak of agnostics and atheists, at all Papal audiences. Thousands of non-Catholics are granted private audiences and special Apostolic benedictions, in which they do not officially believe, but which they fervently welcome. They buy rosaries and holy medals for their friends. Many are tempted to forget past theological controversies, envious of the unquestioning and peaceful faith of the Catholic masses. Non-Catholics often admit that they receive, from their visits to Rome and the sight of the Holy Father at close quarters, a spiritual uplift which is often stronger than that experienced by Catholics, who are accustomed and therefore inured to such ceremonies. The Pope has once again become a great spiritual leader, a symbolic figure, the moral head of all the forces of good against evil.

Catholics, of course, undertake the voyage not only to see him but also to visit the traditional places of worship, the great basilicas, sanctuaries, shrines, and also to gain indulgences. Catholics and non-Catholics flock to Assisi, where the poetic memory of Saint Francis is still fragrant and where Giotto's frescoes depicting his life are well preserved. They go to Loreto, where the Holy Virgin's cottage can still be seen, brought through the air by angels from Asia Minor. Pilgrims sometimes visit Saint Michael's sanctuary on Monte Gargano, the spur of Italy. It was founded in a deep cave, where the Prince of Angels appeared in the eleventh century to Norman knights on their way back from the Holy Land. Others go to Syracuse, in Sicily, where a new, inexpensive, and ugly bust of the Virgin, a mass-produced article currently sold in all department stores in Italy, is known to have wept, a few years ago, shedding abundant tears which, according to the chemical analysis of the municipal administration, contained all the ingredients of real human tears.

There is now a special rush to the village of San Giovanni Rotondo, in Apulia, not far from Saint Michael's cave. Non-stop buses leave Rome for the once obscure hamlet every day during the tourist season. People go (as so many have done in past centuries) to worship a living saint. He is Father Pio da Pietralcina, a bearded Capuchin. He lives a simple and holy life. Since 1918, he has been blessed with the stigmata on feet, hands and ribs. Those on his hands he keeps modestly hidden under mittens. Stigmata, to be sure, are only the first signs of sainthood and not the surest nor worthiest of all. Even some Protestants and heretics have been known to have had them. The Church does not acknowledge their validity; it does not consider Padre Pio a saint because of them. Surer signs of sanctity, of course, are levitation, ubiquity, an exceptionally ascetic life and miracles.

Father Pio does not fly. It is perhaps the only saintly feat he has not yet performed. But he is renowned for ubiquity and miraculous cures. Without ever leaving his convent cell, he has appeared a number of times simultaneously to trustworthy witnesses miles from each other and carried on conversation with all of them. Once a well-known cardinal even saw him kneeling in Saint Peter's, in Rome, lost in prayer. He has become visible in the bedrooms of the sick and dying, in prison cells and hospital wards, after his help had been invoked. When he cannot go (apparently his personal appearances are not without some limitations), he sometimes sends a strange perfume in his stead, which pervades the whole room and is smelled by everybody present, including the incredulous, reminding them invariably of fresh wood violets. It is the well-known 'odour of sanctity' described by many authorities since the early Middle Ages. Many of the despairing people who invoked him were cured of mortal and sometimes incurable diseases, as numerous doctors' certificates testify, or were freed from distress and anguish.

The little town of San Giovanni Rotondo is now the centre of feverish activities, some of them questionable, exploiting his name and presence. The Church takes a diffident view of most of them, warns the faithful against possible exploitation, and periodically sends inspectors to report on what is going on. There is a large hospital, financed with foreign money. There are inns, hostels, restaurants, shops selling all kinds of relics and mementoes, shady intermediaries who promise anybody a meeting with Father Pio and even a miracle, for a little extra money.

He himself seems unconscious of all this and takes no part in it. He says mass very early in the morning, as he has always done, in front of a vast crowd, which includes one-day tourists, pilgrims seeking grace, sufferers asking for a release from their sufferings and many devout followers who have left everything behind to live near him in poverty. The mass celebrated by him lasts more than an hour, as he pronounces every word with clarity and great devotion, and sometimes loses himself for long minutes in rapture. He exchanges words, after mass, with a few people who have obtained a meeting with him. His conversation is good-humoured and witty, not at all the forbidding sayings of an ascetic or mystic saint, but rather those of a good country priest of peasant extraction, which he is.

Among his followers there is a former American bomber pilot. During the last war, on his way back from a mission in the Balkans, he wanted to jettison the unused bombs before landing in Foggia. Over San Giovanni Rotondo, as he was on the point of opening the hatch, an immense figure suddenly appeared in the clouds, almost a cloud itself, the figure of a bearded monk, with upraised arms, imperiously commanding him not to drop the bombs. The pilot, greatly impressed, could not help obeying. Several years later, when his adventure was almost forgotten and was nothing more than a dubious after-dinner anecdote, he happened to read about Father Pio in an old magazine. Suddenly he understood the meaning of what he had seen and what had happened to him. He came to Apulia, met the holy friar, and was converted to the Catholic faith.

*

Perhaps just as many people still come for exactly opposite reasons. Italy to them is one of the last countries in the Western world where the great god Pan is not dead, where life is still gloriously pagan, where Christianity has not deeply disturbed the happy traditions and customs of ancient Greece and Rome, and where the Renaissance has not spent itself. Religion, they point out, is but a thin veneer over older customs. Many of the saints, venerated as powerful protectors of this or that village, are, in fact, but the local gods disguised. Sometimes their names give them away. On the flanks of Mount Aetna, in Sicily, for instance, people worship a 'Santa Venerina', who, among other gifts, has the power to make barren women fertile, like the Venus of old, *Venere* in Italian. And is there not a relation between the name of the patron saint of Naples, the venerated bishop Januarius, whose dried-up blood becomes liquid twice a year, whose relics many times stopped Vesuvius' lava at the very gates of the city during the fiercest eruptions, and the Roman protector of all portals and doors, Janus? The Church, they say, knows or suspects all this, but, in its great wisdom, allows it to go on, since it does not interfere with fundamental doctrines. It takes almost as much work and bother to unmake a saint as to make one. Only two lost their rank recently, after years of priestly research and deliberation. One was the old and glorious Saint George, protector, among many things and places, of the Republic of Genoa and of the Kingdom of England, the saint whose image is on every golden sovereign. The other was Saint Philomena, an erudite mistake of the early nineteenth century, born of the misreading of an old inscription.

Foreigners come to Rome to taste *la dolce vita* in Via Veneto, in night clubs, in villas on the Via Appia, in film studios, or artists' ateliers in Via Margutta. Some play nymph and faun on solitary beaches, in secluded caves and woods, where they can bathe in the nude, drink the wine, eat simple food with their hands, consort with *contadini* and fishermen, living close to nature and in harmony with the vagaries and caprices of human instincts. For these people, Italy is the world's earthly paradise, where sin is unknown, man is still a divine animal and all loves are pure; the right milieu for legal, illegal, natural, seminatural, unnatural or merely bizarre honeymoons, affairs, liaisons, and escapades.

To Italy come the mature ladies who still feel young inside and long to renew the thrills of their adolescence, and mature gentlemen who pine for the love of uncomfortably young girls. To Italy flock ladies or gentlemen in pairs of the same sex, middle-aged couples who settle down somewhere to the regular rountine of bourgeois housekeeping: one shops, the other cooks, one washes, the other mends the socks or stockings, and they both shine the silverware. Or the lone men on the prowl who find it easier and safer to seduce penniless peasant boys, sailors or firemen in Italy than elsewhere.

Others are longing for things that have kept their

natural flavour, those simple flavours which industrial civilization is now supplanting with conventional ones. They like the guileless wines, the local cheeses which are unknown a few miles away, the freshly-picked fruit warmed by the sun; the sea urchins, split in half with a rusty knife when still dripping salt water, and eaten with a few drops of lemon juice; the *pane casareccio*, or home-baked bread; the passion of the hairy peasant girls smelling of healthy sweat. These people above all relish what they believe are the simple and genuine emotions of the Italians who are apparently unashamed of them and seldom try to hide them. There is a tense, dramatic quality, a shameless directness, about the Italians which is refreshing to foreigners accustomed to nordic self-control, to feigned or real frigidity. These people still seek, like Stendhal, 'that combination of love, sensuality, and sincerity' which apparently still characterizes the race. Here 'a man who plays a rôle is as rare . . . as a natural and simple man in Paris', and, one might add, anywhere else in the northern hemisphere. They also believe with Stendhal that 'music lives only in Italy', together with other sensual arts, and that 'in this beautiful country one must only make love; other pleasures of the soul are cramped here. Love here is delicious. Anywhere else it is only a bad copy.'

*

Italy is today again the teacher of many arts. Italians have maintained, or have newly invented, a variety of crafts and skills which are still rare and precious in the contemporary world. Foreigners learn the art of carving marble, training show horses to jump, racing Grand Prix cars, making pitiless films about sex-mad and disinherited characters in the slums, designing special bodies for elegant automobiles, designing shirts, clothes, shoes, and all sorts of contemporary gadgets, designing modern buildings in the *bravura* style of Pier Luigi Nervi, the great master of concrete structures. Young pianists from all over the world, severely selected, study free with Benedetti Michelangeli, the mysterious Italian maestro, in a castle which he keeps near Turin. Young opera singers, composers, directors, and conductors work hard in winter as

apprentices at the Rome Opera and put on their gradua-
tion shows in the main theatre at Spoleto, at the end of
the year, when Gian Carlo Menotti is not using it. Art
students live and work in the ancient and glorious Academies which many foreign nations keep for the purpose.
Some are supported by the West: the American Academy
on the Janicular Hill, the French Villa Medici in Trinità
dei Monti, the Belgian, West German, Spanish, and
Danish Academies, here and there in the city. Others
are still surprisingly kept by Marxist popular democracies
and by the non-committed nations: the Hungarian, Polish,
Rumanian and Egyptian Academies.

Some of these pupils eventually finish by doing things
alla Italiana more conscientiously than the natives and
beating them at their own game. It happens almost every
year at the Rome horse show, when foreigners riding with
the Italian jumping style beat the local champions, or at
Monza, when the foreign drivers drive their Ferraris or
Maseratis to victory ahead of their local rivals. For many
more expatriate residents, Italians are pupils, as they have
often been in the past. Television and musical comedy
choreography is the monopoly of the young and well-paid
Americans. Russian émigré choreographers and scene
designers work in many opera houses and theatres. American film directors make vast historical potboilers in Tech-
nicolor for Italian producers. There are branch offices of
American universities where business management and
public administration are taught to the natives with mis-
sionary zeal. American Quakers roam the countryside
teaching illiterates how to read and write. Soviet theore-
ticians and organizers occasionally give a hand to the local
Communists. German technicians, engineers, and chemists,
and American management consultants work in Italian
factories. English and American advertising firms have
offices in Milan and Rome. Swiss graphic arts experts,
Hungarian and Spanish football coaches are widely employed. All these people, like Sir John Hawkwood of old,
find life pleasant and invigorating, even if their Italian
pupils sometimes seem obstinate in their ways and do not
improve easily.

*

Perhaps few things illustrate the contradictory character of the motives driving some foreigners to Italy better than the contrast between snobs and non-snobs. The snobs come here, as they have come for several centuries, as to their own paradise. Italy is the happy hunting ground of the newly rich and the insecure name-dropper. These can easily re-create a life of long ago, a life of royal splendour which would be impossibly expensive and pretentiously ridiculous in their home towns. Furnished palaces with historical names can be leased in no time. Nobody wants them. Liveries can be bought or hired within a few hours, servants engaged by the day or the year to fill them, including an impressive *maggiordomo* and good cooks. In an emergency all this can be staged overnight by specialized firms. A number of important-sounding guests, with names going back to the Crusades or related to famous Popes, can be gathered with a little patience but no special difficulty. Such people, like characters in nineteenth-century novels, still have practically nothing to do, wear their clothes well, and have impeccable manners. They have little money, regal tastes, and like being expensively entertained. Sometimes invitations to some of the biggest affairs are broadcast all over Europe and the United States. Women journalists and gossip columnists from as far away as London, Chicago or Hollywood flock in to describe the dinner or the ball with glowing phrases. Such things usually leave the Italians cold. They are not even mentioned in the local press.

The non-snobs flock here to enjoy the company and the relaxed attitude of the inhabitants, completely indifferent as they are to status symbols. The tiring game of extracting social recognition from others and expensively impressing the world with one's own fortune, name or rank, is played by a relatively small minority of Italians, mostly people with foreign ties or blood, who ape foreign manners and have been educated abroad, or brought up in Italy, years ago, by Edwardian nannies from England. Madame de Staël discovered long ago that Italians as a rule were not impressed by titles and appearance. Being rich, noble by marriage, and famous, she could not hide a certain irritation. She complained: 'Distinctions in rank have little effect in Italy. . . . People are hardly susceptible to aristocratic prejudices, and as society considers itself the judge of nothing, it permits everything. . . . There is no *salon*, there are no little daily devices with which to shine.' Stendhal also pointed out that 'a marquise of the highest nobility may be the friend of a simple drawing teacher. . . . Vanity is but one of the passions, far from being the ruling one. . . . A man living on an income of fifteen hundred francs speaks to a man who has an income of six million as simply as he would to an equal. This would be thought incredible in England.'

J. P. Morgan the elder died in Rome, at the Grand Hotel, where he stayed at least once a year. He came principally to eat in small *trattorie*, where nobody knew who the fat American gentleman with the bulbous nose was, and to roam the streets at night, endlessly talking, as he could not do in New York or London, to one of his dearest friends, the impecunious Italian journalist Salvatore Cortesi, about the meaning of life, death, love and God. At the beginning of the century, the charm of places like Capri and Taormina, before they were improved and transformed into ordinary and expensive resorts, was the moral and social equality of all, which, at the time, could not be enjoyed anywhere else. Russian revolutionaries, millionaires from Germany and the United States, English lords, penniless painters, poets, or vagabonds, local loafers, peasants, sailors or fishermen, all dressed alike in the same cheap cotton clothes, often ate in the same *osterie*, drank the same wines, wasted the time in idle talk together and led the same kind of life.

Important people still find today the refreshing restful pleasures of obscurity and simplicity. The King of Sweden, together with his family, pursues his hobby, which is archaeology. Dressed in old clothes, without attracting attention, he digs for Etruscan tombs in search of little bronzes and pottery. The Queen of the Netherlands has built herself a simple cottage by the sea, at Porto Ercole. Bettina, the widowed friend of Aly Khan, bought herself a piece of the coast of Sardinia. While the famous enjoy the pleasure of being ordinary mortals for a change, obscure people find a different kind of satisfaction: they escape from the torture of being obscure in places where others enjoy the limelight. They also relish an added attraction. In little picturesque villages, still known only to few, but which may become celebrated ten or twenty years from now, in places where the great go about in shabby clothes and speak to everybody, it is usually easier for the simple foreigner to be taken for the great or the equivalent of the great and to strike up acquaintances which would be difficult or impossible anywhere else.

*

Many of the historical reasons for coming to Italy are entirely imaginary. The Holy See, to be sure, is only to be found in Rome, Vesuvius in Naples, the ruins of Pompeii at Pompeii, the art treasures of Florence in Florence, but some of the other very important attractions can also be found elsewhere. They are often more conveniently situated, sometimes the equal of, or better than, those in Italy. Take the climate, for instance, sung by poets through the centuries, at all times one of the principal pretexts for the voyage. 'Sunny Italy,' foreigners used to say. The definition was obviously created by the English, the Russians, and the Scandinavians, people whose native weather was irremediably bad, the worst in the civilized world. What these people meant was that in Italy, surprisingly enough for them, the sun shone in summer. The sun of course shines in summer in many other places, too. How many poor northerners fell victims to this misleading *lieu commun*, who, suffering from an affliction of the lungs, were sent to Rome, Florence, or Pisa, to spend the winter, where they declined and perished in the rain, sleet, cold and humid air? Among the victims of this prejudice we can also reckon hundreds of imaginary characters in nineteenth-century novels. Oswald, Lord Nelvil, the preposterous hero of Madame de Staël's *Corinne*, was one: he had to leave his native Edinburgh, because 'his health was perturbed by a deep sensation of pain, and the doctors, fearing his lungs were attacked, had ordered him the air of the Midi'. He did not improve.

In fact, the climate of Northern Italy is about the same as that of most continental European countries. Milan and Turin are colder in winter than Copenhagen, warmer in summer than Valetta or Algiers. Central and Southern

Italy have about the same climate as other Mediterranean countries, milder on the coast than inland, not as good as in Hong Kong or in the Crimea. Winter is undoubtedly more comfortable in Egypt, Florida, the Sahara, the oases of Libya, Morocco, and Algeria. Rome notoriously has one of the most unpleasant weathers of all, *scirocco* for almost two hundred days a year, a sultry southern wind which fills the sky with low, grey, dampish clouds, makes mildew blossom almost everywhere, puts liverish stains of humidity on the walls, makes people feel weak, impotent, irascible, their heads filled with cotton wool. Norman Douglas, who named a book after it, called the wind 'the withering blast whose hot and clammy touch hastens death and putrefaction'. Venice is under a dreary rain most of the autumn, winter, and the beginning of spring. There is no sadder atmosphere in the world, especially when the wind turns south-east and the city smells vaguely of rotten cabbages and stagnant waters. Oscar Wilde, who was there on such a day, and rode in a black gondola, said dejectedly that he had felt as if he had 'travelled through sewers in a coffin'. The city inspired mostly thoughts of death to Thomas Mann.

Or take another of the traditional reasons for the trip, good food. As a rule, food is good in Italy. It is always beyond reproach in a few famous restaurants and *trattorie;* very rarely it is mediocre, almost never bad. It has character. It is seldom ambiguous or pretentious. Things frankly smell, look, and taste as they should, every component sharply differentiated and true to its nature. No velvety sauce dims their appearance or their flavour. Everything is eaten fresh and in its proper season, when it is at its absolute best. No fruit or vegetable comes from a hothouse, with the damp paper taste of artificial products. Nothing is picked before its time and allowed to ripen in storage. Nothing is frozen, nothing is chemically preserved. The colours are gay: the yellow of the *risotto alla milanese*, the red of tomato salad or spaghetti with tomato sauce, the green of broccoli, the white of Tuscan beans, the bishop purple of boiled octopus, the gold of *fettuccine al doppio burro* are all clean hues, as pure as the colours of flags or children's crayons. Pizzas are painters' palettes ready to portray a summer sunset. The wines are resplendent like jewels when the sun shines through the glasses: no subtle nuance betrays the vigour of their tints or their bouquets.

A good meal is good in Italy, better in fact than anything one gets in more efficient countries in the north, better than in Spain, infinitely better than in Greece. But food and wines, it must be admitted, are not quite as good as in France. Italian cuisine merely presents Nature at its best. French cuisine is a challenge to Nature, it subverts Nature, it creates a new Nature of its own. It is an art. What does it matter that Italian wines are exactly what the juice of particular grapes becomes after fermentation, the products of diligence, when the French ones are often creations of genius, wise mélanges of various crus, some vulgar and some extremely rare, manipulated by experts? They undoubtedly manage such things better in France.

Or take the ruins. Some of Italy's ruins are admittedly unique. There are perhaps more Greek temples still standing on their original pillars and more Greek remnants of all kinds in Southern Italy, the Magna Graecia of old, than in all of Little Greece. But there are older and sometimes more famous and awe-inspiring monuments strewn all over the world, from the jungle of Yucatan to Ankhor Vat, from the desert of Mesopotamia to Iran, from Egypt to India. Great palaces, museums, celebrated masterpieces can be viewed and admired in many places, all over the world, as good as and sometimes better than those in Italy, from Spain's Escorial and El Prado to Leningrad's Winter Palace and Hermitage. Or take art. Contemporary art is livelier and more arresting in Paris and New York. There an ambitious young artist can not only study but make himself known and a collector has a wide range to choose from. La Scala is undoubtedly the greatest opera house in the world. But good opera can be seen and heard in Vienna, London, and New York, and good symphonic music can be found in Vienna, Munich, Berlin, Düsseldorf, Cologne, Frankfurt, Paris, London, New York, Boston, and a score of other American cities, not to speak of the Soviet Union. Ballet is bad in Italy. It is infinitely better in Moscow, Leningrad, New York, London and even Copenhagen.

Is it spectacular landscapes, majestic mountains, irides-
cent bays, waterfalls, coquettish lakes, pretty islands that
travellers think they cannot do without? Of course, natural
beauty and famous views are abundant in Italy. Such
things, however, are not unknown elsewhere. Nature is
usually more inspiring even in the United States, wherever man has not meddled with it. Italy has no century-
old woods, which turn all sorts of hues in the autumn,
from gold to crimson, as they do in upper New York State
or in New England; Italy has no canyons and no deserts.
Rio de Janeiro, Istanbul and Hong Kong are as beautiful
as the bay of Naples. The Alps look just as impressive
from the opposite slopes in France, Switzerland and
Austria. Other mountains are as tall, steep, craggy; some
are more remote, wild and unattainable. Lakes surrounded
by wooded slopes can be counted by the hundred in other
parts of Europe, many as pretty as the Italian ones.
Waterfalls are romantic, to be sure, but puny and slender
in comparison with the best in Africa and America.
Italian rivers are little brooks when measured against
the four or five mighty rivers of the rest of the world.
Islands? The Greek islands are more numerous, wilder,
more remote and warmer all the year around.

Some confess that it is *la dolce vita* which attracts
them. Only the name is new. The sweet life has always
attracted travellers, to Venice in the months of the famous
Carnival and elsewhere at different times of the year, down
the centuries. But is *la dolce vita* really more *dolce* in
Italy than elsewhere? Is it more *dolce* than in Paris, for
instance, Las Vegas, New York, Munich, or Hollywood?
Comparisons are impossible. Unfortunately gay life is
something that cannot always be found by travelling to
definite spots in the world. It is often a quality a man
carries with him, a capacity to provoke light-hearted
adventure wherever he goes. Many visitors are disappointed in Rome, when they discover that life can be
as prim and proper there as it was back home, or as it is
for most Romans.

Is Italy, then, as some claim, the ideal place to enjoy
the inefficient and lax enforcement of laws, a refuge from
the tyranny of income tax and other fiscal impositions?
The world is filled with pleasant little republics or prin-

cipalities where the well-to-do foreign resident is respected
and considered beyond the pale of the law, and where a
good friend in the right place or a gift in time to an
official will save a lot of trouble. As for the pure avoidance
of taxes, there are better places than Italy. The rich
Italians themselves prefer Switzerland to their own country. Monte Carlo, Luxemburg and Liechtenstein are
celebrated hiding places for conspicuous fortunes. Or do
these foreigners want the flattering comfort of a warm-
hearted, hospitable, obliging, willing, picturesque and
skilful populace, ready to supply craftsmen, artisans and
sycophants with little trouble? Such endearing people
exist in many countries, everywhere, in fact, where an
ancient and refined civilization has decayed without yet
giving birth to a local version of modern industrialized
society.

Obviously such explanations are only good as far as
they go. People do not always, of course, expect to find
in Italy the absolute best. Sheer superiority does not
interest them as much as the special quality which imbues
everything, animate or inanimate, in Italy and nowhere
else. It is vulgarly known, in tourist bureau advertising,
as 'the charm of Italy': it notoriously adds value and
interest to obvious attractions, it makes them all better
here than elsewhere, just as salt makes ordinary tastes
sharper and clearer. Even sorrows become precious.
Heinrich Heine noted: 'Simply letting yourself live is
beautiful in Italy. In these marble *palazzi* sighs have a
more romantic echo than in our modest brick houses; in
the shade of these laurel bushes it is more pleasant to
weep than under our gloomy fir trees; it is sweeter to
day-dream following the shapes of Italian clouds than
under the ash-grey dome of a German sky, a work-day
sky in which even clouds take on the solemn and sulky
expression of little burghers and yawn with boredom.
. . . What is, after all, pleasure if not an extraordinarily
sweet pain?' What is it? 'The charm of Italy,' concluded
Stendhal, 'is akin to that of being in love.' He should
have known what he was talking about as he had dedicated most of his life to a painstaking study of both
subjects. The two, love and the charm of Italy, are similar
and complementary. One intensifies the other. Love in

Italy is notoriously more satisfactory. Italy seen through lovers' eyes is more enchanting.

Is Italy love? Or is Italy, as some say, art? Like the Italian scene, art, too, can be intoxicating, can transform people, can transport them far from themselves, can be delightfully aphrodisiac. 'Art,' says Walter Pater, with words which could be applied equally to Italy and to love, 'gives nothing but the highest quality to your moments as they pass.' But can an ancient country, a peninsula stretching from the Alps to the Mediterranean, filled with fifty million busy people and their historical problems, be seriously compared to a delicate sentiment, to a primeval urge, or to the highest flowering of the human spirit? Can geography be mixed up with psychology or with aesthetics?

*

Henry James suspected that the pleasure of Italy was inseparably tied to the human element, the people who had created the landscape almost with their own hands in the course of so many centuries. It was for him, 'the incomparable wrought fusion, fusion of human history and moral passion with the elements of earth and air, of colour, composition, and form; that constitute her appeal and give it supreme heroic grace'. He stopped one day in the dull little town of Velletri, south of Rome, for a few aimless hours. It was a dreary place. There was nothing to see. And yet he was fascinated. 'There was a narrow raised terrace, with steps, in front of the best of two or three local cafés,' he wrote, 'and in the soft enclosed, the warm waning light of June, various benign contemplative worthies sat at disburdened tables and, while they smoked long black weeds, enjoyed us under those probable workings of subtlety with which we invest so many quite unimaginably blank (I dare say) Italian simplicities. The charm was, as always in Italy, in the tone and the air and the happy hazard of things, which made any positive pretensions or claimed importance a comparative trifling question. . . . We lay at our ease in the bosom of the past, we practised intimacy, an intimacy so much greater than the mere accidental and ostensible: the difficulty for the right and grateful expression of which makes the old, the familar tax on the luxury of loving Italy.'

Others felt this undeniable link between the people and the attraction of the place, between the people's moods, habits, looks, approach to life and the pleasure of Italy. William Dean Howells, the *Italianizant* who had chosen, as a prize for having written the campaign biography of Lincoln, to be appointed consul in Venice, noted: 'It was their lovely ways, far more than their monuments of history and art, that made return to the Florentines delightful. I would rather have had a perpetuity of the *cameriere's* smile when he came up with our coffee in the morning than Donatello's San Giorgio, if either were purchasable; and the face of the old chambermaid, full of motherly affection, was better than the façade of Santa Maria Novella.' He loved 'the delightfully natural human beings one could always be sure of in this land of human nature unabashed'. 'It is their manners as a whole,' Stendhal noted, 'their natural ways, bonhomie, the great art of being happy which is here practised with this added charm, that the good people do not know that it is an art, the most difficult of all.'

It is not quite true, of course. The Italians know that everything in their country is governed by their experience, the product of their industry, imbued with their spirit. They know that there is no need, really, to distinguish or to choose between the smile on the face of a *cameriere* and Donatello's San Giorgio, between the 'composition and classicism' and landscaped hill about Florence. They are all works of art, the 'great art of being happy' and of making other people happy, an art which embraces and inspires all others in Italy, the only art worth learning, but which can never be really mastered, the art of inhabiting the earth.

❋

This, finally, is the ultimate motive, the one that gives strength, urgency and validity to all other motives, the answer to Milton's question, 'Why Italy?' People still come as they came for centuries because they are attracted by a certain quality in Italian life. Whether they know what it is or not, it somehow quickens their blood. It still gives them a Saturnian feeling of liberation. Italians around them seem to understand things which still perplex other people, to have explored short cuts, a few of which are a trifle shabby and questionable, but useful to avoid life's roughest spots. They seem to be trying to work out a sure *système* to break the bank of history. The *système* is not quite perfect. It seems to work well only when the stakes are low but it warms people's hearts and gives them the illusion of cheating fate. The Italians seem happy. They show a porpoiselike eagerness and zest in everything they do which are contagious. One of Goethe's travelling companions tried to teach him the secret: 'Why think?' he told the young poet. 'Man must never think. Thinking makes you grow older. Man must have many things, a great confusion, in his head.' One must allow contradictory tendencies to proliferate, one must cultivate opposite ideals, one must follow reason alone, one must not fret over the imperfections of life on earth. One must carry on. The pleasure of Italy comes from living in a world made by man, for man, on man's measurements.

CHAPTER FOUR

The Importance of Spectacle

THE extraordinary animation is what strikes one at first, the vigorous ant-hill life of the natives. Streets, squares, marketplaces teem with people, noisy, elated, gay, energetic, busy people. There are uniformed *carabinieri* watching everything and everybody through half-closed eyelids, fat priests strolling slowly, peasants dressed in rough velvet clothes, smart young soldiers on leave, housewives carrying heavy shopping bags, desperate youths with long hair and blue jeans, swarms of pretty girls and children playing between everybody's legs. Ladies lower little baskets on a string from a fourth-storey window, in the manner of anchorites from the top of Egyptian pillars, for the postman to put the mail in, or the baker his bread. Begging monks pleadingly push little wooden boxes under everybody's nose. A hunchback sells lottery tickets, 'last numbers left, sure to win'.

Ladies come out of shops to check the colour of some material in the full light of the sun. Vendors extol the advantages of their wares in loud voices (watermelons are always 'good to eat, drink, and wash one's face with'). Craftsmen carry on their work in the open air, in front of their shops, and sing or chat with passing friends: mechanics dive under disembowelled cars, cobblers hammer shoe leather, carpenters polish table-tops with the sweeping gestures of a conductor directing an *adagio cantabile*. A waiter changes table-cloths and snaps each in turn in the sunshine with a twist of his wrists. Sometimes a religious procession goes by: a musical band and *carabinieri* in full uniform with red and blue feathers over their cocked hats, precede chanting priests in lace surplices, girls in white veils, little boys with angels' wings attached to their shoulders, and the chief priest under the ancient velvet canopy, uncertainly held aloft over his head by devout gentlemen. Or a funeral may pass: prancing black horses, their harness decorated with black plumes and silver ornaments, a glass-enclosed hearse surmounted by a flight of golden wooden angels, more black feathers and sundry symbols of eternal life, followed by weeping relatives and friends.

Carts, shop-windows and stalls are loaded with vegetables, flowers, fruits, toys, clothes, shoes and fishes in the colourful confusion and disarray of gifts pouring out of a cornucopia. There are white cauliflowers in the north, green cauliflowers in Rome, and purple in Catania; short and green *zucchini* everywhere or white and six-foot-long *zucchini* in Naples, artichokes with thorns on the Riviera and without thorns in the south. There are pyramids of oranges, some sliced to show the bloody flesh preferred by Italians. There are fishes: coral pink mullets, cuttle-fish made of glistening alabaster, long swordfish or tuna-fish in Sicily, sleek sturgeons near the mouth of the Po river, soles along the Adriatic, entangled octopus still writhing in agony. The *salumerie* windows are worthy of the brush of a *natura morta* painter from Bergamo, a city distinguished for its food and a school of painting completely dedicated to it: triumphal arches of *prosciutti*, *mortadelle* hanging from the ceiling like Venetian lanterns, festoons of *zamponi, caciocavalli*, and *provoloni; mozzarelle* swimming in milk, pillars of Parmesan cheese wheels painted funeral black, large jars of olives, mushrooms in oil, picked cucumbers, barrels of anchovies in brine.

Everything is displayed everywhere, in dramatic and artistic disorder. Flowered cotton material is unrolled from its board and thrown at the observer as if in anger. Spaghetti in sheaves are tied at the waist with white, red, and green patriotic ribbons. *Fiaschi* of wine or olive oil are decorated with medals like war heroes. In the butchers' windows, pale calves' heads, with eyes closed and lips curled in secret merriment, hold a lemon or a carnation between their teeth in death-defying insouciance. Even a hernia truss, shown in the window of an orthopaedist's shop, bedecked with little flags and colourful ribbons, becomes a gay and desirable object.

The noise is usually deafening. People chat, whistle, swear, sing, curse, cry, howl, weep, call to each other and shout, carrying on elaborate discussions or delicate negotiations. Mothers murmur endearing baby words to their little children and ask bystanders to be witnesses to their darlings' charm and pigheadedness. Other mothers call their sons from top-storey windows with voices carrying to the next province. Bells clang with deep bronze notes from the top of the belfry above, drowning every other sound. Somebody is always practising the cornet or the trombone. At times the same popular song or famous operatic aria comes apparently from everywhere, from radios in every shop, from the open windows of apartments, from under the tables in the café, from the pockets of clients, from the abdomens of passing housewives. *Vespas*, cars, motorcycles, trucks go by with roaring engines.

The air is in fact filled with so much noise that one must usually talk in a very loud voice to be understood, thereby increasing the total uproar. Lovers sometimes have to whisper 'I love you' to each other in the tones of newsboys selling the afternoon papers. Italians on their death beds, in rooms facing especially noisy squares or streets, are known to have renounced leaving their last wishes and advice to weeping relatives, being too weak to make themselves heard. It is, however, a gay and happy noise, magnified by the stone walls, the absence of greenery, the narrowness of the streets. It goes on from dawn to the small hours of the night, when the last strollers stop under your bedroom window to debate a fine point of politics or the personality of a common friend, both speaking at the same time at the top of their voices.

The show can be so engrossing that many people spend most of their lives just looking at it. There are usually café tables strategically placed in such a way that nothing of importance will escape the leisurely drinker of *espresso* or *aperitivo*. Reserved old ladies peer unseen at the spectacle through the wooden slats of green-painted blinds. Nothing escapes their sharp eyes; they draw deductions from every detail: a woman's purchases, a girl's new dress, a new smile on the face of a young man, a strange car from out of town, a boy's whistle to a third-storey window. There are free benches or little walls in the sun for the elderly. There are balconies along the façades of all houses, as convenient as boxes at the theatre. You can place an armchair there, or stand leaning on your elbows, and see the days, the years or your whole life go by, as you watch a cavalcade with thousands of characters and hundreds of subplots.

What makes all such scenes more intensely fascinating is perhaps the transparency of Italian faces. Conversations can be followed at a distance by merely watching the changing expressions of those taking part in them. You can read joy, sorrow, hope, anger, relief, boredom, despair, love, and disappointment as easily as large-printed words on a wall poster. Undisguised emotions, some sincere and some feigned, follow each other on an Italian's face as swiftly as the shadows of clouds over a meadow on a windy day in spring. A waiter taking an order for lunch, for instance, will show the following series of moods in quick succession: (1) bored obsequiousness and professional courtesy, as he hands a menu to the new client; (2) resignation, as he whips out his pencil and keeps it poised on his pad waiting for the usual, dull, unimaginative order; (3) slight curiosity, if the client looks thoughtful, coughs and asks a few pertinent questions; (4) incredulous attention, if the client shows himself really difficult to please, somewhat circumspect in weighing possible choices; this may be followed by (5) a look of alertness, eagerness and pleasure if the client proves himself a knowing expert, or by (6) a return to the bored obsequiousness of the beginning if the order turns out to be, after all, the ordinary thing.

Reading facial expressions is an important art in Italy, to be learned in childhood, perhaps more important for survival than the art of reading print. Spoken words may be sometimes at variance with the grimaces that accompany them. The words should then be overlooked. Only the face counts. Italians are often disconcerted, unhappy and lonely in the north of Europe, and seldom know what is going on, surrounded as they are by blank faces on which little can be read and that little seldom exciting. They wrongly conclude that, as the people show no feelings, they have no feelings worth showing. The proverbial impassivity of the English is believed to be a definite proof of coldness and insensibility. The Italians' excessive

64

facility to express emotions is, strangely enough, a drawback for actors. Perhaps they are too richly endowed by Nature: they have more natural gifts and talent than necessary. Their florid acting turns too readily into hamming when not under rigid control. The best spend years to unlearn what many of their foreign colleagues have to learn. Orson Welles once acutely observed that Italy is full of actors, fifty million of them, in fact, and they are almost all good; there are only a few bad ones, and they are on the stage and in the films.

*

Then there are the gestures. Italian gestures are justly famous. Indeed Italians use them more abundantly, efficiently, and imaginatively than other people. They employ them to emphasize or clarify whatever is said, to suggest words and meanings it is not prudent to express with words, sometimes simply to convey a message at great distance, where the voice could not carry. In the hurried world of today gestures are also employed more and more as time-saving devices. Motorists no longer slow down and waste precious seconds to shout intelligible and elaborate insults to each other or to pedestrians, as they used to do but a few years ago. Now they merely extend one hand in the general direction of the person to whom they want to address the message, a hand with all fingers folded except the forefinger and the little finger. It conveys the suggestion that the other man does, should or will shortly wear horns, in other words be cuckolded by his wife, fiancée or mistress. A few gestures are as arbitrary and conventional as the deaf and dumb alphabet or the sign language of American Indians. Most of them, however, are based on natural and instinctive movements, common to the majority of men, certainly common to all Western men, elaborated, intensified, stylized, sharpened, made into art. Like all great traditional arts, this one too can generally be understood by the inexperienced at first sight.

The mimicry is not, as many think, always exaggerated and dramatic, emphatic contortions of arms and body, rolling of eyes, convulsive agitation of hands and fingers. Probaby the acting of opera singers, directly derived from the Italians' natural mimicry, spread this erroneous impression. The best gestures are often so economical as to be almost imperceptible. Sicilians, for instance, are known to convey a vast range of grave and sometimes mortal messages practically without stirring a muscle of their faces or moving their hands. For them, a slowly raised chin means 'I don't know' or, more often, 'Perhaps I know but I will not tell you.' It is the answer policemen always get when questioning possible witnesses of a Mafia killing which took place in front of hundreds of people in a busy market square. It is also the answer a harmless stranger gets from diffident Sicilian peasants when he asks the way to the nearest village.

The extended fingers of one hand moving slowly back and forth under the raised chin means: 'I couldn't care less. It's no business of mine. Count me out.' This is the gesture made in 1860 by the grandfather of Signor O. O. of Messina as an answer to Garibaldi. The general, who had conquered Sicily with his volunteers and was moving on to the mainland, had seen him, a robust youth at the time, dozing on a little stone wall, in the shadow of a carob tree, along a country lane. He reined in his horse and asked him: 'Young man, will you not join us in our fight to free our brothers in Southern Italy from the bloody tyranny of the Bourbon kings? How can you sleep when your country needs you? Awake and to arms!' The young man silently made the gesture. Garibaldi spurred his horse on.

The lifting of one single eyebrow means, 'I'm ready to take what decisions are necessary.' The slow closing of both eyes in an otherwise immobile and expressionless face signifies resignation in front of the inevitable, acceptance of a difficult and unpleasant duty, as, for instance: 'We warned him again and again. The man is stubborn. He does not want to listen to reason. We will do our duty.'

One of the most economical and eloquent of Sicilian gestures I saw one day in the lobby of the Hotel des Palmes, in Palermo. A man entered from the street. He obviously wanted everybody to know immediately, beyond doubt, that he was a gentleman, *un gran signore*, a man of means and authority, accustomed to being attended on. He looked around as if searching for a friend among the people loitering in the room, took off his overcoat, held it at arm's length for a fraction of a second, and, without bothering to see whether a servant was at his side, dropped it. A real *signore* always has somebody ready to receive his coat when he takes it off. He never needs to check. The coat, of course, did not drop to the floor. A bell-boy was there to catch it.

Strangely enough, no serious study has ever been made of the subject. One man alone, that I know of, a priest and antiquarian from Naples, Canon Andrea de Jorio, attempted to catalogue the gestures of his countrymen. He began by trying to read a meaning in the scenes painted on Greek vases and Roman frescoes or depicted in mosaics and bas reliefs collected in the Bourbon Museum in Naples. He asked himself what these gods and mortals would be saying if they were modern Neapolitans and what a contemporary deaf Neapolitan would make of their mimicry. To begin with, he identified and collected hundreds of such signs from life around him, described them, had them drawn and engraved by an artist, then catalogued and double-indexed them. After many years, in 1832, he published the result of his life-work in one thick volume, dedicated to Frederick William of Hohenzollern, hereditary Prince of Prussia. The slightly misleading title is *La mimica degli antichi investigata nel gestire napoletano* (The Mimicry of Ancient People Interpreted Through the Gestures of Neapolitans).

The interpretation of the ancient people's mimicry fills only a short section. The bulk is dedicated to a practically complete and unique list of all the signs necessary to express anything, or almost anything, in Naples and elsewhere, without opening one's mouth. It is a very rare volume. It is not included in bibliographies, encyclopaedias, lists of rare books for sale, or catalogues of Italian libraries. It is unknown to specialists and scholars. The only copy I know of is in my hands. I stole it from the library of an old and unsuspecting English gentleman.

A glance at the contents proves how natural, easily understood, universal, and timeless such gestures really are. As they have changed little since 1832, it is probable, as the Canon tried to demonstrate, that they may still be more or less what they were in ancient times. Take the chapter headed 'Rage, anger.' It lists ten principal ways of silently expressing such emotions. They are, to quote only the headings and not the elaborate descriptions: (1) 'biting one's lips'; (2) 'biting one's hands and single fingers'; (3) 'tearing one's hair'; (4) 'scratching one's face'; (5) 'firmly enclosing one fist in the other hand and rubbing it with such force that the joints crack'; (6) 'gnashing one's teeth with wide open lips'; (7) 'moving one's lips with a shuddering, nervous rhythm'; (8) 'stamping the ground with violence'; (9) 'beating palm against palm, as if to applaud, once or twice only, with force'. The only gesture not easily understood is number 10, 'pretending to bite one's elbows'. It is the pantomime of an Italian idiomatic saying. It means, in words, 'I will do anything to avenge myself, even the impossible, of which biting my elbows is a hyperbolic example.'

The chapter headed 'No, denial, negation' lists thirteen ways of expressing the same concept, ranged in a scale of growing intensity. The first and simpler ones are: 'raising one's eyebrows as far as they will go and in one quick motion'; 'turning one's face away from the object that is being refused'; 'moving one's head to left and right'; 'lifting one's lower lip over the upper, or lowering one corner of the lower lip'. The erudite Canon only listed nine ways of demonstrating 'love', all chaste. His eyes were probably averted from the more provocative examples, to be seen in abundance all around him, in the Neapolitan streets, in his day as they are now.

Often enough, a simple gesture, accompanied by suitable facial expressions, takes the place not of a few words but of a whole and eloquent speech. This, for instance: imagine two gentlemen sitting at a café table. The first is explaining at great length some intricate question which interests him, perhaps how the world will shortly be changed for the better by some new and impending development. He may be saying: 'This continent of ours, Europe, old, decrepit Europe, all divided into different nations, each nation subdivided into provinces, each nation and each province living its own petty life, speaking its incomprehensible dialect, nurturing its ideas, prejudices, defects, hatreds. . . . Each of us gloating over the memories of the defeats inflicted by us on our neighbours and completely oblivious of the defeats our neighbours inflicted on us. . . . How easy life would become if we were to fuse into one whole, Europa, the Christendom of old, the dream of Charlemagne, of Metternich, of many great men, and, why not? the dream of Hitler too. . . .' The second gentleman is listening patiently, looking intently at the first's face. At a certain moment, as if overwhelmed by the abundance of his friend's arguments or the facility of his optimism, he slowly lifts one hand, perpendicularly, in a straight line, from the table, as far as it will go, higher than his head. Meanwhile he utters only one sound, a prolonged 'eeeeeeh', like a sigh. His eyes never leave the other man's face. His expression is placid, slightly tired, vaguely incredulous. The mimicry means: 'How quickly you rush to conclusions, my friend, how complicated your reasoning, how unreasonable your hopes, when we all know the world has always been the same and all bright solutions to our problems have in turn produced more and different problems, more serious and unbearable problems than the ones we were accustomed to.'

*

The extraordinary animation, the vivid colours, the disorderly abundance of all God's things, the military uniforms and clerical robes, the expressive faces, the revealing gesticulation, the noise: these are among everybody's first superficial impressions in Italy, anywhere in Italy, in the north as well as the south, in big cities as well as in sleepy villages, in modern centres as well as in decrepit and miserable hamlets forgotten by history. There are, of course, deep regional differences, of which the traveller becomes aware little by little. A cattle fair at Lugo in Romagna, not far from Bologna, is obviously not the same as a cattle fair in Paestum. Lugo is a medieval town near the mouth of the Po river, with a brick-red castle and old baroque churches, at the heart of bountifully fertile lands criss-crossed by canals and ditches. The farmers there are big and fat, with red, shining faces, brown hair and light-coloured eyes. The cattle are well-fed, happy, and heavy. Paestum, at the mouth of the Sele river, south of Salerno, is the centre of a hitherto sterile and arid plain, once cursed with malaria, which has been only partly reclaimed and irrigated since the end of the war. The peasants are swarthy, lean, with burning black eyes and shining white teeth. The cattle are small and bony. Still, the cheerful and good-natured fervour, the feverish activity are the same in both places.

Or take Rome. Via Veneto is one of the great streets of Europe, one of the principal thoroughfares of a great capital. In reality, it is the enlargement of the *corso* of any Italian small town. On both sides are café tables crowded with customers who watch the strollers going back and forth, at apéritif time or after the theatre. Among the strollers are herds of tourists, Italian and foreign, and, against this anonymous background, the habitual native characters. One can learn to recognize a few by sight, after a while, and follow their lives through months and years. There are the lean, the ambitious and handsome young men, who arrive one day from the suburbs or the provinces with one suit on their back and a few lire. They manage to make a few drinking friends, meet one powerful person, meet his mistress, gain his confidence, gain her favours, meet a few more powerful persons through them, and slowly rise, like gas bubbles of putrefaction in a muddy marsh. You can check their rising practically day by day. First they buy another suit, then a second-hand car, a few better suits, the first expensive car. In the end, they sport the smartest clothes on the Via, the most beautiful and bejewelled women, a glib and condescending manner, and the fastest and most glittering cars. How long does it take? Sometimes just the time to introduce a millionaire to an independent film producer and a pretty actress, or a high government official to a contractor of public works.

There are the defeated and shabby old men (how smartly and insolently they wore their uniforms, boots, and decorations when they were young, under Mussolini, how quickly they disappeared for a time after the war), who now try to hide their decay, loneliness and flabby bellies. There are flocks of unknown starlets (some arrive daily fresh from the country), who walk back and forth hoping to be noticed by one of the new great directors. After a while, they merely hope to be noticed by any old director, maybe the kind that makes historical potboilers in colour for the South American and Middle Eastern markets, who will offer them two or three days' shooting, with one or two close-ups, and a few spoken lines. In the end, most of them only hope to be noticed by just a man, a solitary man with the price of a good dinner on him and maybe a little *cadeau* in the morning. Some end by jumping from their boarding-house windows. You recognize their faces in the newspapers the next day and learn their names for the first time. A few become world-famous: they stop coming to Via Veneto, except two or three times a year, and then only surrounded by friends, photographers and women noticeably not half as beautiful as they. The old actresses, often drunk (how lovely and frail they were only yesterday), come more often, accompanied by insolent young lovers. There are hundreds of female and male prostitutes; photographers for the better scandal and blackmail magazines waiting for a world-wide celebrity to show up drunk, to quarrel with a friend and be arrested. They are often satisfied. There are black market pedlars of contraband cigarettes or dope, actors' agents, pimps, or simple Roman bourgeois taking the air. One can follow many parallel lives, in Via Veneto, an episode at a time, year after year, with no effort, by merely sitting at a café table, as one does in the main street or in a *piazza* everywhere in Italy.

Even where Italy is superficially less like Italy and more like any other nordic European country, an acute observer cannot fail to discover some of the national characteristics under the alien surface. Milan, for instance, the steel and glass capital of industry, commerce, and finance, here and there looks like Zürich, Düsseldorf, or Madison Avenue. The crowds look well-fed, well-dressed, purposeful, efficient and busy. People rush about with a frown on their faces as if they had but a few minutes to find a doctor and save a human life. They sometimes gulp food at snack bars without sitting down. The business men you interview are often glacially uncommunicative, laconic and reserved. They do not move their pale hands and roll their eyes when they speak. They manage world-wide enterprises, compete with the Japanese and the Germans, launch bright new projects, build dams and bridges in Africa and Asia, talk about millions of dolars. The

71

buildings where they work are higher than anything in
Europe, more daring and modern than those in New York.

Is this Italy? you ask yourself. Then you walk about
the city and explore the older quarters, the forgotten
squares where the housewives do their shopping. Or you
discover the Galleria. It is the crossing of two streets at
right angles, glass-covered like a Victorian hothouse, in
the centre of the city. Café tables line both sides, filled
with leisurely customers observing the people going by,
as in Piazza San Marco, in Via Veneto, in Via Caracciolo
in Naples, or in hundreds of other streets. Loiterers dis-
cuss grave matters and wave their hands to emphasize
some important point. Some are opera singers without a
job, waiting for an engagement to drop from the sky, to
sing *Rigoletto* or *Trovatore* in the provinces, abroad, in
South America, anywhere. Other strollers are visibly from
the country, red-faced, fat, solid. They are farmers and
brokers who have gathered there on certain days of the
week to trade grain, ever since the Galleria was built
almost a hundred years ago. They buy and sell actively
and shrewdly, shaking hands to close each deal, and
marking it down in their little notebooks. You can tell
who wins or loses by watching their faces. The noise and
the gestures fill the empty space. Or you may wander
down Via Monte Napoleone, a short street of elegant and
expensive shops, at apéritif time. Handsome and well-
dressed young men stroll there with feline steps, to look
disdainfully at women; handsome and well-dressed women
stroll languorously to look at and be looked at by men.
Brand-new *gran turismo* cars, each one a unique model,
the most costly in the world, go by slowly or are parked
along the kerb. Here again you can follow what goes on
by watching faces. You can recognize the newly-born
flirtation or the tired old liaison; the hopeful girl pursuing
the bored man; the eager youth in attendance on the
mature and wise beauty.

When you observe things more closely, in Milan, even
the things which want to appear foreign, extremely efficient and modern, the powerful businessmen, the aerial
skyscrapers reflecting the passing clouds in their hundreds
of windows, the elevated autostrade running along on
concrete crutches, the complex industrial plants apparently

invented by mad engineers or science-fiction writers, you begin to notice that many things are a little too much and too emphatically what they are supposed to be. In fact Milan, in its newer quarters, is a little more like Zürich, Düsseldorf, and Madison Avenue than Zürich, Düsseldorf, or Madison Avenue themselves. You are in Italy after all.

*

The fact that everybody, or almost everybody, seems to be doing his job with whole-hearted dedication and enthusiasm is what impresses travellers next. This does not mean that Italians do everything with efficiency, speed and thoroughness. They do not. They merely do it with visible pleasure, as if work were not man's punishment. Often in other countries, one is waited on by people who obviously believe they were destined for better things but were forced by cruel fate to accept a degrading occupation, so degrading in fact as to bring them in contact with repulsive people like you. This never happens in Italy. Nobody is rude to strangers. Nobody looks bored, surly or mutinous. This discovery gives you a pleasant feeling. It also puzzles you, after a while. Is it really true, you ask yourself, that Italians escape from the common lot? Can it be that they are happy, each doing in life exactly what he wants to do, what his hopes conceived for him, what Providence put him on earth to achieve?

The evident delight and eagerness with which things are done are contagious. Cheerful faces surround you as soon as you cross the border. Cheerful customs inspectors wave away technicalities connected with the *carnet de douane* of your car or the cigars in your suitcase. Cheerful porters carry your bags. In the hotel a cheerful concierge or director finds you a room in a full house as if you were his own dear cousin, cheerful waiters suggest in a low voice not to take the fish today, as if they were really interested in your health. You begin to think that everybody, no matter how humble, degrading, or insignificant his position, has, after all, a dignity all his own, the dignity of the man who does not envy anybody and finds himself at ease with his conscience.

Take the singers of Neapolitan songs in the open-air restaurants. Many have no voice, a rough musical ear, a bad memory for words; they barely make a living with what money the customers toss them; they sometimes feed themselves with warmed-up left-overs from the kitchen. But they sing with incredible gusto. They improvise variations, infuse sweet sentiment in the languorous passages, become effervescent and sprightly in the gay ones, spin out long notes through their round little mouths, as if they were real tenors. They choose the proper song for each table: little dance tunes for the young, lonesome love laments for the solitary couples and old numbers for the aged and nostalgic, exactly as if they were highly-paid entertainers under steady contract. Or take the majestic and motherly ladies who oversee public lavatories in parks or restaurants. They graciously open doors, hand you soap and towels as if they were flowers, exchange a few courtly words, and finally accept a modest tip with a queenly nod and a smile. What better way to spend one's life, they seem to think, than amidst the shining porcelain, the roar of many waters, the perfume of such delicate soaps, in contact with such distinguished people?

In previous centuries, foreign sculptors in Italy were always carried away by the skill, humility and eagerness of their marble-cutters, the men who translated their rough clay models into lasting stone and often improved them. In the same way, in Rome, today, foreign film directors, sober and efficient men in their homelands, often incapable of any sustained flights of imagination, are known to become intoxicated and to acquire a weird feeling of omnipotence when working with their local collaborators, a court of compliant assistant directors, cameramen, stage designers, architects, builders of sets, mechanics, carpenters, and electricians. The meekest soon discovers himself almost turning into a Tiberius, Nero or Caligula, a divine autocrat giving impossible and capricious orders to devoted slaves. He finds that anything, anything at all, which would take months of haggling elsewhere, can be done at once, in a matter of hours. There are apparently no obstacles to the free expression of his ideas, no petty chicanery from the front office, no financial difficulties, no trade union rules to hold up his inspiration. Finally he can prove himself the great artist Providence intended him to be.

The script can be revised, improved, enlarged at any time, whenever a good idea strikes him, even on the spur of the moment, on the set, while shooting. New sets can be ordered for scenes invented during a sleepless night, disrupting whole schedules. Episodes can be whipped up to exploit some bit of natural scenery the director has seen in the country or to employ the undiscovered talents of a little blonde girl he has met at a party. There is an enthusiastic feeling of improvisation which makes the work exciting. Sometimes a good suggestion comes from the make-up man or an electrician perched with his lights under the roof, and is immediately adopted. 'This is the stuff the *Teatro dell'arte* was made of,' says the delirious director. Every new idea, new turn in the plot, or new scene he suggests is welcomed with cries of enthusiasm from the Italian collaborators, who rush about feverishly giving immediate orders. '*Che ci vuole?*' they say, which means that nothing is impossible.

These people naturally do not dislike to see their precarious jobs prolonged, perhaps indefinitely. A morning shooting often turns into a whole day, sometimes goes on all night, if necessary, without interruptions and without anybody complaining. No one seems to remember he needs food and sleep and has a home, a family and a bed to go back to. In this way a film scheduled to be finished in six weeks often takes three or four months. A few are never finished. Only rarely do these happy improvisations and new ideas manage to improve a film. Many, in the end, turn out to be too long, slow, involved, amateurish and incomprehensible. A lot of work must be done to them, back home in the cutting room, to shorten them; often a voice off-screen must be added to explain the inexplicable jumps in the narration. Not a few Napoleonic directors have found their Waterloo in Rome.

Even ordinary foreigners, who have nothing much to do, who while away their time and their income as agreeably as possible, become fascinated by the opportunities and ease of Italian life. As they rent a house, hire a servant or two, order a suit and a few shirts, have a few pieces of furniture made by a cabinet maker on the basis of a vague sketch on the back of an envelope or a picture in a magazine or look for some rare antique, they are inevitably carried away by everyone's docile and enthusiastic collaboration. They begin to discover a new kind of freedom. One can order anything, or almost anything, made or done, and it costs no more, or only a little more, than what one has to accept from superior powers in other countries. Life is malleable, a soft, yielding matter which can be shaped to any form. Possibilities seem infinite and inexhaustible. Any whim can be satisfied, provided one has money, and it does not take too much money, at that. One can really express oneself in Italy.

Take the prostitutes. Experienced travellers, and the Italians themselves, naturally enough, believe that no professional courtesan in Europe beats the Italian. She has qualities all her own. She is often soft-spoken, gentle, at times even slightly timid and a little awkward. She appears anxious to please. She can be motherly, sisterly, wifely and also, suddenly, turn into a shameless bacchante, a delirious and skilful voluptuary. She has inherited from her immemorial past the knowledge of a great number of delicate refinements, but hides her art under an engaging appearance of embarrassed clumsiness. *Ars,* she has learned from the ancient Romans, even if she cannot say it with the old words, *est celare artem.* Great art must be guided by an invisible technique; it must seem the spontaneous blossom of the moment's mood and impulse.

Money seems not to be her immediate aim in life, as it does not seem to be the aim of all great artists. Of course, she does what she does for a few thousand lire. But somehow she gives the impression that, a few times, this time especially, the payment is a pure formality, a gross necessity. The perfection of her performance seems to be her real aim, and pleasure, the delicate pleasure of effortless love, pleasure for herself, of course, but also the pleasure she reads on a man's radiant face. What she apparently wants above all is to create a moment of pure and fragile illusion. At the end, she will toss the money away without counting it, and perhaps waste a few precious minutes talking to the client as if to an old friend. She will show him a picture of her little son, whom she keeps in the country with her peasant mother. She will notice a spot on the man's coat and take it off with benzene. She may pass a carnation through his button-hole. Often enough, her last kiss on the doorstep will be surprisingly chaste and affectionate, by no means perfunctory or lascivious. There is nothing hard, nothing commercial, nothing arid about her. She is a proud girl.

The traveller (after gathering these superficial impressions, before really plunging deeply into Italian life) is at first tempted to conclude that what he has been told and has read was all wrong. Italians are transparent people, he thinks, incapable of dissimulation and hypocrisy. He dives with joy and relief into this new and heady atmosphere, even though he cannot easily define the various elements which compose it. Only later he begins to suspect that there may be, with all this, a theatrical quality which enhances but slightly distorts all values.

CHAPTER FIVE

Illusion and Cagliostro

CLEARLY, then, the surface of Italian life, often gay and playful, sometimes bleak and tragic, has many of the characteristics of a show, a show in both meanings of the word. It is, first of all, almost always entertaining, moving, unreservedly picturesque, self-explanatory, animated, and engaging, as all good shows are, secondarily, all its effects are skilfully, if not always consciously, contrived and graduated to convey a certain message to, and arouse particular emotions in, the bystanders. Only the dull can refrain from smiling, gaping, or wiping a tear from their cheeks, as the case may be. Only the stupid can misinterpret the patent meaning of what they see.

The staging of scenes and the expression of sentiments inevitably tend to become more elaborate when the public is present. Watch an Italian mother fondle her baby. If she is alone, she is tender and solicitous like any other mother, in a matter-of-fact way. As soon as somebody enters the room, she will immediately enact a tasteful impersonation of Mother Love. Her face will suddenly shine, tears of affection will fill her eyes, she will crush the infant to her breast, sing to him, fondle him and make up poetic pet names. An Italian will often utter grave and sincere words (dictated by wrath, jealousy, the defence of his interests and dignity, or passionate love) and, at the same time, look out of the corner of his eye to check the impression he is making on his public.

The striving for effects, which can often be perceived in things made by God, is always present in those made, adapted and corrected by man: in the tiny and timid smile of a begging child; in the vast and majestic façade of a famous church or palazzo; in the green glass carafe of red wine on a pink table-cloth near two yellow lemons by the dark blue sea. The old bearded fishermen who sit on the sea wall smoking their clay pipes look ready to be photographed in colour for a travel poster. The forsaken appearance of a Sicilian village square, with its immense baroque church, the lounging unemployed men, the cadaverous donkeys, is a concrete dramatization of doom and hopelessness. The chrome and glass geometry of a northern industrial town is an equally concrete dramatization of efficient modernity.

The first purpose of the show is to make life acceptable. Life in the raw can be notoriously meaningless and frightening. Italians feel uncomfortable when surrounded by nature. They have for centuries cut down ancient woods where the pagan deities found their last refuge and solitary majestic trees. They long ago invented ways to force vegetation to obey their will: they pruned bushes into sculptured forms, they created gardens which were as similar to green cities as possible. Gabriele d'Annunzio, who was perhaps more Italian than any other Italian, spent the last years of his life passionately uprooting trees and bushes in his beautiful garden on Lake Garda (planted years before by a nature-loving German) to put in their place stone pillars, stone walls, marble arches and allegoric statuary. He even transported and installed among the flower beds the iron prow of a first world war torpedo boat. Italians long ago devised ways to make water design harmonious arabesques in fountains. The art of teaching horses apparently impossible things, which is still cultivated in Vienna by the *Spanische Schule* riders, was perfected in Naples by a man named Pignatelli almost four hundred years ago.

Dull and insignificant moments in life must be made decorous and agreeable with suitable decorations and rituals. Ugly things must be hidden, unpleasant and tragic facts swept under the carpet whenever possible. Everything must be made to sparkle, a simple meal, an ordinary transaction, a dreary speech, a cowardly capitulation must be embellished and ennobled with euphemisms, adornments and pathos. These practices were not (as many think) developed by people who find life rewarding and exhilarating, but by a pessimistic, realistic, resigned and frightened people. They believe man's ills cannot be cured but only assuaged, catastrophes cannot be averted but only mitigated. They prefer to glide elegantly over the surface of life and leave the depths unplumbed.

This eternal search for shallow pleasures and distractions, this dressing up at all costs of reality could become cloying and revolting if they were not accompanied by *garbo*. *Garbo* is another Italian word which cannot be translated exactly, as it describes a quality particularly necessary and appreciated here. It is, for instance, the careful circumspection with which one slowly changes political allegiance when things are on the verge of becoming dangerous; the tact with which unpleasant news must be gently announced; the grace with which the tailor cuts a coat to flatter the lines of the body; the sympathetic caution with which agonizing love affairs are finished off; the ability with which a *prefetto* gradually restores order in a rebellious province without provoking resentments. Without *garbo* a rousing patriotic speech would become rhetorical, a flamboyant declaration of love sickening, an elaborately adorned building loathsome, a florid musical composition unbearable. *Garbo* keeps everything within the boundaries of credibility and taste.

It is impossible not to be enchanted and fascinated by the show. In Italy a man is never alone with his thoughts, always feels himself immersed in humanity, everything around him is clear and open. Such picturesque performances by natural elements, landscapes, human beings and architecture constitute a kind of perpetual entertainment. Everything tells its own pathetic story. You are anxious to hear the next instalment. Nobody ever becomes surfeited with these delights. Even the natives cannot bear to be away from them for long. When they emigrate, they choose, if they can, to surround themselves, in the new country, with their own countrymen, familiar noises, gestures and facial expressions. They sometimes settle in dramatic landscapes resembling those they left behind, as they did generations ago in California. Neapolitans think other people die when they see Naples: what is certain is that the Neapolitans themselves decline visibly when they leave it.

Foreigners are doubly affected. They have never felt such a heady sensation. Like the inexperienced watching their first film, they are taken in by the life-like shadows

and carried away by the emotions evoked; they suspect
there must be a trick somewhere, but do not bother to
discover it. They seldom ask themselves why life in Italy
should be so moving, why the Italians should be the
actors, playwrights, choreographers, and *metteurs-en-scène*
of their own national drama; they just enjoy the show.
Once foreigners begin to understand that things are not
always exactly what they look like, that reality does not
have to be dull and ugly, they are no longer the same.
This sensation is important. It is a discovery which has
influenced more than ordinary travellers. It has subtly
transformed great writers who have come in contact with
Italy and, through them, the spirit of Europe. The new
animation which was felt in the work of men like Chaucer,
Milton, Goethe and Gogol, on their return, or even of
men who never left home, like Shakespeare and Pushkin,
and who knew about Italy from hearsay, was due only
in part to the fact that these writers may have studied
the language, imitated literary models, adopted new techniques, but, above all, that they had become aware of
the exhilarating Italian secret, that life can be ennobled
as a representation of life, that it can be made into a
work of art.

*

Polite lies and flattery can be utilitarian on occasion but,
most of the time, must be honestly classified among the
devices disinterestedly designed to make life decorous
and agreeable. They are the lubricants that make human
relations run more smoothly. Flattery somehow makes the
wariest of men feel bigger, more confident, and therefore
more indulgent, generous and almost magnanimous. It is
so common in Italy as to go practically unnoticed. One
breathes it as one breathes the scent of violets in woods
in the spring, without recognizing exactly what it is that
gives one such a delicate sensation. Everybody is constantly being vaguely praised by everybody else. A decrepit man is always told he looks years younger; any old
hag that she is beautiful, more beautiful this year than
last, today than yesterday, tonight more than this morning. Almost imperceptible flattery is in the eagerness with
which your orders are obeyed, or the obsequiousness with

which your advice is sought in matters in which you have no particular experience. It is in the use of academic or other titles; people affix them to your name, as if to prove that you so visibly deserve such honours that it is impossible you have not been awarded them. A middle-class man is called *dottore* in his youth and becomes a *commendatore,* or *knight commander,* when over forty. Ordinary letters are addressed to the 'most egregious', 'illustrious', 'celebrated', 'eminent', 'renowned' Signore, or simply to N.H., the abbreviation for *Nobil Uomo.* Tailors praise your build. Dentists exclaim: 'You have the teeth of an ancient Roman!' The doctor cannot help remarking that he has rarely encountered an influenza as baffling as yours. The antique dealer, the jeweller, the waiter, the butcher, everybody will exclaim that your taste is exquisite, that it is a pleasure to serve you, that they would not sell what you are buying to anybody and certainly not at the ridiculous price you are asked.

Naturally nobody takes such transparent homages seriously. Nobody, for instance, pays attention to the implicit flattery contained in every-day greetings. A friend of mine was saluted in Naples (the capital of hyperbolic and meaningless flattery) with the simple and courteous formula: 'Sir, consider me the last button on the livery of your last lackey.' What could be more tasteful? My friend, not being a Neapolitan, was taken aback. He did not know what to say. He mumbled incoherent monosyllables. The correct answer to that one, of course, is: 'Sir, the last button on the livery of my last lackey is of diamonds.'

Most polite lies, like flattery, are too transparent really to further the liar's interest. When the shoemaker convincingly says, one hand on his heart, 'Of course, sir, you will have your new shoes on Thursday, without fail. Do not worry!' he is aware that he cannot fulfil his promise. The shoes will not be ready on time. But he is lying not for himself. He is lying for you. He wants you to feel at peace until Thursday, at least, warmed by the hope that your shoes will arrive. Norman Douglas long ago derided this kindly habit. He wrote (in *Siren Land*): ' "Can you supply me with something to eat, fair Costanza?" "How not? Whatever you command." Whatever you command: fairy-like bubbles of southern politeness which, when pricked, evaporate into different macaroni.' It cannot be denied that in the few minutes preceding the appearance of the macaroni, as in the few days before Thursday, the expectation has added something to a man's life.

Even instruments of precision like speedometers and clocks are made to lie in Italy for your happiness. The instrument in your car always marks a figure which is between ten and twenty per cent above the actual speed at which you are travelling. It is meant to make you feel proud of your automobile and your driving skill, but also to make you slow down sooner than you would otherwise and possibly save your life. The clocks on railway stations are all five minutes fast; everybody knows it, of course; and yet travellers, who would arrive on time even if they walked, are stupidly encouraged to quicken their step. Only foreigners are sometimes discouraged sooner than necessary and miss their trains. The electric clocks on the trains themselves, on the other hand, are often a few minutes slow, to give passengers the illusion they arrive on time when they are late, or a little ahead.

*

Transparent deceptions are constantly employed to give a man the most precious of all Italian sensations, that of being a unique specimen of humanity, a distinct personality deserving special consideration. An Italian considers it a duty to cultivate such illusions in fellow human beings, but, above all, he considers it a duty to himself. Nobody in Italy ever confesses to being 'an average man'; everybody persuades himself he is, sometimes for intricate and improbable reasons, one of the gods' favoured sons. This sensation can be bolstered up not only with words but in many other ways. Take the matter of theatre tickets. To pay the full price for a theatrical performance is equivalent to admitting that one is nobody, has no friends and enjoys no particular powers. It is not surprising that Italian theatres are half-filled with non-paying customers and the other half with customers who pay a reduced price. (People who hold free tickets are known as *Portoghesi*, not because the natives of Portugal are especially addicted to the habit, but because, several centuries ago, a gala performance given in Rome in honour of a Portuguese mission was swamped by Romans who, as they entered, brazenly declared themselves Portuguese.) Similarly nobody pays the full price for railway tickets. All kinds of people travel free; most of the others enjoy vast discounts; only a few *grands seigneurs*, foreigners or naive Italians pay the full fare. This naturally creates complicated problems of accounting. It has been calculated that, if everybody paid, all fares could be halved.

Northern Italians love to tell the following joke about the Neapolitans' compulsion to make anybody feel a privileged person. It is the story of a Milanese buying a stamp in Naples. He walks out into the street carrying a letter, looking for a tobacco shop where stamps are sold, when he meets a Neapolitan acquaintance, who immediately grasps the situation. 'You want a stamp?' he says. 'You know where to buy it? Anywhere? How silly of you. It is lucky you met me. You must be careful these days. I know a good place, the best place in town—what am I saying?—in all Southern Italy. An old-fashioned tobacconist. He is honest, reliable, not one of those money-mad modern tobacconists. I will take you to him.' As he enters the shop, leading the Milanese, he winks visibly and addresses the man behind the counter: 'Giuseppe, this is a friend of mine, from Milano, who must be served with all due consideration. This is his problem. He wants a stamp, a thirty-lire stamp, for a most important letter which must be mailed immediately. I told him only you could give him entire satisfaction. Have you still some of those good thirty-lire stamps, those very good ones, which you sold me last week? Let him have one, please, one of the best.'

Less needy Italians successfully conceal the same ingratiating technique under a cloak of professional impassivity. Suave businessmen from the north confidentially offer some of their clients exceptionally encouraging deals, fabulous opportunities in profitable ventures, at particularly favourable conditions, 'just for you'. In reality most of these things are as difficult to obtain as thirty-lire stamps for thirty lire.

*

The show however is not always purely disinterested. It is often enacted also for the promotion of the actor's interests and those of his family, friends, and protégés. How many impossible things become probable here, how many insuperable difficulties can be smoothed over with the right clothes, the right facial expressions, the right *mise-en-scène*, the right words? With them anybody at all can quickly gain the attention, benevolence, and sympathy of the public at large or of a single important person. Alastair Reid, at a meeting of literary men gathered at Formentor, in 1962, to award two prizes to unknown writers, admired this particular technique. 'The Italians held forth,' he wrote, 'with such persuasive eloquence that no one could bear to impose on them the time limit of seven minutes that had been agreed on. (On one occasion, Vittorini stopped dramatically in mid-phrase to observe that he had outrun his time. "Go on, go on!" cried the bedazzled throng, and he did for a good ten minutes more.) Their every appearance was a performance, their every utterance a stylist's delight.' (The Italians that year managed to have one of the prizes awarded to one of their candidates, a struggling young woman writer, a protégée of Moravia.)

Sometimes the show is put up by a whole city, which wants to appear either prosperous or miserable, as the occasion requires. Rome was made to appear more modern, wealthy, and powerful with the addition of whole cardboard buildings, built like film sets, on the occasion of Hitler's visit, in 1938, in the fashion of Potemkin's villages. (Trilussa, the dialect poet, wrote a famous epigram on the occasion: *Roma de travertino, refatta de cartone, saluta l'imbianchino, suo prossimo padrone*, or 'Rome of travertine, re-made with cardboard, greets the house painter who will be her next master.') Hitler was notoriously impressed. Sometimes the show is put up by the whole country. After the war, Italian officials rushed to New York, some to describe the hunger, poverty, ruin and hopeless desperation of Italy, in order to get free grants of grain, cotton, coal, oil, and other raw materials from the American government, while others rushed to New York to describe an entirely different picture, the feverish activities, the new hope, the eagerness, the upsurge of energies, the fervid initiatives, the faith in the future of their countrymen, in order to get ordinary loans.

Sometimes the same men were entrusted with both missions. When passing from one office to another, or from a party with government officials to another party with private bankers, they quickly changed facial expressions and tone of voice. Of course, they never lied. Both pictures were true.

❋

Such behaviour was recommended long ago by one famous book. Few Italians, it is true, ever read it. Perhaps the author's teachings sank so deep into his countrymen's conscience that they are now part of their very nature, or, more probably, he, being Italian, merely codified what everybody more or less knew then and would still know centuries later. The book, by Baldassar Castiglione, is *Il libro del cortegiano*, printed in Venice in 1528. It was translated into English soon after as *The Book of the Courtier*; it became famous as the perfect guide for young members of the English Establishment practically until Edward VII's times. Castiglione teaches many accomplishments necessary to win and keep the favours of one's masters and to get ahead in the world: how to be at home in the tilting yard, the banquet-hall, the ladies' boudoir and the council chamber.

He was well suited to write such a treatise. His father was a wealthy count. His mother belonged to the almost royal house of Gonzaga. Born in 1478, at Casatico, in the duchy of Mantua, he was very carefully brought up and became a man of varied accomplishments, in all of which he was good but in none of which he was uncouth enough to excel: he was a soldier, politician, scholar, diplomat, author of renowned Latin poems, sportsman, art critic, and connoisseur, *homme à femmes*. He was at home in the principal courts of Europe. He visited London, in 1506, to accept the investiture of the Garter from Henry VII, as proxy for his master, the duke Guidobaldo d'Urbino. He was a friend of the best-known figures of his day, including Raphael, who painted his portrait, which now hangs in the Louvre. His advice is always practical and shrewd.

This is what he has to say, for instance, about facing dangers at war, in the language of his English translator:

'Where the Courtier is at skirmish, or assault, or battle upon the land, or in such other places of enterprise, he ought to work the matter wisely in separating himself from the multitude, and undertake the notable and bold feats which he has to do, with as little company as he can, and in the sight of noble men that be of most estimation in the camp, and especially in the presence and (if it were possible) before the very eyes of his king or great personage he is in service withall: for indeed it is meet to set forth to the show things well done.'

Castiglione is a gentleman and does not invite his reader to shirk his duty. A man, however, must not waste his heroism: he must undertake whatever dangerous task 'he has to do', seeing to it, with *garbo*, that his performance is not confused among many others, but staged well in sight of a choice and influential public, so that his daring shall not be in vain and his courage shall not go unrewarded. Are the arts of the courtier really honest? Castiglione reassured his reader that the skills he teaches, if properly employed, are not necessarily dishonourable: they are no more dishonourable than the dexterity with which the better sportsman defeats his opponent in a match ('Will you not say also that he who beats his fellow . . . at fencing . . . beguiles him because he has more art than the other?') or than the ability of the talented jeweller, who makes a precious stone 'much fairer' by setting it properly ('Will you say that the goldsmith deceives the eyes of them that look at a jewel?').

The devices are not always animated by the ignoble desire to deceive and bedazzle observers. Often, to put up a show becomes the only pathetic way to revolt against destiny, to face life's injustices with one of the few weapons available to a desperate and brave people, their imagination. To be powerful and rich, of course, is, for an individual as well as a nation, more desirable and satisfactory than to be weak and poor. Italians know it as well as anybody else. For some reason it has always been extremely difficult for them, individually and nationally, to conquer power and wealth. What were they to do? They staged an almost perfect imitation of the real thing. In normal times, after all, when there are no conflicts, power and the show of power can be considered equivalent. The mere shadow of power, if convincingly projected, can be as frightening as power itself. By its use, one may gain a few years or decades of tranquillity, and that is all one wants. In a crisis, of course, only real power can defend one. But crises are rare, seldom come unannounced, and can be delayed or avoided by a tactful change of policy. This is a risky game. It may last a certain length of time, perhaps a very long time, but not forever. At some point, real power destroys make-believe power and everything ends in catastrophe. But the show is better than nothing, better than the supine acceptance of immediate defeat.

Similarly, it is infinitely better to be rich than to seem rich. But if a man or a nation does not have the virtues and opportunities necessary to conquer and amass wealth, what is he or it to do? The art of appearing rich has been cultivated in Italy as nowhere else. Little provincial towns, capitals of tiny principalities in past centuries, like Lucca, Modena, Parma, Mantua, Ferrara, boast immense princely palaces, castles, vast churches, and stately opera houses, all disproportionate, sometimes ridiculously so, to the size of the principality, its means, and its population. There were in Naples penniless aristocratic families who could not afford carriages: they only owned the doors, with their coats of arms splendidly painted on them, which they attached to hired coaches on the rare days when they needed to parade in public. There were, here and there, decayed families who saved every lira, living in but a few rooms of their *palazzi* and eating boiled potatoes with the servants in the kitchen, in order to throw a big ball on one day of the year. The gilded salons were then thrown open, thousands of candles illuminated the gloom, flunkeys hired for the day stood in ancient liveries on the marble stairways holding silver candelabra in red peasant hands, two orchestras alternately filled the air with melodies, the champagne flowed freely. There are still today gentlemen buried in obscure country villages, where they manage what estates they have left, who emerge once a year, to go to Monte Carlo, Paris, or Biarritz for a few days, where they stay in the most celebrated hotels, dine with bejewelled ladies, entertain fabulously wealthy guests, are entertained in turn, tip lavishly, and then go back to their hiding places for another year of skimping.

One must bear this in mind even today, when the country has reached, for the first time in history, an unwonted opulence. Italians wear good clothes, drive shining cars and fill expensive restaurants. New companies erect stately steel and glass buildings for their head offices. Some of these people (not all, of course) own little more than the clothes on their back, the part of their car they have already paid for and the money with which to buy their expensive meals. Some of the companies dedicate a large part of their financial resources to the construction and the decoration of their resplendent new offices. Sociologists have recorded that the first expenditures made by the illiterate non-skilled workers in the South, when they get their first steady job in centuries, are strictly dedicated to superfluous and gaudy purchases: wrist watches, radios, television sets, and fancy clothes. Apparently the things they want above all are the show of prosperity and the reassurance they can read in the eyes of their envious neighbours. Only later do they improve their houses, buy some furniture, blankets, sheets, pots and pans. The last thing they spend money on is better food. Better food is invisible.

*

The suspicion that what surrounds one in Italy may be a show can be disturbing. It perplexes Italian adolescents, who have had a sheltered education, when they grow up. The pleasure foreigners feel at first is embittered, when they prolong their stay, by doubt and diffidence. Foreign diplomats in Rome disconsolately say: 'Italy is the opposite of Russia. In Moscow nothing is known yet everything is clear. In Rome everything is public, there are no secrets, everybody talks, things are at times flamboyantly enacted, yet one understands nothing.' To avoid making mistakes, some people conclude too hurriedly that everything here is only make-believe, nothing is ever what it looks like, and one can never trust appearances; everything then takes on a double outline as it does to a drunken man. These cautious people are just as easily misled as the naïve. Appearances in Italy are not always illusory. Is the young man less in love with his young lady if he courts her in a dramatic way? Is the man who watches the public's reaction from the corner of his eye less dominated by wrath, jealousy or love? Is the Sicilian village less miserable because it looks so evidently miserable? Is the army less powerful if it is pompously paraded? Not necessarily, of course, not always. In fact, the thing and its representation often coincide exactly. They may also coincide approximately, or may not coincide at all. There is no sure way of telling.

*

Take a very common example, the embarrassment of a pretty foreign girl who meets her Italian lover in an Italianate garden or a gondola under the moon. The man softly murmurs reassuring and entreating words into her ears. Meanwhile his hands seem animated by a life of their own. They caress her, attract her near him, tickle her hair at the nape, and boldly slip under her dress. His cheeks brush hers. He becomes more ardent, voluptuous and commanding. He is difficult to resist. What can she make of the performance? What is he, really? He may be an honest lover like any other, perhaps a little more skilful. He may be, at the opposite end of the scale, an accomplished performer, a complete impostor. He may also be anything in between. Reality and representation may differ by a mere hairbreadth, like the two images in a camera telemeter. He himself often does not know where truth ends and invention begins. He may sincerely think he is in love but may only be a lukewarm and temporary *innamorato* carried away by emotions and his ability. Or he may have found the challenge to his skill or daring too strong to resist in an especially difficult situation, matched with a particularly virtuous woman. Or he may be desperately in love. Whatever his feelings, his performance is almost always delightful, moving and tactful. Only rarely it may be irritating. The poor girl can only give in within reason, play her own rôle, keep her head, and enjoy the show.

One does not have to be a pretty woman, a diplomat, or a businessman to meet the problem. Ordinary sightseers face it. Everything must be interpreted in a similar fashion. Monuments, to begin with. The biggest in Italy is dedicated to Victor Emmanuel II, the Father of His Country, in the Piazza Venezia, in Rome. It is, obviously, and visibly, what it purports to be, the massive tribute of a grateful people to the king and military leader responsible for their liberation and the foundation of the Italian unified national state, in 1861. Its grandiose architecture is an early twentieth-century, or Belle Époque, copy of Roman Imperial style. We must overlook the fact that, since it was inaugurated in 1911, hundreds of film sets have aped its example and numberless *papier maché* reproductions of the same colonnades and tympana have somewhat spoiled the original effect for us.

Then one examines it a little more closely. Why was such a huge pile erected in the very heart of ancient Rome, on the most sacred of the seven hills? Why was it not built in a park, outside the city, on a less revered height, possibly on Monte Mario? Why does it conceal and practically swallow the Campidoglio? Was the sight of the famous hill disturbing to the pride of modern Italians? (One knows, of course, why the marble is so irremediably white. It is not the traditional stone of Rome, travertine. It was quarried near Brescia, in North Italy, for the good reason that the prime minister of the time, Zanardelli, was from Brescia.) Why is its style so self-consciously imperial?

By and by one begins to perceive another monument, underneath the first. The excessive size of the construction, its position, its architecture reveal the insecurity which surrounded the patriotic minority who managed to achieve Italian unity and tried to strengthen it against almost overwhelming opposition. They clearly wanted to celebrate a National Hero to cancel out many of the heroes of the past, a patriot to obliterate all non-patriotic Italians, a king to annul all republican partisans of the Risorgimento. If Victor Emmanuel II had not existed, or if he had not been as brave and generous a king as he was, one suspects the governing élite of the time would have invented him, attributing to him the Plutarchian virtues he should have possesesed. In the end, one concludes that the monument is not only the sincere tribute of a grateful people to the memory of their great king, but also the theatrical representation of such a tribute.

Or take some of the churches. Take the biggest and most

revered of them all, Saint Peter's. It is undoubtedly an impressive place of worship. All of the greatest artists since the Renaissance laboured to make it so. Michelangelo was one of its architects. All the paraphernalia and personnel necessary for ritual communication with the deity are abundantly available. Grandiose ceremonies are staged periodically, according to a very ancient liturgy, dedicated to the revealed mysteries and holy traditions of the Roman Catholic Church. Hundreds of unbelievers are converted yearly within its walls. Thousands of believers are confirmed daily in their faith and comforted. But, when one compares it to other churches, elsewhere, and to a few very old small ones in Rome itself, one finds it perhaps too ornate, mundane, rhetorical, and vast to conciliate the intimate emotions usually connected with religious fervour.

One can pray there only with some difficulty. One is distracted by the colours of the rare marbles, the complicated architecture, the miniature perfection of the sculptures, the gesticulation of the statues, the celestial music, the coming and going of herds of indifferent sightseers. One begins to understand, at a certain point, that it is not only a great basilica, a place of worship, the seat of the Holy Roman Church, but also the dramatic representation of all this. One discovers that it is not merely designed to inspire religious emotions but also to impress the onlooker with the power, the majesty, the wealth and the solidity of the Church and, therefore, the glory of God himself. If you then happen to come across one of the secret storehouses where the necessary decorations and machines for the various ceremonies are kept, you cannot escape an irreverent conclusion: Saint Peter's is also God's own holy playhouse.

*

The search for the secondary level of everything Italian becomes a game, at a certain point. Is the hungry beggar in the street real or a good imitation? How much is Signor A, the celebrated contemporary politician, whose picture daily appears in the press, a real statesman, and how much, instead, the skilful impersonation of one? How truly is Signor B a great novelist, Signor C a great actor,

Signor D a great film director, Signor E a great poet? Of course there is no simple answer. Most of these eminent gentlemen may be, in their particular callings, what they seem. They certainly are, at the same time, and in varying degrees, good impersonations. A few may be clever impostors, some, on the other hand, may be even greater than their public character; others may be great but in a different way.

D'Annunzio, for instance, lived like a Renaissance prince, was a voluptuary surrounded by borzois, a gaudy clutter of antiques, brocades, rare Oriental perfumes and flamboyant but inexpensive jewellery; dressed like a London clubman; preferably slept with duchesses, world-famous actresses, and mad Russian ladies; wrote exquisitely wrought prose and poetry; rode to hounds. His politics were of the extreme right. In reality he was a penniless provincial character of genius, the son of a small merchant from Pescara.

Alberto Moravia, on the other hand, wears turtle-neck sweaters and shabby clothes; often writes the awkward language spoken by uncultured people, freely employing words children are punished for pronouncing; publicly escorts unemployed starlets, unknown lady poets just out of school, and the daughters of metal workers and bricklayers. His politics are of the extreme left. In reality he is the son of a wealthy bourgeois family, decently brought up according to the rigid standards of the first decades of this century (there are pictures of him in Little Lord Fauntleroy and sailor suits), who could easily live on the income from his properties, inherited from his father, who was a hard-working construction engineer.

Both men, d'Annunzio and Moravia, are extraordinary writers, both typical representatives of their respective generations. Both tried to become spokesmen for a class and a kind of life which was not theirs. The perfection of these performances is such that it is usually almost impossible to determine at first sight how close the real and fictitious characters are to each other. An exact valuation often takes some time. Meanwhile one must behave with caution.

*

This is, it must be admitted, more or less true in many other countries. It has been true at all times. There have always been eminent men who played their own rôles with skill. Impersonation has been an essential part of the métier of mighty personages in all epochs. Nero died thinking he had been a great actor playing the rôle of a Roman Emperor. Louis XIV was proverbially faithful all his life to his duties as a showman. Many men managed to persuade the crowds of their own greatness; others only the more naïve, from a distance, and not for long. Great historical events often took the form of ceremonial display. There have always been monuments and edifices which were at the same time what they were and representations of themselves. Take the old castles, anywhere in Europe: how much strictly military value had they and how much were they designed to impress the enemy with their impregnability?

This is also true in Italy. But there is a fundamental difference. In other parts of the world substance always takes precedence and its external aspect is considered useful but secondary. Here, on the other hand, the show is as important as, many times more important than, reality. This is perhaps due to the fact that the climate has allowed Italians to live mostly outside their houses, in the streets and *piazze;* they judge men and events less by what they read or learn, and far more by what they see, hear, touch and smell. Or because they are naturally inclined towards arranging a spectacle, acting a character, staging a drama; or because they are more pleased by display than others, to the point that they do not countenance life when it is reduced to unadorned truth. It may be because the show can be a satisfactory *ersatz* for many things they lack, or because they love, above all, a good actor who can stir them, a good dramatic situation which can make them feel the emotions only art can evoke well. Whatever the reason, the result is that at all times form and substance are considered one and the same thing. One cannot exist without the other. The expression is the thing expressed.

This reliance on symbols and spectacles must be clearly grasped if one wants to understand Italy, Italian history, manners, civilization, habits, and to foresee the future. It must by no means be overlooked by anyone who does not want to delude himself. It is the fundamental trait of the national character. It helps people to solve most of their problems. It governs public and private life. It shapes policy and political designs. It is, incidentally, one of the reasons why the Italians have always excelled in all activities in which the appearance is predominant: architecture, decoration, landscape gardening, the figurative arts, pageantry, fireworks, ceremonies, opera, and now industrial design, stage jewellery, fashions, and the cinema. Italian medieval armour was the most beautiful in Europe: it was highly decorated, elegantly shaped, well-designed, but too light and thin to be used in combat. In war the Italians themselves preferred the German armour, which was ugly but practical. It was safer.

Inevitably Italians are tempted to applaud more those performances which stray dangerously farthest from reality, those which make do with the scantiest of materials, those which do not even pretend to imitate existing models and still manage to be effective, convincing, stirring or entertaining. Take imitation marble. Since the earliest days local craftsmen have been unique in their ability to counterfeit the real thing. Half the marble one sees in churches or patrician *palazzi* is in fact but smooth plaster deceptively painted. It is not necessarily always cheaper than the real thing: at times it can be infinitely more expensive and inconvenient. Of all the imitation marbles, Italians appreciate more those which really imitate nothing at all, but create a combination of colours which never existed in nature. What is specially prized is the daring of their makers, their Promethean challenge to God.

The word for such dexterity is *virtuosismo*. The greatest of all, Nicolò Paganini, often finished playing his most complicated sonatas after breaking all the strings of his violin except one. Down the centuries, Italian *virtuosi* have been famous for having produced floods of *trompe l'œil*, *trompe* the mind, and *trompe* the heart. They have filled libraries with admirable love poems inspired by no vulgar passion but by a highly developed ability to make harmonious and technically perfect combinations of words. They can write impeccable essays proving the absolute opposite of what everybody knows is the truth; impeccable scientific papers knowingly based on slightly spurious data; historical studies in which the facts disagreeing with the author's thesis are carefully neglected. Some criminal lawyers take special pride in having those clients acquitted who they know are really guilty.

Many see through the deception and yet applaud the adroitness of the performer. It takes a great man to do such things. Anybody can make an omelette with eggs. Only a genius can make one without. *Virtuosismo* is not necessarily an empty display of ability. It often has a practical value. Take warfare during the Renaissance. As it was practised abroad, it consisted of the earnest and bloody clash of vast armies. He who killed more enemies carried the day. In Italy it was an elegant and practically bloodless pantomime. Highly paid *condottieri*, at the head of picturesque but small companies of armed men, staged the outward appearance of armed conflict, decorating the stage with beautiful props, flags, coloured tents, caparisoned horses, plumes; the action was accompanied by suitable martial music, rolls of drums, heartening songs and blood-chilling cries. They convincingly manœuvred their few men back and forth, pursued each other across vast provinces, conquered each other's fortresses. Victory was decided by secret negotiations and the offer of bribes. It was, after all, a very civilized and entertaining way of waging war. It often left matters as undecided as warfare practised elsewhere, but cost less in money, human lives and suffering.

Italians have been suspected of duplicity in every epoch. They are believed to excel in such disreputable and dubious fields as diplomacy, the conduct of intrigues, fraudulent speculations and the organization of swindles. Severe foreigners point out that the arts of political deception were codified by the Italians and that some of the most famous international adventurers were Italians—such names as Giacomo Casanova and the Count of Cagliostro are often quoted to prove the point. These accusations are old, so old that some go back to the Middle Ages and some probably to earlier times, rooted in racial and religious prejudices and misunderstandings. But there is some truth in some of them.

It must be admitted, first of all, that the virtues of the Italians, like those of other peoples, may at times degenerate into their corresponding vices. The parsimony of the French easily turns into avarice; the reserve of the English into deaf and dumb isolation; the animated activity of the Americans into senseless agitation. It is not surprising, therefore, that the possession of a knack to correct and embellish the appearance of life may at times tempt some Italians to utilize it to mystify their neighbours for their own private advantage. But something always prevents an Italian from achieving a lasting, world-wide, stupendous swindle. He is usually the victim of his own machinations. Italian adventurers, founders of counterfeit religions and dishonest financiers on a large scale are few and insignificant when compared to those born in other countries. None of the internationally famous scandals of the past is connected with an Italian name. John Law was a Scotsman; no Italian was involved in the South Sea Bubble, the speculation in tulip bulbs in the Netherlands, the scandal of the Panama Canal company shares in Paris at the end of the last century, the Stavisky case in France between the two world wars or the growth and collapse of the empire of Kreuger, the Swedish match king.

There is no doubt that the Italian Giacomo Casanova had the qualities for a career as an international adventurer and swindler, comparable to the best foreign examples, but it can be proved that what prevented him from reaching ultimate success was, curiously enough, his most typical Italian characteristics. He was tall, handsome, with a spacious forehead and a Roman nose, the looks of a gentleman, and an air of authority about him. He was untiringly vigorous and healthy. He was also clever, wrote well and fluently, played several musical instruments, spoke and wrote several languages with ease, Italian and French with elegance. He had read a great deal, quoted glibly from the Latin and Greek classics and contemporary authors; he could converse as an equal with philosophers, poets, and novelists. He visited Voltaire to dispute with him on some minor point. He pleased women at first sight, women of all ages and conditions, and usually succeeded in rendering them helpless and defenceless in front of his pressing entreaties. His physical capacity to satisfy the most exacting mistress by renewing his homages to her a practically unlimited number of times through the night and the following day, with only short *entr'actes* between the exertions, is not as surprising as the feat of psychological endurance: he was never bored, never embittered by experience, sincerely admired one woman after another, and slipped into bed at a moment's notice with the fat, the lean, the young, the old, the dirty, the *soignée*, the lady, the chambermaid, the strumpet, the nun, always admirably animated, till very late in life, by the same schoolboyish eagerness.

He spoke in a very persuasive manner and often impersonated any character he chose. 'My secret is simple: I always say the truth, and people naturally believe me,' he lied in his memoirs. His truths were, to say the least, improbable and, at times, blatantly absurd, yet most people trusted him for a time. He had no scruples of any kind, in any field, to embarrass him. He died penniless, alone, far from his native land. He was saved from destitution by a charitable friend, Graf Waldstein, who gave him a dreary job as librarian in his castle at Dux, in Bohemia. The great adventurer's last years were embittered by humiliating squabbles with the Graf's servants, who played backstairs tricks and practical jokes on the defenceless old man.

•

The other notorious Italian adventurer usually mentioned in the same breath with Casanova, was born Giuseppe Balsamo but called himself Count Alessandro di Cagliostro (Cagliostro was the family name of a married aunt who had been his godmother). His success is almost inexplicable. He is described as short, fat, ugly, dark-skinned, unwashed, with a sullen and suspicious expression on a vulgar face. He was arrogant, rude, boastful and given to outbursts of frantic rage. He had no known mistress. He was a faithful husband. Practically illiterate, he spoke only one language really well, the Sicilian dialect, and all others with a heavy Sicilian accent. 'There is,' wrote Lavater to young Goethe, 'nothing seductive about him.' Goethe was so interested in the famous charlatan that, when he was in Palermo, he went out of his way to prove to himself beyond doubt that the Count of Cagliostro and Giuseppe Balsamo were the same person. (Cagliostro had denied it and was to deny it to his end.) He searched for the family and found them to be poor, honest, God-fearing people, in a spotlessly clean kitchen. Cagliostro's mother plaintively asked the young German poet, if he should ever meet her son in the North, to remind him that he still owed money to her since the last time he had been home, years before, when he had pawned some of her jewellery and had never redeemed it. 'We are told,' the relatives said to Goethe, 'that Giuseppe has made a fortune and now lives like a very rich man. What luck would be ours if he returned here and took care of us!' It was the candid expression of an aspiration which is still universal in Sicily—to be supported by a rich relative.

Giuseppe Balsamo was born in Palermo in 1743. He entered a convent where the good brothers, who dedicated their lives to healing the sick, taught him the rudiments of medical arts which were to be useful to him later in life. He ran away after a while and grew up in the streets, making ends meet by practising many illegal trades. He dabbled in the primitive magic practices of the poor and illiterate, who obscurely still preserved pre-Christian and Moslem traditions and beliefs. He sold potions, made incantations, evoked demons, prepared amulets, told the future, healed the sick and endeavoured to kill his clients' enemies from afar for a small price. Above all he practised an art for which he had a special talent and which he went on perfecting all his life: he reproduced any signature with such perfection that he often deceived the original signer, and could counterfeit all sorts of difficult documents. In 1768 he decided Palermo had nothing more to teach him and left to seek his fortune in the world.

He emigrated to Rome where he met and married Lorenza Feliciani, the daughter of a small artisan. Lorenza was so beautiful as to be practically irresistible. She was still described as 'seductive' by sober and reliable witnesses twenty years later. What his unsavoury and repellent aspect had prevented him from attempting he could now do with the aid of his wife. Smiling Lorenza attracted and reassured wealthy men. Some slept with her and paid her well, some merely basked in the radiance of her beauty. They were all fleeced by her husband. Cagliostro sometimes feigned terrible attacks of jealousy and blackmailed some customer (in London he blackmailed a married Quaker with no difficulty), but more often he just placidly counted the money coming in. (It was not an unusual practice at the time. The husband of a well-known eighteenth-century ballerina used to say: '*Les cornes c'est comme les dents. Ça fait mal quand ça pousse et puis l'on mange avec.*') At the same time, he continued to practise his own arts.

The young couple travelled through Europe, as all good adventurers had to. Everywhere they lived in luxury and were encouraged and aided by the rich and important friends Lorenza soon gathered around her: in Saint Petersburg it was Potemkin himself who protected them. Wherever he stopped, Cagliostro organized a lodge of a Masonic rite of his own invention, the 'Egyptian Order', which possessed magical secrets no other order had ever heard of. All his wife's friends were usually enrolled with elaborate ceremonies. Among the many advantages of the order was the possibility of purchasing from the Grand Copht, the leader himself, one of his two famous elixirs. The first, the less expensive brand, merely stopped a man's age at the moment he took the first sip; the second managed to turn time backwards and rejuvenated the customer by a matter of ten, twenty, or thirty years, according to the dose. The success of the two potions was immense. Cagliostro filled Europe with his bottles.

He himself, as he liked to point out, was living proof of the success of his secret formulæ. He was thousands of years old. He remembered everything he had seen in his centuries-old life. He would reminisce about the construction of the Pyramids, the Roman emperors he had met, and what Jesus Christ had told him. No great personage of the past escaped his friendship. He was probably the greatest name-dropper in history. The manufacture of his elixirs was among his lesser activities. He conducted magic rites and experiments of all kinds, turned lead into gold in front of sceptical audiences, communicated with superior spirits, healed the sick, and foretold the future. Some of this was pure quackery. Some, however, showed him to possess mysterious, metaphysical powers of sorts. He really healed many sick clients and a few of his prophecies came true. Fleeing from France in 1785 he predicted the revolution, the destruction of the Bastille, and the coming of 'a great Prince who would reform religion'.

Cardinal de Rohan was convinced that he had seen him actually manufacture gold in the cardinal's own palace in Strasbourg and construct from tiny stones a huge diamond worth 25,000 livres. 'He will make me,' proclaimed Rohan, 'the richest man in Europe', and placed a marble bust of the magician, inscribed with the words 'The divine Cagliostro', on the staircase of his country palace at Saverne. In Paris, a city notoriously hospitable to quacks, he and his wife had a great success. Lorenza adopted the name of Serafina and pretended to be an ageless spirit from another world. He cured wealthy patrons and crowds of paupers who waited for him at the gate of his house every morning. Unfortunately, his friendship with the gullible cardinal involved him in the famous affair of the Queen's necklace. As a result, he and Lorenza were locked in the Bastille. Being innocent of this particular crime, he was quickly able to prove it; the Cagliostros were freed, but obliged by the police to leave Paris immediately.

This incident was the beginning of the end. The couple meandered once again through Europe, but without success. The old charm was gone. He had become too notorious. Too many people thought he was a humbug. The couple ended up in Rome, almost twenty years after leaving the city. This was his final mistake. He failed as a healer; the Romans were neither as ill nor as gullible as the Parisians. He tried, as a last resort, to set up a Roman lodge of his famous Egyptian Order. He invited all the best people, including high prelates, to an introductory meeting at the Villa Malta. (The villa is next to the Villa Medici. It belonged to the Knights of Malta, later became the residence of Prince von Bülow, who was German ambassador in Rome in 1914, and is now owned by the Jesuit Order.)

A sceptical eye-witness, the abbé Lucantonio Benedetti, has left us a minute description of Cagliostro's last desperate effort to ward off ruin. The count, short, thick-set, dark, appeared sitting on a tripod, like the Sybil of old, and gave what probably was his set speech for such occasions. 'It is fitting that I reveal who I am, that I open up my past. . . . I see the endless desert, the giant palms project their shadows on the sand, the Nile flow quietly, the Sphinxes, the obelisks, the columns rise majestically. Here are the wonderful walls, the temples rising in great numbers. . . . It is the sacred city, Memphis. . . . The victorious king is entering the gates, Thotmes III the Glorious, after having defeated the Syrians and the Canaanites. . . . *Io vedo* . . . But now I am in another city, here is the sacred temple where Jehovah was adored. . . . The new god has vanquished the old. . . . I hear voices, people are acclaiming the prophet, the son of God. . . . Who is he? He is the Christ. Ah, I see him, at the wedding feast of Cana, turning water into wine. . . .'

The abbé added: 'Here he gave a great cry and jumped from his tripod. He shouted: "He was not the only one to perform that miracle. I will show you. I will reveal to you the mysteries, nothing is unknown to me, I know all, I am immortal, antediluvian. . . . *Ego sum qui sum.*"' He proceeded to add a few drops of magic liquid into a carafe of water and turned it into wine ('sparkling like Orvieto', the abbé duly noted), which he declared to be the famous Falerno of the ancient Romans. 'A few people tasted it and called it excellent,' the abbé wrote, who did not touch it. The count then spoke of other secret powers he possessed and of his magic elixirs. He distributed samples of elixir number one to a few elderly gentlemen in the audience, whose eyes immediately shone and whose cheeks became pink. (The abbé wrote in his diary: 'The elixir had about the same visible effect of a good glass of Montefiascone.')

Finally, he gave the demonstration of his power to transform small diamonds into big ones. He borrowed a ring from the French ambassador, the same Cardinal de Bernis who had been Casanova's friend in Venice and Paris, put it in a crucible, poured various liquids and powders over it, spoke words which he said were Egyptian and Hebrew, and finally handed the cardinal his ring with a stone more than twice the original size. 'The cardinal cried out that a miracle had been performed,' wrote the abbé Benedetti, 'but I believe the second ring had nothing to do with the first and that the second stone was but a piece of rock crystal.'

The meeting was a failure. Cagliostro was arrested and imprisoned in Castel Sant'Angelo, by order of the Holy Office, not for being a swindler but for impiety, heresy and practices offensive to the Church and the Christian religion. His wife turned witness for the prosecution, to save her neck. He was tried and sentenced to death. The sentence was later commuted to life imprisonment. Cagliostro was locked in a small cell in the impregnable castle San Leo, near Rimini. He died a short time before the French revolutionary armies, who had invaded the Papal states and were liberating all the prisoners of the Papal tyranny along their way, could reach him.

*

An old English lady I knew, who spent most of her life in Rome, used to wag a finger and say: 'There is some Cagliostro and some Casanova in every Italian, even in those you'd suspect the least.' The fact, which, of course, did not displease her, is not entirely exact. Casanova and Cagliostro, it is true, could not have been born elsewhere. Their adventurous lives were, in a way, a retaliation *all'Italiana* against a world that had made them poor, powerless, despised, and members of a nation that offered to them at the time, only a life of poverty, buffoonery, and sordid humiliation. They also had the common Italian defect, that they could not employ their particular gifts to construct something solid, to transform their lives in a stable way, to conquer durable honours, wealth, prestige, and power, as adventurers from other lands would have done.

Something always stopped them. They practised their art for art's sake. They distributed treasures with the same ease with which they amassed them. They were contented with but the appearance of success. Their careers, however, belong to Europe and not to Italy. They had to go abroad to find customers in sufficient numbers. Their achievements depended in part on the absence of other Italians in their entourage and among their customers. Their victims could only be foreigners.

The credulity of their easy public spoiled them in the end and made them over-confident. Their *virtuosismo* led them astray. They overreached themselves, making their stories more and more daringly incredible. That is why, every time they touched Italian soil, they came to grief: Casanova was once jailed in Venice and twice forced to flee, Cagliostro met his final defeat in Rome. Both of them were not such good Italians as those who never left the country, lived a quiet life, and used their powers in a discreet and inconspicuous way, without ending up in prison or in a solitary cell in a remote castle, leaving a spotless name and a tidy fortune to their descendants. Not to become notorious is the most important rule.

These are (to sum them all up) the most easily identifiable reasons why Italians love their own show, why they prefer often to live in their own ambiguous world of make-believe, among *papier mâché* reproductions of reality, flowery but insincere words, in the penumbra of half truths, among the convulsive gesticulations of unfelt sentiments and emotions. First of all, they do it to tame and prettify savage nature, to make life bearable, dignified, significant, and pleasant, for others and themselves. They do it, then, for their own private ends; a good show makes a man *simpatico* to powerful people, helps him get on in the world and obtain what he wants, solves many problems, lubricates the wheels of society, protects him from the envy of his enemies and the arrogance of the mighty. They do it to avenge themselves on unjust fate.

In difficult times, under bloody tyrannies, the show can also be used as a defence. It is, often enough, the only defence. During the last few months of the last war, when Italy was the battle ground of foreign armies and divided by civil war, I was living on a lonely part of the coast of Tuscany, near Porto Santo Stefano. Allied bombers rained bombs on us night and day. During a lull, a German navy captain and some officers came to pay me a visit: they carefully looked over the house to see if there was anything suspicious, talked obscurely among themselves, finally relaxed, sat down, and drank some wine. I drank with them. The captain sighed and said: 'You don't know, sir, how insidious life in Italy today can be for men like us. Everybody, literally everybody you meet can be an enemy, a deadly enemy.' I said nothing. He went on: 'Not everybody is like you, sir. I can see from your face that you wish for the victory of your country and its German allies. There are many, you will not believe this, who want our defeat, but there is absolutely no way to tell them apart from the others.'

I was left speechless. The captain was honestly disconsolate. The fact that the Italians did not go around carrying large signs, reading 'Loyal ally of Nazi Germany' or 'Despicable traitor wishing for the defeat of his country and its allies', seemed to him incredible. How could he really tell friends from foes? Was he a mind reader? How could he reward the good Italians and shoot the others on sight, when they all smiled to him in about the same way, talked mildly about the weather and the war, expressed the same vague hopes in speedy victory and peace, lifted their glasses to Mussolini and Hitler, and looked about as honest and reliable as all Italians did to a good German? In my case, obviously, he felt he could rest secure. Why? He did not know I was on a Fascist government list of suspects to be arrested on sight and possibly shot (such lists were long and had practically no importance in the front lines; they often lay forgotten in their unopened envelopes). He could not know that I had been busy with underground work and was at the time giving partisans all the help I could. How could he, if I did not tell him?

The case, I admit, is too extreme to be used as a typical illustration. The captain, without a doubt, was less perspicacious than most of his countrymen. He might also have been tired, confused by the incessant bombings, dejected and frightened. He might have been stupid. Still, his sincere and heart-breaking lamentations will remain with me as the most memorable example I have ever encountered of a northerner's bewilderment in front of the complexity of Italian life. His words also proved to me, incidentally, how thoroughly Italian I was, in spite of my foreign travels and education, since I was able, practically without speaking, to convince a poor, guileless, candid Nazi that I was openly and firmly on the side of the Axis.

CHAPTER SIX

The Other Face of the Coin

BEHIND the turbulent and picturesque agitation of Italy, behind the amiable, festive, and touching spectacle, behind the skilful performances, real life is something else. It can be sordid, tragic, and pitiless. It is often an anguished, sometimes a mortally dangerous game. It is always difficult. The cradle of every newly-born baby is surrounded by a number of evil and all-powerful genii, determined to make his existence a miserable one. He must try to ward them off and to defeat them, if he can, when he grows up. His is a desperate job, with only a few and feeble good influences to help him.

The first of the evil spirits is poverty. Italy is still a very poor country today, poorer as a whole than any other western European country except Spain. (The average standard of living has been calculated to be at present about what it was in the United States in 1914, in France in 1924, and in Britain in 1927.) The Mezzogiorno is still by far the most miserable region. In spite of the vast sums invested by the government over the past decade, the poverty of the Meridionali as a whole is still only a little less acute than that of the population of North Africa. The majority of them still manage to eat only enough to stave off death; it is an improvement, of course, on what they could afford in the past. In the newly-built factories, the management compels the workers to consume one square meal a day in the canteens to be sure they have absorbed an adequate amount of calories and are strong enough to carry on their work. It is well-known that, should they be allowed to lunch at home, they would eat practically nothing, as they would have to share their food with many famished relatives. Then there is the shoddy poverty of most of the northern industrial slums; the melancholy and concealed poverty of better-paid workers, the more modest employees, and the lower middle class in general, who often save every lira in order not to conquer status symbols but to give their sons a superior education and allow them to go to the university; their sons' angry poverty, the cultural proletarians, who earn less than unskilled workers as teachers, municipal doctors or veterinary surgeons in country towns and villages, petty bureaucrats, police officials, trade union organizers, and party hacks.

There is the poverty of the decayed and proud aristocrats, owners of once prosperous lands ruined by price drops, agrarian reform or foreign competition, the poverty of the dispossessed élites of yesterday and the day before. All these *déclassés* join with the cultural proletarians to form the cadres of the fanatic mass movements of the extreme left and the extreme right. Even where there is no actual poverty, among reasonably prosperous people, there is always the fear of its possibility which casts its gloomy shadow over everything. The rich tend to behave as if wealth were a precious medicine in times of epidemics. Many cling pathetically to it and defend it by every means, legal or illegal.

The second of the evil genii is ignorance. Millions of people, between ten and thirty per cent of the population, are still illiterate. The figure varies according to the definition of illiteracy. Is a man who cannot read and can write only his name literate or illiterate? Is a man who went to school but forgot everything, or who can only occasionally make out a few familiar words on a wall poster, literate or illiterate? Even the undeniably literate are seldom very proficient. Fewer newspapers per million of the population are sold in Italy than in any other country of western Europe. The cultured minority itself, as a rule, still possesses only an old-fashioned, provincial and inadequate culture.

Practically nobody, except cabinet ministers, journalists, diplomats, businessmen, a few scholars, and the rich, has the possibility of travelling abroad to study foreign habits and compare foreign countries with their own. The widespread ignorance of real conditions in the rest of the world feeds unjustified prides and prejudices, excessive admiration or absurd contempt for foreigners. The new politicians, improvised since the end of the war, have mostly been compelled to become real experts in one art alone, the most difficult of all, that of getting themselves elected by an inconstant electorate and of jockeying for high position within their parties, in Parliament, and in the government. They have all been frenziedly occupied with day-to-day chores, signing thousands of letters every day, conferring, flying to international conferences, travelling through the provinces, making speeches of all kinds for all occasions; too busy not only to make a serious examination of the national problems, to devise modern solutions for them, to survey the wheezy functioning of the State apparatus, and to analyse the causes of its decay, but even at times to read the newspapers. These are read for them by underlings, who cull a few paragraphs for their perusal. Political business is carried on mostly by ear.

The most erudite Italians, the university professors, the depositors of the nation's culture, lack funds to purchase books and to carry on simple scientific experiments. University laboratories are ridiculously inadequate, the libraries pitifully small and out of date. The salaries being offensively tiny, professors must make a living. They take on extra jobs, as consultants for business concerns, or as practitioners of the professions they teach, doctors, economists, lawyers, geologists, engineers, surgeons. This becomes their main activity. Their academic rank, the 'prof.' on their visiting cards, merely serves them to earn bigger fees. They have little time for anything else also because they must live where they make their money and commute to the provincial cities where they have their chairs. They lecture and run. Many keep abreast of progress abroad by desultorily reading specialized magazines. Only a few heroic ones somehow manage to study seriously, find the money necessary to carry on their scientific research, become world authorities in their field and win Nobel Prizes. Even the Church is alarmed at the low level of erudition of the ordinary clergy and the parish priests, whose worldly and theological knowledge is often much below that of their French and German colleagues.

The third evil spirit is injustice. There are too many laws in Italy. A tropical tangle of statutes, rules, norms, regulations, customs, some hundreds of years old, some

voted last week by Parliament and signed this very
morning by the President, could paralyse every activity
in the land, stop trains, planes, cars, and ships, shut
every shop, industrial plant, hospital, school, and office, if
they were suddenly applied. The late Luigi Einaudi, Italy's
foremost economist and ex-President of the Republic,
calculated that, if every tax on the statute books was fully
collected, the State would absorb 110 per cent of the
national income. It has been proved that the laws, being
so numerous, contradictory and ambiguous, could allow
a determined government to carry out any kind of revolution, of the extreme left or the extreme right, by merely
selecting a few appropriate statutes and applying them to
their ultimate consequences. Nobody knows how many of
them are still valid, nobody knows for certain what some
of them really mean. Often, not even recourse to the
records of what the law-makers said, years before, when
debating them in Parliament, reveals their significance
and precise purpose. They are generated in a continuous
stream by a curious Italian superstition: when things go
wrong, problems are baffling, and nothing else avails, a
new law is usually passed, often too difficult and complicated to be applied properly, in the hope that it will have
thaumaturgic effects, that it will act like an incantation
and ward off that particular evil. Some, of course, are
useful. A few are good. Many useless or unpractical ones
have been forgotten, 'abrogated by desuetude' is the technical term, but all can be suddenly rescued from oblivion,
dusted, and used at any time for the benefit of a powerful group, as weapons for the destruction of its enemies.

Courts do very little to disentangle the confusion. Few
Italians in their right mind expect anything but erratic
justice from them. The current rule is never to sue when
one is in the right. It is too risky. One should go to court
only when one knows one is in the wrong and on the
defensive. 'The judge,' experts explain, 'may easily make a
mistake and award you the verdict. And anyway, the
controversy will drag on for years, from one postponement
to the next. Your opponents may lose patience and come
to a compromise.' Trials last interminably, also because
the judges are few, badly paid, with practically no staff
to help them. They are usually intelligent, erudite and

honest men, who somehow try to cope with mountains of legal papers literally threatening to bury them; they pile up daily on their tables, chairs, the floors of their dingy offices, along the walls, and rise to the height of a tall man. The magistrates have no secretaries, often no telephones. Second-hand typewriters are bought by the clerks with their own money, and used surreptitiously, as the law says that all documents should be written in long hand, with steel pen and ink, in order to be valid.

In a solemn speech in January 1963, one of Italy's highest magistrates complained that many judges in Rome lacked an office of their own, lacked desks, lacked chairs. The dearth of chairs was especially bothersome as lengthy proceedings could not be carried on standing up. Most controversies are settled privately by an agreement between the lawyers. Creditors often accept ruinous settlements, a token sum or a small part of what is owed them, rather than wait years for a larger amount. *'Pochi, maledetti, e subito'*, is the rule, or 'few lire, damned, and on the spot'. Even such substitute arrangements are expensive. Poor people can scarcely afford them. They often prefer to be the victims of an injustice, submitting to obvious wrongs, and forget the whole thing, rather than go to all the trouble and expense of litigation. Some day, they hope, should the opportunity arise, they will get even somehow with their enemies. One never knows; *'Dio non paga il sabato,'* they say, 'God does not pay on Saturday'.

Bureaucracy should, of course, interpret and administer many of the laws. Bureaucrats should, as a start, at least know what the laws are. But they are badly paid, badly chosen, badly organized and badly treated. As a rule they are impatient, overbearing, hurried, ignorant, indifferent to other people's problems, insolent, and sometimes corrupt. There are a few, however, without whom the State apparatus would stop functioning altogether, who are intelligent and efficient. They know no better than the others what the laws are, but devise short cuts through the tangle of red tape and obsolete regulations; they keep the masses of paper slowly moving; they manage to solve some problems. There are two or three in every large bureau, who cheerfully do everybody's work. The others place their hats on the hat-stand, to prove they have not left the building, and go for walks, go home, or to another and better-paid job. The few good ones are obviously not enough. Things inevitably get delayed. Claims for damage done by Garibaldi and his Redshirts to property in Sicily in 1860, for instance, were still being paid in 1954, ninety-six years later, in lire which had lost all value and meaning, to heirs who barely remembered the reason why they were entitled to receive such pitifully small sums of money. Nobody thanks the good bureaucrats for their zeal, and they are not rewarded for their efficiency. State regulations say that all salaries are fixed solely according to seniority; the few good employees, their many bad and indifferent colleagues, all follow the same predetermined career from beginning to end; they get the same rises on the same day, are promoted and named *cavaliere* at the same time, and are pensioned at the same age. Nobody can ever be fired for inefficiency. A bureaucrat can only be fired for the most scandalous and flagrant crimes, like robbing the safe, purloining funds, or killing the *capo ufficio*.

Italians of all classes (unless they are important people with powerful friends) spend a substantial part of their time standing in angry queues, in front of office windows, or waiting endlessly merely to have some simple right recognized. What their rights are, nobody knows for sure. Uncertainty is used, in Italy, as *instrumentum regni*. The Republic has multiplied the bureaucracy of the old Kingdom, partly because the tasks of the modern State have increased, but also in order to give steady jobs to many supporters of the parties in power. When the country is separated into little self-governing regions, as the constitution commands, each little sovereign region will then have its own little government and will pass its own complicated laws. Each will be legitimately entitled to float loans, pile up debts, organize its own offices and regulations. The number of bureaucrats and queues will increase proportionately.

Fear is the fourth evil spirit. It is the offspring of the others, of poverty, ignorance and injustice, but more powerful, far-reaching and harmful than all of them. Fear lurks in every fold of Italian life, even where one does not suspect it. There is the fear of the lowly, the poor and the down-trodden, for their overbearing masters; the fear of the high-born, the mighty and the rich for their unreliable and mutinous subjects and the fear on two fronts of the middle class for both the mighty and the explosive masses. Fear silently settles almost all questions, exasperates political decisions, fans discontent into raging revolts. It dominates many men's lives, distorts characters, robs a firm man of his will, an honest man of his virtues, a free man of his independence, a sincere man of his love for truth, a proud man of his dignity, an intelligent man of logic and consistency. It forces many a loyal man to betray his friends and his convictions. It kills all hopes and teaches sordid resignation.

Italians first of all fear sudden and violent death. The vigorous passions of a turbulent and restless people are always ready to flare up unexpectedly like hot coals under the ashes. Italy is a blood-stained country. Almost every day of the year jealous husbands kill their adulterous wives and their lovers; about as many wives kill their adulterous husbands and their mistresses; fathers or older brothers kill the seducers of defenceless and guileless virgins; virgins kill the men trying to rape them; desperate young lovers commit suicide together in pairs, or separately one at a time. This steady massacre, inspired by love, which has been going on for centuries, has surely cost more lives than the many pestilences and catastrophes which have ravaged the country, and the wars fought on Italian soil.

Money, honour, prestige, politics and the desperate struggle for power or survival also exact their daily human sacrifices. Dismissed workers kill their employers; ruined businessmen kill themselves or their competitors; angry tax-payers kill the tax-collector; failed students kill their teachers; Mafia men kill their rivals, stool-pigeons, policemen and bystanders. Fascists kill Communists and Communists kill Fascists; rioting workers kill policemen and strike-breakers with stones, clubs, steel pipes wrapped in newspapers or stevedores' hooks; policemen kill rioting workers. Veteran Communist leaders are frightened by the violence of the younger men who, when called upon to stage a peaceful demonstration, smash everything in sight, overturn trams and cars, viciously beat up innocent by-standers, and get themselves senselessly killed.

The world of vice also demands its daily victims. Street-walkers are found dead with silk stockings wound tight round their necks or knives stuck in their ribs, on their unmade beds or in country lanes; fatherly homosexuals are found in public parks with their heads smashed in and pockets turned out; on deserted beaches, naked call-girls are found at dawn drowned in a few inches of water. Prostitutes kill their pimps, whom they usually primly call *'il mio fidanzato'*, my fiancé; pimps and dope-peddlers kill each other over territorial disputes. Thousands die every year in the most devastating and spectacular car crashes in the western world. Others die in train accidents. Then there are recurring earthquakes, floods, landslides, tidal waves.

Even when violent death is not lurking in the shadows, when things look pleasant and peaceful and life seems secure, prosperous and easy, an Italian must remain on the alert and move with circumspection. The country is about as large as California, but less fertile and less en-dowed with natural resources. The inhabitants are in-credibly numerous, fifty million of them. The competition at every level and in every field is intense, ruthless, and without pause. Jobs of all kinds were few until very re-cently. Now ordinary jobs are plentiful, but the good ones are still scarce. Those most sought after are still very rare. There is, as a result of all this, not much elbow-room. The country has often been compared to 'a plate of soup surrounded by too many spoons'. It is no wonder that table-manners are as bad as they are.

An Italian learns from childhood that he must keep his mouth shut and think twice before doing anything at all. Everything he touches may be a booby-trap; the next step he takes may lead him over a mine-field; every word he pronounces or writes may be used against him some day. He must also pay attention to the unknown people who may be photographed in a group with him at some cere-mony or on an outing; at a later date the picture may turn out to be the damaging proof of complicity with scoundrels or of compromising political allegiances, and may eventually destroy him. In the last two years of the Fascist régime, prudent journalists, who did not dare or could not afford to leave their jobs, stopped signing their articles and bitterly said, '*Chi si firma è perduto*' ('Whoever signs is lost'), which was the paraphrase of one of Mussolini's arrogant slogans, '*Chi si ferma è perduto*' ('Whoever stops is lost'). Those who either defiantly signed their Fascist articles to the end or left their jobs for jail or the underground movement were not few but they were especially brave.

An Italian must know how to take care of himself and his kinsfolk in the most outlandish circumstances and foresee all future emergencies. Peasants somehow knew exactly what to do in front of approaching armies, during the last war. 'Cattle and women up the mountains,' they ordered as their forefathers had done so many times. He must know that he must count only on himself alone. The moment he relaxes and thinks good times are here to stay, he is lost. Good times have never lasted long in Italy.

Fortune is notoriously fickle and history restless. '*Pourvou que ça doure*,' Madame Letizia Bonaparte used to mutter in her Corsican accent, when her son Napoleon ruled all Europe. Rachele Mussolini repeated the same concept in different words and a Romagnuol accent, during the twenty years of her husband's fortune. The old king, Victor Emmanuel III, used to look with gloomy diffidence at the vast crowds gathered to cheer him and said to his aide-de-camp that about the same number would come to his execution and would cheer just as lustily. He could never forget that his father, the 'good king' Umberto, was shot and killed in 1900 by a man called Bresci, an Italian anarchist from Paterson, New Jersey.

Fear has taught Italians to go through life as warily as experienced scouts through the forest, looking ahead and behind, right and left, listening to the smallest murmurs, feeling the ground ahead for concealed traps, taking notice of signs on the bark of trees, of broken twigs, and bent grass. Perhaps one of the best examples of their capacity to come out alive from the most difficult ordeals is the life of Palmiro Togliatti, the Communist leader. In the twenties, after Mussolini marched on Rome, he went into exile and was sent to Moscow as the Italian party representative in the Comintern. He lived in the Hotel Lux, in Gorki Street, with all the international leaders. He worked daily with the heroes of the Russian revolution, Zinoviev, Bukharin, Stalin, Molotov, Trotski. They all befriended him, the inconspicuous, little, bespectacled Italian, whose only known weakness was running after the young girls who arrived from the West, couriers or secretaries. He never left Moscow, except once to go to Spain during the civil war and several times to Paris.

At the end, he emerged as one of the few survivors of his generation, the most authoritative interpreter of Marxism-Leninism in the West. All the others who sat with him in the Comintern were dead, most of them killed by Stalin, some by their disorderly and adventurous lives, only a few by simple old age. The circumspect and taciturn Togliatti, the son of the administrator of a State-owned orphan asylum for the sons of low bureaucrats on the island of Sardinia, was one of the few endowed with the knowledge necessary for survival. He knew which way the ideological wind was going to blow, who was going to be the next boss, who was really powerful and who only seemed to be, what friends to drop, what enemies to acquire, what snares to avoid. The arts of the ill-paid and insecure Italian cultural proletarian were more than a match for the Asian cunning, ruthlessness and cruelty in the top echelons of international Communism.

The rich and powerful are naturally afraid for their fortunes, privileges, honoured positions in society and, often enough, for their lives. They are so timid and insecure that most of them are always tempted to follow a demagogue who promises them solid and enduring security. This is nothing new. In the Middle Ages, the wealthy, known as the *popolo grasso,* or the fat people, were always the target for the hatred of the poor, known as the *popolo minuto* or *popolo magro,* the minute or lean people. The fat ones organized parties, ruthlessly played power politics and hired murderers to free them of their enemies. They built their *palazzi* as strong as fortresses. Still today the doors of some of these ancient mansions, now occupied mostly by harmless banks, insurance companies, government bureaus or foreign embassies, can be barricaded in a matter of minutes; the ground-floor windows are defended by stout iron grills; easy passage to the roof could allow men to pour boiling oil or molten lead on assailants; inconspicuous slits are predisposed here and there for the careful aiming of crossbows and guns. To the left of the main entrance of the Quirinale, which was once the Popes' seat as temporal sovereigns, later the King of Italy's royal palace, and now the President's official residence, there still stands a strong round tower, made of red bricks, with sufficient louvres cut in the thick walls for a well-aimed concentration of fire on an attacking crowd, if the need should again arise.

Wealthy Italians also know that they must always be ready for any emergency. A new law could suddenly expropriate some of their property or all of it. A revolution may break out. They must be prepared to flee the country at any time. This has happened in the past and may happen again: throughout the centuries exiles from some city-states filled other Italian city-states, plotting endlessly for their return at the head of friendly armies. The Liberals and Democrats returned from exile with the Piedmontese armies during the Risorgimento, when the country was unified, in the nineteenth century; the anti-fascist émigrés returned with the Allied armies at the end of the last war. In 1944 many, compromised by Fascism or afraid of a revolution, fled abroad or hid in convents and came back only when things became safe again. Many are ready to go today: they keep yachts in nearby ports or will make for the Swiss border in their fast cars at the first rustling of the leaves.

The fear of the rich is nothing to that of the poor. They have no protection, no private armies, no treasures at home or abroad, no *palazzi*, no influential friends. They have but their miserable jobs and their lives to lose. They do not like the way things are run and have been run for a long time, but they are also frightened by change. Even the revolutionaries are afraid of revolution: they talk and write truculently of the next blood bath but do little to bring it about. Stalin sneered at Togliatti for his timidity and once said to Tito: 'Togliatti will never start a revolution. Look at him. He is a lawyer, a professor.' He thought the Italian was the best man in the Comintern to write subtle and astutely worded documents and no more. The poor know that they are the first victims of any crisis or disturbances, even of those of their own making. When Fascism collapsed, after the fury of the first few days, when Mussolini, his mistress, and many members of his last government were shot, few of the great and famous personages were arrested, tried, and executed, but thousands of unknown little men were killed at random or arrested, put in concentration camps, tried and condemned to death as directly responsible for starting the war and provoking the ruin of their country.

*

Fear can also be detected behind the Italians' peculiar passion for geometrical patterns, neat architectural designs, and symmetry in general, which is part of their love for show—mainly the fear of the uncontrollable and unpredictable hazards of life and nature; fear and also its shadow, a pathetic desire for reassurance. This compulsive predilection for regularity can be seen everywhere. It is only rarely utilitarian and seldom satisfies strictly functional needs, as almost always it is merely meant to please the eye and comfort the heart. Fruit and vegetable dealers spend precious minutes of the morning building fragile pyramids of their wares which they will have to demolish in the course of the day. The new maid will stubbornly remove every piece of furniture in your room from its accustomed place, every morning, to satisfy her ideal of symmetrical decorum. She will arrange the bibelots on the mantelpiece until it will look like the parody of an altar. Old gardens leave nothing to chance and unbridled nature. Their complicated patterns of hedges, gravel walks, fountains, statues, always strictly symmetrical, often puzzle the visitor, because they can only be fully admired by people flying over them in balloons, who see them as elaborate tapestries.

Streets, *piazze*, avenues, public parks, *corsi* have been planned in rigid symmetry; almost identical churches, like Chinese *potiches*, flank the opening of an avenue, several streets converge on the same obelisk or monument, similar or identical fountains beckon to each other at the two ends of a long *corso*. The cultivated countryside is always unnecessarily neat. Saplings in newly-planted woods are always set in military rows. The same obsession with regular patterns can also be traced in invisible things, in absurd rules and regulations which balance prohibitions to this group with prohibitions to that one; in the elaborate outlines of scholarly treatises, in the organizational charts of government bureaus and military units. The greatest Italian literary masterpiece, Dante's *Divina Commedia*, is so well-ordered that students reading it must buy a plan showing the exact position of Hell, Purgatory and Paradise. It is composed of an introductory canto and three parts, each of thirty-three cantos, each ending with the same word, '*stelle*'.

The word for this is *sistemazione*. To *sistemare* all things is considered to be the foremost, perhaps the unique, mission of man on earth. *Sistemare* and *sistemazione* cannot be exactly translated. The latest dictionary bravely attempts a few well-meaning suggestions, as inaccurate as random artillery shots. *Sistemare* means, according to its authors, 'to arrange, regulate, settle', and *sistemazione*, naturally enough, 'regularization, arrangement, settlement'. The English terms are not colloquial and are mainly used in official prose, editorials and scholarly dissertations. The Italian words are, on the contrary, as common as bread and cheese. They occur in everyday conversation. To begin with, *sistemare* means to defeat nature. Italians *sistemano* mountain torrents, marshy land, wild animals, spoiled children and unruly populations. '*Ti sistemo io*' is a much abused threat. It means, 'I will curb your rebellious instincts'.

The words are also often used in the sense of 'conquest of security'. *La sistemazione*, or, more frequently, *una sistemazione*, any kind of *sistemazione*, is the dream of most Italians. It does not necessarily signify hard work, responsibility, good wages, and the possibility of getting ahead, but often nothing more than a mediocre but durable position, protected from unforeseen events, with a predictable career, some moral authority, and a pension at the end. (The advice of a dying Roman father to his sons is famous. 'My sons,' he said, 'you must all try to have an occupation in life. Life without an occupation is contemptible and meaningless. But always remember this:

you must never allow your occupation to degenerate into work.') Fathers all over Italy want to *sistemare* their sons, mothers want to *sistemare* their daughters, with good and steady husbands, not too rich or handsome, as rich and handsome husbands do not take easily to a definite *sistemazione*. The girls themselves, the pretty girls in bikinis who win beauty contests on summer beaches, and the ugly ones, clothed in black cotton smocks down to their ankles, who work in offices, do not often dream, like girls in other countries, of a career in the films, the intoxicating love of muscular gentlemen, a wealthy and nomadic existence. They prefer *una sistemazione*. International courtesans as well as tired street-walkers want to *sistemarsi* where their past is unknown, they can pose as widows and respectably bring up their illegitimate children. Industrialists often dream of being able to *sistemare* competition, by establishing strong cartels and iron-bound agreements. The royal government before the war used to *sistemare* the colonies: pioneers, gamblers, adventurers, soldiers of fortune and speculators were strictly forbidden to go there.

The passion for *sistemazione* is also curiously common among the rebellious non-conformists and the outlaws. The *bandito* Giuliano, who flourished in Sicily just after the war, gave proper military titles to his henchmen and was surrounded by a primitive but rigid etiquette. *Poètes maudits* and avant-garde writers, painters, and film directors who shock the world with their daring, often marry good cooks and good housekeepers, who raise their children well and try to save money; the food they eat is never avant-garde. After the March on Rome, in 1922, almost all the Blackshirts, rebels who sang blood-curdling songs about their contempt for death, the authorities, laws and conventions ('Life thou art my friend, death thou art my mistress'), brandished hand-grenades, daggers and machine-guns, and had skulls and bones embroidered on their chests, had one main ambition, besides establishing a new régime, that of becoming regular bureaucrats, with a good and steady salary and a pension in the end. It was nothing new. In 1860, when the Redshirts of Garibaldi reached Naples, after having miraculously liberated all of Sicily and Southern Italy in a few months, many of them also demanded to be *sistemati* in the regular army. Some of the brave partisans who heroically contributed to the defeat of the Germans in Italy also requested to be enrolled as policemen, firemen, soldiers or bureaucrats, as soon as the war ended.

*

Some of this national obsession can also be found, in various degrees, in the ideologies of the political parties most popular in Italy, those which have obtained the largest percentage of votes in every election since the war. They are, reading from left to right, the Communists, the Socialists, the Christian Democrats, and the Fascists, or, as they prefer to call themselves, the *Movimento Sociale Italiano*. Together, these now represent about 85 per cent of the electorate. None are especially interested in freedom. Fascists, Communists, and left-wing revolutionary Socialists notoriously deride liberty as a silly and sentimental weakness of their enemies, a *petit bourgeois* prejudice, which can be utilized to provoke disorders, to disrupt the functioning of the State and carry on preparations for their particular revolutions with greater ease. Christian Democrats and right-wing Socialists, on the other hand, praise liberty, mention it a number of times in every speech, exalt it in their anthems and marching songs; the Christian Democrats even have its Latin name inscribed on their escutcheon, '*Libertas*'. But when these parties' ideals are analysed, they appear so confined by limitations, provisos, theological preoccupations, controls, class prejudices and arbitrary shackles, that one must conclude they are really wary of liberty, want only a little of it, at best, safely diluted, and, at times, none at all.

All mass parties of right and left (and a good many Christian Democrats) dream of different but all equally stable futures, with little or few surprises; societies in which people will be divided along well-defined horizontal strata, as neatly as the oranges and apples in the fruit and vegetable dealers' pyramids, each man knowing where his place is and will be, from his birth to the end of his life; decisions of every kind, private, moral, cultural, economic, political, taken by wise leaders who alone know what is good for the country, as they alone possess all the information; leaders selected not by the blind and haphazard choice of the voting booth, but, more intelligently, through the secret intrigues, the infighting and the ruthless struggles of power politics.

The people, these parties promise, will no longer have to worry about abstract ideas, policies, intricate and technical problems, of which they know little and in which they are not interested, anyway. Bureaucracy will do most of the work. Naturally enough, Italians who vote *en masse* for these parties are too wise not to know that such ideals might presumably function in more efficient and disciplined countries but never in their own. They know that, should one of these parties gain absolute power, it would at most be able to superimpose on Italian reality a shining façade of new buildings, parades, uniforms, celebrations, mass meetings, speeches and slogans, under which the shoddy life would imperturbably go on, the clever ones making money and having an easy time, all others carrying on as well as they can. It has happened a number of times in the past and would almost certainly happen again. They also know that the idea of entrusting the future entirely to bureaucracy, if reasonable in other countries, is madness in their own, where the bureaucrats have always shown themselves the least able to run anything efficiently, honestly, and equitably. Nevertheless, the hope of defeating fear, the mirage of a final *sistemazione* to end all *sistemazioni*, the dream of constructing a perfect and everlasting *papier mâché* State, is so fascinating that they keep on voting for the same mass parties election after election.

CHAPTER SEVEN

Cola di Rienzo or the Obsession of Antiquity

THERE ARE, throughout Italian history, many characters who personify the national reliance on make-believe as an instrument of policy. But only one of them can be considered the Italian hero in all his perfection, who possessed all the typical attributes in their utmost purity. These are: literary, artistic, vague and contradictory ideas, practically unrelated to the contemporary world; the vast ambition to dominate all Italy, to re-establish the Empire and, in the end, to dominate the rest of Europe; the dream of building a 'new State', inspired by ancient history, in which peace, law and virtue would prevail; a genuine love for his people, his country and their glorious past, a love so intense it could be confused with self-love, as if he identified himself with Italy and the Italians; and the desire to avenge his people's ruin and humiliation, which he attributed solely to the wickedness of others. This man recklessly flung challenges to all the great powers of the day, tried to awaken his countrymen to a new sense of their mission, and dragged them reluctantly into wars neither he nor they were prepared to fight.

At first he frightened enemies, comforted friends, aroused the admiration of some of the best contemporary minds, and enchanted the multitudes. He was the greatest orator of his times, carried on all public business from a balcony, addressing himself to the crowds massed in front of him. He seemed irresistible. His principal device was showmanship: the use of symbolism, pageantry, ceremonies, parades on horse and on foot, uniforms, sonorous titles for himself and his followers. He was driven once from power. Brought back by foreign soldiers, he was killed, in the end, by the very people he had tried to make great and powerful. His body was hung from the feet, head downwards, in a public square, mocked and jeered by the same people who had praised him as their saviour and applauded him only a few days before. His name was Cola di Rienzo, or Nicholas son of Lawrence.

He was born in Rome, in 1313 or 1314, in the Regola quarter, near the church of Saint Thomas, hard by the Ghetto. His father was an innkeeper, his mother a washerwoman. (Mussolini's father had been a blacksmith at first but later opened a wineshop. Garibaldi's mother had been a washerwoman.) Cola liked to think he was of better blood than the rest of his family. He boasted he was the bastard son of Henry VII, the emperor who had been visiting Rome at the appropriate time and had been a guest at Lorenzo's inn, incognito, for a few days. Cola's bearing and appearance confirmed his pretensions. As a young man he was handsome, bore himself with dignity, spoke persuasively, enlivening his speech with suitable quotations and poetic images. 'On his lips,' says the contemporary chronicler, 'laughter had a fantastic quality'. He was brought up in the country, at Anagni, after the death of his mother, by some relatives, but came back when he was twenty, a brooding youth, lost in the contemplation of ancient ruins, the reading of Latin inscriptions, and the interpretation of freshly unearthed statuary.

He collected antiquities, especially cammei, some of which he later mentioned in his writings: the portraits of Scipio, Caesar, Metellus, Marcellus and Fabius. He read what classic authors he could find, Livy, Sallust, Cicero, Seneca and Valerius Maximus. He also studied the Bible. Till the last days of his life, he knew by heart whole passages from all these books. The pagan writers and the Christian texts and legends formed in his self-taught mind a strange confusion of medieval mysticism and Roman glory. He often spoke to the people, at random, gathering them around him in the streets, and stirring them with the evocation of their past and their present humiliation. 'Where are now these Romans?' he would exclaim. 'Their virtue, their justice, their power? Why was I not born in those happy times?'

The times could not have been sadder. Rome was in a desperate condition. It had been abandoned by the Popes in 1305, after Clement V had preferred to settle in Avignon rather than face his own rebellious subjects. No effective government was left in the city. Without law, the people, high and low, defended themselves as best they could from robbers, arsonists, rapists and murderers. Each of the great noble families had a fortress in the town and impregnable castles in the surrounding territories. The Orsini owned Castel Sant'Angelo and dominated the quarters around Monte Giordano, Pompey's theatre, and Campo dei Fiori. The citadel of the Colonnas was near the church of the Holy Apostles, by the Quirinale hill, where they still live today; they dominated the Corso all the way to the Piazza del Popolo. They all maintained private armies of horse and foot soldiers, led by sons, grandsons, and other relations. They imposed their own law and order within their jurisdiction, fighting interminable wars among themselves. When things went well, they lived in Rome with great pomp, but when the odds were against them, or when the sultry *scirocco* became oppressive, they retreated to the country, with all their women, children, treasures, cattle and retinues.

Poor Romans without means purchased protection and peace by giving their allegiance to the noble family ruling over their part of the town. When a Roman moved, he shifted his loyalties with the furniture. Humble commoners had to serve in the little private armies, from time to time, but could always ask for help, when necessary, to defeat an attack or, if aid was slow, to avenge a wrong and carry out retaliation. Of course, human life had little value. Women were raped, houses burned down, convents raided, cattle abducted, money stolen as a matter of course. Every morning corpses were swept from the streets and thrown into the Tiber with the refuse. The physical condition of the buildings was just as desperate. The Basilica of Saint John Lateran was roofless; the Milvian bridge in ruins, destroyed by the Orsini who owned and controlled the only other bridge, near Castel Sant'Angelo; the belfry of Saint Peter's had been devastated by lightning; many churches, bridges and papal *palazzi* were abandoned in various degrees of decay, damaged by fire, old age, the weather, sacking and the repeated pilfering of stonework, statuary and tiles.

In 1342, young Cola, the promising orator, was sent by his countrymen to Avignon as a member of an embassy to the Pope. He harangued Clement VI, pointing out that as long as law and order were in the hands of those who had least interest in defending them, the unruly barons, the city would know no peace. He was especially keen on the subject, as he had recently lost a brother, killed by unknown murderers, and this private grief had turned his thoughts to the ills of the city. His vigorous words in defence of the people did not please the members of the baronial families who composed the rest of the embassy and whose relatives were among the members of the papal court. He was thrown out into the streets, in disgrace, and lived in Avignon a few months as a pauper. But his brilliant ideas, his ornate mind, his culture and his eloquence seduced the poet Petrarch, who was more or less in love with the same dream, that of reviving the glories of the past and re-establishing in Rome the capital of united Italy and of all Europe. The two men strengthened each other's convictions and became life-long friends. Thanks to Petrarch's intercession, and the fact that the old Pope had died in the meantime, Cola returned to favour, was named an apostolic notary and sent back to Rome.

His job was one which most Italians fancy: he had a steady income of five gold florins a month, some authority, underlings to do the real work and time to pursue his private studies. Cola walked about, met all sorts of people, meditated on the causes of the decay of Rome, denounced them, made beautiful speeches that moved his hearers to tears. He refused to write with a goose quill, as he thought it was beneath the dignity of an apostolic notary, and had a pen made for him out of silver, possibly inventing the first metallic pen in history. Above all, he cultivated a following among the common people, the tradesmen, the merchants, the petty bourgeoisie, the low clergy, the intellectuals, tied together loosely by their admiration for the leader and dissatisfaction with existing conditions.

He called himself at the time, 'the tribune of widows, orphans and the poor'. He was possibly also the inventor of the political cartoon: he often had pictures painted on suitable walls, depicting complicated allegories, to drive home some particular point, each female figure clearly labelled Rome, Christendom, Italy, Religion, the Empire and so forth. Noblemen often invited him to dinner in their town forts, to make him talk of their sins. One night, at the house of Giovanni Colonna, he boasted: 'One day I shall be a great lord or emperor.' Then, pointing to each in turn, he went on: 'I shall imprison you, behead you, quarter you, torture you and hang you.' They all laughed uproariously when he said these words, not suspecting that that was exactly what he was going to attempt to do before long.

The night of Saturday, May 9, 1347, he spent in the church of Sant'Angelo in Peschiera, listening to twenty masses dedicated to the Holy Ghost. In the morning he emerged bare-headed but fully armed. The impressive pageantry was carefully staged. Surrounded by his armed companions and protected by a hundred hired soldiers, preceded by four flags, he marched on the Campidoglio, the seat of the nominal and ineffective government of the city, a few minutes away. The first flag, dedicated to liberty, was red (it was perhaps the first appearance of a revolutionary red flag in history) with gold-embroidered letters and figures, Rome sitting on two lions, holding the globe in one hand, a palm in the other, and the legend *Roma caput mundi*. The second flag was white, dedicated to justice, with Saint Paul wearing a crown and carrying a sword. The third was also white, with Saint Peter holding the keys, symbols of concord and peace. The fourth was the banner of Saint George, so old and ragged it had to be carried in a wooden box on top of a pole.

The cortège, soon joined by loafers, street urchins, beggars and inquisitive Romans, arrived on the hill and occupied the building by surprise. Nobody was defending it. Most of the noble families had heard about the secret plot but thought it was a comical invention of the mad notary, not to be taken seriously. The most powerful, the Colonna clan, was out of town. They had gone *en masse* to Tarquinia to procure wheat which was scarce at the time. Stefano the elder, the head of the family, who was then about eighty years old, returned at full speed, a few days later. When he heard the news, he disdainfully said: 'If this madman continues to bother me, I shall have him thrown from the windows of the Campidoglio.'

Cola went to the Campidoglio balcony, after seizing

the building, and spoke. He was surrounded by armed
men, his flags, relatives, henchmen and followers. He
made a memorable speech on the wretchedness of Romans,
their past glories and the urgent need to establish a firm
government. The crowd roared its approval. He then
asked one of his relatives to read aloud the new constitution, which he had prepared. Finally he stepped forward
and asked the people who they wanted to elect as the
head of the new state. 'You,' they shouted, waving their
arms frantically.

He immediately got down to business. He first assumed
a high-sounding title, 'Nicholas, the severe and merciful,
tribune of liberty, peace and justice, liberator of the holy
Roman republic'. Then he organized a people's militia,
of 360 horse and 1,300 foot, civilians from all quarters
of the city who were to rush with their arms to the Capitol when they heard the great bell boom. He proceeded
to hang robbers and murderers, including a few prominent noblemen, and decreed that henceforth no private
forts and fortified emplacements were to be tolerated
within the walls, that all noble families were to be held
responsible for the safety of wayfarers along the roads
crossing their lands and that they were forbidden to give
asylum to bandits and criminals of any kind. All bridges,
narrow passes, gates and fortified emplacements in Rome
itself were to be manned by the people's militia. Those
that were not considered necessary were to be demolished.

Whoever did not obey his orders was to be exiled to
his country estates and was never to set foot in Rome.
Two weeks later, to make sure, he summoned all heads
of noble families to his presence. Most of them appeared.
He received them dressed in a scarlet cloak over his
armour, the symbol of his newly-acquired authority, and
led them to an altar in front of which he had placed the
insignia of the Church. He asked them all to swear over
the Bible and a consecrated host that they would avoid
all aggression against him, his government, his soldiers
and the people at large. They gave their oaths, thus accepting implicitly the end of feudal rule, the restoration
of the 'republic', the legitimacy of his authority and the
validity of the new constitution. He made the anti-feudal
revolution obvious to all when he prohibited commoners

from giving oaths of allegiance to noble lords, putting escutcheons on private houses or shops for their protection, and addressing noblemen as My Lord, or *Mio Signore*.

Things went well enough for a time. 'Never perhaps has the energy and effect of a single mind been more remarkably felt than in the sudden, though transient, reformation of Rome,' noted Gibbon, who was born a few centuries too soon to witness similar sudden and equally transient reformations of Rome. 'A den of robbers was converted to the discipline of a camp or convent: patient to hear, swift to redress, inexorable to punish, his tribunal was always accessible to the poor and stranger; nor could birth, or dignity, or the immunities of the Church, protect the offender or his accomplices.' An anonymous contemporary chronicler understandably exaggerated when he wrote: 'The woods began to rejoice that they were no longer infested with robbers; the oxen began to plough; the pilgrims visited the sanctuaries; the roads and inns were replenished with travellers; trade, plenty and good faith were restored in the markets; and a purse of gold could be exposed without danger in the midst of the highway.'

Cola, after a few weeks of peaceful rule, finally began to reveal a little more of his plans. His first aim was to unite all Italy into one great federation under his leadership. This he proceeded to do not by waging wars or carrying on vast political intrigues but by correspondence, so to speak, by sending swift and trusted messengers with noble letters in eloquent Latin prose to the governments of the many Italian cities, republics and small principalities. These men travelled on foot, unarmed, carrying a white stick in their hand for recognition, and were welcomed almost everywhere with great demonstrations of joy. Friendly and respectful, but evasive, answers soon began to be received, followed by ambassadors of princes and free cities. The low-born notary assumed more and more the dignity of a legitimate official sovereign and power began to corrupt him. His titles became more sonorous and florid, and embraced more and more territory as the time passed. He was known at this time as 'Nicholas, severe and merciful, deliverer of Rome, defender of Italy, friend of mankind, and of liberty, peace and justice, tribune august'.

He rode a white horse about the city, a privilege reserved for popes and royal princes; his clothes were of white silk embroidered with gold, the papal colours; in front of him walked one hundred foot soldiers from his own native quarter, Regola; over his head flew always the great banner of the republic, designed by him, a sun with a circle of stars and a dove with olive branches. He went once to Saint Peter's with great pomp and people came from all quarters to line his route and admire him. The cortège was preceded by a detachment of his cavalry, well-dressed and armed, then came officials of his government, followed by a man carrying a cup of gold, then more cavalry, musicians on horses with silver trumpets and tymbals, and heralds. One man carried a naked sword, another threw gold and silver coins to the populace, with an assistant on either side holding bags filled with money, something which had been seen before only when emperors entered Rome.

The tribune rode alone, dressed in half yellow and half green velvet lined with fur. In his right hand he carried the rod of justice, a sceptre of polished steel, crowned with a globe and a cross of gold which enclosed a small fragment of the true cross. Behind him a man kept the great banner raised over his head. At his sides fifty men from the village of Vitorchiano (the faithful allies of Rome who still today take part in all municipal ceremonies) walked, dressed in furs, carrying halberds, and looking, as a contemporary witness says, 'like armed bears'. A cortège of friends and supporters came last. At about the same time, his plebeian relations all changed names and professions; his uncle, a barber, dressed like a knight and called himself Messer Rosso. In July Cola began dating his missives according to a new era, Year One of the Restoration of the Roman Republic. He went no further, as his rule lasted only seven months, from May till Christmas, 1347. Mussolini, who imitated this practice six centuries later, was able to go farther. He proudly wrote, on a photograph he gave a journalist three days before his death, 'Anno XXIII E.F.' or Fascist Era.

The first really ambitious show Cola staged was to celebrate his acceptance of knighthood in the church of Saint John Lateran, on August 1. It was a bizarre show, as it was weighed down by too many allegories at the same time: it was to surround him with the mystic medieval halo of ecclesiastical consecration, to make him a nobleman, and, at the same time, to revive imperial Roman memories; but especially it was meant to establish, with the greatest solemnity, a turning point in history, a revolution in contemporary political principles, a new age. An interminable cortège went from the Campidoglio to the old basilica on July 31, through streets decorated with flowers, arches of foliage, and precious tapestries, between vast applauding crowds. Jugglers entertained the onlookers, street singers sang songs, poems were declaimed by popular poets, musicians blew trumpets, played drums and strummed lutes. Cola led the procession on his white horse, followed by ecclesiastical, civil, and military dignitaries in rich clothes, each group with its own banner. Cola's wife came on foot, attended by gentlewomen: flowers were strewn in front of them. Some of the foreign ambassadors changed their clothes several times along the way, throwing what they discarded to the populace.

When the parade reached the church, everybody was dismissed until the next day. The tribune disappeared from sight. Inside he took a ritual bath in the porphyry sarcophagus in which, legend says, the Emperor Constantine was miraculously cured of his leprosy by Pope Sylvester. This was considered at once a shocking sacrilege and was later used as one of the charges for Cola's excommunication; he merely meant it as a symbol of his new power, which drew its confused strength from Christian, feudal and ancient Roman roots. He then lay down on a luxurious state-bed, prepared near the high altar (one leg gave way under his weight; the incident was taken as an omen of bad luck), and slept till morning.

The following day he was knighted with a pompous ritual of his own invention. At the end, he showed himself to the people from the balcony in a majestic attitude, wearing an imperial purple robe with gold spurs (the mark of knighthood and noble birth) and carrying a naked sword. Back in the church he finally revealed to his guests and the public the meaning of the celebration and for the first time disclosed his political plans in their entirety. Rising from his throne, he proclaimed in a loud voice: 'We summon to our tribunal Pope Clement, and command him to reside in his diocese of Rome. We also summon the sacred college of cardinals. We also summon the two pretenders, Charles of Bohemia and Louis of Bavaria, who style themselves emperors.[1] We likewise summon all the electors of Germany to inform us on what pretence they have usurped the inalienable rights of the Roman people, to elect the lawful sovereign of the empire.' Unsheathing his new sword, he brandished it three times in three directions, repeating 'This too is mine!' each time.

The revolutionary significance of his words and gestures could not be clearer. He wanted nothing less than to re-establish Rome as the official capital of the world, *caput mundi*, make the Roman people once more arbiters of their own destiny, and revive the Roman empire in its ancient form. He wanted the Pope reduced to the subordinate position of bishop of the eternal city and head of a world-wide spiritual organization, and no longer to be temporal sovereign of his Italian possessions; he branded both emperors as usurpers, since only the Roman people could elect a legal one. And who could he be? He could only be one man, the present head of the Roman republic, the people's choice, in other words, himself, Cola, the son of Lawrence the innkeeper. Without visible force with which to fight and defeat his enemies, he had at one stroke challenged all the available powers of the day, the Roman nobles and feudalism, the Pope and the Church, Germany, and the Empire.

Later that day he offered his guests and the Roman citizens one of the largest and most expensive banquets ever seen in those days of chronic famines. The Lateran Palace had been transformed for the occasion: walls had been torn down, new stairways built, courtyards, porticoes and rooms spread with tables, eighty kitchens installed to prepare all kinds of elaborate food. Red wine flowed from one and water from the other nostril of the bronze horse of the equestrian statue of Marcus Aurelius, which was

[1] They were both claiming, at the time, to be the one and only legitimate emperor; one was supported by German feudal chiefs and the other by the Pope.

then in front of the Lateran Palace and was still believed to be the statue of Constantine, the first Christian emperor. In the middle of the main dining-room an immense cake was built, shaped like a castle, from whose windows and doors new dishes appeared as if by magic.

A subsequent day was appointed for another dazzling show, his coronation. That ceremony too was overloaded with fantastic meanings: it adopted some of the features from the traditional coronation of poets on the Campidoglio and some from the coronation of ancient Roman heroes when they were carried in triumph through Rome. Six crowns were successively placed on Cola's head by six eminent priests, representing the gifts of the Holy Ghost, which then apparently numbered only six and not yet seven. A ruffian in ragged clothes tore each crown except the last from his head as soon as it was placed there. He too was a badly remembered relic of the past (in the old days, the soldiers and the people were free to jeer and address irreverent remarks and insults to the military leader who was being carried in triumph), and symbolized the impermanent quality of all worldly honours. The last crown made of silver, which the ragged pauper did not take away, was placed on his head by the prior of the Hospital of the Holy Ghost (it still exists; its telephone number is 652257) who also handed him a sceptre. Finally, old Goffredo degli Scotti, the nobleman who had knighted him a few days before, gave him a silver globe on which was a cross and said: 'Most high tribune, accept and exercise justice, give us peace and liberty.'

That day Cola's ambitions reached their maddest point. Not content with having ideally conquered, for the time being, a position higher than the Pope's and the Emperor's, he dared to compare himself to Jesus Christ. In a little speech he alluded to his age, thirty-three, the age of the Saviour at His death, as a sign that for him too a great fate was in store. A holy monk, who had been one of his supporters, wept bitterly at this and said: 'Now is our master cast down from heaven. I never saw a man so proud. By the aid of the Holy Ghost he has driven the tyrants from the city without drawing a sword. Why is he so arrogant and ungrateful to the Most Holy?'

All the preceding weeks the chancery had been working frantically, preparing letters for foreign princes of ever-ascending rank, and studying their replies. Cola even sent an embassy to the King of England and one to the King of France directing them to stop the war between them, as it had been doing 'great damage to all Christendom'. A third letter was sent to the Pope in Avignon, commanding him to reconcile the two sovereigns without delay. An embassy arrived from King Louis of Hungary, asking Cola to intervene in his favour in a difficult family quarrel: his brother, King Andrew, husband of Queen Joan of Naples, had been murdered and he asked for permission to cross the Roman territory with his army in order to avenge the wrong done to his family. Another embassy arrived from Queen Joan, almost at the same time, asking the tribune to protect her and to intercede on her behalf with the King of Hungary. Cola promised to do what he could, inserting in his replies admirable and rare quotations from the Bible. To and from all Italian cities went messages, in preparation for a solemn congress of lawyers to be convened in Rome, which would proclaim in erudite juridical terms the rights of the Roman people (all Italians had, meanwhile, been made honorary Roman citizens). Once the supremacy of the city was clearly established by a congress of eminent lawyers, lawyer Cola had no doubt that nobody would ever dare challenge it.

To consolidate his rule, he invited all the heads of the noble families to dinner. Old Stefano Colonna, at the table, felt the hem of the tribune's dress, and said with contempt: 'It would be better for you to wear the honest clothes of the common people rather than this pompous apparel.' Cola became furious, had them all imprisoned, ordered the great hall decorated with red and white hangings (the colours suitable for a sentence of death), summoned the executioner and sent a priest to confess the prisoners. (Stefano Colonna refused the administrations of the confessor, disdainfully saying he was not yet ready to die.) But then Cola, as usual, became frightened at what he was about to do and changed his mind. He set them all free in exchange for a pledge not to break the peace, gave them gifts, said it had all been a joke and led them in mounted procession through the city as a public sign of reconciliation. This was the fatal mistake that destroyed him. The contemporary chronicler knew it as well as the people when he said: 'This man has lighted a fire he will not be able to put out.' (The chronicler drove the point home with an earthy proverb, which cannot be printed here in English: '*Che vale petere e poi culo stringere? Faticasi le natiche.*') From that day on, the feudal chiefs of Rome knew they could not trust Cola and had better call their soldiers to arms, man their castles and prepare for war.

The war eventually destroyed him. The Roman nobles were the key to his designs. He was forced to fight them to keep his power in Rome. Without the support of Rome he would lose the support of the outlying districts. Without those, his ambitions in Italy were ended. Without a united Italy he could not face the Pope or the Emperor or bend either to his wishes with the aid of the other. He fought a desultory and amateurish war against the noble families, with some incidental successes, but could not hope ever to destroy his enemy, comfortably ensconced in so many fortified towns, far from the city. The people, in the end, tired of his madness, his expenses, his inconclusive warring, the pomp, the ceremonies, the show, the empty eloquence, and the scarcity of food, longed for the bad old days, before the 'new State' was established, the days which suddenly seemed peaceful and prosperous in retrospect. They mutinied. Scared by an unimportant but noisy street riot, without trying to defend himself and his government, he left the city at the head of the few soldiers who had remained faithful to him. It was December 5, 1347.

Cola returned seven years later, on August 1, 1354, at the head of a mercenary army led by two French captains, the brothers Monréal. He had wandered through Europe as a pilgrim, finally visited the emperor in Prague, who promptly imprisoned him as a dangerous revolutionary and heretic and sent him in chains to the Pope. In the end, after much writing of eloquent Latin letters and much skilful debating, he gained the emperor's trust and friendship and the Pope's pardon. He was sent back to Italy with the papal legate, the Spanish cardinal Gil d'Albornoz, who was to reconquer and pacify the papal states for the Church. Cola offered to go ahead of the main army to Rome where he had heard the people were anxiously awaiting him. In fact he was acclaimed as the liberator. The Roman cavalry welcomed him along the road, at Monte Mario, waving olive branches. The people of the city cheered him, 'as if,' says the chronicler, 'he were Scipio Africanus.'

He was led once more to the Campidoglio through streets decorated with tapestries and with gold and silver ornaments. He spoke again from the balcony and again the people waved their arms and shouted his name. But he was no longer the same man. He was flabby and fat. 'In the society of Germans and Bohemians he is said to have contracted the habits of intemperance and cruelty,' says Gibbon. 'Adversity had chilled his enthusiasm without fortifying his reason or virtue.' He had become avaricious, cowardly, suspicious and cruel. He often had his enemies, or those he suspected of being his enemies, condemned to death after a mock trial, sometimes only in order to confiscate their wealth. He again waged insensate and inconclusive wars against the well-fortified barons, as he had done seven years before, until he had again spent all his money, the mercenary soldiers were on the verge of mutiny, and the people of Rome once more ready to revolt. He imposed heavy taxes on them, spent public money freely for himself, his friends and his mad schemes and did nothing to prevent trade from languishing and famine from tormenting the city. On October 8 sporadic riots broke out. The people were shouting '*Viva il popolo!*' They gathered at the foot of the Capitol hill, crying 'Death to the traitor Cola!'

Cola was at first unimpressed. He refused to have the bell of the Commune sounded and went on the balcony to reassure and placate the crowd; dressed as a knight, with the great banner of the republic as usual over his head, he lifted his arm, asking for silence in which to speak. The shouting increased. Stones were thrown at him. His hand was pierced by an arrow. He hurried back into the building, frightened and undecided on what to do next. He repeatedly and mechanically put on his helmet as if meaning bravely to face the revolt in arms with his men, then took it off as if to change his clothes and flee.

Meanwhile the people were setting fire to the palaces: flames were already devouring the wooden stairway. Cola finally made up his mind. He entrusted his life to his acting ability. He took off his armour, cut his beard with scissors, painted his face black, put on the old clothes of a gardener, took on his back a mattress, to protect himself from flying embers, and sneaked out of the building.

He had already passed the last door, and was mingling with the crowd, shouting in heavy peasant dialect, 'Down with the traitor!' and 'Let's go upstairs to steal, there are many things there!' when somebody saw the golden bracelets still around his wrists and the rings on his fingers. He was recognized and killed. His dead body was struck time and again with pikes, spears, lances and pitchforks, then dragged along the Corso, to San Marcello, where it was hung by the feet. Two days and two nights it was left there, stoned and spat upon by jeering boys, until it was finally burned near the ruins of Augustine's mausoleum over a bonfire of dried thistle.

*

It was easy for Gibbon to dismiss Cola as just another 'mixture of the knave and madman'. We now know better. Mad knaves abound at all times in all countries, but few, very few indeed manage to leave their permanent marks on history. To do that they have to be more than just insane adventurers, although, as a rule, they must be that, too. They must, also, be the unconscious and docile instruments of the gods, unknowingly attuned to the secret harmonies of the universe, somewhat like the people who, the Neapolitans say, can *dare i numeri*, give numbers; these are usually old monks, beggars, idlers, ragged women, rag-pickers who do not know and could not tell you what numbers will be extracted the following Saturday in the national lottery but somehow infallibly indicate them. You must follow them and observe them closely. A few casual words or absent-minded actions of theirs, if properly interpreted according to ancient methods, may at times reveal the correct answer and enrich you.

Men like Cola are unconscious interpreters of their times and have an intuitive and prophetic understanding of what their countrymen long for. You must ignore their explanations, which are often ridiculous. You must watch them. Listen to them talk to the crowds. They speak as if they are giving words to the crowd's own dumb sentiments. They awaken an echo in men's hearts. They drive them to great deeds. People willingly die for such men, good people who do not like to die and would not die for simple knaves and madmen. Men like that somehow identify the great themes history is going to propose like dowsers feeling secret veins of water underground. Cola's ideas were a disorderly and laughable hodgepodge. But inadvertently he managed to put his finger on most of the great motifs which would dominate Italian history for centuries and most of which still dominate it today.

He sensed the necessity for popular government, justice (or the same law for every man), good administration, order, liberty and the end of bloody feudal anarchy, not so much because it was bloody and feudal, but because it was inefficient. He wanted to give Italy a unified government five centuries before the Italians managed to do so. He learned what so many were sadly to learn later to their cost, that every time a man was to attempt to solve the Italian political problem he risked heresy and excommunication. Cola understood that Italy had to be unified and strong in order to fight on two fronts, against the foreign oppressors, the Germans' imperial authority on one side, and on the other, the Church's political power and the Popes' temporal aspirations. He was considered by many enthusiastic scholars, centuries later, to have been one of Italy's earliest patriots, a prophet of national ideals, a forerunner of the Risorgimento, second only to Dante, Petrarch, and Machiavelli.

Cola was Italian. He spoke eloquently, wore handsome clothes, invented flags, staged the most tremendous feats and ceremonies of his day, sent elegant letters to all and sundry, put his trust in fragile juridical formulas and historical precedents, but neglected to build a real republic, with a real army, appoint good captains, secure sufficient funds for military campaigns, draw up suitable plans for defeating or intimidating his enemies. He never for a moment suspected that it was not enough to build a life-like persuasive façade. The façade and reality, for him too, were one and the same thing.

As a result, his achievement had the practical flimsiness and spiritual durability of a work of art. That is why, perhaps, he appealed mostly to artists, to such men as Byron (who dedicated a part of *Childe Harold* to him), Bulwer Lytton (who wrote the novel *Rienzi, the Last of the Roman Tribunes*), Richard Wagner (who composed the opera *Rienzi*), and Gabriele d'Annunzio, who spent precious hours compiling Cola's biography, the only historical work he ever did. Cola also appealed to other 'knaves and madmen' of destiny. In Napoleon's carriage, as he trundled his way back from Moscow, there was a copy of a book called *Conjuration de Nicholas, dit de Rienzi,* by the abbé Jean Antoine du Cerceau, printed in Paris, in 1733.

CHAPTER EIGHT

Mussolini or the Limitations of Showmanship

*Nobody knows his servants as badly as their master;
nobody knows his subjects as badly as their ruler;
because they do not show themselves as they do to
others; they always strive to disguise themselves and
to seem different from what they truly are.*

FRANCESCO GUICCIARDINI

A N OLD socialist from Bologna, Aldo Parini, a modest
man, who had been a good friend of Benito Mussolini in the early days, asked to see him just before the
last war. Il Duce received him at the Palazzo Venezia.
Parini had nothing to ask for himself; he had a job, and
was no longer interested, he said, in politics. He pleaded
with the dictator, however, to help some of their ancient
comrades, brave and honest men who had fought, with
them, the socialist battles at the beginning of the century,
and who were now penniless, unable to get a job, and
persecuted by the police. Could he not give orders to leave
them in peace so that they could make a living? Could
he not perhaps assign the oldest and poorest of them a
small pension out of secret funds? Mussolini liked playing
the magnanimous and generous prince. He reassured his
old comrade that all he was asking for would be done, and
took down the names of the needy socialists. Then he
started talking about things in general.

'He was dressed in a white linen suit. It was summer.
His face was sunburned,' the old socialist told me years
later, after Mussolini's death. 'He swaggered, made faces,
pushed his chin forward, bent his knees, hands on hips,
as cavalry officers used to do, all in good humour. He
recalled some forgotten mutual friends. He boasted about
the achievements of his régime. I said nothing. Then he
told me: "You are a stubborn fool, not becoming one of us.
Why don't you join the Fascist Party?" I felt that if I had
said yes, I was tired of living apart from the rest of my

countrymen, he would have given me a party card then and there. It would have solved many problems. I wanted, however, to be true to my youth, and said no, I was happy as I was and needed nothing. He insisted. Finally I blurted out what was in my mind. I said: "This régime of yours, I am afraid, will end badly. Such things always do. Benito, you'll die like Cola di Rienzo." At these words, which I meant seriously but said in a facetious tone, Mussolini made one of his grimaces, expressing mock horror, then laughed and looked at his hands, spread out in front of him, fingers wide apart, the thick and short hands of a peasant. What he said I will never forget. He said: "I wear no rings, you see. It will not happen to me."'

*

Mussolini was born at Dovia di Predappio, near Forlì, in Romagna, on July 29, 1883. His father was a blacksmith, an ardent revolutionary (a 'primeval socialist', as somebody called him), who named his first-born son Benito after Benito Juarez, the Mexican leader of the rebellion against Maximilian; his mother was a long-suffering school-teacher. He was brought up hating the Church, the army, the king, the *carabinieri*, the law, the rich, the well-educated, the well-washed, the successful, any kind of authority, all the things he was later to defend, and to hate at times even the proletarian revolutionaries who disappointed him: he often called them 'socialist noodles'. He was a turbulent boy, determined to be first in everything, proud, quarrelsome, boastful, superstitious and not always very brave. A friendly biographer wrote: 'He picked quarrels for the sake of the fight; when he won at games he wanted more than the stake, when he lost he refused to pay.' He was expelled from two schools for having knifed two school-mates. Many of his companions hated him. A few loved him dearly, almost fanatically, and followed him as their leader. Old men in Romagna still remember his harsh childish charm, his winning smiles, and his fierce loyalty to his friends and followers. He was always persuaded that a great destiny was reserved for him. 'One day,' he said to his mother when he was still a boy, 'I will make the earth tremble.' He did.

He became a school-teacher in 1901. The following

year he fled to Switzerland to avoid conscription: it was at the time a duty for a serious revolutionary. In Lausanne he tried, once or twice, actually to become a member of the working class by getting a job as a labourer but discovered that he did not like hard work. He much preferred reading revolutionary literature and talking. He read voraciously and indiscriminately, mostly pre-Marxist or non-Marxist rebels, including Nietzsche, Sorel and Schopenhauer. Of Marx he apparently read only the Manifesto. He preached indiscriminate violence—atheism, class warfare, the 'myth of the general strike', and revolution for revolution's sake—to his countrymen, mostly poor immigrant bricklayers, who were so impressed they elected him secretary of their trade union. He sought the company of other revolutionaries who were at the time mostly Russian nihilists, anarchists, and social democrats. They called him familiarly Benitushka; he called himself more dramatically an 'apostle of violence'.

He never washed, shaved seldom, wore his thinning hair long on his neck and lived wherever he could. Once he inhabited an abandoned packing case under a bridge together with a young girl. The police watched him and arrested him several times. Angelica Balabanova, the Russian socialist, befriended him and was charmed by him for a time. She understood that, under the blustering, blasphemous and rebellious talk, he was a timid man, uneasy when in the presence of people he suspected to be his social or intellectual superiors. In reality he watched himself playing the great rôle he was inventing as he went along, hamming at it with gusto; no earnest revolutionary in Switzerland at the time was as visibly frightening as he was. Certainly not Lenin, who diligently impersonated a little professor.

Mussolini returned to Italy in 1904; an heir had been born to the king and so an amnesty had been granted. He became a village school-teacher, served in the Army as a *bersagliere* (he turned out to be a good soldier, after all), earned a new diploma as teacher of French in high schools, and did odd jobs as a journalist, socialist agitator and organizer. He began to improve his oratory, slowly developing a technique which was to make him one of the best and most moving speakers in Italy. He paid little attention to the logic and truth of what he said as long as it was energetic and stirring. His gestures had rhythm and vigour. He used short, staccato sentences, with no clear connection between them, often with long and dramatic pauses, sometimes changing voice and expression in a crescendo of violence and ending in a tornado of vituperations. When his audience was carried away by his oratory he would sometimes stop and put to them a rhetorical question. They roared their answer. This established a sort of heated dialogue, through which the spectators became involved in decisions they had no time to meditate on. By means of violent writings and incendiary eloquence, he rose in the socialist party organization until, by 1912, he was made editor of the party organ, *Avanti!*

He was a very successful editor. The paper's circulation rose from 50,000 copies to 200,000 under his leadership. The rôle of the journalist was one of the few in his life he did not have to act, because he really was one, perhaps the best popular journalist of his day in Italy, addressing himself not to the sober cultured minority, but to the practically illiterate masses, easily swept by primitive emotions. Those very qualities which made him an excellent rabble-rousing editor made him a disastrous statesman: his intuitive and superficial intelligence; his capacity to oversimplify and dramatize; a day-by-day interest only in the most striking events; a strictly partisan point of view; the disregard for truth, accuracy, objectivity and consistency when they interfered with his aims; the talent for doing his job undisturbed by scruples, doubts or criticisms; and above all, an instinctive ability to ride the emotional wave of the day, whatever it was, to know what people wanted to be told, and by what low collective passions they would more easily be swept away. If the Italians had been a newspaper-reading public like the English, *Avanti!* would have easily reached a circulation of two or three million copies. As it was, 200,000 was considered a miracle.

He went to live in Milan with his family, which consisted of his common-law wife Rachele (socialists at the time refused to acknowledge the existence of Church and State and got 'married' without a civil or religious ceremony) who was the very young daughter of his father's mistress, and his little girl, Edda, who looked like him, two large black eyes in a pale and bony face. He was only a little better dressed than the 'apostle of violence' of his Lausanne days. He still washed seldom, shaved only twice a week, wore the same suit until it fell to pieces and neglected to tie his shoe-laces. He made strange grimaces when he talked, used violent and unprintable words, had an impatient temper, but managed, as he had done in his schooldays, to attract faithful friends and fanatical followers, some of whom clung to him to the end.

There was something about him that startled and fascinated almost everybody, including some of his enemies. Most people who knew him well, who spoke frequently with him, who worked for him, were the victims of this inexplicable charm. Men literally fell in love with him as if he were a woman, unreasoningly and blindly, ready to forgive him everything, his rudeness, his errors, his lies, his pretentiousness, his obstinacy and his ignorance. One of the men who had worked for him since 1914, Manlio Morgagni, committed suicide in July 1943, after writing these words on a piece of paper: 'Il Duce has resigned. My life is finished. Viva Mussolini!' He also attracted many women. He treated them roughly, as he had the peasant girls of Forlì, sometimes taking them without preliminary explanations on the hard floor of his study or standing them up against a wall. Only a few of them sensed his timidity, his lack of security, his desire for admiration and affection. Those lasted some time. The others, mesmerized and frightened, were soon dismissed.

My first impression of him, years later in 1932, during some army manœuvres, was a disturbing one. He wore a white yachting cap, a wing collar, the double-breasted jacket of a businessman, grey-green army breeches, and black boots. He looked like a circus performer in off hours. Perhaps his clothes were meant to symbolize the multifarious variety of his interests: horses, business, the sea, the economic life of the nation, and the army. He looked small, thick, rude, and stubborn. I remember the large ivory-coloured bald head, the bulging black eyes in the pale face, the protruding jaw, the yellow teeth set wide apart (a sign of good luck, according to popular belief), a little potato-like excrescence on his cranium, and the large black mole under his chin. He moved his arms and legs as a wrestler does to make his clothes fit better.

I wrote in my diary: 'He is the engineer at the throttle, we are the passengers on the train. Will he always be able to see if the bridges ahead are still standing or have been washed away? Let us hope for the best.' It is true that I had not been exposed to his charms as I had not talked to him. I had merely watched him for days, from a short distance, at army observation posts. He was, of course, playing the rôle of the man with an indomitable will 'whom,' large black letters on village houses proclaimed at the time throughout Italy, 'neither God nor man will bend.' In reality, he was, as he had always been, obstinate, deaf to criticism, self-willed, suspicious, but also erratic, undecided most of the time, prone to adopt the most recent opinion he heard. He was trying to hide his irresolution and fear. This I was too young and inexperienced to know. I took him at his face value.

He had certainly been irresolute during the fateful summer of 1914. Italy was tied to the Austrian and German empires by the Triple Alliance. The right wing, the conservatives, the general staff, the business and financial interests and the government were in favour of maintaining strict neutrality. The younger people, avant-garde artists, trade unionists, anarchists, students, republicans, democrats, nationalists, the hot-heads of the right, and the more moderate socialists, were all, for different reasons, in favour of war on the side of France and Great Britain. Socialist doctrines, as usual, were no certain guide. Workers should have been against a bourgeois, capitalist war, but they also had a theoretical duty to encourage a catastrophe which would have accelerated the proletarian revolution. The editor of *Avanti!* at first repeated the old slogans: 'Down with war! Down with armaments! Long live the international brotherhood of workers!' He denounced war-mongers. He organized a referendum among his readers: 'Are you for war or peace?' He headed one of his violent articles: 'Who drives us to war betrays us.' But then the journalist in him wavered, when he felt he would lose followers by supporting the cautious government policy. Pacifism was unpopular with those he wanted to lead, the younger generation of rebels. After a few months, on October 18, 1914, without taking orders from or consulting the party leaders, he published an editorial urging war. He was immediately dismissed from his job and expelled from the party in a stormy session. He walked out crying dramatically: 'You hate me because you cannot help loving me!'

With foreign and Italian money, he started a new newspaper of his own, *Popolo d'Italia*, which came out on November 14. He immediately managed to gather behind him more followers than he had had when editing *Avanti!* and more readers. Italy entered the war on May 24, 1915. He also went to war, when his class was called, and served well as a corporal in the *bersaglieri*, until he was wounded. (It was noticed that he went about Milan on crutches long after they should have become useless.) After the war, when the frail structure of Italian political unity was endangered by civil strife, economic difficulties and the collapse of the existing method of government, he used his paper to give vent to all the passions, to rally all the hot-headed veterans of all parties who found it difficult to go back to dull civilian pursuits, the very young men who felt they had been cheated by not having been in the war, and all those who had wanted a revolution, any kind of revolution, so long as it was not a socialist and Marxist one. On March 23, 1919, in Milan, he founded something called *I Fascii*, a vague but determined organization which adopted a fiery and contradictory programme, so contradictory in fact that it attracted dissatisfied and restless men from the right and the left, anarchists and conservatives, businessmen and artists. Arturo Toscanini was one of them. The confusion of the programme reflected the disorderly but brilliant mind of the leader, his lack of principles and his perennial irresolution. Here and there, in other cities, in the provinces, in towns, in villages, bands of young men sprang up, to fight socialists and communists in the streets. The movement quickly found conservative support. Street fighting became a common occurrence.

Mussolini was generally considered the truculent and arrogant leader of all this, the man who rode the storm. In reality, he was secretly reluctant as usual and devoured by doubts; but he put up a good front. The expression on his face was resolute. He scowled and clenched his teeth. His working table at the *Popolo d'Italia* was covered with an arsenal of weapons, hand-grenades, pistols of various calibres, muskets, knives. (He loved weapons until late in his career. In the waiting-room of his study in the Palazzo Venezia there were often a couple of duelling pistols and a couple of duelling sabres, to intimidate his visitors.) His articles bristled with insults for the cautious and timid. He often wore a black shirt, like his followers.[1] He wrote arrogant articles, heaping insults on grave and prudent statesmen, challenging his enemies to fight, forecasting the most glorious future for the party. But he never took a personal part in a street brawl. Manœuvring behind the scenes, skilfully keeping all doors open, he negotiated with the socialists and the conservatives, at the same time as he was fighting them both; with the monarchists and the republicans; with the government and the opposition. His genius was proved above all by the fact that he maintained himself at the head of a mass party composed of many different factions, always managing to defeat all his possible rivals, until practically the very end, twenty-five years later.

None of this was visible from a distance. His public figure was one thing, the fearless leader braving danger at the head of his fighting men, his private figure was another, known only to few. (The discrepancy was naturally known to his wife, Rachele, who later used to complain to him, as one of his sons told me many years ago: 'You bend forty million Italians to your will but you are not able to make your own sons obey you.') His vacillating character was well-known to the leaders of the party who decided to march on Rome, in October 1922; Balbo told him: 'We are going, either with you or without you. Make up your mind.' He remained prudently behind in Milan while the Blackshirts straggled through the rain into the capital, without meeting any opposition. He arrived the

[1] The Italian habit of wearing a shirt of a distinct colour as a political uniform was started by Garibaldi in Montevideo in 1843, who dressed his Italian Legion, then fighting for the independence of Uruguay, with an old stock of unsold red shirts made originally for slaughter-house workers. Black shirts had been used in Italy by workers in the railways, steel mills, and machinery shops.

next day in a Wagons-Lits compartment, after he had
been summoned by the king for consultations. He presented himself at the Quirinale symbolically attired in a
tight morning coat he had borrowed, spats and a black
shirt, a blend of tradition and revolution. He said: 'Your
Majesty must excuse me for wearing a black shirt, but I
have just returned from the battle which we had to fight,
fortunately without shedding any blood. . . .'

*

There is a disturbing mystery about Mussolini's career.
He was dictator of Italy for about two decades, exactly
from October 28, 1922, till July 25, 1943. Two decades is
almost the time lag between two generations, the years
necessary for schoolchildren to become mature men, and
for mature men to become old. He himself was thirty-
nine when he took power and sixty only a few days after
he had to relinquish it. In the end, he was leading a
country different from that in which he conquered power,
a new country which he had shaped according to his
wishes, organized according to his theories, staffed by men
educated and selected by him and his lieutenants. His
powers were limitless: where his legal prerogatives ended,
his undisputed authority and immense personal prestige
began. He ran the only political party officially in existence,
so capillary and widespread that it interfered with the
daily habits of millions of people from dawn to dusk and
even later at night (he wanted Italians to produce more
and more children and granted advantages and prizes to
large families), and from the cradle to the tomb. He
decided the contents of newspapers, books, magazines,
radio programmes, films, encyclopaedias. He had no opposition to contend with.

He was sole legislator, judge, censor, policeman, ambassador, general. He was the Head of the Government,
President of the Grand Council, President of the Council
of Ministers, and, at one time or another, occupied most
of the seats around the council table himself. He was on
and off, for years, Minister of the Interior, of Foreign
Affairs, of the Army, the Navy, and the Air Force; he
managed economic affairs as Minister of Corporations.
The ministries he did not run he controlled indirectly.

Everything was conceived by him as a preparation for the ultimate test, the biggest world war ever seen, which he did little to avoid, foresaw with accuracy years before, and practically welcomed. The armed forces he led as commander-in-chief had been organized, trained, and armed by him for the conflict; they were supported by the economic and industrial organization he had shaped with that sole aim in view; encouraged by the propaganda machine he had invented and run for two decades; led by him during the war, through successive strategic moves, conceived and decided by him and by generals of his own choosing.

He was practically defeated by one man alone, himself. He found himself impotent in front of the overwhelming enemies he had evoked, and of the arrogant ally he had encouraged and cultivated, with the scarce resources he himself had predisposed, the industries he had encouraged, and the weapons he had designed and built. He was left in the lurch by himself as Foreign Minister (his grasp of the world situation had been highly over-optimistic), as Minister of the Armed Forces (he had chosen the wrong commanders, strategies and weapons), as Minister of the Interior (he underestimated the will of the Italian people to suffer and die for a war they did not understand), as Minister of Propaganda (he had believed his own newspapers), and as Head of the Fascist Party (he glibly thought he had worked out all the answers to the riddles of the modern world).

Italian artillerymen in the Western Desert fired Austrian guns of first world war vintage, built by the Skoda works in 1908 or thereabout, against the very modern American and British models. Mussolini lacked raw materials, fuel and food to fight a long war, and he lacked merchant ships with which to supply the far-flung theatres he had chosen to fight in, since many Italian ships in foreign waters, not having been informed about their country's entry into the war, were immediately impounded. His tanks were small, weak, slow, tinny affairs, which could be pierced by machine-gun fire; he had chosen them because they were cheaper and, for the same price, he could have more of them. He said they were faster than the heavier models, more 'attuned to the quick reflexes of the Italian soldiers'. He had no aircraft carriers. His planes were good but too few to count; he could not replace them fast enough. They were clever toys, elegant models laboriously made by hand by ingenious mechanics for peacetime reviews, rather than industrial products which could be turned out fast enough to produce results. His navy, which had somehow managed to run itself for years, was relatively efficient, but certainly not big and advanced enough to stand up to the combined strength of the fleets he attacked. It lacked radar and, what is worse, it never suspected such an invention existed, which made Italian ships sitting ducks for the British, at long range or at night.

The army was at first disciplined and in good spirits. The cliché of Italian soldiers running away was not true in the beginning. The men sacrificed themselves even after it was amply clear the whole thing was a macabre and hopeless joke. Of course, nobody likes fighting against overwhelming odds. The men tried their best, armed as they were for a short colonial adventure against disarmed backward people, but certainly not to face the biggest, richest, most numerous and advanced armies in the world. The navy sacrificed its ships and one half of all officers in the desperate attempt to save its honour. What was missing in Italy was often not the courage or the will to fight but any kind of serious plans and organization behind the fighting men.

Even if the experiment had not ended in catastrophe, historians would probably have wondered at the curious scarcity of concrete achievements during the twenty years of Fascist rule. What had Mussolini really done with his time? He promoted public works, to be sure, built harbours, railways, roads, schools, *autostrade*, monuments, aqueducts, hospitals, irrigation and drainage networks, public buildings, bridges and so forth. Some of these things were good and useful: they were admired and envied by friends and enemies. And yet, in retrospect, the result of all this activity seems meagre. To get the exact measure of his achievements one must, first of all, subtract from the total all that would have been accomplished by any government in his place. It is difficult to believe that, without a dictator, dirt roads would not have been covered with asphalt, as they were all over Europe at the same time. Some marshes had been reclaimed, aqueducts and railways built, industries promoted in Italy by the liberal governments before the Fascist *coup d'état* and, even before them, by the Bourbons of Naples and by the Popes' inefficient governments. When all the projects which, hypothetically, would have been undertaken anyway are subtracted from the total, Mussolini's contributions, while still important, shrink perceptibly. They shrink a little more when one considers how many projects were plain mistakes, decided for political and spectacular reasons rather than the hope of practical results; and how much money disappeared into the pockets of dishonest contractors. As a result the sum total of the Fascist achievements in this field seems out of proportion to the noise surrounding them, their fame and their moral cost.

In reality, behind the scenery of modernization and industrial investments, millions of Italians still lived a life of prehistoric squalor, and most of the fundamental problems of the country had been left practically untouched. One Mussolini really solved, peace with the Church. A few problems had somehow solved themselves, with the passage of time. Of some others only the visible symptoms had been attacked, never the deep-seated causes, too complicated and dull to interest a flashy, amateurish, hurried and journalistic leader. The problems which only a dictator could solve, the really hard ones, were left intact or became more serious and ingrained, problems like illiteracy, the Mafia, malaria, banditry, the social and political backwardness of the southern provinces, unequal distribution of income, primitive agriculture and an inadequate industrial structure.

His approach to many of the great contemporary difficulties was somewhat optimistic and facile. The very first instructions I received, in 1930, when I joined the *Corriere della Sera* bureau in London, were: 'Do not mention the world economic crisis.' They were his own words relayed to all journalists, his own way to settle one of the greatest difficulties of the times. I remember asking myself what would have happened if the Italian press had stopped mentioning the Atlantic Ocean: would Italians have drowned trying to go to New York on bicycles? When I went to Sardinia, a few years later, I was told I was to write about anything, anything at all, except two things, bandits and malaria. They were then the two most important phenomena of life in the island. They could easily be kept out of newspapers. But, I wondered, how could they be avoided in official documents and statistics? They were not, of course. They only had different names. The bandits were called *latitanti*, or fugitives from justice, and malaria was *febbre intermittente*, or intermittent fever. While urgent problems went unsolved, a number of imaginary ones were invented yearly and brilliantly eliminated: Italians were forbidden to shake hands (only the Fascist salute was allowed), foreign words were abolished from street signs and ordinary usage (the Pensione Milton of Rome became Miltone), and the *lei*, the formal address in the third person singular, was strictly prohibited by law and abolished in all grammars.

What is the explanation for the inaction and ineffectiveness of Fascism, and why did it fail? Mussolini was not stupid. He was shrewd, quick to learn, wary, astute. He could grasp a complex situation in a few minutes, face resolute opponents with success, usually take what intuitive decision any situation required. Perhaps he did not work hard enough. The suspicion came to me one day, many years ago, in Rome. I had given a lift to a soldier in my car. 'Where to?' I asked him. 'Palazzo Venezia,' he said. I asked him why. He explained simply that he was from the same town as Mussolini's office cook, and that he had to deliver a package her people had given him. 'Do you ever see Il Duce?' I asked idly. I, of course, saw him often, as a journalist, but only at formal ceremonies, surrounded by his retinue, and in uniform. 'Oh yes,' said the soldier calmly. 'I see him all the time. He is always in the courtyard, talking to drivers and the doormen.' I was stunned. I had probably stumbled on one of the darkest state secrets of the time. We now know that the light in his study was kept on until very late at night even when he was not there, which was often, to give people the illusion that he was sleeplessly attending to their welfare. Even so, he worked hard enough.

He liked work. He knew everything that went on in Italy (he got his first news report in the morning from the chief of Police and the general commanding the *cara-binieri*), knew everybody (important people and people who wanted to be thought important went to see him several times a year), was kept *au courant* of the smallest secrets (telephones were tapped not only to defeat the enemies of the régime and to uncover the devious plans of foreign emissaries, but also to provide him with gossip), read everything that was easy to read, newspapers, maga-zines, books, saw every film, and met all the distinguished foreigners who went through Rome. If he was not the great statesman he wanted to appear, he certainly was a good politician, busy with the numberless chores of his calling, and a good journalist, keeping abreast of every development gathering information for future use.

The explanation of his failure is perhaps that he was not a failure. He lost the war, power, his country, his mistress, his place in history, and his life, but he suc-ceeded in what he had wanted to do since he took power. It was not to make his country safe and prosperous. It was not, obviously, to organize Italy for a modern war and for victory. He had dedicated his life just to putting up a good show, a stirring show. He had managed to do it extremely well. He should not be compared to Crom-well, Washington, Cavour, Bismarck, or Talleyrand, but to men like Ernesto Rossi and Tommaso Salvini, the emi-nent actors, and to P. T. Barnum. He was a flamboyant interpreter of heroic rôles in the style of great nineteenth-century tragedians or operatic baritones. Paolo Monelli, the author of the best life of Mussolini, wrote: 'The Italians saw in him only the tenor for whom they raved as they had years before for Caruso and Tamagno. As one does with tenors, they enjoyed his good long notes and the melody without paying any attention to the words, but, if they had listened more carefully, they would not have been surprised by the catastrophe later. He had announced it.'

He played a versatile and multifaced rôle, that of Mus-solini, a heroic mixture of the Renaissance *condottiere*, cold Machiavellian thinker, Lenin-like leader of a revolu-tionary minority, steely-minded dictator, humanitarian despot, Casanova lover, and Nietzschean superman. He added later to his repertoire the Napoleonic genius, with well-known results, and, just before he died, the socialist renovator of society. He was none of these things. In the end, like an old actor, he no longer remembered what he really was, felt, believed, and wanted. Ugo Ojetti, an erudite art critic, writer and man of taste, who liked him, used to say in the thirties: 'I cannot help thinking, when I see him, how much his face must ache at night when he retires.' That he was conscious of playing rôles all the time could be discerned by any attentive observer: he walked, strutted or strode like a tragedian wearing an ancient costume; he pivoted on one spurred boot heel as if he were always trailing a long purple cloak behind him. He never tired but never looked at ease.

His success seemed incredible. He was more popular in Italy than anybody had ever been and probably will ever be. His pictures were cut out of newspapers and magazines and pasted on the walls of poor peasant cottages, at the side of the Madonna and Saint Joseph. Schoolgirls fell in love with him as with a film star. His more memorable words were written large on village houses for all to read. One of his collaborators exclaimed, after listening to him announce from the balcony that Ethiopia had been conquered and that Rome had again become the Capital of an Empire, in May 1936: 'He is like a god. . . .' 'Like a god? No, no,' said another. 'He *is* a god.'

I remember him, one day, during military manœuvres in the Langhe, in 1932, walking through a vast bare plain of yellow stubble surrounded by distant green hills, trees, and the steeples of village churches. Peasants came running from all sides, red-faced, panting, to see him, touch him, shout to him. One of his secretaries followed him with a leather envelope, the exact size of thousand-lire bills, to hand banknotes to the more miserable with the gesture of a gambler dealing out cards. Soon enough Mussolini was leading a parade of thousands of frenzied and gesticulating followers. He showed no expression on his face except the usual wooden determination. Mothers lifted babies high for him to see and possibly to touch, as they had done to kings in the Middle Ages. At one point a few nuns came running, their long black veils flying in the wind, carrying baskets of freshly-picked peaches to offer him. He accepted their homage without thanking them, without turning his

head or smiling, and handed the fruit to his retinue. Nobody who saw it will ever forget the sight of city squares
filled with crowds listening to him; the heads were as
close together as tesserae in a mosaic, all eyes turned to
one focal point, the balcony or stand from which he was
speaking. It was an ominous and frightening sight.

We laugh now when we see him in old newsreels. Possibly his showmanship was like some wines which do not
last or travel well, but which are excellent when con-
sumed the year they are made in their native surroundings.
His technique was flamboyant, juvenile, ridiculous, but
highly effective: it pleased his public, the plebeian and
illiterate masses from which he had sprung, the patriarchal Italians of the villages and the countryside who
longed for the ancient peace they had lost with the industrial revolution and the first world war; the 'bigoted and
reactionary' *petite bourgeoisie*, as Mario Missiroli called
it, who wanted to attend to their little affairs and let other
people worry about vast problems; the half-baked intellectuals and the frustrated nationalists who felt humiliated,
born and living in a third-rate country with a first-rate
glorious name, a country easily beaten by less glorious but
more efficient rivals. His technique was obviously not
meant for men of taste and culture. In Italy these were,
anyway, a minority which did not count; many, like Benedetto Croce, their leader, firmly resisted the régime; many
faced death in exile or life imprisonment; many col-
laborated with it, either intimidated and frightened or
ready to exploit what opportunities the régime offered.

The job had been an easy one in the beginning. There
was practically no gap between the spectacle and reality.
Many things were being done. Some of the easier problems
were effectively dealt with. The country was improving.
Living conditions were getting better. He had inherited a
good bureaucracy from the previous governments. He was
then still ready to listen to good advice. Later the job
became more and more difficult: the international situation grew more menacing and complicated. The gap between the flamboyant representations, the ceremonies, the
fiery speeches and the plain and ugly facts widened dangerously. After twenty years of dictatorship, people did
not know he was not really solving any problems. People

were drugged by propaganda and stirring shows. Most of them had lost or forgotten the capacity to judge things independently. Those who were alarmed at the way things were going consoled themselves by thinking that he was always there, in the Palazzo Venezia, the 'sleepless one', working hard, seeing to it that nothing irrevocably bad would happen. His reassuring face looked at everybody from each wall, from every film screen. Many secretly trusted him to avoid a real show-down, a catastrophe. Had he not made Italy a first-rate power, well-armed, well-commanded, feared by her enemies? Was he not the greatest man ever born in Italy? Was he not, like all of them, no fool?

*

Trying to find out what really happened, one gets lost in a complex psychological labyrinth, bewildered by an Italian play of mirrors reflecting each other's distorted images. There is no doubt, to begin with, that Mussolini deceived the people. He used deceit as a tool to govern with. The thing is not deplorable in principle. All great statesmen have had recourse to occasional distortions, mis-interpretations and outright lies. Mussolini merely lied more than all other past statesmen, a little more than some of his contemporary competitors, less than Hitler anyway; he enjoyed a monopoly and was able to multiply his lies by making good use of the newest communication techniques. His slanted views and fabrications filled newspapers, posters, the radio, the film screens, many books, magazines, and even the conversations between people who did not know each other very well. After such unprecedented mass attacks, it is not surprising that the majority of his captive audience believed most of what he wanted them to believe.

He was not entirely a ruthless and cold-blooded souls-engineer, a push-button politician who heartlessly manipulated people's emotions, beliefs, hopes, in his own interest, to further his schemes. He could be described as such only when he tried to convince his people of things he knew were utterly false; this happened often enough, but not always. He, too, was an Italian. He, too, loved a good show, enjoyed a good military parade, was comforted by a naval review, or strengthened by a vast ocean-like meeting in a city square. He, too, believed his own slogans. He, too, was amazed by the fake statistics, thrilled by empty boasts, stirred to tears by his own oratory. He, too, confused appearances for reality, the veneer for the solid wood. Truth, for him also, was what it looked like and what most people liked to believe.

His show was necessarily always new and startling. Only by keeping his public interested, thrilled, puzzled, frightened and entertained, could he make them forget the sacrifice of their liberty and their miserable poverty, unite a solid majority of them behind him, dishearten and divide the opposition, assure internal order and international prestige. Obviously, the choice of a sober policy imposing real sacrifices and a stern discipline, the admission that difficulties could not be annulled by the use of words, sleight-of-hand tricks and optimistic communiqués, but needed a lot of grim studying, careful planning, and hard work, would have probably cost him his job. He was not the man to conceive such a dreary programme, anyway, or to carry it through. Boredom would have destroyed him. Therefore one may say that not all his performing was his own, dictated by his caprice. Much of it was demanded by the people themselves; most of the time he had to give them also the lies they expected, the myths they wanted badly to believe in, in a critical and dramatic phase of their history, just as the character he impersonated was not wholly of his own choosing, but also one many Italians had been expecting, the impersonation of their secret longings, and which placated their obscure anxieties. Signs proclaimed all over Italy: 'Duce, you are all of us!' It was, in a way, true.

He could not help being corrupted by his own spectacle and people who surrounded him. Roman emperors all began to deteriorate the day they were raised to the imperial dignity. Many great leaders in the past, drunk with their own great importance and vast intelligence, thinking themselves infallible, surrounded by sycophants, eventually stumbled and committed a fatal mistake. At one point, they all took too big a risk. Napoleon attacked Russia and Hitler tried to fight two wars on two fronts. But Napoleon and Hitler commanded the most efficient and powerful military machines of their times, which had hitherto defeated all their enemies. They both had a reasonable chance; they both came close to winning, against heavy odds.

Mussolini never had a chance. It is true, he thought the war was almost over when he entered it, in June 1940; he counted on the aid of his mighty ally in an emergency; he trusted his intuition and his luck. But any reasonably prudent dictator should also have been prepared for unforeseen circumstances. He was not. He should have known that Germans sometimes lost wars and that they had an even chance of losing this one if it lasted long enough. He had suspected it, for a while, in the beginning when Italy was still neutral, and knew it at the end. He explained to friends and collaborators. 'Germans, of course, are militarists, not soldiers. They are going to lose. If they had as much political as strategic genius, they would have been the masters of the world centuries ago.' What he never knew was what every military attaché in every foreign embassy in Rome knew, that Italy was ridiculously and tragically unprepared. What blinded him?

He never even suspected that practically nothing was behind his show. He never knew how really weak, disarmed and demoralized the country was. He honestly thought he could play a rôle with his ineffective army, his servile generals, his Biedermeier guns, his toy planes, his tin tanks, and his ramshackle industries. This is an inexplicable state of affairs. He was no fool. He was not mad. While a little worn out and prematurely aged by his intense life, his love affairs (Claretta Petacci had come into his life in 1936, when he was 53 and she 24), and his bad health (he suffered from nervous stomach cramps, which gave him great pain in moments of crisis), he was on the whole still well aware of what was going on. He was badly informed, that is all. But he wanted to be badly informed. He knew nothing about Italy's military preparations. He had kept himself in the dark. He had been deceived by himself. But he had been aided by his ministers, his generals, the shows, the parades, the mass meetings and the people.

He had tried, from time to time, in the beginning, to pierce the curtain of official obsequiousness and official half-truths and deceptions. As long as his brother Arnaldo was alive (he died in 1931) and as long as he saw some outspoken old friends and collaborators, he was not yet dangerously detached from reality. But gradually the heady atmosphere of high position got the better of him. Somehow he was not capable of protecting himself from its deleterious effects. The master of make-believe could not always detect make-believe when practised by others on him. This, of course, is the heart of the matter. His resistance to deception, which was never very strong, gradually dwindled and eventually disappeared altogether. When people warned him against adulation, he shrugged his shoulders. In one of the first months of his government, in 1923, an old ambassador returned from Geneva, where he had represented Italy at a meeting on the control of poison gases. As the venerable gentleman entered the younger man's room, Mussolini did not look up from his desk and went on writing. Finally, after long minutes, he lifted his eyes from the paper and, jutting his chin forward, asked disdainfully: 'What are the most dangerous gases, ambassador?' The ambassador gravely answered: 'Incense is the most lethal of all, your excellency.' He was soon put on the retired list. As the years went by, Mussolini became completely addicted to the artificial paradise he had created for others. He needed bigger and bigger doses of flattery and deception each year. In the end the most sickening and improbable lies, as long as they adulated his idea of himself and confirmed his prejudices, seemed to him the plain and unadorned expression of objective truth.

All great personages, of course, are surrounded by fawning courtiers. Flatterers are especially common in Italy, where the people have always employed such arts offensively, to gain advantages, destroy rivals, and conquer power and wealth; and defensively, as the squid uses ink, to blind and confound powerful men, dictators and tyrants. But most great personages are aware of the danger surrounding them. All men in authority, in Italy, any kind of authority, even village mayors, know that the smiles, the praises, the gifts, the applause are not for them but for their rank. Most of them manage to protect themselves from disaster. Mussolini never learned. He was too

convinced of his own infallibility. He liked only the men
who did not warn him of the dangers facing him and
never tried to tell him the truth. As a result the only
people approaching him were the best flatterers of the
kingdom. They were not all dishonest. Some were just
fools who believed what they said. Some desperately
hoped that what they said was true, that he really was
the greatest man alive and that all would turn out for the
best in the end. They flattered him also to reassure themselves. Others were just unscrupulous crooks.

In the end he lived within a private imaginary world
of his own. The cities he visited had been carefully prepared a long time before his arrival: he was shown only
the things and the people that would please and comfort
him. Everything else was efficiently hidden. He did not
know the enthusiastic crowds cheering him were rein-
forced by regiments of black-shirted policemen and by
thousands of extras brought from the provinces the day
before. He did not know that some of the new buildings,
public works, or villages he opened were abandoned and
began decaying the following day, that some of the
aqueducts never carried water, and that all the numberless
divisions he was passing in review were more or less always
the same few, transported here and there.

The technique was so smooth that it even deceived
Hitler. Preparations for his visit in 1938 went on for six
months. All Italy was to show the German dictator a new
face. Nothing was to be left that was 'nineteenth century,
homely, familiar'. The country was transformed. Streets
where the parades were to pass were redesigned and reconstructed like film sets, houses were painted and
decorated along the railway line from the Brenner to
Rome. The soldiers taking part in the reviews had been
hand-picked. Most of them were to be blue-eyed and
tall, to show the visitors that Italians, too, were Aryans.
(Only the king could not be changed, to Mussolini's annoy-
ance. He was very small and not impressive. He was,
strangely enough, the only nordic one of them all, with
so much Austrian and German blood in him, showing
through his light blue eyes.) The parading soldiers were
armed with all the weapons existing in the country. They
were all dressed in brand-new uniforms.

It is well known that Hitler's favourable opinion of his partner, of Italian military preparations, and the people's devotion to the régime and to the Axis, made him commit several miscalculations, one of which probably cost him the war. He believed, in the end, that he lost the Russian campaign because he had started four weeks too late; he was four weeks late because he wasted time to rescue the Italians bogged down in Albania, in their ill-prepared attack on Greece. If this were true, Mussolini could be considered the greatest negative military genius the world has ever seen, who defeated two great nations single-handed, his own and Germany.

Il Duce enjoyed the show more than Hitler did. He always chuckled when he read the writings on house-walls, as if the words were really the expression of the people's will. He also read with relish the reports of ambassadors from abroad, strictly announcing the things he wanted to believe. He read his own newspapers with great pleasure. It was easy to fool him. Once, during the war, he looked at some figures in a report, pretending to be the total number of new guns his army possessed, and protested. There were not that many new guns in Italy. He knew. His Under-secretary for War, an astute general, quickly replied: 'No, Duce, there has been a mistake. These are the guns our industries are planning to produce in the near future.' He was reassured.

*

Mussolini fell from power on July 25, 1943. The Allied armies had invaded Sicily only a few days before. All overseas possessions were lost. The Italian army had been destroyed in Russia, in the Balkans, and in Africa. Italy was battered and paralysed by mass air-bombardments. The Germans themselves were only carrying on defensive retreats, economically, sparing whatever resources and men they had left. All the big Fascist chiefs took part in a fateful meeting of the Grand Council, presided over by Il Duce, who looked tired, haggard, and senile. He made an objective, or almost objective, exposition of the situation, showing that he had kept a good journalist's superficial grasp of things to the end, in spite of all, but talked as if he were talking of other countries, other wars, other leaders, other times. His henchmen demanded that the command of all armed forces be turned over to the king. Mussolini pleaded with them, cajoled them, threatened them, pointing to some files, presumably filled with compromising secrets, which he had on the table beside him, pleaded with them to respect his old age. ('I shall be 60 in a few days,' he said.) Finally he acquiesced. He accepted his demotion.

The following day Victor Emmanuel received him in his private villa and ordered his arrest. There was no Fascist revolt when the news spread. No faithful followers rose in arms. Nobody kept the Fascist oath: 'I swear to defend the revolution with my blood.' Nothing happened. The show was over, that was all. The dictator had been defeated by the Italians in the most costly way for them, but the only way. The people rejoiced tumultuously. Mussolini was transported here and there, to some islands at first, then to a resort hotel in the mountains of Abruzzi he had built for skiers, in search of a place the Germans could not reach. The Germans found him anyway, in spite of the fact that there was no road to the hotel and only a cable railway connected it with the lowlands. They used gliders. Mussolini arrived at Hitler's headquarters in East Prussia, thanked his liberator, donned his old uniform, and was named president of a puppet régime, the Fascist Republic of North Italy.

His headquarters were on Lake Garda, comfortably on the direct road to the Brenner Pass, in case of sudden retreat. His last few months of life were dismal. He knew everything was lost, he was a failure, his régime had plunged Italy into the wrong war, at the wrong time, with practically no weapons; and those few moral and material resources which existed, including the heroic courage of thousands of men, were squandered in insensate expeditions dictated by an amateur strategist's desire to show to his ally that he, too, was a master-mind. Sometimes he tried to find alibis: the fault was the Italians', he said, their soft character, their dislike of vigorous action; they were not the descendants of the ancient Romans but of foreign slaves, mongrels, serfs. He dreamed of a return to power, when he would take revenge on all his enemies, made possible by the secret weapons which the Germans had prepared. He paid practically no attention to current affairs, read many books, wrote an enormous quantity of insignificant articles, essays, apologias, memoirs, including some for children's publications. He was interested in but one thing, the position he would have in history. Jesus Christ, Napoleon, Caesar? he asked his visitors guardedly. He never mentioned Cola di Rienzo. He never mentioned Barnum, either. He visited Claretta Petacci in a little villa nearby almost every day. He was sick, weak, and dispirited. He knew the end had come.

The end indeed came on April 25, 1945. The Germans had signed a secret armistice with the Allies, behind his back, and were giving themselves up to the Allies as prisoners of war. He tried to negotiate his own armistice through the Archbishop of Milan but soon realized he had no power and no other open possibility than that of giving himself up. He had counted on the loyalty of the people of Milan who had cheered him in the streets with practically the old enthusiasm only a few months before in January, and had wildly applauded a speech he had made in a theatre. But the people were now all against him. It was dangerous to stay in the city. He decided to escape with a handful of faithful followers to Valtellina or to Switzerland. To the end, as usual, he vacillated and could not make up his mind. How should his adventure finish?

Like Cola he was undecided: heroic death or bourgeois escape? Valtellina is a narrow Italian valley which penetrates into Swiss territory like a wedge; it can be defended on a small front by few men, as it is protected to the left and right. He could easily make a last stand there, with a few companions, or, if he changed his mind, reach foreign soil with only a few hours' march through the mountains. In the end, like Cola, he decided to trust his art as an actor: to disguise himself and flee. He made up his mind to go directly to Switzerland, without wasting time in more futile and bloody heroics, carrying all his money and all his most useful documents, those he would employ to frighten Allied statesmen and to defend himself if he were tried as a war criminal. He was found and arrested by partisans on the road going north along the shore of Lake Como, hiding in a German truck, dressed in the heavy coat of a German petty officer and a German helmet. Claretta Petacci was arrested with him.

They were both shot against the ornate gate of a pompous villa, the next morning. The woman had tried to shield his body and was mown down with him. The money and documents disappeared for ever. The bodies were taken to Milan and hung, like Cola's, feet high, from a petrol station roof, alongside those of all the other Fascist chiefs caught and killed on the same road, on their way to Switzerland. Thirteen years before he had told Emil Ludwig: 'Everybody dies the death that corresponds to his character.' He had deluded the people, that was his crime. But his fatal error was that he had not known that the people were also deluding him. They led him to the catastrophe which was the only way they knew to get rid of him.

CHAPTER NINE

Realism and Guicciardini

THE PROBLEM the people faced under Fascism was as old as Italy: how to survive and possibly prosper in the midst of corruption, civil wars, revolutions and foreign invasions, under bloody tyrants and their greedy courtiers, without the protection of the law. Most of the methods evolved by the Italians are unsatisfactory. They are partial solutions at best. A few individuals manage to prosper in a decaying world, but the better they fare the worse the world becomes. And yet what is a man to do? He cannot change his countrymen. He cannot choose the times he is born in. He is powerless to deflect the tides of history. He can only try to defend himself from their blind violence, keep his mouth shut and mind his own business. The greatest Italian authority in these arts is Francesco Guicciardini, lawyer, diplomat, statesman, historian and thinker from Florence, who tested and refined them during his busy and successful life. He confided his experience in a secret notebook, *I Ricordi*, which was only published centuries after his death. It is the best handbook yet written for navigating in treacherous times. It is still invaluable today.

Montaigne, no mean practitioner himself of the related French arts of *savoir faire* and *savoir vivre*, called him, affectionately, '*mon Guichardin*'. Even Machiavelli, whose name has become proverbial as that of the heartless codifier of the Italian rules of the game, paid homage to his rival, for whom he felt not only the highest esteem, a rare sentiment among competitors, but also admiration, friendship, and even love. 'I love Messer Francesco Guicciardini, I love my fatherland more than my soul,' he once wrote. He could not go higher, as he loved his little fatherland, Florence, and his large fatherland, Italy, literally more than his own soul.

The two men have been compared repeatedly through

the centuries. The parallel is almost irresistible. After all, they were both Florentines, born in the same city at about the same time (Machiavelli in 1469 and Guicciardini in 1482); both started young, when the popular republic of Florence employed them as ambassadors; both pursued political careers, and were fascinated by the technique of governing men and achieving power. Both, in the end, were defeated and chose to retire to their country estates, where they studied, wrote historical works and meditated on history's immutable and mysterious laws; both reached the conclusion that men and things were what they were and that all reasonable plans of action had to start from that assumption. The two friends believed that the pursuit of success was an absolute imperative, for individuals as well as states, the only sensible goal for action. 'He who has no position in life,' Machiavelli wrote, 'cannot even get a dog to bark at him.'

In spite of these superficial similarities they were profoundly different. Machiavelli, the older man, kept some of the youthful illusions of an earlier and happier age. He was an artist, above all, who wrote perhaps the most beautiful, lean and muscular prose in all Italian literature, at times bitter, biting, ironical and light, at other times solemn, grave and sonorous, but always limpid. He lived an irregular, almost bohemian life. He was a brilliant failure, never really managing to achieve his ends: he never made love to the women he wanted, satisfied his ambitions, reached the top in his political career and was never taken seriously as a thinker during his lifetime. He died penniless: he never even succeeded in persuading the republic of Florence to pay his arrears and to reimburse him for his expenses. He never managed to get his immortal works published. He was the permanent victim of political changes: he had made no headway when Florence was democratically ruled by the people; but, when the despotic Medici came back to power, he was arrested and tortured with four turns of the rack as a suspect republican; later, when the republic was once more restored, he was wrongly considered with suspicion and excluded from public business as a supporter of the Medici. Such is the fate of very intelligent men who are, however, not intelligent enough to conceal their intelligence and lull other people's fears and suspicions to sleep.

Machiavelli was, in reality, too much of a dreamer and an optimist to achieve practical results. He thought there were sure ways to solve the Italian national problem; he believed history could be re-routed, fate averted, the people changed, of course not by means of moral teachings, crusades, reforms, and prayers, but of realistic expedients and devices. He thought (just as Stendhal was naïvely to believe, three hundred years later, that all the ills of Italy would vanish the day a bicameral parliamentary system was adopted) that a militia of conscripted citizens, which would do away with the need for mercenary armies led by corruptible *condottieri*, would make the country invincible. (This proposal was rejected by the more experienced Guicciardini, when he was governor of the Romagna, as too abstract and dangerous; he thought that nobody could stop the citizens, once armed, from making war on each other.) Machiavelli hoped, above all, for the coming of a Great Leader, a superman who could perform the miracle of uniting Italy and ruling over her with a firm hand, and could keep foreign armies and local enemies at bay by the employment of all the arts and tools of contemporary statesmanship, poisons, deceit, terror, bribes, spies, and, when necessary, justice.

Guicciardini was no light-minded artist. He led no bohemian life. He entertained no illusions. Born a wealthy patrician, he was well brought up and educated. His virtuous youth had been spent, as he himself wrote, 'without corruption, levity, or waste of time'. His only known vice was women, for whom he had a long and persistent, though secret, weakness, women of all conditions and ages. (He never liked his wife, whom he had married for political reasons and always left at home.) He seemed so aloof, reserved and forbidding, that he provoked the hatred of all who knew him only superficially. He had learned his first lessons in the art of surviving and prospering in treacherous times from his father Piero. Piero was unsinkable. He managed to have a good reputation, but not so good as to frighten others; he managed to get appointed to high positions but not high enough to provoke envy and criticism. He had always felt the wind turning with sufficient anticipation to prepare himself without vulgar haste. He flourished under all régimes, popular and aristocratic, democratic and tyrannical.

Francesco had the same keen sense of political meteorology and managed to float just as surely most of his life, through some of the most complicated and deadly convulsions of Italian history, perhaps with even more dignity and ease than his father. To float, to prosper, to wield power were his only aims. He occupied some of the highest offices in the country with dignity, reaching almost regal powers. He acquired a solid reputation, seriously cultivated historical and political studies, and enlarged his private fortune. He got everything he wanted by honest means, not courting powerful personages, or courting them so discreetly as to be undetected. 'I always allow appointments to run after me and not vice-versa,' he disdainfully wrote. This was due to luck, his character and upbringing, his uncanny knowledge of human nature, and his ability and prudence which made him a desirable man to employ by anybody in difficult posts. Even those who hated him still admired him: 'Messer Francesco,' wrote Benedetto Varchi, the Florentine chronicler who loathed him, 'besides his wealth, his degree of knowledge, besides being governor or lieutenant of the Pope, was also famous for the practical knowledge he possessed of human actions, which he discussed and judged with great perception.'

These, briefly, were the stages of his rapid career. He was a struggling lawyer of twenty-nine when the republic of Florence appointed him ambassador to the King of Spain. In 1515, when he was thirty-three, he was sent by the republic to greet Pope Leo X, another Florentine, formerly Cardinal Giovanni de Medici. Leo, who had a keen nose for able men, took him into his favour and three years later appointed him Governor of the rebellious cities of Reggio and Modena. In 1521 Parma was added to his rule. The young and inexperienced democrat from Florence knew enough to surround himself with princely pomp, an impressive retinue, and escorts of cavalry and foot soldiers whenever he appeared in public. He was an efficient governor. He acted ruthlessly against all rebel subjects, not only those who sided with the emperor and were, therefore, open game, but also against those who sided with the pope, had friends at the Roman court, and could make the governor's life difficult. He disarmed everybody, arrested and tortured suspects, whatever their rank, executed robbers and murderers, generally enforced law and order, paved the main streets with stone, and balanced the budget. The Pope who succeeded Leo (after the short reign of another) was also a Medici, Clement VII; he named forty-one-year-old Francesco Governor of the vast province of Romagna and, three years later, Lieutenant-General of the papal armies.

In 1531 he was promoted to the Governorship of Bologna, the most important of all the papal Lord-Lieutenantcies. After the death of Clement, in 1534, he resigned and came back to Florence, to play local politics as a faithful henchman of the Medici family. With his support, Alessandro de Medici conquered power. He was a cruel, stupid, avaricious and dissolute tyrant, who ordered most of the pretty girls and handsome matrons of Florence to be brought to his bedroom, and was hated by everybody, including Guicciardini, who nevertheless served him loyally. Alessandro was murdered. Messer Francesco then used all his political skill and influence to bring to power another tyrant, the young Cosimo de Medici, belonging to a cadet branch of the family, and procured for him from Charles V the imperial title of 'Grand Duke', thus destroying the very name, if not the memory, of Florentine republican liberties.

This was his only mistake. Cosimo was a boy of seventeen, much addicted to sports and frivolous pursuits. Guicciardini thought he would just amuse himself with the 12,000 gold florins which were to be paid to him every year and leave matters of state to him. (Benedetto Varchi graphically describes Messer Francesco's unconsciously revealing his secret designs: 'Lowering his face and raising his eyes, Guicciardini said: "Twelve thousand gold florins—*è un bello spendere*, a nice enough sum to spend!"' The gesture would be still good for the villain in an Italian opera or costume film.) What Guicciardini did not know was that Cosimo was a political *enfant prodige*, a precocious teenage statesman. With decent modesty and becoming show of deference, the inexperienced youth had used the circumspect and shrewd veteran, one of the greatest politicians of all times, as his ladder to mount the throne, and then kicked the ladder away.

Guicciardini retired decorously to his villa near Arcetri, called *Il Finocchieto*, the fennel patch, to oversee his peasants, improve his wine, study, meditate, sum up his experiences, and write some of the best books of history in Italian literature. He died of a stroke at the age of fifty-eight.

What is striking and instructive about Messer Francesco is the wide discrepancy between his personal thoughts and beliefs, and his public acts. What is even more striking and instructive is the fact that he was not surprised or troubled by the discrepancy which he placidly accepted as one of the facts of life. He never allowed his private intimate convictions to interfere with the business on hand. He was, for instance, privately a devoted and religious man, honest and honourable, brought up strictly within the Catholic faith. In his youth he had even thought of becoming a priest. He wanted religion to return to ancient piety and moral zeal. As a good Christian, he despised the temporal power of the Popes, which had transformed the Vicar of Christ into a worldly princeling playing dirty Renaissance politics. He denounced in his secret notebook the corruption which power, wealth and ambition inevitably furthered among priests. Yet he served two Popes' unholy schemes and helped consolidate and enlarge the material domains of the Church.

He calmly explained in his *Ricordi*:

'No man hates the ambition and avarice of priests more than I do; for these vices, odious in themselves, are most unseemly in men who make a profession of living in contact with God. . . . My position under several Popes has compelled me to desire their aggrandisement for the sake of my own profit. Otherwise, I should have loved Martin Luther like myself—not that I might break loose from the laws which Christianity . . . imposes on us, but that I might see . . . villains . . . forced to live either without vices or without power.'

Although he hated tyranny above all, he did nothing to free Florence from tyrants and helped to destroy the city's liberty forever. He merely expressed his disapproval of tyrants in his journal and went on with the task in hand. He was too wise to allow himself to dream and to hope. Could he trust the men who plotted to re-establish free institutions? Of course not. Francesco sadly wrote:

'Do not take too seriously most people (not all of them, of course) who preach the advantages of liberty, because, if they hoped to find an advantageous position in a tyrannical state, they would rush there by the quickest post. In almost all men, the concern for their own interest is stronger than love of glory and honour.'

And:

'I do not blame those who, enflamed by love of country, defy dangers to establish liberty and popular rule, though I think that what they do is extremely risky. Few revolutions succeed, and, when they do, you often discover they did not gain you what you hoped for, and you condemn yourself to perpetual fear, as the parties you defeated may always regain power and work for your ruin.'

One had to learn to live with tyrants. Here are a few hints on how to prosper under them.

'No rules are useful when living under a bloody and bestial tyrant, except perhaps one, the same which is useful in times of plague: flee as far as you can. But when the tyrant is obliged to be relatively moderate and respectful, out of caution, necessity, or political convenience, a wise man must try to appear capable and courageous, although for the time being resigned to things as they are. . . . The tyrant will then flatter him, not to offer him any cause to desire a different government. This the tyrant would not do if he knew the man to be restless, for if he thought there was absolutely no way to keep him quiet, he would think only of how best to kill and put him out of the way.'

'I believe that a good citizen and patriot should maintain good relations with the tyrant not only for his own safety, but also for the benefit of everybody else. By seeing the tyrant often and gaining his trust, he may at times favour a good initiative and forestall a bad one. Those who blame this behaviour are mad. It is best, however, not to be among the tyrant's most intimate confidants. Thus you enjoy the advantages of his power and, when he meets his ruin, you will not be swept away with the rest.'

Prudent behaviour inevitably involves some dissimulation. How should a moral man envisage this necessity? Here is Messer Francesco meditating on this eternal problem:

'Everybody likes open, truthful and frank persons. To be open, truthful and frank is a noble and generous thing, although often harmful. On the other hand, dissimulation and deception are useful and often indispensable, because of the evil nature of men. These arts are, however, despised and hated by everybody. Therefore I do not know which behaviour to choose. I would suggest truthfulness should be ordinarily preferred, without abandoning deception altogether. That is, in the ordinary circumstances of life, use truthfulness in such a way as to gain the reputation of a guileless man. In a few important cases, use deceit. Deceit is the more fruitful and successful the more you enjoy the reputation of an honest and truthful man; you are more easily believed.'

The Guicciardini basic formula is this: 'Those men conduct their affairs well who keep in front of their eyes their own private interest and measure all their actions according to its necessities.' It is the way to survive and prosper in treacherous times. He added that unfortunately too many short-sighted men 'think that their interest lies mainly in the accumulation of wealth and not also in keeping a good reputation and a good name'. Messer Francesco knew better. He knew that without some renown and respect a man could amass riches but rarely preserve or increase them. He also knew that the lofty ideals he cherished would not interfere with his personal success only if he considered them his own private prejudices. He could speak of piety, honour, liberty, justice, morality, and the hope to see Italy freed from foreign oppressors to a few trusted friends, teach them to his children and grandchildren, write about them in his notebooks, within the four walls of his house, behind locked doors. But his decisions in the world were never to be dictated by a desire to change it. He could be compared to a seasoned captain who naturally would prefer to sail over a smooth sea, driven by favourable breezes in the right direction, but is prepared to adapt himself to whatever conditions will prevail. To arrive safely with any weather is his only goal. *Navigare* is a word employed often in the metaphorical sense, meaning to cut the sails and set the course according to the prevailing political winds, knowing that it is beyond man's power to change them. When Giovanni Musco, the Sicilian dialect comedian, was asked by Mussolini whether he was a Fascist he answered cryptically: '*Marinaio sugno*, I am a sailor.'

*

Italians do not need to read Guicciardini. In fact few of them ever do. They learned long ago to beware privately of their own show and to be sober and clear-eyed realists in all circumstances. They mind their own business. They behave with circumspection, caution and even cynicism. They are incredulous: they do not want to be fooled by seductive appearances and honeyed words. They cannot afford to be carried away by emotions. They keep them under control. This does not mean that they are cold people. When it is safe to do so, they enjoy genuine and unrestrained emotions as well as anybody. But they know that the free expression of genuine emotions is a luxury for the privileged, often a dangerous and expensive luxury. Only saints, heroes, poets, gentlemen of means, foreigners, madmen, and the poor, who have nothing to lose, can afford to give way to their emotions. Ordinary people must usually choose between the unrestrained expression of counterfeit emotions and the controlled expression of real ones. Though they have forgotten one of their old proverbs, which Lord Chesterfield quoted to his son, they still obey it; they keep *volto sciolto e pensiero stretto*, an open countenance and closed thoughts, for the same reasons that the façades of their houses are often cheerfully inviting but their front doors are always double-locked.

Like anybody else, they, too, would naturally prefer the world to be different: an Arcadia where the sheep could lie with the wolf, where everybody could say and write what he thought, and men were all brothers. But they know that those who delude themselves are almost sure to meet a bad end: they know the world is an ugly and pitiless place, and adapt themselves, without useless recriminations, to its inviolable laws. They good-humouredly make the best of their lot, whatever it may be, as soldiers do in a solitary outpost surrounded by the enemy, who grumble, shirk unnecessary dangers, make their dug-outs comfortable, adorn them with pictures and flowers, hoping for salvation but also resigned to death.

Only few Italians find solace in actual rebellion. Not all of the many members of the Communist party want to start a revolution. Most of them want to enjoy the privileged status of revolutionaries in a frightened capitalist society. Those few who want to set up a Marxist state know sadly that their revolution, as Guicciardini pointed out, would not modify the fundamental injustices of life. Revolt, anyway, gets one nowhere, tears one away from safe and anonymous obscurity, and makes one's life unnecessarily difficult. In the most favourable circumstances, on the rare occasions when it is successful, it may eventually improve one's great-grandchildren's lot, but almost never one's own. This is why many Italian rebels and revolutionaries always were and still are the best of men, more disinterested and worthy of admiration than others. Most people in Italy, in fact, believe that the *condition humaine* is a sentence without pardon and amnesties, that original sin cannot be washed away, that man cannot easily change his fate and that, in the end, he must pay for whatever relief he may gain with other and worse troubles.

For all these reasons they tend to be concrete people, never allowing their imagination to stray too far, preoccupied with concrete problems, situations, men and things as they are. They cultivate tangible pleasures, the pleasures of the senses, and, when they can, those, just as substantial, which wealth and power afford. The imperative which they implicitly obey in all their decisions is *non farsi far fesso*, not to be made a fool of. To be *fesso* is the ultimate ignominy, as credulity is the unmentionable sin. The *fesso* is betrayed by his wife, buys gold bricks, falls for deceptions and intrigues, and often accepts the wolf's invitation to lie down with him. The *fesso*, incidentally, also obeys the laws, pays the taxes, believes what he reads in the papers, keeps his promises, and generally does his duty. Fortunately, there are still enough *fessi* in Italy, mostly in the north, to keep the country alive; without them everything would probably stop; and yet few would admire or praise them. Their number is therefore diminishing. Nobody knows what will happen when they disappear altogether.

This intense preoccupation with solid, measurable, sensible reality is readily perceived by anybody having even a superficial acquaintance with Italian life. It can be read in the ambiguous political decisions of every day, in the astute way in which business negotiations are conducted. It can also be confirmed simply by overhearing the conversation at the next café table, in a train compartment, or in any waiting-room. Average Italians talk mostly about what many other people talk about, food, money, the art of fornication, work, clothes, appearances, amusements, how to defend oneself from the schemes of rivals and the rigours of the law. Only the very young talk about art, virtue, justice, dreams, liberty, and ideals. The emphasis is always on the solid, the down-to-earth, the material, with a wealth of precise and substantial details. The people they describe are seldom virtuous, disinterested and generous; the loves, seldom pure and spiritual. The characters they mention, living politicians or dead historical figures, are always blandly accused of all sorts of crimes, homosexuality, adultery, the seduction of minors, corruption, nepotism, treason, cowardice, the plundering of public funds, or, the worst crime of all, stupidity. Why was a certain man appointed to a certain post? The last explanation they accept is that he may be capable of fulfilling some of its functions. It pleases them to think that it is because he is somebody's brother-in-law, has come across documents which would ruin the man who appointed him, belongs to an all-embracing secret society, or made love to a powerful man's mistress.

After the war, for instance, everybody tried hard to find a suitable answer to the puzzling problem: why was the United States showering billions of dollars on their country? Communists were certain that it was part of a master-plan to impoverish, starve, enslave, and destroy the Italian proletariat. Non-Communists could not make up their minds. Were the Americans mad? Many possible explanations were debated and discarded. At the end, most people said: 'Why should they, who won the war, enrich us, who lost it? They must have their own reasons. Whatever they are, there is no doubt the Americans are serving their own interests. Therefore, there is no need for us to be grateful to them.' There is a large part of reality which the realistic Italians never really grasp; there are many things they do not see for being too clear-sighted.

•

A few years ago a small English family rented an unpretentious villa near Florence. They had modest means, no ambitions, and tranquil ways. The father was a scholar, read a lot, and wrote an interminable book. The wife took good care of her two children, cultivated her garden, and typed her husband's manuscript. Florence and its surrounding hills have been a traditional refuge for people like them, studious and mild-mannered Anglo-Saxons who found life in their countries too hectic and exhausting. This particular family settled down comfortably: they liked the landscapes, the simple *contadini*, the long walks in the country. They were happy.

A maid helped them with the household duties. Elvira, a simple peasant girl, whom they treated as one of them. They taught her to read and write and to brush her teeth twice a day. As the months passed, the girl began visibly to swell. One day she could no longer postpone confessing what they had already guessed, that she was expecting a child. She wept copiously, tore her hair, told them she was not worthy of their trust, that they would be right to dismiss her and send her out into the street. She said she wanted to die, that she had to die, in any case, as she had no place to go, and her own father would kill her if he found her out. Her lover, the cause of her condition, had emigrated months before, and could not be traced; there was absolutely no way to get him back to marry her.

The Englishman consoled her as best he could, his wife took her in her arms, the children embraced her. The couple assured her that, according to their more modern and enlightened views, it was no shame to be an unwed mother, just a *contretemps*, and that she was not the first nor the last to whom such an accident had occurred. She was to stop worrying, it was bad for her.

From then on they were going to take care of everything. She would stay in the house, do whatever light duties she could, look after her health; in the end the child would be born in a good clinic in Florence, at their expense, and then both mother and baby could come back and live with them for ever after. The Englishman even generously proposed that he be godfather and his wife godmother at the christening, if the difference in religion did not prevent it. The maid dried her tears and smiled.

When she returned with her baby, the Englishman sent for her father, told him what had happened, reassured him, explained that everything was all right, and invited him and the whole family for the *festa* of the christening. At the end of his little speech he looked benignly on the old peasant, feeling justly proud of being ready to alleviate other people's sorrows with his modest means and to do what he could to make poor Elvira and her baby secure and happy. He was also understandably proud of showing this simple Tuscan *contadino* how generous and civilized the English could be in such matters. Maybe the lesson would not be wasted, maybe it would be remembered in similar cases in the future, and help modify the harsh and primitive local customs.

The old man looked grim and suspicious, as he listened to the foreigner's halting words with the strange accent, shook his head, and said nothing. Of course, he was too intelligent to believe the incredible fairy stories he had been told. Why should an Englishman, obviously a very wealthy and well-born gentleman, want to take care of that shameless and lying strumpet, Elvira, who should be better dead than alive to dishonour her family, as everybody would agree who knew anything about life? Why, then, had the Englishman not kicked her out of his house? Why had he spent all that good money on fancy doctors, a room in an expensive clinic, chicken broths, talcum powder, and diapers? Why did he want to go on spending more? Why did he want to be godfather? And, above all, why did he waste time telling him all that noble nonsense?

There was, obviously enough, but one true explanation. Anybody could guess it. The Englishman was the father of the newly-born baby. Elvira had probably seduced him, as she was perfectly capable of doing, the shameless *puttana*, or he had taken Elvira into his house to sleep with her. One could understand his reasons, one could even sympathize with him, when one looked at his bony English wife. What a stupid or immoral woman she must be, the peasant thought, to be willing to be godmother to her husband's bastard child, to the fruit of a sinful relation! The ways of foreigners are mysterious. Still, he concluded, whatever had happened, there the matter was and he had to do what was right. He nodded curtly and left.

The following day legal documents began raining on the poor English household. The Englishman, it appeared from the stilted prose, was being sued by Elvira's father for a very large amount of money, money for damages, money to assuage outraged feelings and redeem the dishonour and discredit to the family, money to assure the child and his mother adequate means for life, more money to pay the lawyers and, eventually, the courts. Obviously, Elvira's family considered that they had acquired the right to live comfortably from that day forth on the misfortune and disgrace of the poor girl. The Englishman left the whole matter in the hands of lawyers, gave up the villa, dismissed the maid, and hurriedly departed with his wife and children.

*

This obvious predilection of the Italians for the solid, the all-too-human, the comprehensible, the pleasurable; this constant suspicion of the honourable, the unworldly, the chivalrous, and the noble; this persistent fear of emotional traps; this concentration on private interests and disregard for public welfare; this certainty that all things, no matter how alluring, will end up badly, all these have been constant characteristics of Italian life since time immemorial. They are ancient mental precautions and expedients, unconsciously accepted by almost all, developed by the people in order to get through life unscathed. Numerous foreign scholars, who found them confirmed by abundant examples from the literature and the art of centuries, concluded that these were not expedients but perennial traits, an immutable part of the very nature of the people.

The erudite John Addington Symonds, for example, dedicated to this preference several eloquent passages in his *Renaissance in Italy*. 'When we complain,' he wrote, 'that the Italians are deficient in the highest tragic imagination, that their feeling for nature lacks romance, or that none but their rarest works of art attain sublimity, we are but insisting on the realistic bias which inclined them to things tangible, palpable, experienced, compassable by the senses. . . . Realism, preferring the tangible and concrete to the visionary and abstract, the defined to the indefinite, the sensuous to the ideal, determines the character of their genius in all its manifestations.'

Norman Douglas even thought, curiously enough, that Italians were so preoccupied with practical matters that they became oblivious to pure beauty, the beauty of their own land in particular. 'There are wondrous tints of earth, sky, and sea, in these regions,' he wrote in *Siren Land*, speaking of Capri and the nearby coast, 'flaring sunsets and moons of melodramatic amplitude that roll upon the hilltops or swim exultingly through the aether; amber hued gorges where the shadows sleep through the glittering days of June, and the mad summer riot of vines careening in green frenzy over olives and elms and figs; there are tremulous violet flames hovering about the sun scorched limestone, sea mists that climb in wreathed stateliness among wet clefts, and the sulphurous gleams of a scirocco dawn when fishing boats hang like pallid spectres upon the skyline: there are thousands of joys like these, but the natives do not see them, although, to please foreigners, they sometimes pretend to. . . . The coils of muscle about the shoulders of some stripling as he strains himself to raise a heavy limestone block; a young girl whose swelling form gives promise of fruitful maternity; a waving cornfield, a shower in May, a dish of fat roasted quails—all this is legitimately *bello*: but mountains are mere hindrances to agriculture, unsightly protuberances upon the fair face of the earth; land-caves are useful for storing hay; sea-caves blue or green, for sheltering boats in the rain; the sea itself with all its choral harmonies, is merely a place where fishes are caught.'

*

This attachment to the solid, the substantial, and the real is particularly evident in the old *novelle*, the most typical product of Italian literature, the tales which Shakespeare and other northern poets ransacked for their plots. There are thousands of them. The very word *novella* is concrete. It does not mean story, a fiction of the imagination, a poetic invention, but news, actual news, reports of events which really took place, anecdotes in the life of rich, powerful and famous persons, information received from distant places. Foreign writers were as justified in borrowing ideas for their plays and poems from them as contemporary authors are in borrowing plots from the newspapers. The events in the old *novelle* do not take place in a misty and legendary atmosphere, among vaguely defined and shadowy characters, virtuous knights and noble maidens, driven by honourable motives, as in the stories which were written at about the same time, the late Middle Ages, in other parts of feudal Europe. There are real people in the Italian stories, merchants, monks, artisans, shopkeepers, and princes, human beings of solid flesh and sound appetites, who speak the quick and colourful dialects of the market place and the wine shop.

The lesson the reader drew was not meant to edify him. He did not learn to shun sin, to combat evil, to protect the weak, to control his base instincts, to respect the virtues of others, to reform the world, and prepare himself for salvation in after life; he learned mainly to protect himself from deceit, treachery, the arrogance and the cunning of others; to profit by their weakness, to see through their hypocrisy, and to enjoy the good things in life: the lusty wenches, the blushing maids, the good food, the good wine, the gay companions, and the victorious battles against feebler enemies. The cruel and ruthless ways of the world are accepted as unchangeable. They are seldom judged. The poor in spirit, the gullible, the naïve, the betrayed husband, in other words the *fessi*, are derided. Their sorry fate is considered not only inevitable but just and proper. The rich in spirit, the clever and strong men who use their gifts without scruples or charity, always come out on top, the object of the author's and the reader's admiration and approval. Only a few princes are allowed to be magnanimous and generous. All others live, win, or lose, strictly according to the rules of the game as the Italians understood them at the time and understand them, more or less unchanged, today.

Practically without interruption, through the years, Italians have continued to create works of art dedicated mainly to the praise of the strong and the powerful and the derision of the weak and defeated, or dedicated to the glory of the flesh, and the harmonious and perlaceous beauties of the naked female body; some of these works were coarse, ribald, bawdy, others delicate, thinly veiled, and allusive. Even when these artists tried their hands at more elevated subjects, their real tendencies ineluctably cropped up. In many of their Madonnas one can read the pleasure the painter has found in the fresh look of a pretty peasant girl, rather than his piety. Raphael's Madonnas are portraits of his voluptuous mistress, the baker's daughter, called *La Fornarina*, whose insatiable appetite for love was one of the causes of his early death. In great and more ambitious poems dedicated to religious and epic themes, the noble sentiments easily sound sugary and conventional, the language stilted, and the images contrived and literary. Only when the poets describe the fury of battle, palpable objects, villainous infidels, earthy delights and human passions are they at ease and convincing. How much more comfortable many authors feel in the many irreverent and satirical parodies they wrote of the noble and inspiring poems fashionable in the rest of Europe!

Italians also liked to compose cynical comedies of intrigue and deceit, closely following ancient Roman models so coarse they could not be produced unexpurgated even today. The best of these plays were composed by Nicolò Machiavelli, deriding men of the Church, bourgeois conventions, jealous husbands, and the virtue of women. It is odd that such a great historian and political thinker should waste his time writing pornographic farces, but not as inexplicable as it sounds. Many eminent men of the time, high prelates, statesmen and scholars, dedicated their spare time to the composition of obscene poems in Latin or Italian. Then Machiavelli's plays are not as morally distant from his great books, the *Commentaries on the Decades of Livy* and *The Prince*, as one would think. They are all inspired by failure, disappointment and bitterness: the private failure of an extremely clever man who never managed to become important, the public failure of an extremely clever and civilized nation, his own, which never achieved the unity and discipline necessary to defeat illiterate foreign invaders.

In his political works he challenged, for practical purposes, the validity of lofty and disinterested motives in the conduct of public affairs; in his comedies, he challenged the validity of similarly lofty and disinterested motives in the conduct of private affairs. In both fields, like all good Italians, he played safe: he trembled lest he be made a fool of, a dupe, fatally led to wrong conclusions and a bad end by honourable ideals. He felt much more secure believing that *le pire est toujours certain,* or, as he himself would have said in good Tuscan, *il peggio non è mai morto.* He preferred to take it for granted that all sovereigns were cruel, crafty, and ruthless; that all priests and monks were libertines, whoremongers, gluttons and rapacious money-grubbers, and all women harlots. He considered that he was, at the most, wrong only a very few times, hardly ever.

From the end of the eighteenth century to the end of the nineteenth, Italian writers at last dedicated their genius to something more worthy than the colourful description of worldly pleasures and the activities of men and women pliably and readily adapted to the worst in the world. Finally some authors appeared who believed the Italian people could rebel against their dreary and ignominious lot, correct their national defects, and work to better their moral and material conditions. These poets and novelists exalted spiritual values, religious faith, noble ideals; they praised patriotism, strength of character, courage, honesty, justice and truth. Some foresaw the resurrection of the ancient virile virtues of the people and the spiritual renovation of Italy. Their resounding poems and historical novels, as well as Verdi's heroic music, accompanied a vast moral, political and military upheaval, the revolution of the Risorgimento, the conquest of national independence and unity.

But with the end of the old century and the beginning of the new, after the smoke of battle had cleared, Italians began discovering that they were more or less the same as they had always been, that those who had really believed in the Risorgimento had been a small minority. The ancient traits began to reassert themselves, the old outlook to reappear in print. Writers went back to trusting only the palpable and measurable. Giovanni Verga, the Sicilian novelist, described the harsh avarice of peasants and fishermen as they strived to amass *la roba*, or wealth, in order to become bourgeois in the new liberal State. D'Annunzio felt patriotism no longer as a youthful and clean passion, but as an excuse for bloody, ornate and decadent adventures. Above all he believed in all kinds of physical pleasures, the feel of a panting horse at a gallop between his knees, a swim at dawn in the sea, rare perfumes, the killing of enemies in battle, and the endless delights of women's bodies. The old tradition continues. A few famous Italian writers of today (and some of the best films, which are partly inspired by them) have paid as much attention as their forefathers did to the solid aspects of life and have shown the old familiar suspicion of the ideal and noble. Some of these men have described the pleasures of lust, greed, and ambition with the ancient gusto, sometimes reaching daring refinements which even the Renaissance had not known.

When you consider, however, other contemporary works of art you are tempted to believe that Italians are for the first time no longer what they have always been. These are the leaden avant-garde novels, macabre paintings, disconsolate films and joyless poems which the best critics admire. The old fear of being made a fool of by illusions has now become an obsession. The search for truths which will not betray a man, modest truths if need be, has now reached a dead end. Obviously nothing much is left for a man to believe. Not yesterday's noble ideals, the love of country caricatured by the Fascists, the love of honour, honesty, morality, integrity derided by the current mores; not the hope of a better future in which not even the Communist dare believe any longer. Nothing is left because the last refuge of all Italians, his own *particulare*, his strictly private interest, the pursuit of concrete and measurable things, has been discredited for the first time. These newest Italians apparently do not even believe in the ultimate and fundamental Italian certainty, the flesh. In fact, fornication has, for the first time in centuries, become a tedious and almost repellent diversion in some of the best current Italian novels. Nothing is left, then, than *la noia*, the boredom which Moravia has so acutely analysed. But then you listen to people talk in cafés, watch them diffidently buy fish or fruit in an open-air market, watch them rapturously listening to sonorous band-music, watch old men smile to an unknown pretty girl in the street. . . . You are immediately reassured. The Italians are the same.

CHAPTER TEN

The Pursuit of Life

L ET us consider the solitary Italian, whoever he may be, at the moment he is actually born, on the day, that is, when he realizes that things are seldom what they seem, words not always what they sound like, and most of what he learned in school, in the army, or from his elders, and what he read in many grave books, is complete nonsense. On that day he understands that he will surely come to grief if he carelessly tries to live according to the rules he has been taught, like a blind man groping his way in a room in which the furniture is not where he expects it to be. The rules he has been taught are noble rules. They are probably useful to regulate life in other countries, those immaculate, well-ordered and prosperous countries of the north he has heard about. There, Italians believe, the same law is valid for the weak and the powerful; all officials are incorruptible; the inhabitants are honest, truthful and splendidly defenceless because they have no reason to fear one another. There, Italians believe, taxpayers gladly pay all their taxes without cheating; jobs are always awarded to the best man; medals to the real heroes; the labels of bottles always correspond to their contents, flowers and vegetables always come out as depicted on the seed-envelopes. There life is wonderfully easy. It is a different matter in Italy.

A moment of revelation comes, it must be admitted, practically to everybody and not to Italians alone. A day comes when men of all nations understand that life can be pitiless and ugly. Each has his own way of reaching maturity. Some need the imperceptible passing of the years. It takes but a tiny incident for others; like the shaking of a kaleidoscope it precipitates an abrupt change of the picture. Or it may be a great event that awakens him: he sees his country defeated and humiliated, and his leaders revealed as loathsome fiends or irresponsible imbeciles; he discovers that some of the principles he was taught as eternal were but empty words and that he himself was but a puppet in the hands of cynical realists.

The struggle between what should be and what is, hypocrisy and sincerity, make-believe and reality, notoriously goes on everywhere. Things are nowhere done exactly as the naïve or the young imagine. There is, at all times and in all countries, a behind-the-scenes brutal truth which shocks the uninitiated when they discover it; great decisions are never entirely noble; great leaders in all fields are by no means as witty, handsome, magnanimous and far-sighted as their official biographies make them out. As Lord Acton (who saw such things clearly, as he was born in Naples, the grandson of a Neapolitan prime minister) put it in a letter to Gladstone's youngest daughter Mary: 'Most assuredly, now as heretofore, the Men of the time are in most cases unprincipled and act from motives of interest, or passion, or prejudice cherished and unchecked, of selfish hope and unworthy fear.'

It is, however, possible for an ordinary non-Italian, at normal times, when the whole structure does not collapse on his head, never to wake up and to live his whole life wrapped in consoling illusions, affectionately attached to all the dear nonsense of childhood, revering the proper ideals and heroes. Nothing much happens to him. He may just wonder once in a while why unjust men should be rewarded and honoured more than he, but the matter does not embitter him unduly. In Italy no one can afford to delude himself. The most obscure and unambitious individual will be derided, swindled, betrayed if he does not clearly know his way about. The lower his condition the more vulnerable he is and the quicker he must recognize the real rules governing life in order not to prosper but merely to survive. Only after he has learned them, life will become simple, human, pleasant, easy, rich with many opportunities, and satisfactions more rewarding than life in many other countries. Such rules, of course, are not written anywhere. They are suggested by proverbs, humorous mottoes on ash-trays, innuendoes, winks, or shrugs of the shoulder. Few Italians can avoid learning them, however, as they are taught by fear, humiliation, deception and defeat. These things are met earlier in life and more frequently in Italy than in many other countries.

❋

Poor illiterate boys from the slums and starving children from southern villages obviously know all they need to know even before they begin to speak. Those who never learn to read have a clear uncluttered mind: they do not have to forget what others have to learn. How old are the little boys in Naples who steal bags from parked cars and procure prostitutes for sailors on shore-leave? They are born decrepit. The eight-year-old boy who was kidnapped by the Mafia, a few years ago, with his grandfather, one of the great Sicilian landowners, knew, without being told by anybody, that he must show no fear, see nothing, hear nothing, and later remember nothing of what had happened to him.

Many boys acquire their wisdom in school: they quickly learn how to get ahead smoothly, how to defeat rivals while retaining their friendship, how to pass examinations without working too hard. They know which sentiments to express in their essays in order to please the teacher. The penniless university graduates with their worthless law degrees who, every year, swarm north to Rome, Milan and Turin are as wise as members of the Soviet élite: they know the technique of getting a small foothold in some obscure office, through a relative or friend, manœuvre their way to a better position, surpass their competitors, please whoever is on top at the moment, and patiently crawl from one mediocre job to a better one, until they achieve their purpose. Half the Italian bureaucracy is composed of such men. By these arts southerners in the north gradually conquer commanding positions in private business and industry. Most of them are intelligent and useful men, who work well and deserve the jobs they would not have if they ignored the technique of conquering them.

There are many apparent exceptions, men who seem not to need the arts of getting on: great artists, scholars, scientists, who live among abstract ideas, theoretical problems and imaginary characters, as well as the few rich people who have inherited wealth and manners, the gentlemen. But even they when they want really to get ahead, preserve or enlarge their wealth, authority and status, defend themselves from envious rivals, or when they are devoured by ambition, must sooner or later learn. The real exceptions are found elsewhere. There are a few men of great moral stature, stern and obstinate men who play a lone hand, refuse to pay attention to the rules or who make their own. They struggle on, in the face of hostility or criticism, in their own way, win or loose. Most of them have always lost. They still lose today. A minority, however, manage to triumph somehow, from time to time, as some did in the past. They are the great men of Italy, whom the Italians seldom like when alive but honour when dead. They are considered not quite *simpatici*, because they follow their own stern principles and not the *convenances*.

*

Among the few who learn last are the best educated Italians. They therefore can be considered, at times, less Italian than their countrymen, less able to understand what is going on and speak for their country. They discover Italy with a shock. Take the distinguished Neapolitan general Carlo Filangieri, Prince of Satriano and Duke of Taormina, who was born in 1784 and died in 1867. He was the son of Gaetano Filangieri, one of the outstanding political philosophers of the eighteenth century. Educated at Prytanée, the French military school, he fought brilliantly under Napoleon at Ulm, Marienzell, Austerlitz and Burgos, and under Murat, King of Naples, as his *maréchal du camp*, reaching the rank of general in 1815. He could not bear to hear his countrymen insulted. (He once killed the French general Franceschi in a duel, for merely having called the Neapolitans *bougres*.) On the other hand, he knew exactly what life was like in his native country. He left these words for his son: *'Credimi: per chiunque ha un po' d'onore e un po' di sangue nelle vene è una grande calamità nascere napoletano'* ('Believe me, for any one who has a little honour and a little blood in his veins, it is a great calamity to be born Neapolitan'). By *napoletano* he meant a subject of the King of Naples, a southern Italian in general.

Or take another distinguished example, Massimo d'Azeglio. He was a Piedmontese marquis, well brought up, well educated, honourable, intelligent, a man of the world, a patriot. He became a renowned painter, a novelist of note, an excellent cavalry officer, aide-de-camp to the king, and his prime minister from 1849 till 1852. He married Alessandro Manzoni's daughter and was one of the patriots of the Risorgimento. He knew Italy well. When a very young man, in 1820, he first came to Rome, where he met many foreign travellers, including some distinguished English ladies.

He wrote in *I miei ricordi*:

'With foreigners I experienced a sensation of humiliation so painful that from their friendship came to me more bitterness than satisfaction. I was ashamed of being an Italian! . . . The cold behaviour of the English . . . the tranquil and self-confident pride that could be seen on their countenances . . . looked as if they were intended for me, to make me feel my inferiority, to make me understand that when a nation is the prey of anybody that takes it, when it allows all sorts of people from the four quarters of the world to come to it to amuse themselves, just as hunters migrate to regions where the game abounds, then those who belong to such a nation can be tolerated among foreigners, but cannot be considered their equal, ever.'

The bitter words of Carlo Filangieri and Massimo d'Azeglio are notable because of the eminence of the two men, and also because they were written and printed. Usually such comments were said in private. Giovacchino Rossini, the composer of the *Barbiere di Siviglia* and inventor of a famous steak, used to say to his intimates: 'Thank God for the Spaniards. . . . If there were no Spaniards the Italians would be the last people in Europe.'

Clearly the reactions of the well educated are more vigorous and their deception is more profound. As they reach the day of awakening later than their illiterate compatriots, and are more articulate, they can usually also define and describe their thoughts with greater clarity. On that day, to begin with, they already know what everybody should know everywhere: that life is fundamentally a merciless game; that man should find his protection in the warp and woof of society; that curbs on man's instincts constitute the essence of civilized living. Without such protections man is alone in the world, as alone as a beast of prey or as the prey itself, waiting to be devoured.

These people, however, also discover that all official institutions are weak and unstable in Italy: the law is flexible and unreliable, the State discredited and easily dominated by powerful persons or groups, and society (as conceived elsewhere) has little influence. And yet, somehow, life around them flows easily: man is not always devoured by man; people do defend themselves; the daily work is done; the country can be considered civilized, in fact it is among the most civilized in the world, although admittedly enjoying a peculiar civilization of its own. Man is by no means alone here. He is immersed in humanity. He is aided, comforted, protected in many ways. In fact, life can often be gay, animated and satisfying. It is, anyway, all these things for those who do not insist upon abstract and impartial justice, or expect the legal apparatus to function smoothly. Life for resigned and disenchanted people appears to be no more cruel than in better organized countries, or, at least, not cruel and unjust in the same manner. It is as if the people themselves tried to compensate with their own good will for the lack of rigid rules and legal protections. Genial toleration, sympathy for other men's weaknesses, the feeling of intimate complicity among people secretly fighting the same enemies, a vast and indiscriminate indulgence often bathe all things in a tepid bath of benevolence and soften all harshness. Moral preoccupations seldom cast their gloomy shadows. While the official machinery of collective life is omnipresent (there are policemen in five different uniforms, innumerable forms to fill, stamped papers to be used on all occasions, permits required for the smallest activities, hundreds of law books, and stately government buildings in practically every other street), nothing essential really depends on it. How do Italians really function?

The first basic thing an educated Italian discovers is that feudalism as a moral conception was alien to Italy, and never deeply influenced Italian life. Its external and concrete aspects were naturally accepted, as many foreign fashions always are here, but even they were soon adapted to local tastes and conditions, and transformed into something useful and comprehensible. Chivalry, for instance, was turned mainly into a polite pastime for the upper classes. Only its picturesque trappings were eagerly adopted, the elaborate escutcheons, the titles, the elegant courtesies, and the spectacular tournaments. But its moral precepts were generally ignored. There is no local equivalent to the oath which King Arthur administered to his knights, there is no Italian Bayard, *chevalier sans peur et sans reproche*.

Fewer Italians, in fact, obeyed the highest call of the age of chivalry, actually leaving wives and castles to redeem Christ's sepulchre from the Infidels' possession, than gentlemen from any other nation. The men of Pisa, Amalfi, Genoa and Venice, the four sea-republics, shrewdly made money as contractors and merchants in the Crusades. The Venetians, in particular, habitually rented their ships on charter for the crossing of the Mediterranean to the knights from Germany, England and France, and often craftily routed military operations to where they would do the most good to the interests of the Venetian republic, towards the conquest of ports and islands which could be used later as bases for a leisurely commercial penetration into the Levant.

The Italians were also naturally impervious to most of the ideals which made the medieval world go round: unswerving loyalty to one's chief, allegiance to one's sovereign, and *noblesse oblige*, or the sense of duty towards dependents, inferiors, the weak and defenceless. Foreign words like honour, *honneur*, *Ehre* cannot be translated exactly. The Italian nearest equivalent *onore* is misleading: it mainly means something bestowed from outside, esteem or reverence, rank, dignity, distinction, and almost never 'a fine sense of and strict allegiance to what is due or right (1548)', as the Oxford Dictionary puts it. Machiavelli, for instance, complains: '*Gli uomini non sanno essere onorevolmente tristi*', or 'Men do not know how to be wicked in an *honourable* way'.

All this could have little importance were it not for the fact that the modern world still functions on the remnants of the feudal code. It would go to pieces without them:

there could not be powerful nations, governments, armies and navies, solid military alliances; there could not be vast organizations of any kind, financial combines, or great industries; there could not be sporting competitions without a certain amount of Teutonic chivalry, what little of it, anyway, has percolated down to the nineteenth-century bourgeoisie and finally to us. Reverence for truth, fair play, respect for laws, rules, and regulations; respect for one's opponents; capacity to work in teams; willingness to apply to oneself and one's friends the same rules one applies to all others; loyalty to one's convictions and faith, loyalty to one's party, class, school, country, these are the virtues which not only made the Crusades possible and kept together the mighty empires of old, but still manage somehow to hold modern empires together.

The contemporary capitalistic world is still almost incomprehensible to most Italians, who admire, envy and imitate, often very successfully, its outward aspect, its power, and its practical products, but miss its moral character. They even doubt if it exists at all. Many current rules of fair conduct strike the Italians as pure nonsense. Take the English saying 'never kick a man when he is down'. They do not believe anybody really obeyed it. They know a man should not be kicked if he is old, if he is strong and can immediately kick back, if he can later avenge himself, if he has powerful friends or relatives, if he could be useful some day in any way, or if a policeman is watching. But why not 'when he is down'? When else, if you please, should one kick a man more advantageously? When more safely and effectively? A famous handbook on how to play *scopa*, the most common Italian card game, written in Naples by a Monsignor Chitarella, begins: 'Rule Number One: always try to see your opponent's cards.' It is a good concrete practical rule.

There is, it must be admitted, one small remnant of the age of ancient knights which has been preserved intact in Italy. It is a handbook published for the first time in 1887 and reprinted eighteen times, until practically yesterday. A dog-eared copy is to be found in the library of many middle-class Italians of a certain age. It is seldom a copy which they themselves bought, but one they borrowed in a hurry, years before, and never gave back. One usually needs the book immediately, in an emergency, perhaps in the middle of the night or on a Sunday. It is on rare occasions still used today.

It is called the *Codice cavalleresco italiano* or Italian Code of Chivalry, written by one Jacopo Gelli, a cavalry colonel from Leghorn; it teaches one how to behave when involved, in any capacity, in a dispute among gentlemen. Nothing is left to chance. Every minute variation has been foreseen. No rule has been arbitrarily made up, the author points out, who claims to have merely recorded the customs already valid among honourable men. It naturally begins with definitions: a gentleman is 'the man who, out of a refined moral sensitivity, does not believe that the laws . . . are sufficient to protect his honour, and imposes on himself the rigid observance of special rules which are called the laws of chivalry'; honour is determined from outside, *all'Italiana;* it is defined as 'the esteem and consideration which an honest person has been able to gain in public opinion through his actions, always in agreement with natural and civil laws'. 'The sentiment of honour must dominate all other considerations in a gentleman. It is, however, a vulgar prejudice that the honour of a gentleman can be measured by the number of duels he has fought.'

A man may lose his quality of a gentleman (and become an inferior kind of person, who cannot ask for satisfaction after having been insulted) if he violates ordinary laws; he can also be disqualified by a jury of professional gentlemen for adequate technical reasons, which are laid down. Offences are graduated in a scale of intensity like earthquakes or typhoons. The most serious, fourth degree, are those 'which touch the family'. Controversies started by the highest offences can be terminated only with open letters of abject apologies or a proper duel. Meticulous instructions follow on how to organize all kinds of proper duels.

Loopholes, of course, abound. Gelli points out that the first duty of seconds is not to see that one of their principals kills the other at any price but, if at all possible, to settle the matter without recourse to arms. This is difficult to arrange, as neither party ever wants to apologize. There are, however, several catches. The most widely used is Article 9: 'When the offensive act was not provoked or justified, or when it was caused by an erroneous valuation of facts or by misunderstandings, a solution by way of an armed encounter must be excluded.' What insult cannot be said to have been determined by 'an erroneous valuation of facts'? At the end of the volume are many letters, ready prepared, for the use of all participants, a letter from the offended who charges two friends to defend his interests, a letter of challenge to the offender, known as *cartello di sfida*, and models for sundry other documents.

The book is useful in a practical way. It contains the experience of centuries and indicates tactful and dignified means for solving intricate and annoying disputes which ordinary laws and normal procedures leave unsolved or aggravate. It is obvious that such matters can be handled better by third parties, who examine them and debate them with cool heads, than by the actors themselves. Nobody ever gets killed. If Oscar Wilde had challenged the Marquis of Queensberry, with the aid of this handbook, instead of suing him in court, he would have lived a long and industrious life, almost reaching the day in which his tastes had become openly accepted, respected in good society, and useful in the world of literature and art.

But discussions between four polite friends would easily draw out until doomsday (neither group usually wants to admit defeat and offer satisfactory excuses), were it not for one threat, the highly improbable but real possibility of placing the two gentlemen involved, naked to the waist, on a lawn, at dawn, weapons in hand, surrounded by the proper paraphernalia and personnel. This now happens very rarely, once every three or four years, but cannot be excluded. The threat is not only a vague one to the life of the protagonists. As dueling is strictly forbidden by law, the seconds, the doctors, and the expert who directs the encounter are also liable to end up in jail. This slight preoccupation for their own liberty inevitably quickens the seconds' decisions and facilitates most peaceful settlements.

A friend telephones excitedly, to tell you that he is in trouble; you meet him and a friend of his, the other second, to examine the terms of the dispute; you hurriedly thumb through the nearest copy of Gelli in order to study the possibilities available; you copy the suitable letters at the end of the book (there are only forty-eight hours in which to challenge the offender); you do all this and you cannot help smiling inwardly at the ludicrous and archaic procedures, terminology, and complications. I have a few times been the second of friends (journalists are traditionally supposed to be experts in the matter) and, speaking the proper lines and doing the proper things, have always felt as if I were taking part in a bad costume play.

But when, side by side with the other second, both dressed in dark suits as if for a christening or a board meeting, I have handed the offender the letter I had just copied, and, as he read it and tried excitedly to answer something, stopped him with the traditional formula, 'I'm sorry, we cannot listen to anything you say. Please name two of your friends with whom we two will be glad to talk. We'll be waiting for them all the afternoon. Goodbye,' I could not help feeling, in spite of the preposterous words and the pompous and embarrassing gestures, that the moment still preserved a small and remote solemnity.

I once had to hand such a letter to a Communist journalist in a busy *caffè* in Rome, among the cries of rushing waiters, the hiss of the espresso machines, and the chattering of the clients. (We had not much time before the deadline and that was the only appointment I could get with him. We had lost precious hours debating with experts whether a Communist could be considered a gentleman, something on which Colonel Gelli had nothing to say.) He came in from the rain, shut his umbrella, saw us from far away, smiled, waved to us, and came over, saying 'Are you mad? Why did you have to see me before sundown?' He laughed as he took the letter, not thinking what it could be, perhaps suspecting some sort of stupid joke. Then he read the stilted and antiquated words and became very pale and very grave. Obviously, even for him the little ceremony had some vestigial meaning left. The party did not allow him, in the end, to fight the duel. He regretfully had to disqualify himself.

Colonel Gelli's is admittedly an obsolete and silly way of settling disputes. And yet it survives not only because it may be still useful at times. There is another reason.

The gentlemanly way of settling quarrels according to the code of chivalry has lasted in Italy longer than anywhere else because it agrees with one of the deepest national traits. It is one more way of disregarding official laws, rules, statutes, State-appointed authorities, and to regulate matters according to a private concept of right and wrong, traditional precepts, and the help of one's friends.

*

Very few then are the rules which can help an Italian plot his course and steer a safe line in a country which has never really accepted the moral teaching of feudalism, and in which society, the law and the State have feeble powers. He must defend himself. He begins early by being his own school-teacher (most schools are inadequate) and professor (universities are poor, backward and badly run). Later he must be his own journalist (published news of internal affairs can be so biased that to rely on them is to court disaster), his own literary, film, art, and dramatic critic (reviews rarely reflect the worth of the film, book, or drama, but a number of factors, the personal relation between author and critic, their respective political parties, relative ages, philosophical bias, and so forth), his own strategic expert in times of war (nobody will tell him who is winning and when to run until too late), and his own fiscal expert (to distinguish which are the taxes to be paid fully, which only in part, and which to be ignored altogether). He must at times be his own lawyer, policeman and judge. In short, his security depends not on the combined exertions of his countrymen to which he should add his own but mostly on his individual capacities and native shrewdness.

He soon discovers that he can occupy in society only whichever position he can conquer and defend with his personal authority. His authority depends on many factors, his capacity, talents, energy, determination, but ultimately on his ability to intimidate his enemies and, if the need should arise, to destroy them. There are many ways of doing this in Italy, almost as many as there are *milieus*. In convents, bishoprics, or the Vatican, the means are almost imperceptible; a cold stare, a curt nod, a Latin pun followed by an inaudible chuckle, an obscure article on a small theological point or a compliment bestowed for the wrong reasons may suffice. In the business world and in politics a man can be slandered, cuckolded, demoralized, cut off from powerful contacts, blackmailed, pushed to the verge of ruin, or driven to suicide. In some sections of Sicily, to destroy a man may literally mean to have him blasted off the face of the earth or silently poisoned.

All these techniques need power. There must be power behind the seemingly mild words, the obscure menaces, the decision to cut a man off from the sources of his livelihood. Without power all threats would be risible and bombastic gestures. Nobody can hope to live without power, not necessarily a great and frightening amount of it, but as much as is indispensable for the job in hand, neither more nor less, proportionate to one's needs. A cabinet minister behind his desk and the *usciere* introducing visitors to his presence both dispose of what power is necessary for their respective positions, otherwise neither would be where he is.

This necessity forces each man to obey, in the daily struggle for existence, roughly the same rules which have dominated international relations at all times. Each Italian must learn to face problems with the detached technique with which sovereigns and statesmen determine policy. Few decisions are allowed to be influenced by sentiments, tastes, hazards or hopes, but usually by a careful valuation of the relative strength of the contending parties. The choice between one alliance or another, between hostility or peace, resistance to the last breath or immediate surrender, are the result of a realistic estimate of the forces each side can marshal.

This is one of the reasons why, when negotiating even the smallest deal, Italians must always look at each other's faces. They read in their opponent's eyes (or catch in his voice and choice of words) the signs of his stubborn decision or hidden timidity. They can thus decide when it is safe to increase one's demands, when to stand pat, and when it is more prudent to retreat and accept the other man's conditions. Capitulation, of course, must be done with *garbo*, the retreat (for which a door has always been kept ajar) disguised with ingenious and flattering explanations. People are so unconsciously expert at this difficult art that few describe it. This necessity inevitably has its drawbacks. It slows down and complicates all kinds of transactions. Nothing serious can ever be decided by correspondence. People must travel to look at each other. But it has some advantages: Italians, for instance, were naturally gifted diplomats in the days when diplomacy was still a responsible and exacting trade.

This must be kept in mind by anybody trying to fathom the real reasons for some puzzling Italian decisions, or to foresee some future Italian move. Like all statesmen, after Italians have realistically gauged the relative weight of conflicting parties, they fight a weaker enemy and join a winner. Such rules of conduct make conflicts of all sorts last a shorter time in Italy than elsewhere. The number of worthy and heroic people willing to go on fighting on the side which they believe is right but which public opinion knows will succumb in the end is necessarily small. The rules make some decisions, turning points in history, or revolutions inevitable much too soon, when they could still be avoided, prevented, or deflected. It also often makes their results superficial, unstable and insincere.

Power, personal power, is the key.

CHAPTER ELEVEN

The Power of the Family

THE first source of power is the family. The Italian family is a stronghold in a hostile land: within its walls and among its members, the individual finds consolation, help, advice, provisions, loans, weapons, allies and accomplices to aid him in his pursuits. No Italian who has a family is ever alone. He finds in it a refuge in which to lick his wounds after a defeat, or an arsenal and a staff for his victorious drives. Scholars have always recognized the Italian family as the only fundamental institution in the country, a spontaneous creation of the national genius, adapted through the centuries to changing conditions, the real foundation of whichever social order prevails. In fact, the law, the State and society function only if they do not directly interfere with the family's supreme interests.

Italy has often been defined, with only slight exaggeration, as nothing more than a mosaic of millions of families, sticking together by blind instinct, like colonies of insects, an organic formation rather than a rational construction of written statutes and moral imperatives. There were times in her past, and even in recent, almost contemporary history, when the State was at its lowest and weakest, impoverished and defeated, and yet the inhabitants were feverishly active, happy and prosperous. Some gloomy writers compared the joyous activity of the people and the impotence and disruption of the official institutions at those times to the merry swarming of worms on a corpse. Conversely, there were times, rare times, when the interests of the coalition of families coincided with those of the State, and Italy seemed to foreign observers to be a solid, efficient and powerful nation.

This is, of course, nothing new, surprising, or unique. In many countries and among many people, past and present, where legal authority is weak and the law is resented and resisted, the safety and welfare of the individual are mainly assured by the family. The Chinese, for instance, in their imperial days held the cult of the family more praiseworthy than the love of country and the love of good. This is why the Communist régime of Mao Tse-tung tried to stamp out the family, recognizing it as its most powerful opponent. Similarly, wherever the Jews were allowed to settle in Europe, they outwardly conformed to the local laws and impositions, but in their hearts obeyed only their religious rules and the immemorial code of their family life, which allowed them precariously to survive persecutions.

It is therefore not surprising that the Italians, living, as they have always done, in the insecurity and dangers of an unruly and unpredictable society, are among those who found their main refuge behind the walls of their houses, among their blood-relatives. Italians have, after all, many points of contact with the Chinese: the Chinese, too, love ceremonies, feasts, elaborate rites, deafening noise, fireworks, and good food; love children and produce many of them; their art is also highly decorative and ingenious but not always deep; they fashion lovely things by hand, and are astute negotiators and subtle merchants. The Italians are also, in many ways, similar to the Jews: the Jews have the same disenchanted and practical outlook; are among the few people who laugh at their own foibles; they entertain a wary diffidence for other people's noble intentions and always look for the concrete motives hiding behind them.

There is, however, this fundamental difference between the Italians and most other people who use the family as their private lifeboat in the stormy seas of anarchy. Anarchy in Italy is not simply a way of life, a spontaneous condition of society, a natural development: it is also the deliberate product of man's will, the fruit of his choice; it has been assiduously cultivated and strengthened down the centuries. The strength of the family is not only, therefore, the bulwark against disorder, but, at the same time, one of its principal causes. It has actively fomented chaos in many ways especially by rendering useless the development of strong political institutions. This, of course, brings up a complex problem: do political institutions flourish only where the family is weak, or is it the other way around? Does the family become self-sufficient only where the political institutions are not strong enough? However it may be, political institutions never had much of a chance in Italy. The people gave birth to but a few of them: they had to import most of them ready-made from abroad, from time to time, feudalism, the centralized monarchy, the constitution, the bi-cameral system, liberalism, democracy, socialism, as they are now threatening to borrow the Communists' régime prefabricated from Soviet Russia.

The family was also invincible because it was the sacred ark in which Italians deposited and preserved against alien influences all their ancient ideals. It clearly preserved the national character from contamination. The Italy of the families is definitely the real Italy, the quintessential Italy, distilled from the experiences of centuries, while the Italy of the laws and institutions is partly make-believe, the country Italians would like to believe was or will be but know is not. Will all this continue? Will all régimes the Italians give themselves in the future be inevitably corroded and destroyed by the family? Is this belief the reason why Italians are always compliantly ready to experiment with new political ways and why so many of them do not fear revolutions? Will anarchy ever end in this country? Will the family always predominate? This is, of course, the central riddle of Italian history and political life.

*

What follows is a simplified picture of the Italian family as it is supposed to be, an ideal model drawn for the edification and instruction of the reader. Of course, he is too intelligent not to realize that things are seldom as perfect and typical as this in real life, just as no human body corresponds to the coloured images in anatomy text-books. There are in Italy, too, broken families, dissensions, secessions, rifts, and interminable feuds among relatives; in Sicily, members of the same family often crouch behind prickly-pear hedges with hunting rifles in their hands, waiting to kill each other; in Lombardy, members of the same family almost invariably contest their grandfather's will, with the aid of expensive lawyers and all kinds of chicanery, from one court to another. The excessive tenacity, however, with which relatives fight each other at times proves that they are struggling against their very instincts: even when feuding, they cannot help feeling an almost irresistible urge to conform to ancient precepts and an unusually deep sense of remorse when they violate them.

The majority of families manage to be as faithful to the perfect pattern as possible. Usually the best examples are found among the more old-fashioned people, those who are perhaps more Italian than others, peasants, fishermen, landowners, and petty bourgeois from the small towns, and the provincial and more rigorous aristocracy. Southerners of all classes preserve the traditions almost intact, with more tenacity than northerners. In the industrialized north and in the café society of the big cities, the bad examples set by other countries are being increasingly imitated. And yet even the deviations are superficial. No Italian does, without hesitation and remorse, many things Americans, Englishmen and Frenchmen do as a matter of course. He cannot, for instance, lightly abandon a wife who is the mother of his first-born male child.

The family extracts everybody's first loyalty. It must be defended, enriched, made powerful, respected, and feared by the use of whatever means are necessary, legitimate means, if at all possible, or illegitimate. Nobody should defy it with impunity. Its honour must not be tarnished. All wrongs done to it must be avenged. All enemies must be kept at bay and the dangerous ones deprived of power or destroyed. Every member is duty-bound to do all he can for its welfare, give his property if needed, and, sometimes, when it is absolutely inevitable, sacrifice his life. Men have spent their last penny to save a relative from bankruptcy. The family should by every means be safeguarded from runs of bad luck, the disastrous effects of political mutations, and economic crisis. For this, at least one representative must be a member of the party in power and another of the opposition. A well-run family must split in all civil wars. It must be made to prosper for generations, possibly till the end of time. There must be children, of course, lots of children, especially sons who can carry on the name. Nothing should be spared to produce them. Everything is done for them in Italy. They are the protagonists of Italian life. Their smallest wishes are satisfied. A crowd will always gather around a pretty baby. Humble parents go without food, clothes, and comforts in order to pamper their sons, and to see that they go to school and reach a higher rung in the social ladder. The climbing is not hurried, it is done in successive waves, one generation after the other, till the highest pinnacles are reached.

One fundamental point which escapes most foreigners must be understood and remembered. Most Italians still obey a double standard. There is one code valid within the family circle, with relatives and honorary relatives, intimate friends and close associates, and there is another code regulating life outside. Within, they assiduously demonstrate all the qualities which are not usually attributed to them by superficial observers: they are relatively reliable, honest, truthful, just, obedient, generous, disciplined, brave, and capable of self-sacrifices. They practise what virtues other men usually dedicate to the welfare of their country at large; the Italians' family loyalty is their true patriotism. In the outside world, amidst the chaos and the disorder of society, they often feel compelled to employ the wiles of underground fighters in enemy-occupied territory. All official and legal authority is considered hostile by them until proved friendly or harmless: if it cannot be ignored, it should be neutralized or deceived if need be.

There have been men in Italy who, in wars not of their liking, often did only what was necessary merely to return alive to their homes and no more, men who could be technically accused of cowardice; the same men often face, when it becomes necessary, in peacetime, almost unbearable sacrifices and mortal dangers for the sake of their parents or children. Fathers, brothers, sons, grandsons (mostly from the south and the islands, but frequently also from the more advanced north) daily risk death to protect their women from outrage and themselves from dishonour. Many of these champions of family respectability end up in prison for life, but with a clear conscience. They carry themselves proudly, head high. They know they have done their duty and have obeyed one of the few valid laws they recognize. They also know that their relatives will take care of their women and children for as long as it will be necessary.

*

The obligation to provide one's family with the wealth and power necessary to defy the centuries explains many peculiar Italian habits, including the custom of ancient Popes of elevating their nephews and kinsmen to high position and enriching them. It is easy now to sneer at nepotism. It should, however, be studied without malevolence. Kings and Popes, like all Italians, unquestionably owed their first loyalty to their families. But a king, as a rule, had many advantages: he came from a family which was already illustrious, powerful and wealthy, and had many useful connections and ramifications; he did not usually have to worry about conquering his throne and knew his eldest son would inherit it as a matter of course and, after him, his eldest son's eldest son; a king usually had plenty of time and opportunities to promote his relatives' interests, enlarge the family's domain and fortune; furthermore, he was surrounded by a traditional élite of experienced men trained to serve him faithfully.

A Pope was, on the other hand, in a difficult position. He usually reached power when already an old man, a decrepit old man at times. He was in a hurry: he had to do for his kinsmen, within a few years, before it was too late, what most royal families had taken centuries to achieve. His people needed practically everything: they were usually obscure, provincial and poor. He did not know what would happen to them after his departure. He had, of course, the power to confer sonorous titles on them all, but titles are worthless without capital and properties. The men surrounding him were adequately loyal but not to him. They served the Holy Father, whoever he was, and would serve his successor just as loyally. Like all *novi homines* in a tight spot the Pope could count only on his blood relations: they knew their fortunes were tied to his.

All this explains the almost unseemly hurry and the

apparent lack of scruples with which many otherwise virtuous Popes, within a few days or hours of their election, provided for their relatives' welfare. Their efforts were usually successful and had long-lasting effects. The great noble families of Rome (few of them of Roman origin) are still the descendants of the Pontiffs. Many of them still manage to be among the richest, amply enjoying the fruits of ancient favours and plunders. Even the unlucky who received worthless land in the Campagna, picturesque pasture-land amidst ruined aqueducts, are now also immensely wealthy: their estates have in this century become priceless property within the city limits.

We possess a few reliable details respecting the incomes of Papal nephews during the sixteenth and seventeenth centuries, when nepotism was already on the wane. They were recorded by Venetian ambassadors, who, being businessmen, were interested in figures. Saint Charles Borromeo, a nephew of Pius IV, was made cardinal at twenty-two years of age, with excellent results, as he was a great and holy man, and was reasonably believed to have enjoyed revenues amounting to 50,000 scudi a year, which he gave to the poor or spent on the endowment of holy institutions. (The Princes Borromeo are a Milanese family. They still enjoy ample means. They live in their own *palazzo*, the Palazzo Borromeo, in the Piazza Borromeo, in Milan.) Giacomo Buoncompagno (the family now spells the name Boncompagni), the bastard son of Gregory XIII, received an estate of 120,000 scudi, while two cardinal nephews of the same Pope had each about 10,000 scudi a year. (The Boncompagni still own *palazzi*, landholdings, and villas. The last of their *palazzi*, a nineteenth-century imitation of the antique, is now the U.S. Embassy in Via Veneto.)

Sixtus V Feretti enriched Cardinal Montalto, his nephew, with an ecclesiastical income of 100,000 scudi. Clement VII Aldobrandini bestowed on two nephews, one a cardinal and one a layman, revenues of about 60,000 scudi apiece in 1599. He is computed to have hoarded altogether for his family a total of about one million scudi. (The Aldobrandini are still among the most affluent in Italy. They own, among many properties, the famous villa in Frascati, where they live today, built for the cardinal nephew, with vast terraced grounds overlooking Rome in the distance. In its gardens Henry James spent 'ineffable hours'. It was requisitioned during the war by the Germans as General Kesselring's headquarters.) Paul V Borghese was believed to have given to his relatives nearly 700,000 scudi in cash, yearly revenues of 24,000 scudi in funds, and 268,000 in revenues from various offices. (The Borghese are still one of the four or five leading families of the Papal aristocracy, connected with other notable clans all over Europe. They still own the Palazzo Borghese, known as the *cembalo di Roma,* or Rome's harpsichord, because of its curious form.)

Cardinal Ludovico Ludovisi, nephew of Gregory XV, had a reputed income of 200,000 scudi, and the whole Ludovisi family (which has merged with the Boncompagni who are now called Boncompagni-Ludovisi) obtained 800,000 scudi in *luoghi di monte,* or Papal government bonds. The fortunes of the Barberini go back to two nephews of Urban VIII, who were said to have enjoyed revenues of about half a million scudi a year. Their total gain from the pontificate reached the record sum of 105,-000 scudi. The Barberini were among the most avid of all papal families. They built castles, stupendous villas, and one *palazzo,* in the Piazza Barberini, designed by Borromini and Bernini, the most famous contemporary architects.

The most illustrious example of how an Italian, reaching a commanding position (and therefore becoming, whatever his age, the head of the family), sees to it that all his relatives are taken care of, is that of the Bonapartes. Napoleon was a *homo novus* if there ever was one, who, like most Popes, knew he could trust only his blood relations and often not even them. As soon as he was able to, he made adequate arrangements for his brothers, sisters, in-laws, and stepson. His older brother Joseph was made King of Naples for a time and later promoted King of Spain; his younger brother Lucien, who mistrusted Napoleon, was made Prince of Canino, a rich fief north of Rome, in the Maremma; his sister Elisa was married to Prince Felice Bacciocchi and was first given the Duchy of Lucca and later the Grand Duchy of Tuscany; his brother Louis became King of Holland; his sister

Pauline married Prince Camillo Borghese; his sister Caroline married Joachim Murat, who was appointed King of Naples; his brother Jérôme, who had married the American beauty Elizabeth Patterson of Baltimore, had to divorce her and marry the not very pretty Catherine of Würtemburg to become King of Westphalia; his stepson Eugène de Beauharnais was an excellent viceroy of Italy.

Less illustrious examples of this tradition can be quoted to this very day. To disseminate relatives in key positions (like sentries in outposts around a fortified camp) not only assures them all good incomes but also guarantees the family from possible attacks. The habit still persists sporadically even in Papal families. Pius XI Ratti merely made his only nephew a count. John XXIII Roncalli did absolutely nothing to improve the status and revenues of his peasant brothers and his working-class nephews. 'They are the relatives of the Pope,' he said simply. 'They dine with me once a year. That should be enough for them.' On the other hand, the nephews of Pius XII Pacelli were made princes (not by him, to be sure, but by King Victor Emmanuel III, to save embarrassment to their uncle), and placed in command of vast business corporations in which the Church has dominating interests. A perusal of current reference books will contribute any number of contemporary examples: brothers, brothers-in-law, sons, sons-in-law or cousins of prominent politicians in the Christian Democrat party are ensconced in comfortable and rewarding positions in State-controlled or nationalized organizations, industries and holding companies, posts for which they seldom had a particular training.

At least one great political leader managed to amass, since the end of the last war, a private fortune comparable to those of Papal families of old, one of the largest in the country. He put it together shrewdly, using his political power, and quickly, within a few years, fighting against time, as he too was an old man. He did it with a clear conscience, clearly for his sons' future and not for himself: he was too near death to want more from life, but they were yet too young to be placed in important and rewarding positions of their own. To be sure, the tradition is also followed in privately controlled business in Italy, as it sometimes is in other countries; it is also widespread in the minor establishments. There are Government bureaus, modest little offices, tawdry hospitals in the provinces, especially in the south, where important places are occupied by people with the same surname or somehow related to those with the same surname. Often, the only way for an ambitious man to succeed is to marry one of the daughters of the men at the top.

Marriages are naturally important, as decisive for the promotion of the influence and prosperity of an ordinary family as they were in royal families of old. Many sons and daughters of prominent political leaders are married to each other, hostages in each other's camp, thus secretly complicating the work of political commentators, who sometimes cannot unravel apparently inexplicable situations unless they know the invisible ties binding the various politicians, not as heads of internal factions, but as fathers-in-law of each other's offspring. Stern fathers no longer oblige rebellious daughters to sacrifice themselves for the family, as Victor Emmanuel II was forced to do in 1859, with his younger daughter, Princess Maria Clotilde, who was to wed Prince Napoleon Bonaparte, known as Plon-Plon, a fat, middle-aged and dissolute man, before Napoleon III would declare war on Austria and help her father conquer Lombardy. Compulsion is rarely necessary nowadays. Somehow, a well-brought-up young lady naturally desires in a man exactly the qualities that will improve her family's fortunes. A young man will look more attractive to her because of his relatives' power in the very world in which she was brought up, business, politics, the armed services, bureaucracy, the universities, or even criminal life.

The great Mafia families of Sicily, for instance, are as intricately bound to each other by a network of old and recent marriage ties as old aristocratic families in the Almanach de Gotha. Only lately has the U.S. Narcotics Bureau become aware of the significance of such connections among immigrants and started exploring them; it diligently drew up genealogical charts of the most notorious families of Sicilian extraction in the United States underworld and discovered that everybody was everybody else's son-in-law, grandfather, stepson, great-uncle, first, second, or third cousin, godfather or godmother, and so forth. Some of these clans in the United States form compact interlocked groups, their descendants intermarrying continuously; others have looser but still solid connections and share some common business interests. Like European powers in the eighteenth and nineteenth centuries, they combine to preserve peace or to make wars, offensive wars to destroy common rivals or conquer new territories for expansion, defensive wars to preserve intact their spheres of influence; negotiate and conclude truces and solemnly sign peace treaties.

❋

The Italian male, the head or heir of the family, is justly famous the world over for his manliness. He jealously defends his independence. No woman submits him to her will. His pride is clearly visible. Watch him promenade down the *corso* of any small town at sunset, or on Sunday morning after mass. How cocky he looks, how close fitting are his clothes, how triumphantly he sweeps his eyes about, how condescendingly he glances at pretty girls from the corner of his lowered eyelids! He is visibly the master of creation.

And what is woman? She was obviously placed on earth to amuse and comfort him, as decorative and unimportant as the dumb girls who aid the magician to do his tricks on the stage. Like all inferior people, like negroes in former colonies, she must by every means be kept in her place, for her own sake, above all. When she does not become the victim of seditious propaganda, she can indeed be pleasant and useful. She is also happier. She knows it, too, and she is grateful to her master. Whenever she starts giving herself airs, she must immediately be taught a lesson. 'A woman,' says an old Italian proverb, 'is like an egg. The more she is beaten, the better she becomes.'

Naturally Italians commiserate with other people who have not been able to subjugate their women or who have allowed them to run rampant. See how tormented and unsatisfied their women are, they say, who feel no rein on their necks and are allowed to do things which were not meant for them! Look at foreign husbands, they say, who treat their women with awe, sometimes with fear, as if they were carnivorous animals: how obedient these men are to their women's whims, and, as a result, how spoiled, intractable, and unhappy their women become! It is rumoured that these husbands hide nothing of their own private lives and thoughts, account for every hour of their days and every penny they make, and even have to ask permission to go out some night with harmless men friends. How much more in accordance with Nature's laws and the will of Providence things are in Italy and how grateful is the Italian woman to be treated as she is!

She knows pratically nothing of her husband's private life. Has he a mistress? Has he two? Does he go from one regular liaison to another or does he have several at the same time? She is troubled by no doubts. She is only rarely jealous: few suspicions touch her. She trustfully waits for his return home and is happy with whatever he tells her. As for herself, she knows she must be very careful and not so much as look at another man. If she did, she would deserve severe punishment, repudiation, and, frequently enough, death. She knows her place in the immutable order of things, as the wives of southern peasants do, who carry heavy weights on their heads and walk for miles behind their men sitting astride the family donkey. At the end of a summer day, southern Italian families sit on the road in front of their door-steps *a prendere il fresco*, to enjoy the cool air. The men smoke, the women knit, and talk among themselves. The men invariably sit facing the street and nod to friends going by, the women sit with their faces decently turned to the house-wall and see nothing but plaster and stones. Only the brazen hussies, who will surely meet bad ends, turn their heads to the street, from time to time.

*

All this, of course, is mostly nonsense. It is the official cant which inexperienced travellers describe in their diaries. Do Italian men believe it? Many do. Most of them, however, harbour secret doubts and fears. A moment comes when every one of them is struck by the fact that most of the women he has affairs with are somebody's wives and that it is not, therefore, materially possible for all the husbands in Italy to stray from marital fidelity while none of the wives do so. There is no escaping the fact that each day a substantial number of proud Italian males, jealous, suspicious, overbearing, proud men, are being made *cornuti,* and become the object of scorn and ridicule. And this has obviously been going on for centuries.

Appearances, as always, are misleading. Men outwardly behave as if matters were permanently ordered according to immutable and unquestioned customs. Women are willing to play the rôle of second-class members of humanity; they patently act as if they really were but fragile, docile and adaptable creatures. Behind the façade things are different. What is the truth? It would be imprudent and dishonest to generalize too sweepingly. There is not one reality but an infinite range of realities, varying with the section of the country, the social class, the background and the individuals, each reality sometimes changing day by day, merging into another; slippery, ambiguous, many-faceted realities all. This, however, can be said for sure, that there is in Italy a neat and permanent division of prerogatives between the sexes. The man is the titular head of the household but by no means the absolute monarch. He is in charge of general policy, definitely responsible for war and peace and for relations with the rest of the world. The wife is officially a subordinate figure, in charge of humbler duties, but her sphere is largely undetermined and wide-ranging.

The arrangement gives no overwhelming authority to either. It gives the woman the greater moral responsibility. It is only thanks to her that households function smoothly. But the centuries have taught her to make her husband forget how important she effectively is. She usually manages things in a subtle, almost imperceptible, way; she assuages his feelings; she avoids open contrasts but generally has the last unspoken word. She keeps her place, of course. She would obviously lose her ascendancy if she forgot it. Her place may be the kitchen (in lower income families), the drawing-room and boudoir (for the more affluent), and, for all, the double-bed at night, but, whatever it is, it is a position of great power. Men run the country but women run men. Italy is, in reality, a crypto-matriarchy.

Things could not be otherwise. Everybody's status,

security, and welfare, depend on power. The first source of power is the family. The strength of the family is determined by many factors—wealth, connections, alliances, prestige, rank, luck—but, above all, by its inner cohesion and ramifications. These are in the hands of women everywhere in the world and in Italy in a special way. Women engineer appropriate and convenient marriages, keep track of distant relations, and see to it, at all times, that everybody does the suitable thing, suitable, that is, not for him and his happiness, but for the family as a whole.

Italian women are aware of their importance. They know that without them the whole structure would collapse like a house of cards within a few hours. They are ant-like in their incessant and undaunted efforts. Days and nights are dedicated to their duties. They devote the same zeal, enthusiasm, and spirit of sacrifice to their families which heroes and heroines dedicate to King, Leader, Flag, Fatherland, Constitution, Revolution, Seven-Year Plan and which saints of both sexes dedicate to the greater glory of God.

While the struggles and martyrdoms of patriots, revolutionaries, and saints have justly been celebrated by many, nobody has ever even tried to describe the vast, obscure, courageous, and awe-inspiring activities of Italian women of all times to keep their men on their feet, their families safe and the country functioning at all. Very few of these women have reached celebrity. (One of the few is Countess Teresa Confalonieri Casati of Milan. Her husband, who had plotted for Italian independence against the Austrian government, was arrested, tried, and condemned to death in 1823. She travelled to Vienna, to kneel at the feet of the Emperor, asking for mercy. She was successful. Her husband was reprieved and imprisoned for life in the Spielberg fortress, in Bohemia. She never exchanged letters with him. She died without seeing him again.)

How many unsung sisters, wives, daughters, mothers, aunts, grandmothers have been mixed up in the tormented lives of Italian men? How many women have secretly given their every thought, their beauty, their hopes, their health, their serenity of mind, for the protection and welfare of their families through so many centuries of convulsions, invasions, defeats, famine, massacres? How many had to lie, carry on intrigues, manœuvres, plots, or forayed far afield to gather precious informations or to conquer useful allies or hostages of some kind? Many nobly gave their lives, either drop by drop, through the years, or at one stroke, if it was necessary. How many of them dared to kill? How many accepted a life of shame? How many have slipped into the cold bed of a powerful person, under every régime, not certainly always for their pleasure, but in order to secure promotion for their husbands or their fathers? What more can a woman do for her family?

*

The fact that woman is the predominant character of Italian life, even if not the most conspicuous, can be read in many small signs. Almost as many popular songs are dedicated every year to *La Mamma* as to voluptuous hussies or romantic beauties. '*Mamma mia!*' is the most common exclamation. What other people call for their mother in time of stress or danger? Do the Germans say '*Mutter*', the French '*Maman*', the English '*Mother of mine*', when faced by a disappointment or an emergency? Wounded Italian soldiers in front-line dressing stations moan '*Mamma, mamma, mamma*', almost inaudibly, like hurt children. '*Mamma,*' say men condemned to death as they wait for the firing squad to fire. The next most common exclamation is '*Madonna*', which is a supernatural equivalent, as *La Madonna* is the universal symbol of suffering and self-sacrificing womanhood.

The Church itself happily encourages this national tendency. Jesus Christ shares, in Italy, His supreme place with His Mother, on almost equal footing. There are perhaps as many churches dedicated to her, in her many manifestations, attributes and specializations, as to Him. The most popular, revered and frequented sanctuaries are hers, famous shrines, the Madonne di Pompei, di Loreto, del Rosario, del Carmine, del Divino Amore. There are more miraculous images of her than anyone else, some wafted on the waves from the East, in ancient times, by supernatural means, a few painted allegedly by Saint John the Evangelist, and many done by the great Italian masters. They are especially helpful in the solutions of particular feminine problems: spinsters pray to them to find a good husband, sterile wives to become pregnant, unhappy wives to give them back their husbands' love, mothers to cure the incurable diseases of their children. Most Italian men are also personally consecrated to Mary: they have Maria among the names given to them at christening. Mary is one of the saints officially entrusted with the protection of Italy. There is at least one day dedicated to her every month, feast days observed not only by the Church but also by Government offices and private business. The whole month of May is her own month, and, at intervals, whole years are consecrated to her.

It must be remembered that Italians were so attached to the cult of the Virgin Mary, so reluctant to neglect her, that they consented, also for her sake, that the unity of Christendom be dismembered by the Protestants, who did not deem her worthy of so much attention. The national devotion to *La Madonna* helped at all times to make reunification of all Christians extremely difficult or almost impossible. It is principally the pressure of the Italian faithful and the zeal of the Italian clergy which prodded the Church to proclaim dogmas concerning *La Madonna,* codifying and sanctifying traditions and legends dear to the hearts of simple people.

*

Italian men are justly suspicious and jealous of their women. It is one of the foremost masculine duties. The stability and good name of the family notoriously depend more on the wife's faithfulness than on her husband's. Italian laws are clear on the subject: adultery committed by a woman is a punishable crime, adultery committed by a man is not, unless it is accompanied by scandalous and outrageous behaviour. Italian history is studded with famous examples of the determination with which husbands, brothers, and sons punish their women for sins which cast discredit or ridicule on their names. Practically every morning the newspapers are still filled with grue-some tales of the kind. Nevertheless the women show no sign of being afraid of punishment.

Fine examples of this tendency are particularly abun-dant in the sixteenth century, that most Italian of all centuries. Take, for instance, the case of beautiful Donna Pellegrina Bentivoglio, who was killed in Bologna in 1598, by order of her husband, Count Ulisse. She was unjustly suspected of having committed adultery. Four masked assassins cut her to pieces, in broad daylight, together with two ladies-in-waiting and her coachman, and left the remains on the road. In 1590, in Naples, Don Carlo Gesualdo, son of the prince of Venosta, assassinated his wife, Donna Maria d'Avalos, in his palace, with his own hands, together with her lover, Don Fabrizio Carafa, Duke of Andria. In 1577, in Milan, Count Giovanni Bor-romeo, a cousin of Cardinal Federigo and of Saint Charles, a most devout man, stabbed his wayward wife, Countess Giulia Sanseverino, at table, during dinner, with three mortal wounds.

Or take what happened to the Massimo family. It is surely one of the noblest and oldest in Rome, whether it is actually descended from the Roman Fabii and Fabius Maximus, Hannibal's conqueror, as they claim, or not. Lelio, the head of the house at the time in question, had six robust sons, all of gigantic stature and herculean strength, by his first wife, a Savelli. After their mother's death, in 1571, their father fell in love with a girl of inferior status—in birth, breeding and past life—to what was proper for a Roman prince at the time. She was a certain Eufrosina, born not far from Gina Lollobrigida's birth-place, in Ciociaria, who had at one time married a man named Corberio. Her remarkable beauty had already at-tracted the attention of Prince Marcantonio Colonna; he had lost his head and murdered her husband, so that he could bring the attractive widow to Rome and establish her in his house as his mistress. To take her away from Colonna, Massimo had to offer more: he married her. This was ob-viously an insult to the honour of the family, which his sons could not endure. On the night of her wedding, in 1585, they refused to welcome her in the house. The next morning, five of them entered her bedroom and shot her dead. Only one of the six did not take part in the murder. Lelio blessed him and cursed the others. After a lapse of a few weeks the old man followed his wife to her grave, killed by a broken heart. The blameless son Pompeo grew up to continue the great line of Massimo. (His contemporary descendant, Vittorio, shows the milder blood he had inherited: he married Dawn Addams, the film star, by whom he has a son, but desiring to divorce her, unlike his ferocious ancestors, he avoided bloodshed and went to court.)

Fathers' maledictions being still effective at the time, old Lelio Massimo's were not hurled in vain. The five sons all met bad ends. The first, Ottavio, was killed by a cannon ball at sea, fighting the Turks. Another, Girolamo, who found refuge in France, was shot in an ambuscade while making love to a noble lady. A third, Alessandro, a soldier in the troops of General Farnese, was shot dead near Paris. A fourth, Luca, the only one arrested in Rome for the murder of his stepmother, was released on the plea that he had avenged the honour of his family. He died, however, poisoned by his own brother, Marcantonio, in 1599. Marcantonio was arrested on suspicion of having killed him, and imprisoned in the Torre di Nona, where he confessed his guilt. He was beheaded in the little square before the bridge of Castel Sant'Angelo.

●

As the centuries progressed, only the lower classes preserved these severe traditions intact. They are practically the only ones who still jealously preserve them today. Among the well-born, manners became gradually milder and more indulgent. Wives entertained their lovers with increasing generosity and insouciance. Husbands necessarily had to deal with the problem of *corna* in a more realistic, civilized, and less bloody fashion, otherwise more than half the adult population would probably have been exterminated. Some of them (like Count Guiccioli of Ravenna, justly famous as the accommodating husband of Lord Byron's lady love, the great poet's 'last attachment') even managed to keep a good temper, a good appetite and make friends with their wives' lovers, who, after all, were taking a load off their shoulders. The witty Count

Papadopoli, the husband of a famous nineteenth-century Venetian beauty, is another good example. Sleeping one night at her side, from the creaking, breathing, and snoring he heard he realized that one of her numerous lovers had been surprised by his arrival and had found refuge under the bed. The count said nothing. In the morning, when coffee was served to him, he lowered one hand with a full cup and, without looking, asked politely: 'Do you take it with sugar or without?' He thought one whole night spent on the floor, directly underneath his mistress's husband, was enough punishment for any man.

There is the case of a jealous and moral gentleman, who disliked being cuckolded, but managed to avoid it without harsh words and bloodshed. He was Baron Bettino Ricasoli, born in 1809, a religious man, dedicated to politics and serious studies in his favourite field, agriculture. He was by no means handsome. In fact he was extremely cross-eyed, but had a tall and lean figure, and carried himself with a military and proud bearing. He was appointed prime minister in 1861, the second prime minister of united Italy, after the death of Count Cavour, but lasted only a short time in this post, as he incessantly quarrelled with the king, Victor Emmanuel II, who was as aristocratically stubborn as he was.

One night, when he had been married only a few months, Bettino, who had been nicknamed *Barone di Ferro*, or Iron Baron (such unbending characters are not necessarily admired in Italy, where *souplesse* is prized above all; the sobriquet has a derisive quality it would not have elsewhere), took his young wife Anna Bonaccorsi to a ball in Florence. There the poor lady was briefly and perfunctorily courted by a young man, who danced with her a few times. The husband immediately told her: 'We must leave, my dear.' He escorted her to their waiting carriage, sat down next to her, and told the coachman: 'To Brolio.' Brolio was the family seat, a lonely and gloomy castle, lost in barren and sterile hills, where none of the Ricasoli had lived for ages. The couple rode in silence through the snow, until dawn, he in his black evening clothes, she shivering in her ball dress. They lived in Brolio for practically the rest of their lives.

To while away the time he reconstructed the manor,

which now looks as if it had been dreamed up by Sir Walter Scott or designed as a background for *Il Trovatore*. He also experimented with planting different qualities of new vines and producing wines with improved processes. (One must have patience and a firm character for such pursuits. It takes approximately five years for a man to taste the first product of a new combination of grapes he has planted.) The baron came across a pleasing mixture of black and white grapes, Sangiovese and Malvasia, and a way to make them ferment in two successive waves, which imparted a novel taste to the *cru*. The wine became popular, was copied by the vineyard owners of the region, the Chianti, and acquired, in the end, a world-wide fame. One of the best Chiantis is still the Ricasoli, of which the Brolio Castle is the choice and most expensive variety. Thus the baron managed to preserve the sanctity of the family, his wife's name and his honour unblemished, to amass a fortune, and to enrich his neighbours, all at the same time.

*

Also in Italy modern life is eroding the splendid solidity of the family. The change could clearly have serious consequences. If the family weakens, will anarchy reign supreme? Or will Italians finally develop a suitable respect for public authorities and institutions? The family seems no longer what it used to be, everywhere but especially in the industrial centres of the north. Naturally the phenomenon is more noticeable there, as the north is closer to the rest of Europe and is the section where the transformation of society is being spurred on by industrialization and the gradual spread of affluence. Northern Italians often live in tiny flats, separated from relatives by vast wastelands of masonry and congested streets, as far apart as if they lived in distant regions. Relatives see each other at ever longer intervals and some of them inevitably get lost and forgotten. Young people want to have their own independent lives, tastes, studies, ambitions and friends, and to live apart from authoritarian parents. Some of the more old-fashioned rites are gradually disappearing, or are performed with little smiles of condescension and irony. Divorce is beginning to be adopted as an upper-class custom. Of course there is still no divorce on the law books, and there never will be. Not only is the Church against it, but the people themselves rightly consider it a barbarous and ruinous institution; the necessity to preserve some solid bulwark against the impermanence of things will always prevent its adoption. Not even the wildest anarchists and left-wing revolutionaries dared to propose it in the past. The Communists today angrily deny they are contemplating it. After all, as everybody knows, the principal purpose of married life is not the impossible satisfaction of adolescent love dreams, not the achievement of romantic ecstasy, not the perfect fusion of two souls, but the foundation of a new family and the reinforcement of existing ones. It is naturally desirable that husband and wife be happy in each other's company, but it is not indispensable. One thing is, however, imperative, that, should one or both of them be tempted to stray from fidelity, he, she, or both manage things in such a way as not to endanger a permanent structure and ruin other people's lives. Erring husbands or wives should by all means give his or her partner all possible chances to deceive himself or herself. Lack of precautions (even transparent ones), the habit of leaving open letters everywhere, or an adolescent urge not to keep secrets and to confess everything, are considered dangerous tendencies which must be repressed.

In Genoa, a few years ago, there lived a middle-aged married banker of steady habits who loved a pretty woman, the wife of a man of modest condition. The banker did not like the emotions of clandestine meetings in rented rooms. He preferred seeing his mistress at leisure in her own comfortable home. When he visited her in the evening, he always said to her husband: 'My dear friend, I have a hunch that this number will win at roulette tonight. Would you mind going down to the club and place this sum of mine on the proper spot?' The husband always went. He came back after two hours and said that, alas, the number had not come up and that he had lost the money. This went on for years. Brutal moralists would have derided this pleasant little ceremony, and blurted out the shocking truth, that the husband regularly pocketed the money, was a low scoundrel making a

living on his misfortune, and that his wife was a low
strumpet. Brutal moralists would have spoiled this delicate and civilized arrangement by demanding that the
wife openly confess her wrongs, the husband divorce her,
and the banker abandon his wife and children to marry
his mistress, thus ruining two families at the same time.

Now, however, many people want brutally to get
divorces at all costs, so as to be able to marry again. As
a result, *ersatz* divorces of sorts have been devised by
ingenious lawyers, for those couples who cannot obtain
an annulment of their religious bonds. After the war, for
instance, by legal subterfuges, many marriages were
dissolved in countries which had reciprocal treaties with
Italy making court sentences in one country also legal, in
certain cases, in the other. Few Italian tribunals, however, dared to accept the validity of the foreign decrees.
At one time, however, a stubborn old judge made them all
valid for a few years, until he retired. He freed thousands
of unhappily married couples. This lone loophole has now
been closed by more explicit legislation and stringent
regulations, but other methods are being explored. These
divorces are naturally easier for unknown and obscure
people, who do not interest newspaper readers and do
not provoke wide scandals. Film stars, well-known politicians, and popular singers have to go without. But when
there is no way out, when no chicanery is possible, more
and more people now take the law into their own hands
and set up house with new partners, without the benefit
of the municipal authorities and the clergy.

This, of course, has happened before. It has always
happened. But there is a difference between what went
on and what is going on now. The illegal couples are no
longer left alone, like lepers, to live a solitary and almost
clandestine life. They are not considered outcasts, like
Anna Karenina and Vronsky. They are accepted, invited
everywhere, looked upon with compassion and commisera-
tion, encouraged as the innocent victims of a cruel and
medieval legislation. The lady is usually called by the
name of her lover, out of courtesy. By means of legal tricks
of various sorts, their children are also illegally given the
man's family name. Such liaisons are now almost entirely
respectable, so respectable and solid, in fact, that many

of these unmarried ladies and gentlemen begin to have love affairs on the side.

*

As in the past on many occasions, the Italians now seem eager, even anxious, to adopt many foreign fashions. Family discipline is visibly relaxing. Does all this really mean that Italy is changing? Behind the frivolous appearances, behind each family's closed doors, a silent, stealthy, and tenacious struggle is going on to preserve the substance of the old ways. The struggle is going on within the very heart of each individual Italian. The outcome, of course, will be presumably what it has always been, a pleasing show of liberal broadmindedness which will not entirely correspond to the invincible reality behind it. The naïve and superficial observers will notice that 'Italy is no longer the country she has been for centuries', that many Italians are now as 'modern' as anyone else, and that a 'deep revolution' has definitely transformed their lives. Deeper and experienced observers will know better. Of course, something of the new ideas will stick, something not quite essential. But the spirit of the old ways will survive somehow. An Italian will still choose to stand by his family, in a crisis, against the *carabinieri*, the police, the courts, public opinion, and even, at times, his own conscience, because the family has for so long been the only reliable vessel on a sea of troubles, which will always float to safety with all its crew and contents. Things may change, to be sure, but they are changing very slowly, or not changing at all; as in shabby old provincial hotels in Italy only the façade and the entrance hall are being renovated while the rest is left intact.

Reassuring signs of the family's undimmed power in the most modern and affluent *milieus* are still abundant. Take the seven brothers C. of Genoa (there were eight but one of them died in a car accident). Together they own shipping lines, olive oil refining plants, various other industries, enterprises, and organizations worth several billion lire. To preserve the family solidarity, by common agreement, each of them owns nothing more than the clothes on his back and those on the backs of his wife and sons, plus the furniture in his house. Everything else is common property. Even the cars belong to a pool and are summoned by telephone when necessary. The brothers consider the patriarchal arrangement the best possible in order to carry on complex, vast, and privately owned enterprises with the least friction. Or take younger brothers in great Sicilian households. In Sicily, the power of the older families still largely depends on the prestige of an inherited title and the income from inherited land. Italian law does not recognize titles and imposes an equal distribution of a large part of the inheritance among all the children. To avoid seeing the common property divided among too many rivulets and vanish within one or two generations, there are younger brothers who, like lay monks, do not marry, or, when they marry, refrain from begetting children, so that the family fortunes, titles, prestige, and authority will go on undiminished to the next generation.

Other examples could easily be quoted; they are to be met with in every conversation, business deal, news item; they are the very core of Italian life. This, for instance, happened not long ago. A literary prize was offered to the author of the best first book of the year. Among several candidates one was specially favoured. He is a brilliant young man who had published by far the best book and had become well known practically overnight. He is the son of a distinguished man of letters who happened to be a member of the jury awarding the prize. The father, who was a scrupulous gentleman, was embarrassed. He did not want to sit in judgment on his son's work. He did not want to condemn his son's rivals. He did not want to dim his son's almost certain victory with suspicions of favouritism and nepotism. He therefore decided not to participate in the jury that year and wrote a dignified letter to his colleagues. He did not explain his scruples (any explanation would have had to include the admission that he thought his son might win, and that explanation too could have been interpreted as a form of pressure). He therefore refrained punctiliously from indicating that his son was in any way worthy of the prize and suggested two or three other names, names of writers obviously not half as good.

One or two of the judges proposed the son. He did not

get the award. The argument that defeated him had no answer in Italy and was accepted by all as final. When one of the judges said: 'We must be mistaken about him. He must not be as good as most of us think, for not even his father thought he deserved the prize. He never even mentioned him in his letter,' they all solemnly agreed. How bad must this son have been, the judges thought, if his own father had not had the courage to do his duty, what his heart dictated, and had been done since time immemorial?

CHAPTER TWELVE

How to Succeed

THE Italian family, this Macedonian phalanx of strict fathers, self-sacrificing mothers, doting grandparents, spinster aunts, in-laws, pimply adolescents, and swarming children, with its unwritten code and stern discipline, can be compared to a ship sailing over dark and treacherous waters infested by invisible and ruthless enemies. The ship does not sail alone: it is usually surrounded by a vast convoy which ensures its safety. The convoy is the organization (legitimate or illegitimate), to which the family loosely happens to belong. It is the group, clan, political party, *camarilla*, sect, trade union, association, open or secret, formed by people with more or less analogous backgrounds, hopes, fears and needs.

There is, to be sure, one substantial difference between such an arrangement and real-life sailing in wartime. The family follows a formation only as long as it promises safety and prosperity. Whenever the captain judges it prudent, the ship will stealthily but unhesitatingly abandon the convoy for another more convenient, less exposed one; perhaps, in an emergency, even an enemy convoy. At rare times, the family will sail alone, for a while at least, waiting to see which side in a battle will show signs of coming out on top, which side offers more objective chances for survival.

Of course similar alliances flourish in every country. They manage to dominate most human activities everywhere. Everywhere, in fact, it is useful to be 'in' in order to succeed in life. All over the world, it is indeed difficult to get ahead without the consent of entrenched côteries. Some of the most famous groups, it is true, are not as powerful as people think; some are pure fiction, or have but a shadowy and imaginary existence; a few are often nothing more than obsessions in the minds of the defeated, who use them to justify their own lack of success. Many, however, undoubtedly do exist; a few have undeniably left their marks in history, like the Masons and the *bouilleurs de crus* in France; the *Grosse Generalstab* in Germany; the Southern slave-owners, the Wall Street bankers in the United States; the English Establishment; and the Soviet Politburo. Some are really as strong and influential in the world of today as people believe. Contemporary art fashions, to mention one instance, are determined by a small group of dealers in Paris and an inner circle of museum directors throughout the world. Nevertheless, no matter how powerful these groups may be anywhere else, they seldom have the far-reaching importance they always had and still have in Italy.

In Italy, powerful groups know no other limit to their power than the power of rival groups. They play a free-for-all game practically without rules and referee. Of course the law is allegedly supreme; the apparatus of a quasi-modern State is visibly omnipresent, with its props, cast of characters, costumes, titles, and institutions, but there are important differences between such dignitaries and organizations and what they are elsewhere. Each branch of the State machinery in Italy is in reality a mighty independent power which must struggle sometimes for its existence, and usually for the prosperity of its protégés and subjects against all other rival branches of the State machinery: they fight savagely at times, but more often surreptitiously, exactly like private pressure groups, for a larger place in the sun, a bigger cut of the budget, more employees, a higher rank and wider prerogatives for their leaders.

When necessary, public institutions join hands to fight, without the particular advantages which the law should give them and armed only with the power they can marshal, all kinds of private groups, defeat them when they are weak, or come to some sort of arrangement when they are strong. The *Polizia* and the *Carabinieri* have been carrying on a running feud for more than a century. (The unusual existence of two rival police forces many Italians believe to be one of the best safeguards to their liberty. One always keeps watch over the other.) In western Sicily the two police forces have carried on a running fight with the Mafia for more than one hundred years. From time to time the Mafia allied themselves to the *Polizia*, or the *Polizia* allied themselves with the *Carabinieri*. When the two joined forces against the outlaws, they managed occasionally to predominate for a time, not because they represented the law but because they happened to be stronger. This fact, that the State does not necessarily have all the odds on its side, must be remembered if one wants to understand the fine points of such struggles as that between customs guards and smugglers, the Ministry of Labour and trade unions, the Ministry of Finance and the reluctant tax-payers, the Ministry of Public Instruction and the teachers and students, the Ministry of Industry and the industrialists.

The Prime Minister himself must have private backing of his own if he wants his orders to be obeyed, backing within his own party, within the bureaucracy, and within the Church, or of one of the powerful factions within the Church (if he is a Christian Democrat), as he can scarcely depend on his constitutional authority alone. There were a few honourable though inexperienced ministers, just after the war, who did not remember all this (they had been in jail or abroad during Fascism and had lost contact with practical affairs) and gallantly tried to impose their will on reluctant and rebellious bureaucrats or on the people without the proper support and alliances. All of them ended up completely isolated in their offices, bewildered and impotent men. Their telephones seldom rang, only close friends and relatives visited them, nobody told them what was going on, and the office boys even neglected to supply them with stationery and to fill their ink-stands with ink. In Italy even the Law, any law, changes meaning and purpose according to the power of the person who applies or violates it; taxes tend to become milder and more easily evaded for the powerful and the well-connected (the terms were synonymous with the rich and well-born, they now mean mostly people personally controlling many votes). Everything, in short, turns out to be, in the end, not a balancing of legal rights but a confrontation of pure power.

*

Some sort of protection is therefore necessary for everybody. Even the little man with no ambitions needs ample help merely to be left alone. The Italian historical weather has always been notably unstable. In practically every generation, tidal waves of political change batter all obstacles and wash the scene clean of everything that does not have a deep enough foundation or is not tied to something solid. Here generosity is notoriously considered a form of weakness; there is little pity for the beaten enemy; the opposition does not openly wait its turn but always vanishes from the earth and goes underground, perhaps only to reappear in the light of day after a generation or two. Century-old institutions disappear; the old élites are uprooted; raw new leaders must learn the job as they go along (a few always start by accumulating their own private fortunes); solid pillars of society are transformed overnight into dangerous subversives; text-books have to be re-written; old traditions, virtues, beliefs are banned and new ones take their place with bewildering rapidity, frequency and confusion.

In these upheavals, even the obscure and harmless men who obey the law and mind their own business are in danger. The slow and stupid men, the honourable men of firm character who are loyal to their ideals and consider it unworthy to adapt themselves to the new circumstances, and the isolated men without friends are inevitably washed away by the raging breakers. A few honest men emigrate, some sacrifice their lives, liberty or property; many go into hiding and live obscurely without prestige, authority and power. The great majority knows better. Events never surprise them. Just as men facing the violent surf join hands in a chain in order not to be carried away, Italians must at all times attach themselves to a strong group of friends. They never know when the next historical storm will break. They only know that those who stand alone are lost.

●

Italians are not, as foreigners believe, individualists. They loyally serve in their own organizations, which are very rarely the official ones. This was recognized, among few others, by Antonio Gramsci, the acute and erudite hunchback who founded the Italian Communist Party in 1921. He left many notes, reflections provoked by his random reading, jotted down in cryptic form while hopelessly ill in Fascist jails. This is one, freely translated and abbreviated: 'It is being affirmed, with complacency by some and with scorn and pessimism by others, that the Italians are a "people of individualists". A few say "fortunately", others say "unfortunately". Are the Italians really individualists? Is it really individualism that makes the ordinary people ignore politics today and made them ignore the interests of the nation as a whole in the past? Is this the reason that made them repeat: "Let France come or let Spain [it is all the same], as long as we eat"? The fact that one does not participate in the life of the community or the State does not necessarily mean that he lives a lone life, the splendidly isolated life of the proud man who counts only on himself to create his own economic and moral world. It merely means that, rather than joining political parties and trades unions, Italians prefer joining organizations of a different type, like cliques, gangs, *camorras, mafias.* This tendency can be observed both among the lower and the higher classes.'

Gramsci, of course, innocently believed all this to be the fatal result of capitalism, in spite of the fact that he knew the phenomenon was far older than capitalism, practically as old as the Italian people themselves, and that, curiously enough, it was almost unknown or did not prevail in the more progressive nations, where capitalism was really strong. He sincerely believed, however, that communism was the only cure, and that, once all the means of production were public property, the Italians would all become law-abiding citizens. He had to cling to his faith in spite of contrary evidence and doubts: to do otherwise was to admit that all his work and sacrifices had been in vain. We know better. Recent experiences show that Italians carry on in the same old way in any form of economic organization. In fact, the more economic activities the State controls the more people rely on friends and accomplices for their protection and to safeguard their power and property. Nothing is as clique-ridden in Italy as a nationalized industry. Gramsci himself did not live to see his own small and heroic party turned, after the last war, into just another vast mutual-aid association *all'italiana*, directed only vaguely by ideological orthodoxy but mostly by agile opportunism.

*

The cliques, camarillas, mafias, cabalas, or as the Italians often call them, *consorterie*, as well as the more honourable but just as unofficial organizations to which the people entrust their security are not always chosen consciously. Sometimes a man happens to be born in one of them. In the past, he found himself the subject of a prince, the citizen of a tiny republic, the member of a historical party, like the Guelphs and the Ghibellines, or a family clan, like the Montagues and Capulets. He somehow knew from birth (nobody needed to tell him) that he was bound to help all other members and had the right to exact help from them. Such spontaneous formations still exist. Southerners in the north, for instance, or northerners in the south automatically behave like members of a secret society and extend brotherly aid to each other on sight. Such bonds are so strict that people who would naturally be enemies back home (born in rival towns or in rival quarters of the same town) immediately become allies and accomplices in alien surroundings. Italians of all regions, north or south, obey the same moral obligations when they meet abroad. They recognize each other without speaking. They do not have to speak. They communicate with imperceptible gestures and are ready on sight to do practically anything for each other.

The instinctive recognition and feeling of complicity could be compared to the sympathy and attraction which sadly draws together men addicted to secret vices, as if being Italian and living the Italian way were also some kind of secret vice, a crime against nature. The same feeling binds almost all Italians under a foreign tyranny perhaps more strongly than the inhabitants of any other country in the same predicament. The French, the Dutch, the Danes naturally tried to help each other against the German occupation during the last war. None however were trained so well by history to violate all laws, to understand each other at a glance and to combine their efforts against the occupying authorities as the Italians.

They already knew all the tricks. Only a tiny and unreliable minority sided with the Wehrmacht. The great majority spontaneously and immediately behaved as if they were all long-lost cousins. Anybody anywhere could find refuge without fear in the first farm house he came to. He knew that the peasants would cheerfully defy death to feed and shelter him. The same privileges were extended to the Allied escaped prisoners, as many of them can testify, not only because of the ideals they represented, but also because they, being persecuted by the Germans, had somehow become honorary Italians.

More often a man must choose what group to join. The range is rarely very wide; nobody is entirely free; his background, tastes, class, talents, character, ambitions will narrow the field still further. There often is, however, a moment in a man's life in which he must take a chance and make up his mind. Some of the associations he can join are old, powerful and nation-wide. Some are village groups. Within the vast associations, there are again other cliques, one inside the other like Chinese ivory balls, among which a man must skilfully find his way.

One, the oldest and the largest of all, containing all sorts of subsidiary factions and bodies, is the worldly organization of the Church, honourable, virtuous, far-reaching, powerful and omnipresent, a State within the State. It obeys its own laws, it offers infinite possibilities, it protects and aids loyal followers, it solves all kinds of problems, it promotes prosperity and security of good men in all kinds of circumstances. It has notoriously always made official life in Italy precarious and feeble. It can afford the timid man a safe life (he can become a parish priest or a monk). It can afford the ambitious man plenty of opportunities (he can become a Vatican diplomat, the confessor of sovereigns and statesmen, the general of a religious order; the head of a Catholic university or publishing house, a high prelate dominating all sorts of spiritual or worldly spheres, a cardinal invested with wide responsibilities, even the Pope himself). A layman, too, can lead a sheltered and happy life with the aid of the Church. It can accompany him, step by step, from birth to death, assuring him a good job and a steady career, protecting him from the envy of rivals, procuring for him, at times, worldly success, fame, political power, and wealth.

The Church is a world in itself, the most labyrinthine and complicated of all human organizations. From the outside, to the stranger, it looks monolithic. Inside it is an entanglement of factions politely and almost imperceptibly fighting each other for the greater glory of God: the Pope and his private advisers against the Curia, the Curia against the bishops, liberal against conservative bishops, all bishops against the lower clergy, the religious orders against the priests, the religious orders among themselves, all tenaciously struggling for supremacy. The lay Catholics are also divided into a bewildering number of groups, from the extremely wealthy Knights of Malta to the Catholic Action and the disinherited left-wing workers' organizations.

Or, until a few years ago, a man could entrust his prosperity to the Masons. They were in Italy a powerful and secret organization (also divided, like the police, into two rival branches) which, until the first world war, furthered many careers and probably controlled most of the highest positions in the Italian State. It protected its adherents in all walks of life. The Masons were anti-clerical and fought the Church's influence in all fields, in politics, the academic world, the armed forces, and business enterprises. They have now practically lost all their power. There are still today many similarly vast institutions, none, however, as powerful and far-reaching as the Church or the Masons of old, which a man can join for protection: political parties, coalitions of economic interests, cultural cliques of all kinds. A man can also become at the same time a member of several associated and kindred groups: he can be, for instance, a protégé of the Jesuits or of the left-wing Catholic Action, a good Christian Democrat politician, and the director of a nationalized industry; he can be a member of the Communist Party in order to control one of the camarillas in the world of art and culture which the Party dominates.

A man can also join smaller groups, of which there are thousands, some less honourable than others, some outright criminal, all powerful in their respective spheres of influence, down to the Sicilian village Mafia. When dealing with an Italian it is always prudent to know exactly where his loyalties lie, to what clique, association or party he belongs, who protects him, who are his friends, and from whom he derives his power. Naturally there are no handbooks listing such indispensable information. The man will often hotly deny his allegiance. Some bodies (the Masons of old, the democratic parties under the Fascist régime, a few financial combinations today) are secret. Nevertheless, the information is usually not difficult to ferret out. Everybody knows.

One of the reasons why a man will deny his allegiance is that, while it is indispensable to belong to some group or *consorterie*, it may become dangerous and compromising in troubled times. It is, therefore, a good rule never to be too conspicuous. One should always try not to be the standard-bearer; one should accept only solid and secondary positions, one should avoid being known as the follower of one man or the absolute champion of one idea. Nobody knows when the next historical storm will break and when what was accepted formerly as an advantage may become a disastrous liability overnight. One should always leave open doors behind one. This is also one of the reasons why one should always try to have friends among one's opponents. (The thing is easy, because there are many among one's opponents who obey the same rule.)

When, in April 1940, a *commissario di polizia* arrested me for being a dangerous enemy of the Fascist régime, he was inordinately polite. While I waited at the Questura to be interrogated, he sent for a good dinner from the nearest *trattoria*, sent to my house for clean shirts, a change of clothes, and some money, and warned me veiledly about what was best to say and not to say when questioned. He courteously drove me in his car to the Regina Coeli prison. I thanked him and asked him why he had been so kind. He frankly said: 'One never knows. Maybe you'll be able to do the same for me, some day.' (The régime was still very powerful and unchallenged at the time. Italy was still neutral. Germany looked likely to win the war. The *commissario* was carefully buying insurance against a most improbable event.)

A few years later, during the last few months of the

war, the Fascist chief of Grosseto, the province in which I lived at the time, sent for me. Italy was then divided. In the south were the legal government, the king, and the Allies; in the north were the Germans, the quisling government and Mussolini. Grosseto still belonged to the north. The Fascist chief kept me waiting for hours in his office, while he dispatched the business on hand. He made me watch him giving orders to hide cattle from the Germans who wanted to requisition them, orders to give shelter to partisans and to warn others of a forthcoming raid. In the end he turned to me and said: 'I hope you will some day be able to tell all you saw and heard today to a court of law.' I did, after the war, in Perugia. He got thirty years.

Plain speaking is often a dangerous practice. Obscurity is the rule in almost all fields. Most newspaper editorials, art criticisms and political speeches are, as a rule, clothed in elegantly ambiguous prose. One must not make unnecessary enemies. One never knows when one's widely accepted and non-controversial opinions will turn out to be compromising and daring. One conceals one's thoughts, unnecessarily at times, because, for one thing, to conceal them is never dangerous while to reveal them might be so. There are often, of course, less discreditable reasons. Concealment in difficult times may be the only way to protect one's liberty, both one's inner liberty, in which things may be thought as one wishes, and one's practical, ordinary, everyday freedom of action. This is the kind of prudence the citizens of Communist countries well know.

This theory has largely been explored, among others, by a distinguished Italian novelist, essayist, and political writer, Guido Piovene, in a recent book entitled *La coda di paglia*, or *The Tail of Straw*. (A 'tail of straw', an old Italian metaphor, supposedly prevents the man who has it from going too near a fire; it is made up of the compromising facts in his past life, which he wants to have forgotten, and which therefore gravely limit his possibilities in the present. He is always afraid somebody will discover buried secrets and divulge them to discredit him.) Piovene was recently attacked by the press because he is now a sincere anti-Fascist and a Communist sympathiser, in spite of the fact that, under Mussolini's dictatorship, he wrote a few articles extolling the dictator's literary style and praising his anti-semitic policy, and had volunteered for the Spanish war on Franco's side. It must be admitted that he had gone too far. Few intelligent men in their right senses went so far. It was not necessary. People managed to get on well and even reach important positions without once praising qualities which Il Duce did not possess and never thought he had, and policies which he himself secretly despised, as they reminded him of his subservience to Hitler. Piovene defends himself by pointing out that perhaps his actions were not strictly necessary, but that their gratuitous quality is his best excuse. He did what he did not merely to preserve his personal liberty but, he claims, also to discredit the régime. He relied on what he calls 'the melancholic faith of hypocrisy'.

'Mine was the experience of bad faith in times of tyranny,' he writes, without however explaining why he is now so eager to renew that hideous experience by siding with the Italian Communist Party in most controversies. 'I do not even pretend that my bad faith was always a conscious one,' he wrote. 'This would have required a strength of character, a coherence, a courage in mendacity, an almost perverted form of sincerity, which are as difficult to achieve as self-sacrifice. . . . I administered to myself tiny drops of conviction not to despise myself too much.' (This, incidentally, is the difference between men like Piovene and Guicciardini. Guicciardini did not want to be deceived. He had the strength of character to prosper in a world which he knew was irremediably wicked and execrable.)

'Being made of infinite duplicity,' Piovene continues, 'the Fascist period appeared to me "psychological" in the extreme, and I mean by this a period in which man could fabricate for himself complicated intellectual instruments in order not to see the simplest truths: man then shut himself within himself and invented deceptions. There was another kind of mystification in my writing. It happened that, while at work, I entered into a state of contemptuous rage which prevented me from moderating my language and drove me far beyond the point at which I should have stopped; I would exaggerate my prose in such a preposterous way that anybody endowed with the least common sense should have seen through it. The justification was: this article is so stupid that I cannot even consider it mine. I had the illusion of cutting it away from myself and attributing it to some idiot rhetorician I had hired for the job. Thus such absurd comparisons came to my mind, as those between Mussolini and Shakespeare or even between Mussolini and Pascal. I could have just as easily written Parmenides or Lucretius. I wanted to escape as far as possible from plausible comparisons.'

Unfortunately, Piovene's deliberately hyperbolic and ridiculous comparisons did not at the time strike the unsuspecting reading public in the way that he now likes to believe. Most people then thought that there must have been some similarity after all between Mussolini and Pascal or Shakespeare, since a well-known critic said so in an authoritative newspaper. Others, the anti-Fascists, thought Piovene was one more toady of the régime. Only his intimate friends knew the truth, that he despised the Fascists; that he was not particularly eager to acquire advantages but merely wanted to avoid troubles; and that he was so inexperienced in such games that he overshot the mark by an unbelievably wide margin.

In spite of his claim to speak for his generation, Piovene cannot be considered entirely typical. It is true that he did then and he now does side with the party that presumably can assure him the greatest peace of mind. This is admittedly what the majority of Italians are at all times supposed to do. But there are a few points that set him apart. He commits the ultimate sin: he confesses, analyses, and discusses his choices in the open, attracting on himself all sorts of abuse from left and right. He thus squanders away what advantages he might gain by his arts. He also never manages to deceive himself or others completely. And he never got anything out of his adaptability.

An old story illustrates this point, a story the Italians invented at the time of the Berlin blockade, when a third world war looked a matter of weeks away and NATO did not yet exist. The Russians (the story goes) one day suddenly attacked Western Europe with overwhelming forces. Local defences were immediately pulverized. The United States naturally were unprepared to offer ready help. They needed the usual number of years to make up their minds, manufacture the equipment and train the men. The Russians therefore easily went unopposed from the Elbe to Gibraltar in a few days, conquered the British Isles, and organized all the occupied territory according to their political prejudices.

They set up Communist régimes and exterminated all anti-Communists. In due time, years later, the Americans landed, defeated the Russians and liberated Europe. New free governments were organized, who proceeded to shoot all Communists. At the end, the continent was practically uninhabited. Only handfuls of Britons, Frenchmen, Germans, Dutch and so forth were left in the vacant spaces and the empty cities. Italy alone was overcrowded. In Italy almost fifty million people were left alive. They had obviously remembered one of their old proverbs, which says 'Brave men and good wines last a short time'.

Or take another bitter story, an older one, also invented by the Italians themselves in the twenties, when the Fascist régime was but a few years old. The Secretary of the Fascist Party visits a large factory, accompanied by the obsequious company director. At the end of the tour all the workers are massed in the yard to listen to a speech. Before addressing them, the Fascist chief looks them over proudly from his podium, and asks the director: 'What are these people's politics?' The director answers: 'One-third of them are Communist, one-third Socialist, and the rest belong to several small parties.' The Fascist's face turned livid. 'What?' he cries. 'And how many of them are Fascist?' The director reassures him quickly: 'All of them, Your Excellency, all of them.'

Many Italians, in reality, are not technically opportunists: they do not find it difficult to weave in and out of political parties, conceal their thoughts, accept and repeat whatever official ideas are being imposed from above merely because they want to avoid risks; they do all this also because they are sceptical. They believe that all ideologies are equally right and wrong, that there is no abstract solution to their problems, that the world can somehow be made to function under whatever political institutions seem easier to accept at the moment, because all of them will always function defectively in Italy, where they have all failed, at one time or another, and will all fail sooner or later. They think a bad republic is no better than a bad monarchy; a corrupt socialist State is no improvement on a corrupt capitalist State. They know Communism would be an Italian travesty of Communism. They believe there is no panacea for their ills.

*

The simple skills necessary merely to survive are not difficult to learn. They are, after all, not exclusively Italian but roughly common to all insecure societies, with, however, untold local refinements and subtleties which cannot be matched elsewhere. Italians become such deft masters, so early in life, in these arts, that they are usually unaware of their existence. As a result, life flows smoothly, conflicts are concealed or attenuated to the point that foreigners once believed they lived here in a heavenly country, almost the best in the world, an Arcadia where nothing harsh ever happened, where people were happy, cheerful and friendly. Some still believe it today.

Let us recapitulate, for the sake of clarity, these elementary rules: one must cultivate one's family, entertain as many useful friends and as few dangerous enemies as one can, and therefore perfect the art of being obliging and *simpatico* at all times and at all costs. One should always be on the *qui vive*, watch the horizon for the smallest cloud and people's faces for the smallest variation of mood; one should join a powerful group, sail with a safe convoy; one should beware of History.

On the negative side these are the things one must avoid: one should never be too conspicuous, daring, confident, explicit, trusting, credulous; one should not officially embrace definite opinions, nor be out of step with the crowd. Above all, one should remember at all times that conflicts are not decided on the basis of the law, abstract considerations of justice or the relative merit of the contestants, but most frequently by a pure confrontation of power. Might is not only very often right, but might is often the equivalent of beauty, culture, intelligence and charm as well. No harm will come to the man who diligently does all these things. No harm but, of course, nothing really good either.

The skills necessary to do more than just survive, the skills indispensable to achieve even a modest success, are infinitely more difficult to define and to teach. The Italians who practise them and reach even a small commanding position are admirable indeed, larger-than-life heroes who can operate among their own countrymen, people who can see through every trick and know how to defend themselves in all circumstances. The virtues necessary to become the head of anything, in Italy, head of a convent, a municipal kennel, a vegetable market Mafia, a secondary railway station, or the mayor of a mountain village, are such that could, in most other countries, easily make a man foreign minister, the alcove favourite of the queen, the chief of staff, or the president of the republic.

There are, of course, no infallible recipes, no tested instructions which can be applied by anybody with the certainty of getting results. Every case is a different one. Like all great artists, most successful men in Italy seem to obey a few general rules but in reality develop their own particular techniques, exploit their own unique talents, adapt themselves brilliantly to the milieu and the circumstances. The general precepts, like those governing all arts when described in popular handbooks, seem deceptively easy to follow. There is nothing esoteric about them. They are approximately the same to which ambitious men have resorted whenever competition was rife, competitors were numerous, ruthless and intelligent, and the positions to conquer were scarce and strenuously defended, in places like Louis XIV's Versailles, Wall Street in its heyday, or Hollywood in the good years.

But courtiers, speculators, and Hollywood arrivistes were rarely condemned exclusively to seek high position and fame in their respective bear pits. They were free, as gamblers are who choose to suffer in a hell of their own making, but who can always leave the green table. There is a final quality about such things in Italy. If a man has a modest ambition and wants to improve his lot, he has no alternative. He knows he must not count merely on his worth and talents; he must compete in a game without rules; the man who wins is the best man exclusively in the art of inventing new ways to paralyse or destroy his opponents; there are no side-lines, no benches to retire to, no sponges to throw in, no ways to escape. The whole nation is one vast battlefield. Most prizes are modest. The risks are mortal.

These, then, are some of the deceptively obvious rules. Rule One: choose the right companions. In order to succeed, a young man must not only join a large and powerful group but also, once in, worm his way to the top, become one of the influential élite, one of the leaders, or even the solitary chief, if he can, in order to use the whole group to serve his own purposes. It is clearly impossible for any man to do so alone. He must have an *entourage* of his own: he must choose a smaller group inside the large group, join it, and eventually influence it. He must recognize, at the start, which of the various existing cliques presents the best chances. Roughly speaking, there is usually a clique of older men well-entrenched in commanding positions who can defend themselves and who allow only their own friends to prosper, and a clique of ambitious young men determined to oust the older men and take their places. The choice of which faction to side with is a difficult and delicate one. Romantic and sentimental prejudices must naturally be overlooked. One cannot afford to make mistakes, as it is almost impossible to change places later, when the outcome is clear, without paying a heavy price.

Rule Two (perhaps the most important of all): choose the right protector. All inner cliques are usually dominated by a few influential men, sometimes by one leader. In all fields there are a few authorities. Any young man who wants to excel must attach himself to the proper mentor, become his aide-de-camp and use him for his own purposes. There are thousands of ways for a young man to seduce a more mature man, just as there are thousands of good ways to seduce women. In this field, too, a man must remember that art is not enough: no seduction is ever a thoroughly cold-blooded one, or one which goes against natural affinities. Women and older men are seldom fools. There are women who cannot be seduced, just as there are older men who, for fear of being stabbed in the back, prefer to surround themselves

with inept and stupid followers, aspirants who will never
amount to anything. Mussolini only liked subservient and
incapable underlings. As a rule, women favour men they
have a natural inclination for and who offer them something in return for their love; protectors prefer young
men who have something in common with them, who
share more or less the same ideas, who admire them and
imitate them. The choice therefore falls on few of the
many aspirants. Still, the use of the art to get oneself
noticed and selected must never be entirely overlooked.
Art must always be employed to accelerate and facilitate
the natural course of nature.

It is curious that, such being the fascinating complications and psychological subtleties of the game, such being
the stakes for which it is necessarily played by everybody
at all levels and ages, a vast literature, based not on the
commonplace pursuits of love and the all-too-familiar intricacies of amorous dalliances but on pure ambition, does
not exist, a literature dedicated to the heart-breaking
courtship of elderly protectors, the penetration of closed
cliques, the infinite manœuvres and labyrinthine intrigues,
the conspiracies, the plots and counterplots necessary to
prosper even modestly in Italian life. Of the two emotions
moving men, love and ambition, the latter undoubtedly is
the more vigorous, longer lasting, more varied, and presents more dramatic possibilities. As a matter of fact, only
two famous novels are dedicated to such matters, against
an Italian background, both written by foreigners: *La
Chartreuse de Parme* by Stendhal, and *The Cabala* by
Thornton Wilder.

How does a young man proceed? He must be around
as much as possible, to begin with. He must be seen. He
must be available. This is one of the reasons why the
waiting-rooms of powerful men are always crowded with
people offering their services and asking for favours,
sometimes merely waiting for hours in order to speak to
the leader for a few minutes, walk a few steps with him,
offer him a match or a cigarette, hold his coat, do whatever will attract his attention and put them in a favourable light. This was deplored by Count Cavour who used
to say: 'The worst of Chambers is always to be preferred
to the best of antechambers.' In fact the power of a man

in any particular period can be measured exactly by the number of people surrounding him. A few favoured ones follow him in the street, anywhere he goes, or on longer trips whenever he travels. Such hangers-on are still known as *clienti*, in the south, from the Latin term used to describe them in old Roman days, *clientes*, people who offer their services and demand aid, protection and advice.

An old politician in Benevento used to hold court, every morning, like a king of old under a tree, in the barber's shop, sitting on the throne-like chair, with his face covered with lather and a towel draped around his shoulders, while the barber shaved him. It was an unforgettable scene. A noisy crowd surrounded him, proffering petitions, asking for help, jobs for grown-up sons, subsidies, pensions, in a great confusion, while a few henchmen defended him from the bolder assailants. The Jupiter-like old man listened, nodded, called every one by name, laughed and gave orders. The practice is not as visible nor as picturesque in the more modern centres. Nevertheless, the great men of business, finance, industry and science in the north are just as much surrounded and courted by *clienti*, though in a more discreet way.

Flattery, of course, utilitarian flattery, has always been the principal way to get attention, to conquer affection and to get ahead. Perhaps the most heroically successful example in history of one poor and friendless Italian promoting at one stroke, with but a few words (four, to be exact), the business on hand and his own career for the rest of his life, is to be found in the memoirs of the Duc de Saint-Simon. (Success in this instance was facilitated by the fact that the powerful man to be flattered was a foreigner, definitely an easier man to seduce than an Italian.) The incident happened near Parma in 1706. The Duke of Parma, Saint-Simon relates, feared that the French armies fighting the Austrians in his territories would ravage them, and wanted to ask the French commander, the Duc de Vendôme, to move his soldiers a few miles away.

The negotiations appeared especially delicate and difficult. Vendôme was known to be a hard man to convince. He was erratic and capricious. A bastard of royal blood, he was, like most royal bastards, suspicious and touchy.

He was furthermore stubborn, clever, lazy, insolent and greedy. He was proud of being a homosexual and paraded his minions and favourites; slept together with his dogs and never disturbed his bitches when they delivered themselves of their puppies in his bed; ate vast quantities of food, mostly rotten fish, which he especially relished, but vomited almost immediately into a basin in front of his guests, without interrupting the conversation. He always used rough and soldierly language; he received his visitors and carried out the business on hand always sitting on his *chaise percée*.

The Duke of Parma decided to send an ambassador who could impress the French commander: the Bishop of Parma, a dignified and tactful old man, in his purple robes, followed by a young abbé. The prelate was treated like everybody else. After listening to a few rough jokes and watching some scandalous scenes, he left in a huff. But the clever abbé, one of the most ambitious men ever born in Italy, stubbornly stayed on. 'Knowing well who was Vendôme,' Saint-Simon writes, 'he decided to please him at all costs in order to conclude the business on hand according to his master's wish. . . . Vendôme treated him as he had done the bishop. *Il se torchait le cul devant lui.* At this sight, the abbé exclaimed "*O culo di angelo!*" and ran to kiss it.' The matter was concluded quickly in a satisfactory way. The abbé, the son of a modest gardener, attached himself to Vendôme, became his adviser, and eventually followed him to Spain. There the abbé became the confidant of the king and queen and was appointed prime minister. A few years later he was named a cardinal by the Pope. He made himself the arbiter of Europe, deciding war and peace among the great powers. His name was Giulio Alberoni.

●

How, then, can Italy function so splendidly at times in a highly competitive and merciless world? How can so many Italians do their work reasonably well when they and their leaders are seldom selected according to objective capacities, talents, and experience, but mostly through their flair for intrigue? How can any kind of organization function at all when riddled with favouritism and clogged up with flattery? How can so many things be done well, so many industries compete with more efficient and tenacious rivals in the international markets, and life apparently flow so smoothly and gaily? Why, if what is described in the preceding pages is true, do Italians not fail at everything they try? What is the secret?

The answer is complex. To begin with there are definite fields in which the Italian rules of advancement are suspended. Only strictly capable men reach the top in surgery, for instance. For some reason, Italians do not mind entrusting their national life to incompetent and intriguing generals, but refuse to entrust their personal lives to inept surgeons. For analogous reasons, they do not encourage bad opera singers, conductors, ballerinas, courtesans, actors, film directors, cooks, tailors and pilots. These people get ahead strictly on their merit.

It must also be remembered that, at times, men who care enough for their work and have the extra energy needed to excel, easily master the procedure necessary to reach the top as an indivisible part of their job. Without subtle arts, they could not begin to develop their possibilities, and all their latent capacities would go unused. They acquire such arts as part of the necessary knowledge, just as they acquire manners and learn to read and write. Their talent puts them in an advantageous position. Talent is, after all, one of the sources of power. Then, as I have explained, older men and cliques prefer to promote the fortunes of men who will be useful to them, men who unite ordinary talents to the skills necessary to further themselves, and often these young men objectively deserve promotion. Finally, in most private enterprises, Western competitive habits struggle with the Italian traditional ways and often prevail. In the top echelons and very big business, of course, where problems are not concerned with technique and efficiency but with pure power, the chiefs emerge in the old-fashioned Italian manner; only in the lower echelons and smaller business concerns do the men who get ahead tend to be strictly those who get results.

The unbearable pressure of free competition, this selection which heartlessly favours only uncouth and rough persons whose only merits are those of passing tests, doing their job well and knowing their business, is naturally resented by most Italians. What kind of a life is that, they ask, in which a man must relentlessly fight for his position and not bask secure in the protection of powerful friends? This is one of the reasons why all kinds of rigid organization of economic life find favour in Italy. The people liked their guilds in the pre-industrial world, which regulated every trade and occupation from apprenticeship to the tomb; Fascism, before the war, which prevented all competition as dangerous to the State and surrounded the country with impassable tariff barriers; and any kind of Socialism today, as long as it allows ambitious men to get ahead as they have always done, using the protection of powerful relatives, personal charm, a facility for flattering people, and a keen eye for favourable openings.

CHAPTER THIRTEEN

The *Problema del Mezzogiorno*

A T this point the reader has been told practically everything that can help illuminate the Italian landscape
for him and dispel many shadows. He has all, or almost
all, the clues, and should be able to work things out for
himself. He will recognize pathetic and picturesque scenes
for what they are and not what they appear to be. Some
of the obscure, contradictory and incomprehensible events
of past history or contemporary politics, whose actual
significance is vainly debated by honest and baffled experts, will unfold and reveal their secret nature, like
Japanese wooden flowers put in water. Foreign diplomats
and journalists, recently arrived in Rome, may attribute
with ease a precise meaning to equivocal official pro-
nouncements, to apparently clear proclamations of political aims and to subtle and puzzling manœuvres. Italo-
philes will know precisely what they are in love with and
why. Not every little detail will be thoroughly clarified,
to be sure. There will always be mists in the dells. A few
facts, characters, events and problems, a few mass emotions and upheavals, in the past and the present, will
always defy interpretation. Not all of Italy is *all'italiana*.
Life never entirely corresponds to rational and logical
man-made schemes.

There will be times when the reader will be mystified.
He may even be misled by a too rigid and unimaginative
application of the keys to Italian living. He must remember that, while things may not always be what they seem
to a naïve onlooker, they are not always or entirely what
cynical and realistic observers believe. It may happen that
the foreigner dismisses some disinterested gesture, some
sincere declaration of friendship and affection, and some
selfless heroic act as nothing more than show. He may
take a tidal wave of collective enthusiasm for a pure
spectacle without significance. He may be rudely sur-

prised by the truth. General Léon de Lamoricière, for instance, commander-in-chief of the Papal Armies, formed by French, Irish, Swiss, German and Belgian volunteers, challenged the Royal Italian Army of Victor Emmanuel II to battle at Castelfidardo, on September 8, 1860, proudly pronouncing the famous last words: *'Les Italiens ne se battent pas,'* 'Italians can't fight'. He knew. He despised them. He had seen them in battle. The Italians trounced him soundly. The Papal domains were lost for ever that very day. And how many observers declared in 1922 that Fascism was but a straw fire which would not last three months? There is every reason why foreigners should be misled by their own caution when the Italians themselves, who know all about the rules governing their conduct, have, down the centuries, so often been deluded, frustrated and paralysed by their own fear of deceiving themselves.

*

The application of some of the principles already outlined can, for instance, clarify the ancient and puzzling *Problema del Mezzogiorno,* or the profound difference between the Two Italies, the North and the South. There is no doubt that all Italians, observed from a distance, have a family resemblance. They all come more or less from the same stock, have predominantly dark hair, dark eyes and vivacious expressions. They have been shaped by similar historical vicissitudes and have developed or sharpened the same talents in order to survive. They all love life and enjoy a good show. They are all similarly wary of the law; they all pursue their type of happiness *alla* Guicciardini, the advancement of their private welfare, or *il particulare,* at the expense of society; they must defend themselves, their family and *consorteria* against the treachery, envy, hatred of men; they use the family as an ark to outlast natural calamities, historical convulsions, and political upheavals. Unlike the inhabitants of better organized nations, they have to rely on their private virtues and public vices, their adaptability, charm, intelligence, shrewdness, the use of their personal power.

All this is the same in the North as in the South. But there is a difference. The difference is important: it is one of the causes of the slower development of the southern economy, in the past century, and of the more rapid growth of the northern economy. It has so far defeated all attempts to bring the two standards of living more or less onto one level. It will always misdirect the spending of at least a part of the vast sums of money the government invests in the South. There is even a danger that the mutual mistrust and misunderstanding which separate the Two Italies may be strengthened and that national unity, which was always fragile at best, may become more unstable than in the past.

The private aims of southerners and northerners are, of course, more or less the same. The northerner, however, thinks that there is one practically sure way to achieve them: the acquisition of wealth, *la ricchezza*. Only wealth can, he believes, lastingly assure the defence and prosperity of the family. The southerner, on the other hand, knows that this can be done only with the acquisition of power, prestige, authority, fame. The northerner of whatever class, therefore, is perpetually trying to acquire wealth in its various forms. He wants a job, a good job, a better job; he wants land, capital, credit, industrial shares, houses, technical and scientific knowledge and expensive and rare university degrees, which assure him better-paid employment and advancement; he brings up his children with these aims in mind, educating them to become well-paid technicians, engineers, specialists. He undergoes any sacrifice in order to gain material advantages for himself and his family. He wants a rich wife, rich daughters- and sons-in-law, rich friends. He is similar to the French bourgeois, almost a pure *homo economicus*.

The southerner, on the other hand, wants above all to be obeyed, admired, respected, feared and envied. He wants wealth too, of course, but as an instrument to influence people, and, for that, the appearance of wealth is as useful as wealth itself. In the South, the little peasant, the illiterate day labourer, the olive-tree pruner, the sulphur miner, as well as the landed proprietor, the noble member of exclusive clubs, the *nouveau riche* owner of recently founded industries, all will cultivate the gratitude of powerful friends and relatives, the fear of their enemies, the respect of everybody, and the reputation of their families.

In Naples and in Milan there are, for example, wholesale fruit and vegetable merchants. They belong more or less to the same class of people. They have roughly the same education. They pay dues to a local association of *grossisti,* which belongs to a national confederation. They may meet at national congresses and even at European Market congresses. They probably know each other and nod when they meet. They consider themselves colleagues in a vague way. Here all similarities cease.

The Neapolitan usually tours the countryside with his henchmen, bullying and protecting peasants in his well-defined sector, and forcing them to sell their products only to him at the prices he fixes. He defends his territory and his vassal farmers from the encroachment of competitors. He carries a gun. He shoots straight. He can kill a man if necessary. He can command killers. As everybody knows that he can enforce his will and defend his power by killing his opponents, he never, or almost never, has the need to shoot. If the farmers were to refuse to sell at his price, he can leave their produce to rot in the field. The farmers never refuse because nobody else would dare buy their products in competition with him. A superficial observer, of course, would not know what exactly was going on, what were his real relations with the farmers and retailers, and would notice none of the invisible threats and fears. Farmers, dealers, henchmen, retailers, competitors, all smile, joke, exchange pleasantries, drink wine, shake hands. They appear to be the best of friends. Only rarely something goes wrong, and the police find an unexplained corpse in a country lane. The culprits are seldom identified. Nobody usually gets killed, however, in Naples, if he is careful and plays the game.

The Milanese is an entirely different kind of man. He resembles his foreign colleagues more than his Neapolitan or Sicilian competitors. He carries no gun, is followed by no henchman, rarely sees the farmers he buys from, almost never tours the countryside. He sits in a modern office, surrounded by dictating machines, graphs on the wall, brisk secretaries. His business is carried on by telephone, with brokers and buyers in Germany, France or Switzerland, by the carload or the trainload, peaches from Verona, apricots from Naples, oranges from Sicily, grapes from Apulia, spring potatoes or cabbages from Tuscany. His only aim is to ship more and more refrigerated railway trucks abroad, filled with more and more of the fresh produce foreigners consume, at the highest possible prices. He naturally makes a lot of money, in good years one hundred or one thousand times more than his Neapolitan colleagues. But the Neapolitan does not mind. He is not unhappy about it. He wants other things than money, rarer and more satisfactory things. He wants to be well known (his sinister nickname must be recognized in the whole province); to be feared (policemen, at times, must forget they saw him go by); to be powerful (politicians must beg for his help at election time). He also wants to be loved (he will redress wrongs and protect unimportant people asking for his aid).

This, of course, is a didactic simplification, an example chosen to prove a point. Nothing is quite so simple in real life. There is no definite moral frontier between the two sections. Not all the South is purely southern, nor is all the North only northern. One finds men in northern Italy who apparently want to increase their power, authority, prestige and rank above anything else. Likewise, it is easy to find hundreds of people, in the South, who seemingly forgo all preoccupations of prestige in order to amass a lot of money. When observed closely, however, these exceptions usually confirm rather than confute the general rule. Frequently, in fact, the northerner who seems to pursue power does so only because power will generate more money, and the southerner who apparently seeks to increase his fortune really wants the added prestige which wealth brings him. There are, for instance, well-known politicians from the North, in Rome, who use their eminent position in the government in order to enrich their families; and southerners who amass possessions in order to become deputies, under-secretaries and cabinet ministers. Generally speaking, southerners tend to make money in order to rule, northerners to rule in order to make money.

The difference may not be identifiable in every individual but is always discernible in the two societies. It permeates every detail. It strengthens the contrasting characteristics of the Two Italies. It widens the gap. Official Italy, in the course of one hundred years, has apparently succeeded merely in unifying names, labels and titles, but not reality. Take a *prefetto*, the functionary appointed by the central government to rule over a province. He is always a southerner: only a southerner likes a badly paid job with power, honours and high protocol precedence. He rates the title of *Eccellenza*, like a bishop, a papal prince or an ambassador, and sits very high at any table. Nothing would be more misleading than to think that the *prefetto* in a northern province has any resemblance to his colleague in the South. In the North he is an inconspicuous bureaucrat. Few remember his name. In the South he is the ruler, a social leader. He goes to banquets, weddings, funerals, and christenings. He is surrounded by courtiers and sycophants. His word, a mere suggestion on the telephone, or a wish whispered as to himself, is law. He can still sometimes swing elections for the government. When he goes by, in his black car, people bow low and take their hats off.

It is pointless to pass judgment on either of these two societies, to determine which is more civilized, which is more likely in the long run to provide the 'greatest good for the greatest number'. There are obviously more material advantages in the North, but they do not compensate for the dangers of spiritual impoverishment, the crude hedonism, the infantile cultural and emotional life, the dreary levelling, the discipline, which are inseparable from an industrialized society. The southerner, on the other hand, employs all his faculties keenly in the daily struggle, he frequently overwhelms his competitors, he enjoys, at times, the pleasures of victory. He has time to pursue idle and wasteful passions. His life is often more intense, human, nearer nature and natural instincts. But these advantages may not compensate him for its squalor, poverty, hopelessness, insecurity and injustice.

It is worth considering what great benefits southerners have contributed to past Italian achievements. A people wholly dedicated to the rational and scientific pursuit of pure wealth inevitably becomes dull. Civilization and the graces of life flourish best where there are dedicated and intelligent people, who cheerfully accept mediocre living conditions for the sake of more satisfactory occupations and who prefer dignity, fame, authority, prestige or ease of conscience to mere money: scholars, poets, artists, novelists, saints, philosophers, jurists, eccentrics, spend-thrift aristocrats. The Mezzogiorno has produced the majority of such characters in Italian life. Italy's debt to them is great. Some of the best novels in contemporary Italy were written by southerners. Italy's greatest playwright, Pirandello, was born in a place aptly called Chaos, near Agrigento, in Sicily. Her greatest philosopher, Croce, and one of her greatest poets, d'Annunzio, were born in the Abruzzi. The State was cheaply run for decades, by generally able and honest southern bureaucrats. The universities were, and are, staffed mainly by southern professors. Her colonies were administered, her courts were manned predominantly by southerners. The Sicilians formed a nucleus of the Foreign Service, where they excelled. Some of the principal publishing houses dedicated to unprofitable culture were in Bari, Naples and Messina. They kept the Italian soul alive in the dark times of the Fascist dictatorship.

The fact that many southern traits and habits may be classified as typical of an 'agrarian', 'feudal', or 'pre-capitalistic' society is only a partial and misleading, though tempting, explanation. It assumes that southerners would be northerners if only they were surrounded with the proper political and economic structures. This is not the case. Industries, for instance, were founded at both ends of Italy at about the same time, the beginning of the nineteenth century. After the unification, under theoretically identical conditions, they declined in the South and flourished in the North. It was said authoritatively that the industrial decay was due to the fact that the South was feudal. The North, of course, was just as feudal. It was said that it was due to the fact that the South had been ruled for centuries by oppressive foreigners: most of the North had been ruled equally by oppressive foreigners.

It was also said that the North was nearer to foreign

markets. In reality it was separated from them by the Alps while the South did not lack good and conveniently located ports. Neither the North nor the South had coal mines and cheap sources of raw materials. It is believed that southern Italians were the victims of northern bureaucracy, impoverished by Piedmontese or Lombard competitors. In reality, the unified State administration quickly became predominantly southern. The political parties were soon also run by southerners. They were the men who really knew how to reach the top. Cabinet ministers, deputies, high officials did what they could to help. The decisive reason is another: the industrial revolution was not congenial to the inhabitants of the Mezzogiorno. They instinctively felt that the gains were not worth the sacrifice. They felt happier at other pursuits.

*

They had clung to their way of life, through thick and thin, in the past, sometimes heroically fighting the invaders and their novelties, sometimes accepting defeat, ignominy, poverty and desperation, in order not to betray their own nature and traditions. Like the Spanish, they sometimes carried on savage guerilla warfare in their mountains; at other times, like the Chinese, they seemed docilely to adopt foreign ways, in order to neutralize, digest and transform them into something unrecognizable, something of their own. The *Code Napoléon*, for instance, was introduced at the time of the First Empire by two French kings, Joseph Bonaparte and Joachim Murat. After a few years it had been so modified by local usage and interpretation that French lawyers could not recognize it. Even railways were adapted to the ways of the South. Tracks in northern Italy unimaginatively followed the shortest and cheapest routes between cities. In the South, they meandered all over the landscape sometimes in order to pass in front of obscure hamlets where a powerful person was born or owned a country residence, sometimes to lengthen the mileage and enrich the contractor responsible for the construction.

Southerners naturally cannot reconstruct the happy days of long ago, when Ferdinand II reigned, the Bourbon king who spoke dialect and knew his people's foibles.

He died in 1859. He used to boast: 'My kingdom is an island, protected by salt water on three sides and holy water on the fourth.' Cold northern winds sweep the land now. Foreign ways are introduced freely. The people must make believe they are like all others. Many of their ancient virtues have now officially become vices. They do not feel at ease among the new techniques of production. They are often beaten and humiliated by duller competitors, who ignore the fine points of the art of living. They cannot resign themselves to becoming *homines economici*, stupidly bent on making money. Yet, at the same time, they cannot endure their condition of 'inferior' or 'backward' people. They are proud of their past. This is the psychological heart of the *Problema del Mezzogiorno*.

*

The *problema* is nothing new. One hundred years ago, it was clearly apparent that the South deserved immediate attention. Cavour's dying words, a few months after the proclamation of the new kingdom, were dedicated to the *poveri napoletani*. In his last delirium the Prime Minister said: 'North Italy has been established. There are no longer Lombards, Piedmontese, Tuscans, Romagnuols, we are all Italians, but there are still the Neapolitans. Oh! There is a lot of corruption in their country. It is not their fault, poor people. They have always been so badly governed. It was the fault of that rascal Ferdinand. We must bring morality to their country, educate the children and the youth, create nurseries and military schools. We must not dream of changing the Neapolitans by insulting them. They ask me for government posts, decorations, promotions. They must work, they must be honest, and then I will give them knighthoods, promotions, decorations. But above all we must allow them no transgressions. Government employees must not be suspected. I will govern them with liberty and will show what ten years of liberty can do in that beautiful country. . . .'

Special laws, special projects of public works, special credits for business ventures, special appropriations for the South have been a constant feature of Italian policy since the beginning of this century. Giolitti and Mussolini dedicated some of the best years of their lives to satisfying the South's claims to particular attention. Since 1950, the new democratic republic has spent in the South more than double what had been spent in the previous half century, and will possibly go on spending a large percentage of the State revenue. Progress has been immense. Nevertheless the old ills are still present.

●

A short journey through any part of southern Italy by train or car will bear out the truth of this. Wherever he goes, the visitor will see a larger number of public structures and buildings erected with public money than in the North or in any other country in Europe. He will see first, chronologically speaking, the Cyclopean structures of his great-grandfather's time, erected by the first Bourbons, Joseph Bonaparte, and Joachim Murat, at the end of the eighteenth century and the beginning of the nineteenth. He will then see the incredible amount of construction done by Ferdinand II. All this still constitutes the majority of basic works: roads, harbours, government buildings, hospitals and schools. Then he will recognize the more familiar and modest buildings of the early Victor Emmanuel III era, the years before the first world war, followed by the more numerous, lavish and 'imperial' attempts of Mussolini to perpetuate his name and the fame of his régime in perennial marble and concrete. Lastly, he will see the glittering new buildings erected by his contemporaries, the Christian Democrat governments of this postwar period.

Each epoch shows a state of disrepair naturally proportionate to its age. In the suburbs of Naples, for instance, some of the oldest factories, built at the beginning of the century, are literally falling down. The plaster is peeling from the walls. It is sometimes impossible to read the name of the firm painted on the façade, obliterated by the sun and dust. Rotten roof-beams bend under the weight of moss-encrusted tiles. Doors hang from rusty hinges. The courtyards are littered with refuse, dilapidated machinery, weather-beaten packing cases, tin cans. The factories still run, of course. Somehow, on the verge of collapse, the wheels turn. The reason is that economic criteria are considered secondary. The factory is seldom a strictly money-making enterprise. It is not meant to function efficiently. Its shoddy products are probably cheap enough to sell on the market, but cheap because the capital came largely from public funds and not loans; the company enjoys special tax facilities, interest is kept low, and little money is spent on modernization, upkeep or renovation. Wages are (or were until a short time ago) lower than elsewhere, miserably low, in fact.

The factories built by the Fascists are somewhat better, if only because they are newer. Even so, they show no sign of improvements and no attempt to keep up with the times and technical progress. The recent post-war factories, dramatically ultra-modern, with plastic roofs and painted in the bright dazzling colours of sherbets, strawberry, peach, pistachio nut, are still in relatively good condition. Even here, however, flakes of plaster and large spots of moisture reveal their dubious future.

This is generally true also of agricultural establishments. Sometimes, near the bright new villages of the *Enti di Riforma* (the State agrarian reform and development organizations which split up the large landholdings into small farms) are the villages of similar State enterprises built back in Fascist days. They are now abandoned. (Most of the new ones are also uninhabited, make-believe villages because southern farmers anyway prefer to live not on the land but in nearby towns.) The old houses have been allowed to decay. No money is spent on their upkeep. They look like the crumbling ruins of some distant and forgotten historical era, disorderly agglomerations of huts and hovels, their roofs sprouting with weeds and wild fig bushes. Occasionally, the roof has caved in, or has been blown off, and the flora proliferates on the walls and the floors. Often doors, windows, roof-beams, sills, and other movable parts have been stolen. The ruined houses of Pompeii and Herculaneum, in the care of the Ministry of Public Instruction, are in far better condition and look newer.

This disregard for upkeep is revealing. Even today the law enabling the *Cassa del Mezzogiorno* to spend billions of lire on the development and modernization of the country contains no provision whatever for maintenance. The older generation, watching the decay of expensive projects, sadly called the region the 'Cemetery of public works'. The definition is still often used today.

The predominance of psychological and uneconomic motives is confirmed by other signs. Often the old or new structures are noticeably too elaborate, massive and expensive for the wretched town and village they serve. On both the Tyrrhenian and Adriatic coasts the traveller's eyes will rest on large harbours, equipped with granite or concrete breakwaters, quays, and adequate storage facilities. Many of these secondary ports are usually empty and silent, no more than sporadic havens for the odd fishing smack when the *buriana* blows. Likewise one comes across immense post offices where only a few letters and postcards are sent or received weekly by a small population of semi-illiterate peasants; or monumental school buildings sheltering a tiny number of children, which naturally cannot be properly heated or cleaned with the miserable sums of money allotted for the purpose. A *carabinieri* barracks in Bari, built by the Fascist régime, on the waterfront, in a location more suitable for a luxurious block of flats or a hotel, is loaded with statuary, sculptured ornaments, statues and columns, which can clearly add nothing to the efficiency of a police station.

This waste is often explained away as 'foresight', the preparation of suitable conveniences for, and the stimulation of, future growth. This is sadly contradicted by the fact that the local population and local activities have, in frequent cases, dwindled instead of increased. Nothing happened before the war and now most of the younger men emigrate, seeking employment in the North. Naturally, there are exceptions, cases of public expenditures which succeeded in creating chains of connected initiatives and investments out of nothing, but these are not many, they are usually strictly functional, and seldom dictated by a desire for prestige. It is not always that the organ manages to create the function. Many such constructions, very old, moderately old, new, or glaringly new, remind one at times of the stately imperial buildings of the Raj in old India, isolated signs of alien power and splendour.

The psychological and spectacular purpose of many of these structures is finally proved by their siting. In Palermo, for instance, there is a brand-new power station, an impressive structure built since the war. (Palermo is specially prone to display investments. After it was conquered by Garibaldi and his thousand Redshirts, in 1860, and became part of the new Kingdom, the city urgently built two opera theatres, both bigger than San Carlo in Naples, la Scala in Milan, and the Opéra in Paris.) The power station was not placed away from the public gaze, behind a hill, suitably masked so that the ugly buildings and high smoke-stacks could be forgotten, and the smoke and fumes become less obnoxious. It has been proudly placed near the harbour, in the heart of the city, thus ruining one of the most beautiful sights of all Italy, a famous panorama dear to ancient poets and painters. It has been placed in precisely the spot where in ancient days a cathedral would have been erected, consecrated to the local patron saint, or, even earlier, a marble temple dedicated to a tutelary god or to Zeus himself, a monument, that is, to whatever power the century believed could endow the city with untold benefits.

Such behaviour, sociologists justly point out, is not typical of southern Italy but of poor men everywhere, who waste what money they can get on superfluous, luxurious and showy things, while skimping on the necessary. Small backward republics, in Africa, or Latin America, which squander their meagre resources on marble monuments to the Founder and neglect building a sewage disposal plant, adequate schools or a hospital, knowingly or unconsciously are doing all they can to increase poverty, illiteracy and disease. When, however, this is done by citizens of an old European nation, many of them noted for their brilliant intelligence and culture, who have all the necessary economic knowledge, in contact with more progressive examples a few hours away, it can be considered no longer the result of blind sociological reflexes but a deliberate choice.

•

The South is no longer the same. It is changing daily, it is being developed, it is improving. The changes have been brought about by an infinite number of factors, only a few of them manœuvred by man. The South is no longer King Ferdinand's 'island': it is part of a contemporary nation, part of Europe, part of the modern world; it has not been sheltered from history and protected from the influx of world-wide trends. The large amounts of money spent in the last few years could not help having an influence. Some of the money at least was well-spent. The rest could not somehow help modify the local scene, even if not always in the direction desired.

Even war has changed things, Southerners have done their duty in strange and distant lands, from 1866 to 1945, in North Italy, the Alps, the deserts of North Africa, Spain, the plateaus of Ethiopia, Albania, Greece and Russia. Many of them also visited India, Great Britain, Germany and the United States as prisoners, during the last war. All people bring back from wars a secret resolution to lead different and more satisfactory lives, and southern veterans were no exception. Emigration of labour to North and South America and to the rest of Europe, which has been going on since the end of the last century, provoked a steady return flow of money, experienced and enriched emigrants, new ideas, new habits, and restlessness. For a century and a half, able and intelligent men from the middle classes emigrated, mostly to North and Central Italy, where they and their descendants now occupy leading positions. Southern soldiers brought back northern wives. The films and television forced the inhabitants of obscure mountain villages to gaze upon an idealized, bourgeois, well-washed, polite, law-abiding and well-fed image of the outside world. Finally the sudden and vigorous upsurge of economic activities in the last few years could not help having its effect. Unemployed and unskilled workers are now going north *en masse*. Those who remain behind obtain steadier employment and higher wages.

The change is visible. Factories rise along the main roads and the railways. More are being built. A few new industries have a difficult time, of course. They were built in a hurry, with no clear ideas, not enough credit, not enough experience, sometimes by dishonest operators. Others produce something which is produced better and cheaper elsewhere. The South believes not in specialization but in emulation. Many plants, however, are flourishing. They are the factories which nature decreed should be built in that particular spot, because of objective reasons. Some of these were erected by northern firms, taking full advantage of the legislation facilitating economic enterprises in the South, and run by northern managers. Others, like the immense steel works in Taranto, were willed and financed by the State. There are now flourishing industrial centres, here and there, comparable to those of northern Europe. A stretch of coast between Syracuse and Augusta, in Eastern Sicily, where the Greek city of Megara is believed once to have been, and where until lately there were only contorted olive trees and flocks of sheep grazing, in front of the wine-dark sea, now looks like Newark, New Jersey, or Galveston, Texas, the plains crowded with chemical factories, aerial tanks, yellow, red, and blue pipes, and intricate metal structures rising in the sky.

New quarters in decrepit cities everywhere look like Brazilia. The very delirious audacity of the architecture reveals, as it does in South America or in Nehru's India, a secret fear of appearing behind the times, anchored to ancient habits, left behind by the march of progress. Even the faces of the people have changed in the cities and more prosperous towns. The women are freer and more smartly dressed. The crowds look better fed and clothed. Street urchins wear shoes. Beggars have disappeared. Eating habits have changed. The younger people are taller and straighter than their fathers: they are determined not to eke out a living, as their ancestors have always done, no longer to resign themselves to the will of God, the favours of the mighty, the caprice of fortune, and the everlasting *miseria*.

Yet, in spite of all these considerable and sometimes incredible improvements, it would be foolhardy to conclude that the *Problema del Mezzogiorno* is definitely on its way to a solution. To begin with, the immense poverty is too old and too deeply rooted really to have disappeared. It has been mostly swept under the carpet. Its pressure still underlies everything. Most of the improvements and modernizations can be observed around a few chosen cities, a few favoured sites, and the most fertile agricultural sections. Everywhere else, where the casual visitor from the north does not usually go, around the corner from a prosperous scene, a stone's throw from the resplendent new hotels, factories or workers' housing projects, a short walk up the hills, almost everywhere in the countryside, the *miseria* is still supreme. It is better *miseria,* often comforted by new, modern conveniences, a road, a public telephone, sometimes an aqueduct, sewers, a new cemetery, a doctor twice a week, a midwife in residence, a *miseria* tempered perhaps by the distribution of American surplus flour and condensed milk to the children, free medicines to the destitute, but *miseria* nevertheless.

Even if it were to disappear, however, the problem would still not be solved. Even if the process of modernization should continue, if everybody had a roof over his head, enough to eat, relative security, medical care, an elementary education and a steady job, the moral aspects of the *problema* would not vanish. The malaise and the restlessness, the feeling of being the victims of historical injustice and the prey of other people's greed, the desire to revolt and break away from the centralized government of Rome would go on.

Southerners, of course, naturally want to live better lives, at about the standard of the average Western European, and to solve some of their most urgent material problems. They want all this but they also want something else. They want to see the gap between North and South dwindle. They want to live as well as northerners. Anything else is not acceptable. Anything else is dishonourable, damaging to their pride. They do not understand why their nordic countrymen, obviously less clever than they, should have such splendid living conditions, such wonderful factories, such awe-inspiring hospitals, and so much money, and why such things should be less impressive in the South.

Southerners will never be placated, and the *problema* buried, until the real and imaginary differences can be erased. There are a number of reasons why this is not easy. To begin with, a part of every lira spent to improve the South goes to the North. From the North come the engineers, the specialists, the managers, the contractors, the skilled workers for many jobs. From the North comes practically all the machinery for new plants and installations, even the humble pump necessary to irrigate a tiny plot of land. From the North, finally, come almost all the consumer goods, shirts, shoes, clothes, furniture, radios, television sets, and motor scooters which southerners increasingly can afford. In fact, even if some of these things are now manufactured in the South, the fact is kept secret, as southern buyers think it is safer and more honourable to wear or consume things made in Milan.

Take the *cassate alla siciliana*. It is a delicious iced cake, a Sicilian specialty, the ultimate result of tradition that goes back to the Arabs, a thousand years ago. In the North, the *cassate* are but poor and shoddy imitations. Sicily now consumes an enormous number of *cassate* industrially produced in Milan. The local product can now be found only in a few old-fashioned *pasticcerie* or cafés. The Milan product has more prestige. It is advertised on television. It can be ordered in any quantity. It is delivered by refrigerated truck to the smallest mountain village. It costs little enough. It is sanitary.

If the Sicilians ever got round to starting a *cassate* factory they would undoubtedly invade Milan with their better product and eventually the rest of Europe and the world. They do not do this, perhaps, because they can seldom set up a financial company big enough for the job. (Nobody in the South likes to be a minority stockholder. Everybody wants to be the boss. Nobody trusts his partners very far.) Southerners, then, do not like to produce what they do best: they prefer to make more prestigious things like steel, machinery, ships, and, if they could, cars. They also submit too easily to the authority of the North, even in cases, like that of the *cassate*, where their own superiority is universally recognized and indisputable.

There is a final reason, the fundamental reason. Southerners think mainly in political, not economic, terms. Even a *cassate* factory could rise in Sicily only through the initiative of some government bureau, the will of an influential cabinet minister, the intervention of an archbishop, or the decision of a political party. Most southern initiatives, in the past centuries, were the king's. They still are. Politics determine what plants will rise and where, what money shall be allotted to them, and which people will run them. It is the slower and duller northerner, without imagination, who has to rely on his own initiative, and is compelled to do things privately, on his own. As a result the race between the southern and the northern economies is uneven. It is a race between a puppet manœuvred by wires from above and a living man. Inevitably, the northern economy is more vigorous and adaptable. It is run by people mostly selected through competition, guided by experience, spurred on by the hope of gain. While the South progresses by feet, the North progresses by miles.

*

As long as the southerners do not really want just prosperity but moral equality with the northerners, they will go on spending most of their efforts and money only incidentally on purely economic aims but mainly on the display of newly-acquired or not yet acquired modernity, power and prestige. Some of their new factories will go on being monuments, not instruments to produce wealth but demonstrations that the city or region is to be considered no longer backward but modern and progressive, among the most modern and progressive in Europe. Such investments naturally do not produce exemplary economic results. Nor do they produce the required psychological effect. They do not bridge the gap between the North and the South. They increase it. Slowly, a few at a time, southerners are reluctantly discovering the bewildering fact that only investments dictated by hated northern criteria can, in the long run, produce stable southern results, the psychological, spectacular, and political effects required. They alone can, in the long run, really solve the *Problema del Mezzogiorno*. The great majority of southerners, of course, have not yet discovered this dreary and disappointing truth. Most of them, however, are the victims of the eternal Italian delusion, of confusing reality with the representation of reality, in their effort to solve an unsolvable problem: how to produce in the Arcadian past of the Bourbon kings and consume in the contemporary world of cheap and abundant industrial goods.

CHAPTER FOURTEEN

Sicily and the Mafia

GOETHE was right when he wrote: 'Without seeing Sicily one cannot get a clear idea of what Italy is.' Sicily is the schoolroom model of Italy for beginners, with every Italian quality and defect magnified, exasperated and brightly coloured. Sicilians, for example, have a genius for *sistemazione* or giving order to chaos: how many of them were law-givers, how many the first in history to indicate a new mode of expression, a new vision of reality, a new conception of the world and man? Archimedes, Stesicorus (whose future eminence as a poet was foretold when a nightingale perched upon his lips and sang), Empedocles and Theocritus (the inventor of pastoral poetry), in the remote past, and, more recently, Bellini, Verga, Pirandello and Lampedusa are obvious names. In the island, the Italian propensity for pomp, pageantry and spectacle becomes convulsed, superhuman, almost grotesque in its magnificence, stupendously overloaded with superfluous ornaments. There is no more elaborate Baroque in all Italy than that of the churches and *palazzi* of Ragusa, Comiso, Noto and Syracuse, ingeniously carved out of the local golden sandstone.

Everywhere in Italy life is more or less slowed down by the exuberant intelligence of the inhabitants: in Sicily it is practically paralysed by it. The intelligence of Sicilians is so exorbitant, in fact, that some of it had always to be exported. Their capacity to grasp situations with lightning speed, invent a way out of intricate tangles, gauge exactly the relative power of contending parties, weave wonderfully complex intrigues, coldly control their smallest acts, emotions and words, but, when it is safe, abandon themselves to generous enthusiasms, their capacity to do all these things is such that they often bewilder continental Italians as easily as continental Italians surprise foreigners from the north of Europe. The islanders are all so expert, in fact, that they neutralize each other. The simplest project, something which could be carried out anywhere else by means of a letter and a couple of conversations, becomes among Sicilians an enterprise of heroic proportions, each participant inventing diabolical schemes of his own to get the better of his opponent and, at the same time, foresee all possible schemes which his opponent will try to employ. The result is almost always the immobility of two wrestlers of equal strangth, the melancholic immutability described by Lampedusa, the 'feeling of death'.

The Sicilians' best virtues, like those of most Italians, are obviously not those of the anonymous organization man of today, but those of the ancient hero fighting, with his little group, the rest of the world. If the native of the mainland is often capable of gallantry and disinterested behaviour, the Sicilian can reach unbelievable heights of fortitude, generosity, selflessness and fearlessness. He can even accept death with open eyes or deal death impassively, without hesitation or regret, whenever he thinks there is nothing else to do, in defence of his particular, strictly Sicilian ideals. If most Italians manage at times to weave skilfully in and out of written laws, most Sicilians appear to avoid them all completely. They are the supreme masters of this skill, recognized by all Italians as the unbeatable champions.

*

Each man's individual rank is determined by the amount of fear he can generate, by the halo of fear that surrounds him. This is especially true in Western Sicily, where fear is the naked fear of death, but it is more subtly and imperceptibly true everywhere in the island. The elusive techniques developed through the ages to acquire status by scaring and intimidating an ever larger number of people are loosely known as the 'way of the Mafia'. The word Mafia notoriously means two things, one, which should be spelled with a lower-case 'm', being the mother of the second, the capital letter Mafia.

The lower-case mafia is a state of mind, a philosophy of life, a conception of society, a moral code, a particular susceptibility, prevailing among all Sicilians. They are taught in the cradle, or are born already knowing, that they must aid each other, side with their friends and fight the common enemies even when the friends are wrong and the enemies are right; each must defend his dignity at all costs and never allow the smallest slights and insults to go unavenged; they must keep secrets, and always beware of official authorities and laws. These principles are shared by all Sicilians, by the upright gentleman and the petty thief, the penniless prince living in his dusty *palazzo* or the heroin smuggler with relatives in the United States, the erudite scholar lost in his researches and the illiterate sulphur miner. These principles are also carefully preserved among Sicilians living in the rest of Italy and abroad. In fact, a Sicilian who does not feel these compulsions should no longer consider himself a Sicilian. In this sense, *mafioso* is anybody bearing himself with visible pride. 'What a *mafioso* horse!' Sicilians will exclaim when seeing a prancing stallion, well-caparisoned, with arched neck, dilated nostrils and fiery eyes. They obviously do not mean the horse is a member of a deadly secret society.

Mafia, in the second and more specialized meaning of the word, is the world-famous illegal organization. It rules over only one part of Sicily: its threats are terrifying in Palermo, Partinico or Agrigento, but are ignored in Messina, Catania and Syracuse. It is not a strictly organized association, with hierarchies, written statutes, headquarters, a ruling élite and an undisputed chief. It is a spontaneous formation like an ant-colony or a beehive, a loose and haphazard collection of single men and heterogeneous groups, each man obeying his entomological rules, each group uppermost in its tiny domain, independent, submitted to the will of its own leader, each group locally imposing its own rigid form of primitive justice. Only in rare times of emergency does the Mafia mobilize and become one loose confederation.

Nobody knows how many *mafiosi* there are. Only a minority of Sicilians are technically *mafiosi*, in the criminal sense of the word. Many do not honestly know whether they are *mafiosi* or not. Western Sicilians must, as a rule, entertain good relations with the Mafia in their native village or city quarter. They have to live there, they must protect their family, job, property or business, and want no trouble. The Mafia is for them a fact of life, one of the permanent conditions of existence, like the climate, the average rainfall or the local patois. It is often impossible to draw a neat dividing line between *Mafiosi* and non-*Mafiosi*.

Take the good friars of Mazzarino, who were recently arrested and tried for having acted as messengers between the Mafia and its intended victims, men who were being blackmailed. The pious fathers patiently explained to the non-Sicilian court that they were by no means to be considered advisers, instigators or accomplices of the criminals. They had only done their best to persuade the intended victims, to whom they brought the Mafia's blackmail message, that it was safer to pay, and pay quickly, in order to save their lives. Were not one or two men, who had stubbornly overlooked the advice, subsequently found dead in solitary country lanes? Yes, of course, the monks had written some of the messages themselves, but only because the *mafiosi* were illiterate and did not own a typewriter.

Furthermore, the friars pointed out that they were by no means responsible for the conditions of law enforcement in Mazzarino. They were not policemen. They took for granted that there were extortionists and potential victims, moneyed men whose only safety was in conforming with the Mafia's demands, and men who could live and prosper out of the fear they could evoke in others. The monks explained they were only doing their duty: they had avoided unnecessary bloodshed. Was theirs not a charitable mission? (The monks were found guilty, nevertheless, and given long prison sentences.)

Everybody, of course, knows (although such things are never admitted openly) that the trouble the Mafia defends one from is almost always contrived and controlled by the Mafia itself. Everybody knows that the tributes he is paying to the local boss could be compared to a tribute to a powerful feudal baron. Everybody is resigned. But the relationship between the Mafia and its victims is not limited to the collection of money. A day always comes when the Mafia also needs some favour in return. On that day, a man discovers he can no longer refuse. A businessman finds he must give a job to an ex-convict, a banker extend a loan to a risky customer, a farmer shelter some unknown men for a few days in a barn without asking questions, an honest man remember distinctly something he never knew or forget something he saw. All these people gradually get so enmeshed in the net, in the hope of avoiding trouble, that they cannot free themselves.

Take another example. A political candidate needs votes; the Mafia can provide as many as he wants in certain districts; he accepts them with some misgivings. Many outstanding politicians have done so, after all. Why should he not? Orlando, perhaps the highest Italian authority on constitutional law, the Sicilian who was prime minister of Italy in 1918, at the end of the first world war, and, one year later, one of the Big Four at Versailles, with Lloyd George, Woodrow Wilson and Georges Clemenceau, had always welcomed Mafia aid. In the first free election held in Italy after the last war, in 1946, a large canvas sign was put up in Partinico, near Palermo, a notorious Mafia stronghold, where he had been elected for the first time in 1897. It said: 'Vote for Vittorio Emanuele Orlando, *l'amico degli amici,* the friend of friends.' It could not have been more explicit. Everybody knew who the 'friends' were.

When a candidate is elected anywhere in the world he must show some gratitude to his electors. He must do things in return for their votes, things he may not always like. What successful candidate does not, after all, run small errands for his constituents? In Sicily he may have to recommend highly unsuitable men for a good job, write letters to cabinet ministers in defence of shady characters, get a man out of jail, block some public works project (like the construction of an aqueduct) which endangers the power and revenue of some *amico* (the owner of springs of water) and so forth. Does this practice of using the Mafia and doing them favours necessarily make a man a member or an accomplice? Moralists think so. Sicilians are uncertain. They define such men, men who can keep a secret, do favours, accept favours, but also have power and authority of their own, not derived from the Mafia, but which make them useful to the

Mafia at times, merely as *uomini rispettati,* men who exact respect from others and who should not be harmed.

Obviously the whole thing is confusing. The two Mafie are closely related. The second Mafia could not flourish if the first were not widespread. A man could scarcely prosper and get to the top in the second if he were not a master of the first. It is difficult to know exactly where one begins and the other ends. They often overlap. The phenomenon has deep roots in history, in the character of the Sicilians, in local habits; its origins disappear down the dim vistas of the centuries.

•

Nobody really knows what the word means, where it came from, where the thing originated, and why the capital-letter Mafia turned out the way it did. Sicilians mention the word reluctantly, and only to make themselves understood when talking to mainland Italians or to foreigners. They prefer to call it the *onorata società,* or honoured association, or some other name. The members are usually known as *gli amici,* the friends, or *gli amici degli amici,* the friends of friends. Sober businessmen in Palermo use a brisk, modern, businesslike term, when mentioning the influential Mafia men they occasionally turn to for help in a difficult predicament: they call them *uomini quali-ficati,* qualified men, specialists.

This much is known of the Mafia's origins: for centuries landowners used to set up private little armies of their own to defend their families and estates from marauding bandits. There were few roads, the island was wretchedly governed by rapacious foreigners, revolt against alien laws and institutions was endemic. These so-called *compagnie d'armi* maintained some sort of primitive justice by drastic means: as they had no courts of law and no prisons they had to punish the smallest crime with the death sentence. Justice was conceived as something innate in man: wrongs were righted, the weak defended, robbers punished, the outraged virgins married off to their seducers, according to what was, in reality, a rough peasant version of the code of chivalry which the Norman invaders had brought to the island in 1070, and which had been kept alive by the *teatro dei pupi,* the puppets' theatre, frequented by grown-ups as well as children, dedicated to the noble feats of Charlemagne's knights.

Even today the more traditional Mafia men try to maintain the fiction that they are not ordinary criminals but the enemies of criminals; that they do not commit crimes but are sometimes regretfully compelled to employ force in order to finance themselves and to enforce their law, which, after all, they explain, has been for centuries the only valid law in Sicily, the only defence against anarchy. In effect, the visible lives of the old high-ranking Mafia men are generally spotless. They are good fathers, good husbands, good sons; their word is sacred; they fastidiously refrain from having anything to do with spying, prostitution, drugs, or dishonest swindles. They never betray a friend. They are always devoted churchmen, who give large sums to the local parish or to the deserving poor. Many have sisters in convents and brothers in holy orders. When considering the *società,* one must not forget this remnant of the Middle Ages, this cherished rhetoric which is not wholly fictitious. It is important. It distinguishes the Sicilian Mafia from strictly criminal organizations or plain rackets, as the American so-called Mafie really are. It also furnishes a noble alibi to honest men for their collaboration.

Most leaders of *compagnie d'armi,* like the sheriffs in Western films, found it convenient at times to recruit new men among the bandits themselves, usually the older bandits who tired of life in the woods, wanted stability and longed for the respectability of family life. They were the only men around who did not fear taking risks. The dividing line between law-breaker and law-enforcer became more and more indistinguishable. It was easy for men to pass from one group to another and back again. The *compagnie d'armi* degenerated. It was tempting for them, so far from any control, to come to a working agreement with their enemies, the outlaws, so that all could co-exist and prosper peacefully. If the bandits played the game, and did their robbing and killing in other territories, they were well taken care of; if they wanted trouble, they were destroyed.

The landowner was usually far away, in Palermo or in

Naples. If he was on the spot and he discovered that his guards were the accomplices of the bandits, he was quickly placed in a distressingly awkward position. He had no choice. He had to accept the will of his men. They protected him, his family, his castle, his cellars and granaries, did they not? What did he care if they played havoc at times with his neighbours' possessions? His guards could impose their will on him. In return for their services, he naturally had to pay them a share of the crops (did one not always do that with governments?), overlook their crimes, defend them from the official authorities with his influence, and see to it that they were never punished for the outrages, kidnappings, extortions, robberies, and murders which they committed elsewhere.

The primordial and arcadian form of the Mafia with its mixture of ruthless brutality and noble sentiments still exists in Sicily wherever large estates survive. The foreign heir or buyer of an isolated estate is soon told, in a confidential, mysterious, courteous but intimidating manner, that to avoid trouble, he had better hire a certain local man as an overseer, without asking too many questions. The man usually turns out to have spent a few years in prison for robbery, arson or murder. Foreigners, in this case, include Sicilians from the east of the island. The native heir or buyer does not have to be told. He knows. He does what is necessary or sells the land to whoever is allowed to buy it from him at whatever price the *amici* decide. If the new owner is so foolish as not to understand the message, he soon grasps its implications: his vines are cut down overnight, his woods and haylofts set on fire, his sheep and cattle stolen, and perhaps one of his children is kidnapped. The police confess themselves impotent and kindly advise him to do what he was told. If he does, he will be *rispettato*: he will be honoured, served hand and foot, surrounded with feudal courtesies, loudly praised everywhere. Unknown men will take their caps off and bow low when he passes. His life will be more than safe: it will be downright paradisiacal.

Other Mafie now exist, more modern, lucrative and powerful. Most of them specialize in exacting a tribute from all sorts of economic activities. There are the cattle and pasture Mafie; citrus grove Mafie; water Mafie (who control the scarce springs, wells, irrigation canals); building Mafie (if the builder does not pay, his scaffolding collapses and his bricklayers fall to their death); commerce Mafie; public works Mafie (who award contracts); wholesale fruit, vegetable, flower, and fish markets Mafie, and so forth. They all function more or less in the same way. They establish order, they prevent pilfering, each in its own territory, and provide protection from all sorts of threats, including the legal authorities, competitors, criminals, revenue agents, and rival Mafia organizations. They fix prices. They arrange contracts. They can see to it, in an emergency, that violators of their laws are surely punished with death. This is rarely necessary. Most of the time the fact that they can condemn any man to death is enough to keep everybody toeing the line.

The supreme heads of these separate organizations are often well-to-do bourgeois, respected lawyers, renowned surgeons, or country proprietors. They have spotless records. Their manners are ingratiating, they use diplomacy rather than force, speak in a low voice and prefer to employ old-fashioned forms of address: '*Bacio le mani*, I kiss your hands.' Their politics are conservative, often reactionary: they resent all social progress which inevitably endangers their power. They want to keep things as they are. They always side with whatever government exists at the moment, as it is only from the government that they can obtain favours. They are *simpatici*. They have to be.

●

The first nucleus of the Mafia is the family. Some families have belonged to the *società degli amici* from time immemorial, each father leaving the domain to his eldest son as naturally as a king leaves his kingdom to his heir. A father always takes part in confidential negotiations with the eldest son at his side. The latter never speaks. He looks, listens, and remembers everything, in case the older man were suddenly killed. Some new families emerge from nothing. Like all new people, they must struggle with the older families, survive, and slowly assert themselves. As the years go by, they accumulate henchmen, vassals, and property, establish solid relations with landowners, businessmen, politicians, policemen and other Mafia families. Their rank is determined, at first, by the number and fearlessness of their male members and, later, by the number of useful connections they establish. In one village several Mafia families can co-exist as long as they do not compete in the same field of activity: each of them must work its particular sector and all of them be ready to unite against a common threat.

A group of powerful families, belonging to the same district, pursuing identical or related activities, sometimes finds it convenient to form a stable union which is known as a *cosca*. It is the second step in the organization. The *cosca* is not an alliance between equals: it is kept together by the recognized supremacy of one family and the leadership of its head. The word *cosca* itself comes from a corruption of the dialect term for artichoke: a composition of separate leaves forming a solid unit. The *cosca* maintains good relations with other *cosche* dedicated to different pursuits. With competing *cosche* it usually comes to a working agreement: boundaries are established, territories defined, pacts negotiated and respected. Only rarely do the *cosche* have to wage war on each other. The war takes the traditional form of all feuds: a man from one group is killed, another from the rival organization is later murdered in revenge, a third is found shot in a country lane, a whole family is exterminated in return, and so on, for years, until the original cause of the feud is practically forgotten.

A feud which cost hundreds of lives almost a century ago, between the *stoppaglieri* of Monreale and the *fratuzzi* of Bagheria, is still remembered. One of the *fratuzzi*, Salvatore d'Amico, who had lost all his family, at one point turned informer. He told the police all he knew and then said: 'I shall die killed by the Mafia. Neither you nor all the police in the Kingdom of Italy will be able to save me.' Eleven days later he was found riddled with bullets, with a cork in his mouth, the symbol of the *stoppaglieri*, and an image of the Madonna del Carmine, the symbol of the *fratuzzi*, on his chest. The two fighting *cosche* had forgotten their enmity for the time strictly necessary to punish him. He had committed what is the ultimate crime for all Mafia men: he had talked to the authorities. This is known as *infamità*. (The man who had betrayed the bandit Salvatore Giuliano was killed a few years ago in the Ucciardone jail of Palermo with a poisoned cup of coffee.)

Many *cosche* pursuing identical or similar activities often join in an alliance called *consorteria*. The group also recognizes one *cosca* as supreme and its leader as everybody's leader. This happens spontaneously, almost gradually, when the *cosche* realize that one of them is more powerful, has more men, more friends, more money, more high-ranking protectors and relations than any of the others, could do untold damage to anybody defying its will and could benefit all those who collaborate and submit. All of the *consorterie* in Sicily finally form the *onorata società*, or the Mafia. It is, as has been said, a fluid and incoherent association, with vague boundaries.

There are all sorts of degrees of affiliation: a family may operate as a unit without necessarily joining forces with other families, a *cosca* may carry on its business for years without joining other *cosche*, and a *consorteria* of *cosche* may dominate its territory independently of the island association. A sort of Mafia patriotism, however, unites all members: they know they owe all possible support to any *amico degli amici* who needs it, for whatever reason even if they have never heard of him, provided he is introduced by a mutual *amico*. Most Mafia men of any importance know hundreds of colleagues of all ranks. The great leaders meet, follow each other's activities from afar, and evaluate exactly each other's worth, as eminent men do in all walks of life. A few chiefs become especially renowned all over Sicily, for their particular qualities of sagacity, prudence, ruthless resolution, and for their successes. In the end, as a matter of course, one man is acknowledged as the most respected, trusted, and revered of all. He can generate more fear than anybody else. He is the head of the Mafia.

There are no exact rules for choosing him, no statutes, no elections, no conclave of big chiefs, no electoral body. What meetings take place are informal. In the old days, of course, in the last century, he always had to fight his way to the top and destroy his most dangerous rivals. The process was wasteful: it took years and cost hundreds of valuable lives. Nowadays he almost always emerges peacefully. His peers usually have known for years he was the best among them. At times, for brief periods, there has not been a single head but several equally revered candidates, a sort of *sede vacante,* an *interregnum.* Business, of course, goes on as usual. The chief is soon found. He is not indispensable anyway. His power is only absolute over his *consorteria;* it is nominal in the rest of the island. He does not give orders, draw up plans of action, conduct negotiations in the name of the Mafia with political powers or foreign agents. At times he may be called upon to settle a dispute, end a feud or define a boundary; very rarely he declares war against rebels in the name of the whole Mafia.

*

Legendary and still revered above all in Sicily is the name of the late Don Vito Cascio Ferro, perhaps the greatest head the Mafia ever had, who reigned from the end of the last century till the late twenties. (Don is the corruption of the Latin *dominus.* It means a little more than *signore.* It is used for noblemen, gentlemen of means, priests, and Mafia leaders.) Don Vito was born in Bisacquino, near Palermo, the son of illiterate peasants. He quickly emerged as a young man of great qualities. There was a natural aura of authority about him: people of all kinds found themselves obeying him and asking for his advice and consent for their projects without knowing why. Don Vito was the first to adapt the archaic and pastoral ways of the country Mafia to the twentieth century and the complex life of a relatively modern city. He organized all crimes, from the largest deals down to the chicken thefts and the purloining of brass coins from alms boxes in the churches. All criminals were more or less indexed in his memory and that of his henchmen; they were all licensed by him, could do nothing without the *società*'s consent, and incidentally without giving the Mafia the customary cut.

Crime there had to be, of course, as there was in every country under every régime. But in the well-ordered world of Don Vito it had to be disciplined, channelled, intelligently employed on occasion for useful purposes, and made to pay taxes. Crime was, after all, only one of the many activities of man. All of them, without exception, were chartered by the Mafia, paid a tribute to the Mafia and could be conscripted, in an emergency, to defend the Mafia's interests. For the first time in Palermo even beggars were no longer the victims of occasional abuses and impositions by petty criminals, but were enrolled in a regular organization and, like all businessmen, had to contribute a regular percentage, no more nor less, of their daily collections, to the *amico* in charge of their sector.

Discipline was such that, when a *uomo rispettato* from the country, an important politician from Rome, or a distinguished foreign guest of Sicily was robbed by mistake within Don Vito's jurisdiction, he gave an order and, in a matter of minutes, the suitcase, the watch, the wallet or the lady's jewellery was returned with apologies. Palermo was not Catania, in the east of the island, where there was no Mafia to control things and anarchy prevailed. Everybody knows what happened there to Mussolini's hat in 1923. It was a disgraceful incident. The dictator, an *uomo rispettato* if ever there was one, had arrived to visit the city and to confer with the authorities about its urgent needs. He shut himself up in the *prefettura* with the *prefetto*, the chief of police and prominent local personalities, for a long meeting. At the end he asked for his hat, a bowler hat. At the time he still dressed like a well-born clubman on the race course, wearing spats, morning clothes, and carrying a stick. Il Duce's hat could never be found. It had been stolen by some irresponsible and unknown petty thief or souvenir hunter.

Discipline in Palermo itself is today no longer what it used to be. A few years ago, after the last war, an English lady friend of the late Prince Don Raimondo Lanza di Trabia missed her expensive fur coat. The prince reassured her, sent for Don Vito's successor, and ordered him to return it. The Lanzas are one of the first families in Sicily. They arrived one thousand years ago, fought at the side of Frederick II of Hohenstaufen, King of Sicily and Emperor, in the thirteenth century. Lanzas have been advisers to kings and emperors, viceroys, generals, and admirals. Don Raimondo's late father was one of the aces of Italian aviation in the first world war. The family owned thousands of acres of land, whole towns, rivers, castles, *palazzi*, and villas. They could demand absolute *rispetto* in Sicily. The Mafia leader apologized humbly and quickly produced all the fur coats stolen in Palermo within the last few days. The lady's own was not among them. It had been stolen by a free-lance, an unknown man, perhaps a stranger from the mainland, who did not fear the *amici*.

Don Vito brought the organization to its highest perfection without undue recourse to violence. The Mafia leader who scatters corpses all over the island in order to achieve his goal is considered as inept as the statesman who has to wage aggressive wars. Don Vito ruled and inspired fear mainly by the use of his great qualities and his natural ascendancy. His awe-inspiring appearance helped him. He was tall, spare, elegantly but sombrely dressed. A long white beard made him resemble a sage, a New England preacher of the last century, or a respected judge. (He was practically illiterate.) His manners were princely, his demeanour humble but majestic. He was well loved by all. Being very generous by nature, he never refused a request for aid and dispensed millions in loans, gifts and general philanthropy. He would personally go out of his way to redress a wrong. When he started on a journey, every mayor, dressed in his best clothes, awaited him at the entrance of his village, kissed his hands, and paid homage, as if he were the king. And he was a king of sorts: under his reign, peace and order were preserved, the Mafia peace, of course, which was not what the official law of the Kingdom of Italy would have imposed, but people did not stop to draw too fine a distinction.

He admitted having killed one man in his long life, only one, and not for money, but for the honour, prestige, and preservation of the *società*. The man had challenged the Mafia as a whole and had to be killed personally by Don Vito and nobody else. He was Giuseppe Petrosino, the head of the Italian squad of the New York Police Department who had come to Palermo in 1909 to study the relations between the *onorata società* and the Black Hand organization among Sicilian immigrants. Petrosino was not Sicilian and did not know the Sicilian ways: he was from Padula, in the province of Salerno, and emigrated to the United States in 1873, when thirteen years old. He thought he was safe as nobody knew of his arrival except the police. Don Vito shot him a few hours after his landing, in the street, in the Piazza Marina, in front of the courthouse.

Don Vito was arrested in 1926, for the first and only time, by *prefetto* Mori, a tough policeman whom Mussolini had charged with the task of destroying the Mafia. Mori waged relentless war on the *società*, employing Mafia-like methods, disregarding all written laws, striking terror in the heart of everybody. He succeeded for a time. Don Vito easily established his authority over the whole prison, as a well-loved general does when incarcerated in a concentration camp among his soldiers. Order and discipline reigned there for the first time. He settled all quarrels and helped the inmates with their private troubles. He sent subsidies to the families of needy prisoners, sent rich dowries to the daughters of *amici* who were getting married, and generally continued to conduct his business from his cell as well as he could in such difficult times. He died in prison, of a broken heart. Until a few years ago one could still read a few words he had carved with a knife on the wall of the corridor of the Ucciardone prison. Prisoners read the sentence and nodded their approval long after his death. Like most memorable sayings of great men, this too expressed a platitude. It said: 'Prison, sickness, and necessity reveal the real heart of a man.' It is still considered a great honour today for an imprisoned Mafia man to occupy the cell in which Don Vito lived the last years of his life.

＊

It is surprising to discover that a man belonging to the Mafia does not know he is doing wrong. This is approximately the way he sees things. Order has to be preserved. Justice must be assured. Unfortunately, men being what they are, it is often necessary to enforce the will of the Mafia by means of violence. At times, one is also unfortunately compelled to finance the operations of the law-enforcing *cosche* by means of extortion, robbery and blackmail. Do not many organizations fighting an unjust or foreign government do the same? People get hurt, of course, but only because they are stubborn. It is often admittedly difficult to restrict the use of such methods to legitimate purposes. There are deplorable abuses. Power corrupts. All Mafia leaders are tempted by their power. Some yield and come to a bad end. The good ones do not. They are able to control their greed. The good ones are unfortunately getting scarcer. Things are no longer what they were in Don Vito's time. The Mafia is losing sight of its traditional aims, more and more of its men seem bent in violating the old rules merely to make money for themselves by all possible means. Discipline is lax. It is not so much the Mafia's fault as the times'. Similar trends are visible everywhere in the modern world. All men are today inclined to serve their private interests and forget moral duties. Nevertheless, good Mafia men still exist. The breed has not disappeared. They want, above all, to be helpful to others. This they consider their mission in life.

This is how one of them sees himself: [1]

'This is the way I was born, signor Danilo. Whenever somebody asks me to do him a favour, I do it, because Nature made me that way. . . . A man comes and says: "I have a quarrel with Tizio. Could you please help me settle it?" I call the person mentioned, or I go to see him, according to the case, and make the two men come to an agreement. It is a power I have. I am neither vain nor ambitious. I open my arms wide to all kinds of men. I cannot say no to anybody. The trouble is never such that I should deny myself. There is a feeling of duty which compels me to aid others. Often, of course, one gains people's gratitude, one makes friends, many friends, and opportunities arise when one can demand some favour in return. . . . Things follow each other, one after the other, in life. . . . My name has spread. . . . All sorts of people ask me how to vote. They feel it is their duty to ask for instructions, in order to show their gratitude for what I have done for them. They are in the dark, they do not know what to do, and want to please me. . . . Tomorrow, for instance, I must leave the threshing, my cattle, all my things, in order to go to Agrigento. I have been asked to recommend a student to his teachers, so that he may surely pass his examinations. You see how things are?'

[1] A verbatim confession, recorded by Danilo Dolci and printed in his book *Waste:* it has been slightly abridged here.

Obviously the teachers are going to give the student pass marks, no matter how ignorant and dumb he may prove to be. They are not fools. They too want to be on the right side of the Mafia man. Who knows when they will need him? He may help one to be promoted or transferred to a better residence. On the other hand, to displease him would be dangerous and, above all, pointless. Many practically illiterate boys will be promoted that same day in the same school, recommended by all sorts of important men. Why not one more? And so it goes, one favour begetting another, one favour creating the gratitude of the favoured who know they will have to do something in return when required, maybe give their votes to one particular candidate. A successful politician in Palermo or Rome can do them many favours. An illiterate chicken-thief in an obscure village can be asked to render a little service to a powerful gentleman, a small matter like purloining a compromising document or shadowing somebody. A killer can be ordered to kill a man. It is an endless chain secretly held together by fear, ostensibly held together by ties of gratitude, friendship and honeyed compliments. This is why the *mafiosi* call themselves *gli amici, gli amici degli amici* and see themselves as a vast benevolent mutual-aid association, only at times reluctantly compelled to destroy stubborn enemies and to violate official laws, in order to preserve the welfare of their members.

＊

A man who considered himself, above all, a benefactor to society, a good Sicilian patriot, and a good Catholic, was Don Calò Vizzini, the last head of the Mafia who could be compared with Don Vito Cascio Ferro; he was not as great as Don Vito, of course, who will remain a shining example for all times, but he was great enough. Don Calò was born in Villalba and died in the same place at seventy-seven years of age, in 1954. His funeral was worthy of a prince. There were bands, lines of priests and monks chanting and swinging censers. There were ink-black horses drawing the hearse, mounds of flowers, and thousands of peasants all dressed in black. There were women crying, old men with red eyes, and children wailing

All the village authorities participated; more authorities came from Agrigento and Palermo; politicians came from all over eastern Sicily and from as far as Rome. Mournful orators pronounced ornate eulogies, extolling the dead man's virtues: he had been the poor man's friend, he had never left a request for help unheeded, he had been selfless and disinterested. The traditional sign nailed at the top of the church's main door ended with the simple words: 'He was a *galantuomo*'. *Galantuomo* means an honest man, a man of his word, a man of character, a reliable man, but also a man of property: he left approximately two billion lire worth of sulphur mines, land, houses and sundry investments. He was also well-connected, for an illiterate peasant. One of his uncles had been a bishop and one of his cousins, titular Bishop of Noto, was the revered founder of the monastic order of *Maria Santissima del Carmelo*. Two of his brothers were priests, one of them a Monsignore.

Don Calò's power, while never equalling that of Don Vito Cascio Ferro, had been great. Nobody has yet succeeded, so many years after his death, in knitting the Mafia together again into one unit as he had done. When you saw him (I knew him well) you could not imagine the amount of fear he could generate. He looked harmless. He was small, slightly bowed by rheumatism, dressed in the velveteen suit of a well-to-do farmer, with a cloth cap on his head. His manners were mild and courteous. Only his eyes gave him away. They were grey-brown, wide awake, watchful, intelligent. It was instructive to see him leave his house in the morning. Villalba's *piazza* is like a little stage, ready for *Cavalleria Rusticana* to begin, with the church on one side, various *palazzi* and shabby houses all around. Don Calò would punctually come out of the little door on the square at matins and peacefully walk back and forth, his hands clasped behind his back, conversing with his brother the Monsignore.

From the shadows along the walls and the tiny side-streets emerged people who had arrived earlier, some from far away, and were waiting to talk to him. They were peasants, old women with black veils on their heads, young *mafiosi*, middle-class men. They all walked along with him in turn, explaining their problems. He listened, then called one of his henchmen, gave a few orders, and summoned the next petitioner. Many kissed his hand in gratitude as they left.

A little later he would sit at the café table, on the *piazza*, and carry on the business of the day while drinking *espresso*, an elderly farmer or cattle dealer like many others. He would nod as somebody reported an entangled business affair or proposed a plan of action. He rarely smiled. Only once in a while he would place his hand on another man's shoulder, as if to reassure, strengthen or console him. His magnanimous and protective manners, the respectful salutes of passers by, the retinue surrounding him, the humility of the people approaching him, the smiles of gratitude on their faces when he spoke to them, all reminded one of an ancient scene, a prince holding court and administering justice in the open air. Of course, the many victims of his reign were not visible, the many corpses found riddled with bullets in the countryside during more than half a century, the widows weeping, the fatherless orphans.

Don Calò's authority was strengthened by the American Army. When the U.S. forces landed in Sicily he was immediately nominated mayor of Villalba and given ample powers. He disposed of military vehicles and supplies. It was said that he had served the Americans well, before their landing, furnishing information to their emissaries, and getting the whole Mafia network ready to collaborate with them. How much truth there was in the rumours it is hard to tell. What is known is that, under the Allied occupation, he resumed all the powers which he had lost under the Fascist régime and reconstructed the *società* as it had not been for a long time, ever since *prefetto* Mori started sending *mafiosi*, including Don Calò himself, to prison or exiling them in one of the forlorn islands along the coast. He ruled, from the day the first American soldier arrived in Villalba until the day of his death, according to the old rules, with an iron hand. He was informed of literally everything that went on in his district (to supply information is one way to gain a man's gratitude), and of most things of importance that went on all over Sicily. No great business transaction was done without his consent. He was, like most old men, extremely conservative in his political views. He supported the Christian Democrats and fought all revolutionary novelties.

The communists and trade union organizers were his personal enemies. He considered them competitors, leaders of rival Mafie. When Girolamo Li Causi, the veteran Communist hero of Sicily, wanted to hold an open-air meeting in the *piazza* of Villalba, Don Calò sent word advising him against it. 'It is unsafe,' he said. Li Causi naturally knew what the mild warning meant. Being a stubborn and proud man, who respected no authorities, not even that of the *amici,* he came anyway and spoke to a small scattered crowd. At one point his speech was cut short by rifle fire: Don Calò's men were shooting at him and his listeners from the roof tops. The small crowd dispersed in a hurry. A few people were wounded including Li Causi himself, in one knee. He was left at first alone lying in the empty *piazza.* Suddenly a shadow crossed his body, an old man bowed over him and, in the silence, asked in a colourless voice: 'Can I do anything for you?' It was Don Calò himself.

*

There are Americans who believe that criminal groups in their country belong to the Sicilian Mafia, are in effect overseas branches of the main organizations, and that they are all directed by orders from Palermo. This myth is shared even by some naïve American criminals of Italian descent, who learned it by reading the newspapers. They sometimes land in Sicily believing not only that they belong to the *società* but that they have a high rank in it. At the most they are *uomini rispettati,* like all moneyed foreigners. Soon enough most of them discover to their dismay that they are considered merely strangers by the real *amici.* One of these gullible Americans was Lucky Luciano. When he arrived in Palermo, deported from the United States, the police official who had to watch his movements said: 'He believes he is a big shot in the Mafia, the poor innocent man.' Lucky Luciano went around with powerful leaders, entertained them, and visibly treated them as friends. They swindled him out of fifteen million lire by persuading him to invest money in a caramel factory. The partnership was rigged in such a way that the more money the factory made the more Lucky Luciano lost. Thus was the mastermind of the American underworld treated in his native island by the real Mafia.

The theory of a world-wide conspiracy with headquarters in Italy is also difficult to eradicate because it is comforting and plausible. It helps explain away mysterious events, accounts for unaccountable loyalties and alliances, and is very useful to justify the curious impotence of some American police organizations. The real nerve centres of the criminal groups are far away, across the seas. The head of the dragon must be cut first. And that is not the job for Americans but for Italians, foreigners, unreliable people, speaking an incomprehensible lingo.

The theory also has deep psychological roots. The international conspiracy of dark, treacherous and devious men, who use secret and unfair methods to achieve their purposes and beat fair-haired and chivalrous opponents, resemble other international conspiracies of dark and cunning men, the Jewish Bankers or the Jesuits, with secret headquarters in faraway countries. Such an organization, of course, does not exist. In order for it to exist and function it would have to be disciplined and centralized. It would be dangerous but easy to discover, penetrate, and destroy. The reason why the real Mafia cannot be fought efficiently is that it is many things at the same time but not one tight and well-run organization. It is a many-headed dragon which can continue to live for a long time with no head at all. And why, anyway, should the Mafia be able to give orders in the United States when it has no influence whatever in Catania, only a few miles away?

There is, however, some foundation for the American myth. The many Sicilian immigrants to the United States undoubtedly brought with them the lower-case mafia. They felt gallant Sicilian sentiments within their breasts and many still do. Many still keep track of their family in the old country and visit them. As all relations must, they help each other in moments of need. Many rich Americans give money for an orphanage, a hospital, a school, an aqueduct to their fathers' native villages. Some send subsidies to relatives or pay for young Italian cousins to go to school at their expense. A few of these Amer-

icans, belonging to the criminal classes, have particular
needs. Occasionally an escaped gangster finds shelter for
a short time in the farmhouse of distant relatives. He does
not stay long, of course: he can be easily spotted and
he never likes the primitive living conditions. A Sicilian
escaped criminal will naturally be helped by his relatives
to land clandestinely in the United States, be provided
with money and false papers. They would help him in
any case, even if he were honest, as long as he was in
need. (One of Salvatore Giuliano's henchmen with relatives in Boston was discovered in Texas, safely serving in
the United States Air Force under an assumed name.)
Cousins or friends collaborate to smuggle drugs out of
Palermo to American ports, but such traffic notoriously
goes on in every port of the world: heroin is carried to
the United States in ships of all flags by men of many
nationalities, and not by Sicilians alone. There are rela-
tionships of all sorts between Sicilian criminals and American criminals of Sicilian descent, but they are haphazard,
spontaneous, disorganized relations, and scarcely amount
to an international conspiracy. Clearly no order from
Palermo can decide vital matters in the United States
underworld.

*

Sicilian immigrants to the United States found themselves
surrounded by an alien and hostile society. They had to
cope with an incomprehensible language, puzzling customs, rigid laws, and what they considered an oppressive
régime. They felt cut off, for reasons they did not quite
understand, from access to the good things in life, wealth
and authority. They clung to what could give them protection and comfort, the Church, the family, and their
ways. They soon discovered that the arts their people had
developed in the old country to neutralize alien laws were
also useful in the new. The forefathers had beaten the
Arabs, the Normans, the Anjou kings, the Spanish, the
Austrians, the Bourbon kings, and the Piedmontese; the
descendants endeavoured to employ the same means to
survive and prosper in America. That they felt themselves
a minority on the defensive is borne out by one of the
names of their criminal organization, *Cosa Nostra.* It

means 'our own affair, something which must be guarded from intruders'. In fact, they discovered that the ancient arts were far more useful in America and went farther. The Americans were generally trustful, unprepared to defend themselves from guile, often unwilling to fight for what they considered small stakes.

All Sicilians in the United States, among whom the criminals were a small minority, followed the same old rules, the only ones they knew anyway, a sharpened version of those all Italians follow. They are not *per se* dishonest, but they can be employed effectively for the achievement of dishonest ends. Of course, the rules are best in fields like politics and big business where power is a predominating factor, less useful where personal capacity rather than pressure is indispensable. They helped many honest Sicilians in the United States and their descendants to reach higher and higher rungs in the social ladder.

In order to beat rival organizations, criminals of Sicilian descent reproduced the kind of illegal groups they had belonged to in the old country and employed the same rules to make them invincible. The convicted American gangster, Joseph Valachi, once explained the facts of life of the Sicilian village, probably as old as Mediterranean civilization, the principles guiding Homeric kings and heroes in their decisions, to a Senate committee and an awe-struck twentieth-century television audience. He patiently pointed out that an isolated man was a dead duck in the American underworld; that he had to belong to a family, his own, or one which accepted him; that families were gathered in large groups, the groups in alliances, and the alliances in a loose federation called *Cosa Nostra*, governed by an unwritten code. When he spoke, officials of the F.B.I. exposed diligently-designed graphs illustrating the ramifications of *Cosa Nostra* families. He revealed that the organization was, more or less, what it had been in Sicily sixty years ago, before Don Vito Cascio Ferro reformed it. It still needs a lot of killing to preserve a precarious peace and to determine who is to be Numero Uno. He also revealed that the Sicilian criminals in America had abandoned the feudal pretences of their fathers. They no longer pretended to be interested above all in peasant justice for the oppressed; they were interested in dollars, and made money in activities which the older men would have considered unworthy of them, brothels and drugs.

His view of things was partial. It could be compared to a panorama of Napoleonic history as seen by an infantry corporal. War is the extension of policy by other means in the Mafia too. Valachi knew nothing of the long negotiations between leaders, the plans they conceived, the truces they had enforced and the successes they achieved without shedding blood. All he knew was what happened when war broke out, the gunmen marched and rebel factions had to be wiped out. He did not know the real triumphs of *Cosa Nostra* were the silent and unsung ones, when the money flowed in peacefully. More and more, in fact, the leaders abandon criminal activities, manage to infiltrate more or less legitimate business, like gambling, or some really legitimate business, where they establish a monopoly. The monopoly, if closely scrutinized, shows the old arts at work. Nobody dares compete with them because they can destroy a rival, in many ways, and, if need be, have him wiped out. Such men Valachi never met. Even the F.B.I. does not know all their names and, if it did, could pin nothing on them. They live far from their activities, legal or illegal. They contact one or two trusted lieutenants to control a vast sector, deal in cash, never use the telephone, travel seldom, give money to charities, and lead unimpeachable private lives.

*

There is no denying that the Mafia in western Sicily is fundamentally a criminal organization, which causes great suffering among the people, condemns a majority of them to a primitive life of shame, squalor, poverty, hunger and fear. It fights and prevents almost all possible progress. Nobody wants to invest his money and improve things when the will of unknown persons can arbitrarily stop all his activities and ruin him at a moment's notice. Only a few *uomini rispettati,* who come to an agreement with the *amici,* dare to do so, and they have to pay a price. Not even a fearless and disinterested politician can triumph against ruthless rivals, if they are supported by such a vast network of powerful friends and accomplices.

The Mafia, however, is not this alone. If it were only a criminal organization, bent merely on robbing and killing for money, it would provoke a wave of resentment; it could be fought and destroyed. It is believed to be also a spontaneous way, developed by the people themselves through many centuries of misrule, to administer a rough and archaic form of justice, a way to keep one kind of peace and ensure the safety of the inhabitants, an *ersatz* of legal government. To defeat it, the State should first make the Law supreme. Sicilians should be made to feel that they are safe to confide in the police. Things being as they are, the police cannot guarantee anybody's immunity, while the *amici* can, and furthermore can also bestow other untold benefits.

The situation is worse now than it ever was. The Mafia is rapidly degenerating. It is a cancer which destroys all healthy tissues. It is the exaggerated, cancerous form of the milder disease prevailing in all Italy. The art of living, of defending oneself with one's own power, of supplementing the defectiveness of the State with one's own private virtues, corrupts, in the end, all forms of sound government, obstructs the functioning of all legitimate organs, and makes the correction of defects in the government apparatus almost impossible.

CHAPTER FIFTEEN

Fornovo and After

*What was this beautiful land in the midst of which
[Charles VIII's soldiers] found themselves, a land
whose princes poisoned while they smiled, whose
luxuriant meadows concealed fever, whose ladies
carried disease upon their lips? To the captains and
the soldiery of France, Italy already appeared a
splendid and fascinating Circe, arrayed with charms,
surrounded with illusions, hiding behind perfumed
thickets her victims changed to brutes and building
the couch of her seductions on the bones of murdered men. Yet she was so beautiful that, halt as
they might for a moment and gaze back with yearn-
ing on the Alps that they had crossed, they found
themselves unable to resist her smile. Forward they
must march through the garden of enchantment,
henceforth taking the precaution to walk with drawn
sword, and, like Orlando in Morgana's park, to stuff
their casques with roses that they might not hear the
siren's voice too clearly. It was thus that Italy began
the part she played through the Renaissance for the
people of the North. 'The White Devil of Italy' is
the title of one of Webster's best tragedies. A white
Devil, a radiant daughter of sin and death, holding
in her hand the fruit of the knowledge of good and
evil, and tempting the nations to eat: this is how
Italy struck the fancy of the men of the sixteenth
century. She was feminine and they were virile; but
she could teach them and they could learn. She gave
them pleasure; they brought force.*

J. A. SYMONDS (*Renaissance in Italy*)

THE year 1492 is one of the notorious watersheds of
history. In that year Columbus discovered America;
Cardinal Roderigo Borgia was elected Pope and took the
name of Alexander VI; Spain became a nation by the
conquest of Granada and directed her unspent impetus
to foreign fields; Lorenzo de' Medici, *Il Magnifico*, died.

These were all irreparable disasters for Italy. The discovery of America (followed a few years later by the opening of the Indian seas) diverted world commerce into new channels; Alexander VI made the German reformation and the English schism inevitable; Spain's consolidation prepared the way for the domination of Europe by Charles V, King of Spain, Archduke of Austria, and Emperor of the Holy Roman Empire; the death of Lorenzo destroyed the fragile construction of balancing alliances, built by him, which had kept Italy at peace and safe from foreign attacks.

That same year Charles VIII of France, who had just come of age, received secret emissaries from Italy. They had been sent by Ludovico il Moro, Lord of Milan, a treacherous man, who thought he would try on the inexperienced young king one of the perennial ploys of Italian politics, that of inviting a foreign potentate to Italy to fight one's enemies. Ludovico's enemy of the day was, for complicated reasons, the King of Naples. The secret emissaries proposed to Charles the conquest of Naples, offered to finance his expedition, and assured him free passage through north Italy on his way south. Charles had been selected because he had a feeble claim to the throne of Naples. (All kings, of course, have feeble claims to practically all thrones. King Victor Emmanuel III of Italy, for instance, had vague pretensions to the throne of the Stuarts, and also called himself to the end, in official documents, 'King of Cyprus and Jerusalem'.) The Milanese emissaries never hoped their absurd and dangerous proposal would get more than a half-hearted welcome. Why, after all, should the King of France, who had many important things to attend to, risk his power, wealth and life so far from home for such a puny prize?

'Providence,' says J. A. Symonds with solemnity, 'deigns frequently to use for the most momentous purpose some pantaloon or puppet, environing with special protection and with the prayers and aspirations of whole peoples a mere mannikin. Such a puppet was Charles VIII.' This is the way Guicciardini describes him: 'From infancy he had been weak in constitution and subject to illnesses. His stature was short and his face was ugly, if you except the dignity and vigour of his glance. His limbs

were so disproportionate that he had less the appearance
of a man than of a monster. Not only was he ignorant of
liberal arts, but he hardly knew his letters. Though eager
to rule, he was in truth made for anything but that: for
while surrounded by dependents, he exercised no authority over them and preserved no kind of majesty.' This
dim-witted and deformed king usually did what his sycophants and counsellors wanted him to do. They were, in
Guicciardini's words, 'men of low estate, body-servants
for the most part'.

Charles did not laugh in the emissaries' face. He did not
reject their proposal as a deadly trap and lock them up in
prison. He listened attentively to their words. In fact, the
more he thought of it the more he liked the idea. The
reason was that it fitted in with an old dream of his own,
inspired by his youthful reading of fashionable romances.
He wanted to defeat the Infidels, conquer Constantinople,
and be crowned the Roman Emperor of the East. To do
that he could use Naples, its army, fleet, treasure, and
handy ports. Of course, he had France to think of first. The
country was restless, the army weak, the treasury empty;
foreign enemies threatened every border. Before he started
on his Italian venture, Charles bought peace from England with Ludovico's money; appeased Emperor Maximilian
by the concession of a few vital provinces; gave Ferdinand
of Spain (a relative of the King of Naples) the strong
places in the Pyrenees, the key of France's defences, as
prize for his neutrality. Once he had made his country
absolutely defenceless, he proceeded to take every able-
bodied man away from it. He gathered a new army, concentrated stores and ships in the ports of Genoa and
Marseilles, and began moving south to Lyons. This was in
1494, 'a year', says Guicciardini, 'most unfortunate for Italy,
the very first of our disastrous years'.

The coming invasion was regarded in Italy with uneasy
fascination. Only a few people thought Charles was mad
and was courting disaster. He would stretch his communication lines to a dangerous point, they said, and, once
he was deep in Italy, his way back to France could easily
be cut and his army destroyed. Many prepared themselves
to welcome the French. In Florence, the friar Savonarola,
divinely inspired though widely off the mark, preached of

Charles as *flagellum Dei*, the scourge of God, appointed to regenerate the Church and purify the founts of spiritual life. A large number of Italians, as they were to do on numerous successive occasions, convinced themselves that the foreign invaders were coming really to rid them of their bad governments and of their dishonest rulers, and to set up model régimes in which worthy natives would finally hold the principal posts. The vast majority were just frightened. They could not help shuddering at the thought of what the impending arrival of the 'barbarians' might bring upon them. They admitted that whatever calamities were in store, they deserved them. In fact, Ludovico il Moro had done no more, in the view of many of his countrymen, than bring down by a breath, as it were, the avalanche which had been long impending.

The princes of Italy, led by the King of Naples, hurriedly started intense diplomatic activity to form a defensive alliance. They visited each other, kissed, exchanged special ambassadors, letters, gifts and orders of chivalry. They swore solemnly they would be true to each other to the end, whatever that was going to be. They drew up excellent military and political plans. They appeared full of confidence. Italy had the best generals, more money, troops, supplies and weapons than France. Military art had no secrets for the Italians. Furthermore, they were fighting on home ground, close to their stores, on terrain they knew foot by foot. They arranged to place bodies of soldiers in strategic spots, where they would do most harm. In spite of the fact that, on paper, the odds were with them, they did not feel at ease. Next to the King of Naples, Pope Alexander was most frightened: he dreaded the assembly of a Council which might possibly depose him from the throne he had bought by simony. So strong was his terror that he even sent ambassadors to the Sultan of Turkey, imploring him for aid against the most Christian King, but Bajazet II was too far off and too busy to be of use.

The defensive plans could easily have been successful if they had been adhered to. But that absolute agreement which is necessary for the execution of any large and effective scheme, always difficult to preserve in any alliance, was impossible among Italians. Nothing, in fact, turned out exactly as planned. Some leaders, of course, were brave, but could do little by themselves. Some were simply inept. Many were sceptical: after more than a century of bloodless battles and parade campaigning, mainly decided by bribes, they thought the French were going to be only a little more difficult than Italians. Others were just careful. What, they reasoned, if Charles was going to win, after all, and decided to punish those who had fought too valiantly against him? One never could tell what barbarians would do. Would it not be better, then, these wise men thought, to put their money on both *pair* and *manque*, to be on both sides at the same time? They had to think of their families. Many princes surreptitiously sent emissaries to the French camp or made friends with French courtiers, while they carried out their orders with studied slowness and without enthusiasm.

Charles VIII left Vienne, in the province of Dauphiné on August 23, 1494, with 3,600 men-at-arms, the flower of French chivalry, 6,000 Breton archers, 6,000 crossbowmen, 8,000 Gascon infantry, 8,000 mercenary Swiss and German soldiers. He crossed the Alps at the Montgenèvre pass, without striking a blow, arrived safely in the plains below, and entered the city of Asti on September 19. The trip could not be done more quickly today on good roads, in peacetime, by men on foot or on horseback. Neither Piedmont nor Montferrat (the first Italian principalities he crossed) stirred to hinder him, for a reason which was typical of Charles' luck. The two ruling princes were children at that time, the Duke of Savoy was twelve years old and the Marquis of Montferrat fourteen. Their mothers and guardians quickly made terms with the French, to avoid trouble, and allowed them a free passage.

From then on it was but a promenade to Naples. The Neapolitan fleet sailed too late to effect a desired rising in Genoa and stop the French supplies from landing. The Neapolitan troops sent north never went further than Cesena, on the Adriatic. Other allied armies were retarded, enfeebled, and divided by the necessity to stop and fight small wars and mutinies. Venice played a watchful game; she aimed to intervene, when everybody else was exhausted, on the side of the winner. Piero de' Medici of Florence, who held the Apennine passes and could have stopped the invaders with little effort (he held the line on which weak and defeated Kesselring easily kept the mighty Allied armies at bay in the winter of 1944), rode as fast as horses would carry him to the French camp and delivered to Charles the keys of all his mountain fortresses, and also those of Sarzana, Pietrasanta, Pisa, and Leghorn. This relieved the French of the difficulty of forcing their way along a narrow plain, hemmed in on one side by the sea and on the other by a high and abrupt mountain range. At the news, the Florentines rose in fury against their lord. When Charles entered the city, on November 17, it was a free republic once again. The people cheered him as their liberator.

He rode, armed at all points, to the palace of the Medici and told the elders he had come as conqueror and not as a guest. He asked for huge sums of money. Money had been one of his persistent worries. He never could have enough. The Florentine secretaries refused his terms. He peevishly insisted. Then Piero Capponi snatched a paper on which they were written and tore it before his eyes. Charles, who had kingly dignity, warned him: 'We shall sound our trumpets.' Capponi answered: 'We will ring our bells.' At the sound of the tocsin each house would have been turned into a fortress, the streets barred by iron chains, and every quarter would have poured forth men by the hundreds. Charles covered his disappointment with a bad pun in Italian. 'Ah, *Ciappon, Ciappon,*' he said, *'voi siete un mal Ciappon.'* The 'bad capon' did not ring his bells, after all. Florence agreed to pay Charles 120,000 florins on condition that he move on.

He reached the Porta del Popolo, in Rome, on December 31, 1494. At three o'clock in the afternoon began the entry of the French army. It was nine at night before the last soldier and the last carriage defiled through the gates, in the glaring light of torches and *flambeaux.* The people cheered themselves hoarse. *'Francia, Francia!'* they cried. The spectacle was indeed magnificent. There were gigantic Germans and Swiss flaunting plumes and emblazoned surcoats, the chivalry of France with silk mantles over their armour and gilded corselets, the king's Scots guard in their strange tartan uniforms, the terrifying German *landsknechte* with their scythe-like halberds. The people cheered also because they hoped the Pope and all his family would soon come to a bad end. Alexander VI prudently shut himself up in Castel Sant'Angelo. How would the conqueror deal with him? At Charles' side were the Cardinals Ascanio Sforza and Giuliano della Rovere (later Pope Julius II), urging him to summon the Council. But one of the king's trusted courtiers, a certain Briçonnet, managed to turn the destinies of Rome, the Borgia family, the Church and all Christendom. The husband of the daughter of the king's silversmith, the father of five children, Briçonnet wanted badly, for some reason, to become a cardinal. He convinced Charles that he should compromise.

The king abandoned the idea of the Council in exchange for money, a few fortresses, a red hat for Briçonnet, the Pope's son Cesare and Djem, the brother of the Sultan of Turkey, as hostages. (How Djem happened to be in Rome is a long story. The Sultan wanted his brother dead but strangely enough did not want to kill him or have him killed in Constantinople. He sent him to the Pope, to keep at a yearly pension of 40,000 ducats, with the secret understanding that Djem would soon be done away with. Nobody wants to see a guest die who pays 40,000 ducats a year. The Muslim prince enjoyed excellent health for a time at the Roman court, where many courtiers and prominent members of the household were killed every week. He died, however, probably poisoned, soon after he became the guest of Charles. It was thought that Alexander, in the end, had preferred to keep faith with the Sultan rather than with the King of France.)

After a month's stay in Rome, he was welcomed, cheered and fêted by the Neapolitans who are always delighted by a change of masters. As he had done everywhere else, Charles dedicated himself to pleasure. He enjoyed dances, tournaments, feasts, banquets, and the love of the most beautiful, ardent and well-born ladies of the city. Soon enough (as all the conquerors of Naples did after a while), he began boring and irritating the people. With his posturing he made himself *antipatico*. He exacted enormous tributes and distributed all profitable offices, titles and fiefs of the kingdom among his retinue.

On May 17 he managed to cover himself with ridicule.

He rehearsed what he hoped would be the crowning triumph of his expedition by parading the streets dressed as the Emperor of the East, with the robes and the paraphernalia he had invented for his coronation in Constantinople. He carried an orb in one hand, a sceptre in the other, and a large crown on his head. (Such premature performances bring bad luck, as all Neapolitans know. What happened, for instance, centuries later, to Mussolini, when he shipped his favourite white horse by plane to North Africa in preparation for his entry as a conqueror in Alexandria? He never entered Alexandria, lost North Africa, and barely managed to get the horse back alive.) A few days after this ill-omened exhibition, news reached Charles that behind his back the Italians had formed a league and were making earnest preparations to cut his retreat and crush him. Naples was obviously becoming a trap. He decided to return home as fast as he had come.

Italian patriots, who had suffered seeing their country trampled and humiliated, aware of what would surely follow if the King of France was not severely punished for his daring, had somehow managed for once to get most of the princes, the Pope, Milan, Florence and Venice to agree to put an army together and challenge the French. Brave people openly spoke of the 'war of Italy against her enemies', of the 'liberty of Italy' which they had to defend, as if 'Italy' really existed, and was not merely, as the Military and Sovereign Order of the Knights of Saint John always properly called this country, 'the Italian language'. But in Italy patriotism has rarely been the predominant moving force. Most members of the league joined it not merely for love of their country but because it looked like the safer, or less unsafe, thing to do at the moment. It was obviously dangerous to back the King of France, at this point, or aid him with one's neutrality. He was at the end of his resources and possibly of his luck. Where could he go from Naples, practically at the dead end of Italy's narrow peninsula? He was no longer the same man: he did not behave as a victorious conqueror should. His decisions were increasingly erratic. He had little money left. His army was tired, discontented, and decimated by syphilis, the new dread disease which the Spanish had brought back from America, and which the French had met in Naples. Alexander Borgia, who was witty, had said that the French had conquered Italy with lumps of chalk and wooden spurs, because they rode unarmed in slippers and sent couriers ahead to mark the doors of the most comfortable houses in which to spend the night. Obviously, the achievements of their conquest could be as easily effaced as the chalk marks they had left behind. It was clearly more prudent in 1495 to join the league.

✻

The army of the Italian league met the French in north Italy, near the village of Fornovo, on July 6, 1495. Fornovo is on the river Taro, at the northern end of the Cisa pass across the Apennines, between Sarzana and Parma. The place was chosen because the French had passed through it on their way to Naples and it was thought they would pass it again on their way home. Near Fornovo the road along the river-bank begins to straighten out and to descend gently to the plain below, after having meandered for many miles through narrow gorges, between precipitous walls of rock. Upstream, the valley would have been a good place for an ambush; downstream, it was wide and flat enough for the manœuvring of cavalry squadrons and the evolutions of foot soldiers, yet narrow enough to constrict all movements within a well-defined battlefield.

The French numbered about 9,500 fighting men, most of them weary with long marches, insufficient food, and weakened by disease. They were afraid of the approaching encounter (they were experienced enough to know that their position was desperate), disheartened because they had to abandon their conquests without honourable reasons, and, having not fought for a long time, had lost the old zest for battle. Their opponents numbered about 30,000 men, all fresh, well-armed and well-provided. They were confident of victory. The Italian-born among them (the overwhelming majority) knew they were fighting a decisive battle for their country, win or lose, all or nothing, on their home ground, against an inferior enemy who had humiliated them all. In command was one of the best generals of the time, Francesco Gonzaga, Marquis of Mantua, surrounded by the men of his family and by a few expert and trusted *condottieri*. Gonzaga had chosen the spot and the time. He had drawn up a clever and apparently unbeatable plan of battle.

The French advanced carefully that morning, knowing they were to meet the enemy at any moment. They were prepared for the usual, the frontal attack which the medieval military technique considered the only form proper for gentlemen. They sent their baggage, supplies, provisions, *impedimenta*, including the royal treasure (a caravan of between 5,000 and 6,000 loaded mules), to the hills parallel to the road, so as not to be encumbered by them during the fight. In the vanguard they placed 350 heavily armed knights, what was left of the flower of the French chivalry, followed by the Swiss infantry, 3,000 men in their typical formation, marching shoulder to shoulder in a solid square bristling with long and sharp spears. The rest of the army, personally led by Charles, followed at regular intervals. The Italians were to be broken up by the French knights, then dispersed by the sturdy Swiss, decimated by the king's guard of Scottish archers and French crossbowmen, and finally given the *coup-de-grâce* by the rearguard of 300 French men-at-arms.

Gonzaga was too clever to do exactly what the French imagined he would do. A frontal attack, of course, might have assured him the victory, as he had numerical superiority, but at a heavy cost in human lives. He preferred a different plan, something new and unusual, which Captain Liddell Hart calls the 'indirect approach' and was employed by all the great victorious generals in history. For this, too, the Italian commander awaited the enemy where the valley widened and there was room to move. This is what he planned. As the French carefully filed in formation along the road on the left bank of the Taro, the Italians were to pin down the vanguard (as he expected) with repeated attacks of light cavalry units. While this was going on, two columns of heavy cavalry, led by Francesco Gonzaga in person and by his best *condottiere,* Bernardino Fortebraccio (whose name fittingly means Strongarm), were to go swiftly up the opposite (or right) bank in a surprise move; they were to ford the river simultaneously at two points, attack the French flank, spread panic, break up their orderly formation, drive them against the side of the hills, cut the column in sections, and massacre each separately. Unfortunately things did not exactly work out as planned. This is what really happened.

The French vanguard was pinned down, for a time at least, by the Stradioti (the swift light horsemen which Venice had recruited and trained in Dalmatia and Albania to fight the raids of the swift light Turkish horsemen across the border). The Stradioti, armed only with scimitars, were not meant to last long against the heavy cavalry and the Swiss. They were ordered only to harass the enemy and to disengage quickly. The time they afforded Gonzaga and Fortebraccio for their enveloping moves was short. But the unusually heavy rains had raised the level of the river that day and had made the fords impassable. Gonzaga tried vainly to cross where he was supposed to do but lost many men and horses, who could not swim encumbered as they were by steel armour, and were washed away by the rushing waters. He made several stubborn attempts, which took up precious time, and finally decided to try once more farther upstream, where the valley was narrower, the river shallower but more impetuous.

His difficulties immediately revealed his plan to the French. They saw the threat to their flank, turned to face it and prepared for the attack. Many of Gonzaga's men managed, in the end, to reach the right bank, but only at the same ford which Fortebraccio's men were using. As a result the two columns got inextricably entangled. Then they found another unexpected obstacle, an almost unsurpassable barrier, a deep canal with steep and slimy banks of clay which fed water to a mill. More knights and horses were lost. More precious minutes were wasted. At this point, the French, who had rearranged their formation, attacked the Italians, to take full advantage of their difficulties, with the desperate courage of men fighting for their lives, far from home, their backs to the wall.

Within a few minutes the fighting became a disorderly massacre at close quarters, the bloodiest battle that had been seen in Italy in two centuries. The lances broke and the men hacked at each other with swords and pikes. What was left of the Gonzaga and Fortebraccio contingents charged time and again, wildly crying, '*Alla morte! Alla morte!*' and '*Italia! Italia!*' The ground was quickly strewn with dying and dead men and horses. Knights who had lost their mounts fought on foot. At one point, in the confused mêlée, Gonzaga sighted Charles fighting desperately at the head of a small group of men (Charles was a brave and able soldier, trained in tournaments). The Italian gathered a few men and charged once more. This could have been the turning-point. He knew it. But when he was on the point of capturing or killing the king, Gonzaga's horse was wounded and he was dismounted. Fortebraccio had been killed a few minutes before. Charles was saved. Gonzaga was left practically alone, on foot, to do what he could merely to save his own life.

The final result was disorderly and confused butchery, complete chaos. When night came, Charles managed to sneak away, with whatever troops he had left, quickly reached Asti and crossed the Alps. Nobody pursued him. Four thousand dead men were left on the battlefield, two-thirds of them Italian.

*

Fornovo is the turning-point in Italian history. The distant consequences of the defeat are still felt today. If the Italians had won, they would probably have discovered then the pride of being a united people, the self-confidence born of defending their common liberty and independence, Italy would have emerged as a reasonably respectable nation, capable of determining her own future, a country which adventurous foreigners would think twice before attacking. Nobody would have ventured lightly across the Alps, for fear of being destroyed. The European powers would have been discouraged from endlessly quarrelling over Italian politics and from cutting slices of Italian soil, with their defenceless and laborious inhabitants, in order to placate dynastic rivalries and satisfy everybody's greed. The history of Italy, Europe, and the world would probably have taken different tacks. The Italian national character would have developed along different lines. The voices of patriots would not have been mocked but respectfully heeded. When unity and independence finally came in the nineteenth century, the old habits were set. They could not change easily—De Commynes records that the fighting proper lasted at Fornovo for a quarter of an hour, the pursuit and the killing of the routed Italians three quarters of an hour more. Thus the destiny of Italy for centuries was gambled away in fifteen minutes.

Why did the Italians lose at Fornovo? Certainly not because they were cowardly. It was the kind of battle they understand and in which they always fight valiantly, a battle in defence of their country and their own honour, against a hated foreign enemy. The odds were on their side. All contemporary reports agree that the men engaged had shown themselves as brave as the French and had faced death heroically even after they realized all hope was lost. There were other reasons for the defeat, which historians never tired of analysing.

First of all, the will of God. Charles had been lucky ever since he had left France, as lucky as a child or a drunken man. Innumerable times he had squeezed through terrible dangers without realizing it. His army could have been stopped, decimated, or destroyed by any one of many causes, avalanches in the Alps, the timely arrival of a body of troops at a mountain pass, the resistance of a single fortress, the revolt of the loyal peasants. His luck was so scandalous that many people (Guicciardini among them) thought the expedition was divinely sustained and guided. The words *'Dieu montrait conduire l'entreprise'*, or 'God seemed to lead the enterprise', recur many times in the *Mémoires* of De Commynes, who had accompanied the king as political adviser. It never rains in July in Italy. It is the month when the countryside is parched, the fields become as hard as city streets, the springs dry up, the cattle show their ribs, and rivers are reduced to small rivulets. The Taro was swollen and impetuous that day as it usually is for only a few weeks in winter. Gonzaga's plan, depending as it did on the swift simultaneous crossing of the river at two points, was, first of all, clearly defeated by Charles' luck and the weather. The ground was spongy, soft, and slippery, bad for all heavy cavalry but decidedly worse for horsemen attacking than for those on the defensive.

The daring novelty of the complex Italian plan undoubtedly contributed to the disastrous conclusion. Gonzaga chose the more difficult terrain downstream also because he could better deploy and move his men about, taking full advantage of his numerical and mental superiority to the French. He had forgotten, however, that, in the kind of battle he had envisaged, in order to execute manœuvres in the open, and eventually to change plans to face unexpected events, he had to have, first of all, a docile instrument in his hands, homogeneous troops, ready and capable to obey orders or to improvise their own movements as the need arose. What he had instead was a random collection of contingents, brought together at the last minute for the encounter, variously trained, experienced, armed and reliable. When things went wrong each body of troops did what it thought best: some rushed to the fray and died, some ran away, some gathered booty, and some waited patiently to be told what to do next or to see who was going to win. Undoubtedly those who sacrificed themselves were many; the Venetian company of infantry commanded by Gerolamo Genova, to mention one unit, did their duty: they rushed where the fighting was heaviest and lost two hundred men out of three hundred. On the other hand, there is no doubt that the Milan contingent of Ludovico il Moro spared themselves, for lack of orders but probably also for political reasons.

But even if the army of the league had been a uniform, docile and disciplined instrument, Gonzaga could not have utilized it. He had planned a modern battle but had taken part in it as an old-fashioned medieval leader. He plunged into the fray, charged time and again at the head of his men, looking for victory or death. He should, of course, have remained safely, to one side, on a hillock, in order to observe the course of the events with calm, and take the only decision which could have saved the day: send the reserves where they would do most good at the opportune moment. This he could not do. Most of the time he was isolated, in contact with but a few men around him, too busy saving his own life and killing Frenchmen to think of the battle as a whole. He was never able to modify his earlier orders and to adapt his plans.

Contemporary chroniclers pointed to the defection of the Stradioti as the principal cause of the defeat. This is, after the rain, the favourite explanation of Italian historians, because it assuages wounded national pride. Where were the Stradioti, after they had stopped harassing the vanguard? They disappeared from view. They had sighted the train of mules with the French baggage on the hills and had started in pursuit. At that tragic moment, when the arrival of one more fresh squadron could have won the battle, the Stradioti were gathering booty: it was valued at 300,000 ducats and included the king's helmet, his sword of office, his seals, part of his archives, the Dauphin's portrait, the portable altar, and several holy relics.

Duodo, their surviving commander, was immediately arrested, tried, and demoted. He defended himself with ability: he was the first to point out, at his trial, that Gonzaga should not have lost himself in the fighting but should have kept to one side, in order to control the reserves. It is to be remembered that the Stradioti were what they were, irregular troops, trained for one kind of war only, the swift hit-and-run raids against enemy camps, caravans, and cavalry. The principal objective in such wars had always been the enemy's treasure, including women, slaves and cattle. The Stradioti followed their instinct and did what they had always done. Being foreigners and mercenaries, serving the republic of Venice for money and a share of the booty, they were not sentimentally involved in the final outcome anyway. What else were they expected to do?

Perhaps the Italians were defeated by their virtues and vices. They had united too late. They should have fought Charles the year before, on his way down and not on his way back. They had wasted twelve precious months with diplomatic manœuvres and exquisite intrigues. When they finally made up their minds and decided to crush the French, they could hurriedly put together only a patchwork collection of random military units. The troops arrived at Fornovo almost on the eve of the encounter, too late in fact for Gonzaga to consider ambushing Charles in the mountains. More men arrived even later, in the days following the battle. The decision to fight where the valley widened was also influenced by non-military motives *all'italiana:* Francesco admitted he tried to keep as close to Parma as possible; he did not trust Parma and was afraid the Parmensi would attack his rear.

Finally Gonzaga's personal virtues and vices were also determinant. He was the best general in Italy but not as good as he himself thought. He designed a battle also to show off his *bravura*. His plan was defined recently by an Italian expert, Piero Pieri, as *'una esasperazione di virtuosismo tattico'*. Obviously, the marquis was keeping an eye out for his own personal aggrandizement. He had yielded to the inveterate Italian temptation of exploiting a national crisis to become a great historical figure, cheered by the multitude, covered with immortal glory. For this, he could not stay to one side and watch the others fight. He needed to show off his own valour, that of his family, and that of his Mantua men-at-arms. They all fought with great courage. Most of them died. In the end Francesco thought he had won. Was he not left in possession of the terrain? Had he not captured the enemy's treasure? Had he not forced the King of France to flee? Back in Mantua, he had a church built to thank God, called it the *Chiesa della Vittoria*, and had a gold medal struck bearing the words *'Ob restitutam Italiae libertatem'*, or 'For the re-establishment of Italian liberty'. Note the word *Italiae*, which showed how aware the contemporaries were of the national significance of the battle. Everybody else, however, knew they had lost the battle, the war, and the liberty of Italy.

*

Charles VIII's expedition could be compared to the Opium War which the English fought against the Chinese Empire in the nineteenth century. It too was a comparatively mild affair, unimportant as such things go. It too started a chain reaction of unpredictable events and opened the way for a long period of foreign interventions, bloody conflicts, civil wars and revolts. The English (like

the French of Charles VIII) showed the world the
impotence of a great nation, the immense booty which
could be gathered with little danger, the passive weakness
of the over-civilized inhabitants, their incapacity to work
in cohesive and coherent bodies, their readiness to resign
themselves pliantly to the ways of rough, brutal and
resolute invaders. The ruin and the humiliation of great
peoples, the Italians and the Chinese, proud of their past
achievements, fanned nationalism, a hidden hatred of the
foreigners, so obviously inferior to the natives in culture,
savoir faire and the arts, a xenophobia without which
many succeeding events could not be easily explained. It
sporadically burst out in savage and bloody revolts,
followed by periods of supine and servile resignation. The
ultimate consequences of all this reach to the present day.
Fascism and the Boxers' rebellion, the Communist victory
in China and the strength of Communism in Italy, all have
many roots, some of them in distant, half-forgotten defeats
and the desire for revenge.

The European powers, however, brought to China an
entirely dissimilar culture, based on science, organization,
and modern weapons; they brought to Italy a more backward but recognizable form of the common culture.
Undoubtedly Francesco Gonzaga was a better general
than Charles. Only the foreigners' determination on the
battlefields, their courage and discipline, were their own,
the virtues of people who could unite behind their leaders.
The weapons and the stratagems employed by the French
and all the other invaders who followed them had been
invented and perfected by the Italians, and this made
their humiliation infinitely more bitter. The war in China
provoked the final collapse of a decrepit Empire, the end
of a civilization which had not developed the means with
which to defend itself. The European invasions of Italy,
on the other hand, while destroying her supremacy in war
and politics, spurred the Italians to greater efforts in the
fields left open to them, those in which they were unchallenged. Some of their greatest triumphs in the arts
and the newly-born sciences were achieved while the wars
were still going on. Decline came later.

*

What happened after Fornovo is intricate and tragic.
Even the diligent old *Encyclopaedia Britannica* groaned
under the burden of having to clarify subsequent events
to its readers and gave up. Its eleventh edition (Cam-
bridge, 1911, Volume XV, page 41), sadly says: 'It is
impossible in this place to follow the tangled intrigues of
the period.' Practically all the available armies of Europe
came to Italy in the thirty-odd years after 1495. The
Austrians, the Germans, the Burgundians, the French,
the Flemish, the Spanish, the Hungarians and sundry
others marched down the Alps or landed from their ships.
Even the Swiss abandoned their peaceful valleys and
their prosperous cows for the Italian battlefields, under
everybody else's flag as mercenaries, or their own, to get
on to a good thing; the Swiss have a notorious instinct for
safe business opportunities. Everybody formed everlasting
alliances with everybody else in turn, broke them, formed
new ones, marched, countermarched, fought, made peace,
and resumed fighting again. At times, when reading the
detailed chronicles of those decades, one's head reels and
one is reminded of the closing scenes of old silent film
comedies, the free-for-all drunken brawls in which everybody slugged everybody else regardless.

The foreigners won or lost in turn. The Italians always
lost. When things were going well, they had to supply
everybody with food, fodder, lodgings for men and animals
and bags of gold coins. Things went well only sporadically. Most of the time the inhabitants were robbed of
their possessions and massacred, their women were raped,
their fields ravaged, their farm-houses demolished, their
stores emptied, their wine barrels shot through, their
churches desecrated, their cattle slaughtered, their beautiful cities sacked, dismantled and burned. Bands of marauding deserters, the scum of Europe, roamed the
countryside. Hunger and the plague spread like stubble
fire. Italians who were not killed at home, in their native
towns and villages, found death on every battlefield. Not
a skirmish was fought in which they were not among the
victims, as actors on both sides and innocent bystanders.

The local princes and republics, unable to form another
military alliance among themselves to defend their country,
always joined this or that coalition of foreigners, to spite

their personal rivals, and sent their subjects in droves to fight and die in innumerable and incomprehensible little side-wars. The Italians who enrolled as mercenaries in other people's armies thought life in camp was better than life anywhere else. What happened in the last eighteen months of the second world war—the Allies of all colours fighting the Germans, the fascists fighting the anti-fascists, the cities turned into rubble, starving children begging, women selling themselves for a piece of bread, men being deported, tortured, killed by the S.S., hunger, despair, corruption and disease spreading—continued after Fornovo for more than thirty years. Nobody seemed to be strong enough to put an end to the senseless destruction.

In 1527, after thirty-three years of bloody troubles, a new Imperial army marched on Rome. Mustered at random, it included German *Landsknechte* who were fanatical Lutherans, recruited with the hope that they would show extra zeal against the Pope, Spanish soldiers who were fanatical Catholics and Italian mercenaries. It was led by the Constable of Bourbon, a traitor to the King of France. Like all Charles V's soldiers, these were not paid; they paid themselves by exacting levies and sacking cities. The Constable was killed as he approached the walls of Rome with a ladder, in a fog, on May 6, 1527, two hours before sunset. Benvenuto Cellini boasted in his *Memoirs* that he had killed him with his own crossbow. No serious historian believes him. The shot was but one of few. There was no resistance. The walls were scaled, the gates opened and Rome conquered in a matter of hours.

For nine months the city was abandoned to the lust, rapacity and cruelty of thirty thousand men without an authoritative commander to check them. The Pope, Clement VII, imprisoned in Castel Sant'Angelo, saw, day and night, the smoke billow from new fires in every quarter of the city, heard the wailing of women and the groans of tortured men mingled with the jests and the songs of drunken soldiers, and murmured to himself the words of Job: 'Because it shut not up the doors of my mother's womb nor his sorrow from mine eyes.' All Europe was shocked by the horrible tales. For months on end, men were being put on the rack to make them reveal the hiding place of their money; women of all conditions and ages, including the nuns, were being raped by lines of jeering men; priceless art treasures were destroyed or dispersed forever; high prelates were kidnapped for ransom and dragged through the streets dressed in precious holy vestments, mounted backwards on donkeys, in sacrilegious parody. The churches were despoiled of all precious or nonprecious objects: holy relics and books were thrown in the streets with the garbage and the rotting corpses. Not even the dead were safe. Julius II's tomb was prised open and his ring stolen from his dessicated finger. The Catholics behaved as viciously as the Protestants, the Italian soldiers as viciously as the foreigners, the Roman populace as viciously as the conquerors.

*

The sack of Rome, the distant consequence of the defeat at Fornovo, was the catastrophe from which Italians never recovered, the trauma which left its indelible marks on their national character. Not one of them ever doubted that it had come about through their own faults. Why had no leader found the energy and courage to stop the motley and disorderly Imperial army on its drunken way south? Why did the people not rise in revolt against the foreign rabble?

The sack of Rome has no exact parallel as an example of national humiliation. It cannot really be compared to the event which first comes to mind, the fall of Paris in 1940. The Paris of the Third Republic was also the most splendid and glorious city in Europe, the storehouse of priceless wealth accumulated through many centuries, the library of the world, the depository of all that was best in old and new arts, the habitat of distinguished men. But Paris was not destroyed and sacked. It emerged intact from its ordeal. It awed its conquerors. The barbarians crowded the museums, filled the concert halls and the Comédie Française, honoured the dead French cultural heroes while they tortured living French patriots. Rome, on the other hand, was spared nothing. There was no mercy for it. Its glorious past, its majestic ruins, the terrible memory of its greatnes, the masterpieces filling *palazzi* and basilicas, the treasures filling libraries and coffers did not protect it from one single abuse. In fact, all its qualities (like the beauty of most of its women, the virtue of some, and the great dignity of a few), made the rape the more irresistible.

But Rome was something infinitely more than Paris in 1940. Rome was also God's seat on earth, the rock on which Christ had established His Church, the centre of a vast spiritual Empire of which all Christians had been subjects until a few years before. Those who laid hands on it did more than perpetrate an ordinary outrage: they committed an irreparable sacrilege. To see their sacred city being defiled, as the Italians did, without being able to lift a finger to avert its doom, was more than a proof of their military and political impotence: it was the betrayal of their moral and spiritual inheritance. The destruction of the city, like the destruction of Jerusalem, was taken to be a clear sign of the wrath of God in retribution for the vices and the sins of the people. It destroyed their soul. It weakened irremediably their pride and their will to live as one nation, because Rome, like Jerusalem, was also the symbol of the national existence. Italians had not achieved unity, but had always felt themselves to be a nation nevertheless formed, not like others, by kings, soldiers and statesmen, but by churchmen, poets, artists and philosophers. This spiritual country which Italians loved desperately had a capital which was Rome, not the stone Rome on the banks of the Tiber, but the ghostly city to be found in books and legends. It had bewitched Dante, Cola, Petrarch. It was to bewitch all great Italians in the future. Rome was the great mother, the womb from which everything Italians held dear had come, without whose possession they could find no peace. Its loss was irreparable.

*

The Emperor Charles V emerged from the fighting as the sole winner. The noise of battle died. The dust settled. He imposed on Italy a heavy Pax Hispanica. The Italians resigned themselves to their state. Nothing could be done against him. He lived far way: nobody could poison him, plot against him, deceive him, trap him; no league could be formed with foreign allies to fight him. He was more powerful than anybody had ever been: he had the greatest navy, the biggest army, more allies than anybody, the largest treasure ever gathered, overseas possessions so vast that there was as yet no map of them. On his empire, as everybody knew, the sun never set. In 1530 he was also elected Emperor of the Holy Roman Empire.

He graciously consented to be crowned at the hands of the Pope at the same time Emperor and King of Italy. The gold crown of the King of Italy, called the 'iron crown' because it is said to contain one of the true nails of the Cross, of remote antiquity (it probably belonged to Constantine), was kept in the Duomo of Monza, near Milan, where Queen Teodolinda of the Longobards had left it. (It is still there.) It was seldom used. It was never moved far from Monza. The crown of the Empire was kept in Saint Peter's, in Rome. Previous emperors (the first had been Charlemagne in 800) had been crowned there or in Saint John Lateran. But Charles could not spare the time to stop in Monza and then go on to Rome. He disdainfully said that he was not accustomed to run after crowns but to have crowns run after him. He gave orders that both be brought to Bologna, which was halfway between Rome and Monza, and Clement VII meet him there. The Pope accepted meekly. In July 1529 the emperor commanded Andrea Doria to meet him in Barcelona, crossed the Mediterranean in a rough passage of fourteen days, landed in Genoa, and proceeded to Bologna.

The meeting of Pope and Emperor was one of the terminal events of Italian history. With pomp and pageantry it established the moral hegemony of the Church and the material dominion of Spain over a large part of Europe. The ceremony closed a miraculous age of unrivalled intellectual splendour and immense suffering in Italy, and inaugurated a new era, a period of more than three centuries of subjection to foreign rulers, during which it can be said that Italy had no history of her own.

Great preparations had been made in Bologna. There was no money, of course, after the events of the past years. The people were gloomy and hostile. It was noticed that when the Pope entered the city none of the population had responded to the cries of *Viva Papa Clemente!* raised by his attendants. The Pope and his court wore mourning.

After the sack of Rome they had sworn never to shave and to wear their beards unshorn in memory of their past sufferings. Yet the municipality and the nobles of the city managed somehow to get enough money together to give the emperor a memorable welcome. Illustrious guests flocked from everywhere. All the great princes of Italy were present. The Pope was attended by the most illustrious cardinals, high prelates from the Curia and the sees. The emperor was followed everywhere by a cortège of courtiers from Spain, Italy and Germany, ambassadors from England, France, Scotland, Hungary, Bohemia and Portugal.

Veronica Gambara threw her apartments open to the numerous men of letters: the poets Bembo, Mauro and Molza could be seen in conversation with witty Berni, learned Vida, stately Trissino and Marcantonio Flaminio. Giovio and Guicciardini were there. What still remained in Italy of Renaissance splendour, wit and fashion, after the sack of Rome, the ruin of her wealthiest cities, and thirty-five years of continuous wars, was concentrated in a sunset blaze of festivities, games, *conversazioni*, banquets, balls.

Francesco Mazzola, called *Il Parmigianino*, painted Charles attended by Fame who crowns his forehead while an infant Hercules hands him the globe. Titian received the honour of several sittings. His life-size portrait of the emperor in full armour, seated on a white charger, has been lost. Others remain. Charles was so pleased with Titian that he personally picked up a brush the painter had dropped, made him a knight, and appointed him painter to the emperor with a regular pension.

People observed that Charles and his suite in their excursions through the streets of Bologna always wore the Spanish habit. While Italians were dressed in the bright and gay colours fashionable at the time, in silks, brocades, velvets, laces, and woollen cloth, of red, green, yellow, pink, blue, the Spanish wore black suits with black silk stockings, black boots or shoes, black velvet caps adorned with black plumes. The gloom was brightened by buttons of jewellery, and, on Charles' breast, by the chain and the hanging lamb of the Order of the Golden Fleece. The Spanish were pale men who never smiled. Charles was

seen to smile only once, at a lady who had thrown a
flower at him from a balcony. Such slight details would
not deserve attention were it not for the fact that Italians,
as they have always done, quickly discarded their varied
and brilliant clothes and adopted the conquerors' fashion,
the funereal black of the Spaniards. It seemed as though the
whole country had put on mourning for its servitude to
foreign tyrants, for its loss of liberty. The very faces of the
people, in the following generation, as we see them in
portraits, took on an expression of sadness and despon-
dency corresponding to their black garments. A poet noticed
the change and wrote:

> Black robes befit our age. Once they were white;
> next many-hued; now dark as Afric's Moor,
> night-black, infernal, traitorous, obscure,
> horrid with ignorance and sick with fright.
>
> For very shame we shun all colours bright,
> who mourn our end—the tyrants we endure,
> the chains, the noose, the lead, the lure—
> our dismal heroes, our souls lost in night.

The reader does not have to be reminded that black
was also the official colour of the Fascist régime. Mussolini
was dressed in black from head to foot and so were all
his ministers.

CHAPTER SIXTEEN

The Perennial Baroque

WHAT happened to Italy is what usually happens to old ladies who were once famous beauties. Just as they relinquish only reluctantly the gestures, curls, witticisms and fashions of their sunset years, Italy still clings to the manners and ideals of the two centuries which followed the coronation of Charles V. This must be kept in mind by anybody trying to understand anything about this confusing country, past events, current developments, art movements, political evolutions, or by anyone wanting to peer into the clouded crystal-ball of the future. He must not allow himself to be deceived (so many things in Italy are perfect *trompe-l'oeil*). He must look beneath the surface. He will then discover that Italian reality is generally still a Baroque reality.

Baroque is a mysterious term. Some scholars (Benedetto Croce among them) believe that it derived from an artificial word (b-a-r-o-c-o) invented by medieval scholars to teach dull pupils a particularly intricate form of logical reasoning, the fourth mode of the second figure of the syllogism, to be exact. Others think it is the old trade name for the oddly-shaped monstrous pearls still known as *perle barocche* in Italy. The two hypotheses are not in contradiction. Somehow the term came to be used metaphorically to describe anything pointlessly complicated, otiose, capricious and eccentric, similar to rarely used syllogisms or irregularly bulging pearls: twisted theories, elliptical and over-ornate poetry, elaborate and gaudy architecture. Later it came to define a whole period in history, the Baroque era, in which Baroque men thought Baroque thoughts, led Baroque lives, surrounded by Baroque art. The age had a more than casual resemblance to our own.

With the Baroque era, all kinds of things which had been lax, spontaneous, comfortable and haphazard before, became rigid, uniform and somewhat inhuman all over Europe. Absolute monarchs flattened out all rivals and ruled practically without opposition; great kings joined in vast but changing alliances, a slow game of dynastic musical chairs. The minor principalities and republics were left without real responsibility and autonomy. They were robbed of their dignity and became impotent, unwilling and embittered vassals. The danger of little wars decreased but the fear of vast conflagrations involving the whole world was ever present. Centralized power developed the instruments for efficient rule: laws were codified and enforced, bureaucracy became powerful and quickly proliferated, with its archives, forms to fill in, rites, and the authority to punish all those who did not submit to it. The little liberties consecrated by usage, the privileges of dignitaries, guilds, towns, universities, religious orders, professions or any individual who disliked being pushed around, were worn thin until only a vestige was left. Man was left practically alone before the will of his sovereign.

All economic activities which were not prohibited were strictly controlled. The king held monopolies of the main indispensable products, which he alone could export or import. Taxes rained down with unprecedented severity to support the armies and the heavy machinery of government. Stable and pyramidal hierarchies were established in all fields. The armies, no longer amateur collections of men chosen at random, happily bent on arson, pillage and rape, acquired organizational charts, uniforms, an iron discipline and a well-defined chain of command. Authorities determined once and for all the only correct spelling of words and rules of grammar, as well as the unbending etiquette of court and private life. Cities were no longer the spontaneous and untidy products of man's needs, passions and tastes: they were designed by the king's architects. The king demanded straight and wide avenues and large squares. Of course, he wanted the Baroque prestige of a great and ornate capital, but also easy passage for his troops to quell riots. Beauty itself, the most elusive of all qualities, was codified down to minutiae. Religious life was strictly regimented. Gone were the wild debates and revolts of the preceding age in both Catholic and Protestant countries. Morality was imposed, dogmas and principles were defined, rites standardized. In both camps orthodoxy was sternly defended. Free thinkers and heretics were persecuted and burned in Rome as well as Geneva. Miguel de Servetus, the Catalan physician and theologian, was condemned to death in the same month by the Sorbonne and the Calvinists.

Society appeared formed of two main layers. At the top there were a few *grands seigneurs*. At the bottom the vast ragged, picturesque and powerless crowds. The *grands seigneurs* derived their power mostly from the favours of the king and from the revenue of their land. They were encouraged to live lavishly, on their estates or at court, and not to dabble in trade, banking, politics, or scholarly pursuits. Cosimo I de Medici, to avoid trouble, forced the great banking and trading families of Florence to invest their capital in country estates and rewarded them with sonorous titles. Titles were much sought after. The nobility cut off from responsibilities inevitably became overbearing, inept and dull. The populace was kept ignorant, poor, superstitious, harassed by tax-collectors, religious authorities, bureaucrats and soldiers. At times the poor broke out in bloody but short-lived and unprofitable riots. Most of the time, they were kept happy in their misery by the distribution of alms, the sale of cheap flour, the splendid performance of public spectacles and the clubs of policemen. The show was all important. This is why the Baroque age is still unsurpassed in the breathtaking beauty of public buildings, churches, parks, residences and cities. It was not an accident that all great architects of the day were also famous scenic designers. Historical events were, whenever possible, staged like sumptuous theatrical productions.

Behind the splendour, the agitation, the shouting, the roll of drums, the flutter of flags and the roar of guns, under the impeccably rational order of the era, lay a heavy feeling of futility and tedium. Men took refuge in distractions which took many forms: secret revolts against all conformism, open or invisible struggles for liberty or its substitutes, the search for free expression of man's unemployed talents in some interstice between forbidden fields. Men travelled to the far end of the world, fought savages, founded colonies, entertained dangerous political thoughts, volunteered in their own or other people's armies, joined new religious cults, the more outlandish and persecuted the better. Others lived, outside all known laws, lives of licentiousness, violence, profligacy, debauch and crime. This is the other face of the Baroque era, the more Baroque face of Baroque life.

*

When the times turned to Baroque, Italy found herself surprisingly at ease for a defeated, dismembered and oppressed country. She took to Baroque with a vengeance. She looked, in the end, more Baroque than any other Baroque country of Europe. She set the style. Her discoveries, *divertissements,* techniques and designs were eagerly imitated. Rome became the world capital of Baroque. This was because Baroque life utilized fully many of the people's latent talents, tastes and inclinations, but also because the elements of Baroque life, oppression, tedium and revolt, were stronger in Italy than anywhere else. While regimentation in other countries had noble justifications, was imposed allegedly to defend national unity and prestige, and to submit all to a common purpose and the supremacy of the law, in Italy it was imposed externally, by two cosmopolitan powers, Spain and the Church, for external reasons, in their own interest and for their own advantage.

Spain was a mighty empire which ruled Italy like one of her many colonies through viceroys and satellite princelings. The Church, as a temporal body, was a small Italian state, one of many, perhaps more bankrupt, corrupt, disorganized, ridden with bandits than most of the others, as ridiculously impotent as any to carry out an independent policy of its own. But it was also an immense spiritual empire, holding sway in every Catholic country, distributing slices of the American continent as if it were its own property, drawing incalculable strength from the loyalty of Catholic princes and the faith of the Catholic multitudes. The foremost of Catholic princes was His Catholic Majesty the King of Spain, the most fanatically devoted to the Holy See were the Spanish people. The two empires buttressed each other. Each of them endeavoured to employ the other to make up for its weaknesses: the Church made use of Spanish soldiers to enforce its decrees and defend Catholic unity; Spain exploited the spiritual hegemony of the Church to keep the people docile. All the time, like all good allies, they struggled for supremacy. The Church won in the end. It always does.

The difference between Baroque in Italy and that in other countries could be compared to that between Communism in the satellite republics, mechanically imposed by foreign armies after a defeat, and Communism in the Soviet Union, the product of the Russians' tortured genius, of their passionate love for their unfortunate country, and of their perennial self-pity. The outward forms of the régime were more emphatic in Italy, the declarations of faith unnecessarily forceful. There was, at the same time, something vaguely degrading and contemptible about obeying the will of the local authorities, as there now is in any eastern European country; and secret revolt, sabotage, insubordination, anarchy, and lawlessness were considered meritorious and manly. Like all oppressed people, the Italians were forbidden to think, act, work and fight for themselves. Responsible jobs were in the hands of foreigners and of faithful servants of the foreigners, the collaborators. For the ordinary natives there were idle and frivolous occupations, insignificant and servile work or the pursuit of private greatness.

The situation grew more and more explosive as the decades passed. The people, notoriously the most restless, unruly, talented in Europe, found themselves with but a few narrow and secondary fields in which to give vent to their energies. The rulers, Spanish viceroys and petty princes, were more avaricious, dull-witted and ignorant than most other rulers, but also more insecure and frightened; nowhere was the populace purposely kept more hungry, superstitious and illiterate; nowhere else was it entertained more lavishly with spectacles and dazzled more expensively with ostentatious architecture. Nowhere else, at the same time, were so many people plagued by a feeling of futility, more anxious to take revenge on their oppressors, more desperately eager to explore unusual ways to escape.

*

The Italians did not face the challenge of the outside world as, for example, the Japanese did when their turn came, in the nineteenth century. The Japanese easily understood their ancient civilization was a decorated paper-screen, too flimsy to defend them. They went to school. They drilled themselves in Western skills, aped Western ways, adopted foreign uniforms, routines, laws, methods. They became so good that they beat the West at its own game. The Italians did the opposite. They were too proud to admit they had to learn from others. And what could these barbarians teach them who had taught the world? Of course the barbarians had gained military glory and political supremacy over Italy. But what did these short-lived advantages amount to when compared to the Italians' triumphs in the arts and the sciences, which challenged the centuries? What were the ephemeral political structures the foreigners set up when compared to the greatest flowering of the Italian political genius, the result of the Italians' devoted collaboration with God Himself, the Holy Roman Catholic Church, which was to last eternally by divine will? The Italians went on cultivating the very virtues which made them invincible, in their own eyes, but which had also made them the foreigners' too easy victims.

Many capable Italians dedicated themselves to the urgent job of shoring up and defending their tottering Church. Some were the holy men the Church needed at the time, saints like Charles Borromeo and Roberto Bellarmine. All the great Popes of the era (some were among the greatest in history) were Italian, as well as most of the famous cardinals, theologians, writers, scholars, preachers, educators, heads of religious orders, who practically constructed, within a few decades, a brand new Catholic church. These men were serving God, to be sure, but, at the same time, Italy, or what was, after all, the greatest Italian institution left standing after the débâcle, the only one which could still awe and dominate foreigners. This, of course, was nothing new. The Church had been, since the early Middle Ages, the rallying point of the Italians against the menace of imperial power. When a town was on the verge of being conquered by a victorious enemy, who threatened to abolish its liberties and rob it of its wealth, the people turned to their bishop, made him the head of the government for the time being, and sent him out to start negotiating with the enemy, to obtain more tolerable conditions. Even after the second world war, the Italians instinctively turned to the Church. They had been defeated, their country had been invaded, their own national state had collapsed, disease and hunger were spreading, and a bloody revolution looked inevitable. The Pope's Rome obviously wielded at all times a world influence infinitely superior to their own.

Other contemporary Italians went on stubbornly with the work in which they had a head start over all rivals, the arts and the sciences. It was after the sack of Rome and the coronation of Charles V in Bologna that Michelangelo painted 'The Last Judgement' in the Sistine Chapel and planned the Cupola over Saint Peter's, Cellini cast his 'Perseus' for the Loggia dei Lanzi in Florence, Palladio raised San Giorgio from the sea in Venice, Titian painted some of his greatest masterpieces, and Sansovino designed some of his most famous buildings. There was, however, something about their work which distinguished it from what they themselves had done but a few years before, a complacent dwelling on fantastic forms, perhaps, an excess of technical skill, a tortured exaggeration, a new kind of *bravura*. When the giants of a past age died, new men almost as good kept up their work. There was an endless procession of them. Tintoretto was born in 1518, Paolo Veronese in 1528, Caravaggio in 1573, Guido Reni, the painter whom our grandfathers believed to have been the greatest of all Italian painters, the 'divine' Guido, in 1575. The Caracci family team of eclectic painters came to Rome from Bologna in 1595. And Pietro da Cortona, Il Guercino, Salvator Rosa, Magnasco followed, a cavalcade of hard-working, versatile, prodigiously fecund artists. They were no longer the sedate and pious craftsmen of an earlier age. Most of them were slightly mad: they went around booted, spurred, with swords and poignards at their sides, like adventurers, and often had to run for their lives after having murdered somebody in a brawl.

Sculptors and architects were in great demand. They reached heights of excellence never seen before. Men like

Bernini, Borromini, Juvara and their followers filled Rome with hundreds of *palazzi* and churches, studded the panorama of the city with new and daring cupolas, built Saint Peter's and the colonnade in front of it, and gave Rome the face it has today. Many went around Italy, or roamed abroad, from capital to capital, building royal palaces, basilicas, cathedrals, and gardens, planning cities, designing avenues, vistas, *piazze* and fountains, until they dropped dead. In everything they did was the same love of dramatic and bewildering effect, which became more and more theatrical as the years passed, the same unprecedented and daring use of technique, the same perfection in all details. It was not an accident that their genius was also dedicated principally to the Church, to the glorification of its triumphs over the infidels and the heretics, through the most spectacular and pyrotechnical display of *virtuosismo* ever seen. Many of these artists were deeply religious: Michelangelo had become obsessed with the salvation of his soul; Carlo Dolci was determined to paint only subjects which might provoke religious ecstasy; Luca Giordano would not travel to Spain without his personal confessor. Others found solace in serving God and also Italy, poor unfortunate Italy.

It was inevitable perhaps that Baroque Italians should invent theatrical forms which were to dazzle the world for centuries. The age was one of display, make-believe and emotions; the only reality was that of the imagination. Ingenious artists designed stage-sets of miraculous splendour and built stage-machinery to produce incredible effects, storms at sea, floods of real water, flying birds or angels, instantaneous changes of décor, fantastic, panoramas stretching apparently to infinity. The *Teatro dell'-arte* was started in Florence by a company of bored actors who called themselves I Gelosi in 1575. They were tired of repeating night after night the same old words written by the author. They invented their own lines and business as they went along, following a tenuous plot. They were brought to Paris by Catherine de Medici for her wedding, and had an immediate tremendous success. They, and other companies imitating them, soon took Europe by storm.

People everywhere laughed at the famous masks:

Arlecchino and Brighella, the astute servants; Pantalone, the rich merchant worried by taxes and greedy relatives; Doctor Balanzon, the parody of all learned men and physicians; Captain Spaventa, the cowardly and boastful soldier. People wept real tears at the pathetic sentiments expressed by Colombina, the pretty maid, or Rosaura, her young and unhappy mistress, and their lovers. The *Teatro dell'arte* influenced all European theatres. Words percolated from the *Teatro* to all common languages. 'Zany' became an English word in 1588—it means John in Venetian dialect; Zani was a variation of Arlecchino. When a Soviet Russian today wants to say that what he is showing you is not a *papier mâché* structure built to deceive foreigners but the real thing, he earnestly assures you it is not *trovarobe*. *Trovarobe* was the man employed to 'find things', to be sure that all the props needed were on the stage at the right time; later he became the stage-manager, responsible for the scenery and the illusions.

Music is notoriously the consolation of oppressed and frightened people. It is the one art in which one can be safely sincere in dangerous times. This Heinrich Heine understood: 'To poor enslaved Italy,' he wrote in his *Reisebilde*, 'words are not allowed. She can only describe the anguish in her heart through music. All her hatred against foreign oppression, her enthusiasm for liberty, all the anguish at her own impotence, her longing for her past greatness, pathetic hopes, watching, waiting for help, all this is transposed into her melodies.' Before Baroque Italians could find a refuge in music, however, they had to invent it. The man who not only started Italian music on its glorious way but also had to save the newly-born creation from immediate death was Palestrina. The clerical authorities of the times looked upon singing in churches with distaste. This was inevitable, as most of the choirs sang holy words to ribald tunes of foreign importation, suggesting the tavern, the dancing room and the brothel. Masses bore the titles of the popular melodies on which they were founded, names more suited for contemporary perfumes than religious tunes: '*A l'ombre d'un buissonet*', '*Baise-moi*', or '*Adieu, mes amours*'. The very explicit words of love ditties and obscene ballads rang out often during religious services, squalled by the tenor, while the bass sang an '*Agnus Dei*' or a '*Benedictus*'. The scandal could not be tolerated any longer. The Council of Trent, in its twenty-second session, on September 17, 1562, decided to 'exclude from churches all such music that introduced anything impure or lascivious'. Could music suggest anything but the impure and lascivious? Pius IV appointed a congregation of eight cardinals to look into the matter.

It was known that four of them were determined to ban all music from the churches. Giovanni Pier Luigi, called Palestrina from his birthplace, was asked to break the deadlock. He was instructed to compose something which had never been tried before, an original mass in sober ecclesiastical style which would inspire strictly holy thoughts. If he failed, as everybody thought he would (Cardinal Charles Borromeo, the Pope's nephew, personally told him so), the choral establishments of the Pontifical Chapel and all other church musical organizations would be disbanded and music excluded from religious services. Palestrina had an apparently simple but almost impossible task. He was to invent a new form of art or to behold the ruin of his own life and the lives of all his colleagues. He composed the now famous 'Mass of Pope Marcellus'. The cardinals heard it, were placated and convinced. Church music was saved for ever in its new form. Italian music was founded at the same time. What if Palestrina had not succeeded? The mind staggers.

At about the same time, a private academy of scholars, dabblers and artists gathered regularly in the Palazzo Vernio, in Florence, for the avowed purpose of reviving the musical declamation of the Greeks. The quest was, of course, vague and visionary. Nobody knows how the Greeks sang. No Greek music came down to us. The Florentine *dilettanti* had only a dim intuition to guide them, the belief that the ancients had read dramatic verse with musical intonations. As the alchemists vainly searching for the philosopher's stone initiated modern chemistry, the Palazzo Vernio friends invented something entirely different from what they were looking for, Opera. One of them, Claudio Monteverdi, developed the *recitativo*, in his *Orfeo*. It was the acorn from which all the operas in history grew. The new theatrical form, decorated with all the artifices, the scenery, the theatrical effects and the costumes of the era, had an immediate success.

Behind it all, however, behind the splendour and ingeniousness of everything, was a tragic feeling of despair, a spiritual frustration so intense as to be embarrassing. Behind religious art, for instance, behind the monumental stateliness of church façades, the unbelievable *virtuosismo* of the engineering, the convulsed agitation of the decorations, the tortured emphasis of all details, the epileptic gestures of the statues, the fluttering of stone cloaks in perennial hurricanes, the exasperated emotions on the faces of painted saints, there is little intimate religious feeling to be seen, but something else, a pathetic preoccupation with proclaiming beyond all possible doubt the victory of the Church over all its enemies and with convincing the world of its invincible supremacy. Behind most of the ornate, eloquent, erudite prose of the time there was little truth and practically no significance: only specialists read it today. Poetry invented new rhythms, new ways of employing words, new and marvellous metaphors; it entertained, cajoled, caressed, and flattered the reader; it evoked lascivious and impossible pleasures. It reminds us of those great machines built at about the same time, vast aviaries filled with wonderfully variegated birds moving their wings and singing melodiously: they look alive but are merely the product of man's cold inventiveness; they repeat themselves endlessly.

Everything, in fact, was done not for itself alone but principally for the effect it would produce. For two centuries or more an immense number of men of genius dedicated their incredible talents to the national belief that the show is, *faute de mieux*, a good substitute for reality: they filled the world with masterpieces in order to find compensation for the insecurity, emptiness, disarray, impotence and despair of their national life, to forget their humiliation and shame, to forget their collective guilt. It was a frenzied search for consolation and revenge against the crude and overbearing foreign devils. The Italians never succeeded in the end in affirming their own kind of greatness. They were always laughed at. Their achievements were thought to be suspicious, inferior, as if they lacked a manly character. As Croce says, 'Italians lost whatever reputation they had for the earnestness of their intellectual production; their talents gave them the name of excellent actors, singers, composers, decorators, versifiers. They were praised as a *"popolo d'artisti"*, or "a people of artists", at times despised as "charlatans" and "clowns".'

*

Some Italians did not resign themselves to impotence, perhaps many more than one imagines. These odd men disliked being entertained, distracted, dazzled, and benefited: resented being kept in ignorance, deceived and exploited. They hated being obliged to depend on the art of living (which is notoriously nothing more arcane than the art of gaining favours from dull, ungrateful and capricious masters) to make a living. One occasionally gets a glimpse of these men's unhappiness. This is what an earnest writer, Battista Guarini, wrote disconsolately to a friend, after receiving the appointment of poet at the court of Ferrara: 'I strove to transform myself into another man, and, like a play-actor, to assume the character, manners and emotions of a past period. Mature in age, I forced myself to appear young; exchanged my melancholy for gaiety; affected loves I did not feel; turned my wisdom into folly, and, in a word, passed from philosopher to poet.' Croce says: 'He who knows the documents of the time does not always see in them serenity and gaiety. One is tempted to affirm that even laughter had been lost, good healthy laughter; men created it artificially by means of burlesque poetry, academic fancies, and heroic-comic poems, games of words rather than spontaneous expressions of joy.'

Proud Italians felt the shame of not being ruled by laws, the protagonists of their national life and arbiters of their destinies, the humiliation of watching the servile and contented condition of the people around them. 'Italy, who had given birth to apostles and martyrs in earlier centuries,' Croce explains, 'and would beget more later, during the Risorgimento, did not produce any in the Baroque age, because such men cannot exist when there is lazy tranquillity and resignation in the spirit.'

There were not many apostles and martyrs, perhaps, but there were many men who suffered because there were none, and found the lack of purpose and the emptiness of their lives unbearable. Many of them emigrated. Even if Italy had no history of her own, individual Italians tried to become historical characters. Some became diplomats and statesmen for foreign sovereigns, like Cardinal Mazarin. Some served in other countries' armies. Italian engineers directed the works at the siege of Antwerp and in the siege of La Rochelle. Alessandro Farnese became one of the great generals of Philip II of Spain and led armies in Flanders and France. Gabriele Serbelloni, a Milanese, defended Malta from the Turks, became a Spanish general in Flanders with the Duke of Alba, fought at Lepanto on the 166th galley, called *La Donzella*, on the extreme left, as master-general of the artillery for the Christian fleet against the Turks. Raimondo Montecuccoli from Modena commanded the imperial armies against Turenne at the battle of Sassbach and wrote treatises on the military arts (he believed in small, well-drilled, light and fast-moving armies). The kingdom of Naples was considered by the Spanish an inexhaustible reservoir of soldiers and officers: thousands of them fought all over Europe and the Americas. Many became renowned Spanish generals.

That these men were fighting for something more than a stipend and a part of the booty was shown by their extreme touchiness in matters relating to the national honour. They were perennially challenging foreigners (mostly French) who ridiculed the bravery and loyalty of the Italian soldiers. The memory of such chivalrous encounters (which the Italian usually won) is kept alive in Italy: school children have to study them. The French, of course, have forgotten them. The first of such pathetic combats took place in 1503 and is known as the *Disfida di Barletta*. Italian knights under Prospero Colonna had joined the Spanish under Consalvo de Cordoba to fight the French for the possession of Apulia. A French captain, called La Motte, was captured and taken to the Spanish camp. At dinner he derided the Italians as cowardly and treacherous, adding that he, with a handful of Frenchmen, was ready to meet any equal number of

Italians on the field, at any time. The encounter took place in a lonely spot between Andria and Corato, thirteen Frenchmen against thirteen Italians, on February 13. The Italians unsaddled all their opponents and were declared winners. Nobody was killed. A stone tablet twenty feet high was raised on the spot to celebrate the event in noble Latin words. French Napoleonic soldiers overturned it one night in 1805; it was proudly set on its feet again by the local population after Waterloo. It is still there, lost in a vineyard, to remind Italians that, even when things looked darkest, all was not lost.

Another similar challenge took place in 1636, in the plains of Crevacuore, near the Tessin river, in northern Italy. There were two squads of thirty men, this time, and they were to fight until all those on one side had been killed or incapacitated. The Italians took the lead. But when their success looked almost assured, all the French soldiers who were watching the encounter joined in. To avoid the danger of a vast and disorderly battle the officers on both sides stopped the fighting. The French commander later apologized for the unchivalrous behaviour of his men. No monument was raised. For centuries there have been countless duels between individual Italians and foreigners for the same reasons. As late as the beginning of the nineteenth century, the Neapolitan Carlo Filangieri challenged and killed a French general who had offended the Neapolitans. On February 19, 1826, in Florence, the exiled Neapolitan general, Gabriele Pepe, challenged the secretary of the French Legation in Tuscany, the poet Alphonse de Lamartine, who had called Italy 'the land of the dead, *la terre des morts*' in a poem. Lamartine was wounded, embraced his opponent, and confessed chivalrously to having been wrong. Pepe became a well-known figure in Florence and finally made a living giving Italian lessons to foreigners. The last of such noble encounters was fought by Victor Emmanuel of Savoy-Aosta, Count of Turin, a cousin of King Victor Emmanuel III. He challenged a French prince, Henri d'Orléans, who had written a few articles for *Le Figaro*, from Ethiopia, in which he had ridiculed the Italian colonial army. The duel was fought at Vaucresson, near

Versailles, on August 15, 1897. Henri d'Orléans was
slightly wounded.

*

Many learned writers have attributed the final warping of
the national character during the Baroque era solely to
ecclesiastical influence. Benedetto Croce pointed out:
'Those very Italians who, a while earlier, had been accused
of being the children of Machiavelli were now thought
to be the disciples of . . . the priests.' The old Neapolitan philosopher clearly smiled at the contradiction. How
could this be? Machiavelli was a notorious *mangiapreti*,
or 'priest-eater', the opponent of Vatican policy, the
author of ribald satires against clerical corruption. How
could the people have changed so radically in such a
short time? The thing was patently absurd. Of course
Croce was right. He was also wrong. The problem is an
intricate one. Only political pamphleteers and journalists
can dare give it a clean-cut, black and white, answer. It
is impossible for anybody else to disentangle the snarled
skein.

In fact sixteenth-century Italians can be considered the
disciples of both Machiavelli and the Church. Machiavelli,
after all, had not made up his theories out of the air,
but had deduced them from the contemporary events in
his country, the behaviour of his countrymen, and his
own built-in prejudices. He never forgot his Catholic upbringing, and his anti-clericalism sprang more from his
love than from hatred of the Church: he pilloried only
unworthy priests and bad monks. Churchmen, too, could
at the same time be accused of obeying Machiavellian
rules, which, after all, represented the common sense of
the era, just as eighteenth-century Americans, even those
who never heard of Franklin's *Poor Richard's Almanack*,
could be said to follow its precepts. In other words, all
of them, Machiavelli, the people, the Popes, the native
cardinals, the Curia, and the native priests, were Italian;
all were sons of their land and of their times. The Church
can rightly be considered the mother of the Baroque age
but also its daughter, the teacher of the Italian people
at the time but also their disciple. Was the Italian char-

acter really warped because of this? Or was the Church's worldly policy not unduly influenced by Italian native habits?

*

Never had the forces of the Devil been so close to victory. The Church was fighting deadly internal and external threats. The internal threats were infinitely more dangerous and more difficult to deal with. After all, the external enemies were well-known, recognizable and could be squarely fought. They were the self-proclaimed rebels, the schismatics, and the heretics. The internal enemies were less easy to identify: they were the indifferent, the incredulous, the materialists, who preferred a few earthy joys in the hand to eternal bliss in the bush. They were superstition, ignorance, corruption, nepotism, simony, careerism, and the disintegration of ecclesiastical discipline. Above all, the Church had to beware also of its good friends, the misguided and enthusiastic faithful who, wanting to cure all ills indiscriminately and in a hurry, risked spreading new and more malignant heresies and causing its final collapse. Things had indeed come to a bad pass if Cardinal Gaspare Contarini himself, a man of undaunted faith and solid doctrine, had to admit: 'I cannot hide my indignation that some of the most illustrious Catholic cities are tainted with moral plague and loose ways to such a point that many monasteries designed to shelter virgins dedicated to God have now been turned into brothels. Can there be anything more abject and infamous?'

We know how the Church, at the time of the Council of Trent, managed miraculously to triumph over all its enemies. It reformed itself, established a new discipline, eradicated many lax and corrupt habits, restored and revived religious faith, stopped the progress of schismatics and heretics, and emerged stronger and greater from the ordeal Rome assumed an air of exemplary behaviour. Gravity of manners, visible signs of piety, a composed and contrite face, ostentation of orthodoxy became fashionable. Sinners had to adopt the famous rule, '*Si non caste tamen caute*', 'If not chastely at least prudently'. Like all institutions desperately fighting for survival, the

Church had to employ energetic means, some of them ruthless and cruel. In order not to be destroyed by its enemies it had to destroy them first, even if, with them, went a number of innocent bystanders. The Holy Inquisition was introduced from Spain, a larger index of forbidden books was promulgated, and the multiform activities of the vigorous and enterprising Jesuits encouraged.

The Holy Inquisition filled its prisons with suspects. 'At Rome,' writes a shocked resident in 1568, 'some are daily burned, hanged or beheaded. Places of confinement are filled to capacity and new ones must be built.' He was, of course, carried away by his emotions. Prisons were probably indiscriminately packed for many years but we know that the actual victims were not many. They were a handful of heroic and stubborn men, Antonio Paleario, Giordano Bruno, Pietro Carnesecchi, and a few others, among whom was one lone Englishman, who was burned to a crisp on August 5, 1581, for grossly insulting the host. Only in a few cases, in the provinces, was extreme vigour displayed. One of the rare important massacres occurred in 1561 near Cosenza, in Calabria, where a colony of about 4,000 Waldensian heretics was practically wiped out. They were killed by sword, fire, famine, torture, imprisonment or were hurled from the summits of high cliffs. A few survivors were sent to row in Spanish galleys.

It must be remembered that Italians, as a rule, find slaughter stupid and repugnant: through the centuries they were more frequently massacred by landing Muslim pirates or foreign invaders than vice versa. They were massacred indiscriminately by the German army during the last few months of the last war but never massacred Germans indiscriminately. There were never witch-hunts and pogroms in Italy. There could never be a Saint Bartholomew's Night in Rome. Some Italians have few objections to the private killings of one's enemies, when the circumstances demand it, but all of them consider the legal death penalty useless and cruel. (There is no death penalty in the law-books today.) The people's dislike of legal persecution and their kind hearts make them indiscriminately help all victims of the authorities: they feel irresistibly drawn to bandits, fugitives from justice, escaped convicts, as well as political refugees. In 1943, 1944 and 1945, at the peril of their lives, they sheltered anti-Fascists, American and English prisoners of war. They saved thousands of Jews from annihilation in eastern Europe by hiding them from their German allies, smuggling them to safety or providing them with false documents.

It is not surprising, therefore, that many sixteenth-century thinkers of doubtful orthodoxy were saved by the aid of their countrymen. Only a few were Italian Protestants. Most of them (like innumerable anti-fascists under the late dictatorship) were warned in time of their forthcoming arrest, perhaps by the very officials who were charged with arresting them. Some were clever enough to feel disfavour in the air, and did not wait for their doom; some managed to satisfy superior authorities with timely concessions and an outward display of conformism. Others ingeniously explained that a scientific thinker could hold one set of opinions as a philosopher and a completely different set as a Christian. Their motto was the celebrated '*Foris ut moris, intus ut libet*', or 'The façade must conform to the style of the day, the interior to one's choice'.

This is how Clelio Calcagnini, professor of *belles lettres* at Ferrara, explained the rules in a letter: 'There are things which it is safer to suppress and conceal rather than to bring before the common people. . . . Now, when the decrees of the Fathers and long usage have introduced other modes, what necessity is there for reviving antiquated practices which have long fallen in desuetude? Let us then, I pray you, allow these things to rest. Not that I disapprove of their being embraced by scholars and lovers of antiquity, but I would not have them communicated to the common people and those who are fond of innovations, lest they give occasion to strife and sedition. . . . Wherefore, in my opinion, the discussion of many points ought to be confined to the initiated. I must deem it safest to "speak with the many and think with the few".' It is well known that many 'spoke with the many and thought with the few' throughout later Italian history. They did so also under the late dictatorship. Benedetto Croce managed to write and publish his work for twenty years in spite of Fascist censorship, because his writing was obscure, learned and appealed to a minority. Mario Missiroli, the great political journalist of the time, used to say to the younger men who considered him a maestro: 'Do not fret about the freedom of the press. Freedom of the press, after all, is necessary only for bad writers.' A good writer can always find a way to convey seditious thoughts cryptically to the initiated.

*

The forces of the Inquisition could not be directed, as in Spain, against masses of heretics but only against a few reckless leaders, and less often against men than books. Dangerous books were confiscated, destroyed, burned, their owners imprisoned and tried. Bookshops went out of business, printers stopped printing. Guards at the frontiers diligently searched travellers for hidden publications. All this, as usual in Italy, was at first done with a flamboyant show of thoroughness. The psychological effect was immediate and devastating. Prudent people turned in suspicious books and denounced others who still kept theirs. Even a man like Latino Latini, a scholar, a protégé of the Vatican, was alarmed. He wrote to a friend in 1559: 'Have you not heard of the peril which threatens the very existence of books? Here there is no one who for many years will dare write. . . . As you love me and yourself, sit and look at your bookcases without opening their doors, and beware lest the very cracks let emanations come to you from the forbidden books of learning.'

Fra Paolo Sarpi, the learned theologian of the republic of Venice, called the Index 'the finest secret device ever invented for applying religion to the purpose of making men stupid', and desperately warned all his friends abroad not to try to smuggle books to him, since they would be found. Forbidden books, however, never stopped coming. A few, as they are now in the Soviet Union, were allowed in for the needs of scholars who could not otherwise refute their false doctrines. Controls became lackadaisical in time, and very lax. As people became more confident, forbidden books were brought in by important persons (whose baggage went unchecked), obscure travellers, pilgrims, merchants, books bound sometimes with the covers of harmless publications, hidden in ships' holds, or mixed with merchandise. Some treatises were copied by hand and circulated and even printed clandestinely.

This has to be kept in mind, before one can determine the real effect of the Index on Italian life in the Baroque era: only a tiny minority of the Italian people read books nowadays and only a few hundred learned specialists read them in the sixteenth century; the book readers never had much influence on their countrymen, anyway, most of whom live in an out-of-doors, speaking, and not an indoors, reading, civilization. Still, the effect of the prohibition was stifling, because the great majority of peace-loving and reasonable men were too easily intimidated. The 'finest secret device' made few men stupid who did not want to become stupid, but undoubtedly encouraged many in their natural inclination for ignorance and the art of shamming correct sentiments and the beliefs approved by the superior authorities.

•

Nothing in Italy appeared more Baroque-Italian than the Company or Society of Jesus. Strictly speaking, of course, it was by no means an Italian institution. It had a soul of Spanish steel. It was invented in 1539, as everybody knows, by a Spanish *hidalgo*, soldier, disciplinarian, a born leader of men, who imbued it with the stern, heroic, and obstinate qualities and prejudices of his people and his class, Don Iñigo Lopez de Recalda, Lord of Loyola and Oñaz, commonly known as Saint Ignatius Loyola, aided by a handful of Spanish and French priests. The first Italian disciples joined him only at a later date. Nevertheless the Society brilliantly identified, interpreted and encouraged the main aspects of Italian Baroque life: conformism, spectacular opulence, dazzling shows, and the ingenious evasion of obnoxious laws.

No lay or ecclesiastical body of Christians had ever been more dedicated to regimentation, more tightly disciplined, rationally organized, systematically run, and successfully standardized. The fathers were instructed in blind obedience to their superior, 'who stood in the place of God', without reference to his wisdom, piety, or discretion. Their general was closely controlled by subordinates he could not dismiss. All Jesuits were interchangeable cogwheels in a vast machine; they spoke all languages and could fit in anywhere. They infiltrated every nook and cranny and dominated society. They were taught to be 'all things to all men'. They influenced the Church, the private lives of obscure millions and the decisions of princes. Similarly, no other institution satisfied so brilliantly the Italian craving for spectacle and opulence and for the emotions which only a good show could produce.

What we know as Baroque style was created by the Society's architects, the good fathers who designed the first Jesuit churches in Rome. It was called the 'Jesuit style' when nobody yet remembered syllogisms or deformed pearls. It is still distrusted and disliked by Protestants and northern Catholics, because it reeks too much of the Mediterranean. The Jesuit churches were designed to envelop the faithful in a dreamlike atmosphere, an intoxicating feast of *son et lumière* and fragrant incense fumes. Never had ornaments been so sumptuous, or marble of all colours, gold and silver been so lavishly employed. Baroque make-believe reached unprecedented heights: marbles were cut on soft folds to imitate velvet or damask, plaster was painted to imitate marble, and not all the gold was gold.

Was the very essence of Baroque style not its perpetual effort to delude and delight? Croce called it *'la ricerca dell'inaspettato e dello stupefacente,'* 'the search for the unexpected and the stupefying'. *'E del poeta il fin la meriviglia,'* 'It is the poet's aim to astonish the crowd', wrote the greatest poet of the times, who used words as deceptively and decoratively as the architects used marbles, Giovanbattista Marino. The Jesuit churches rang with entrancingly sweet music, and their pulpits with studied eloquence, the like of which had never been heard before, a revolutionary departure from the dreary and scholastic rebukes of other priests, an ornate and honeyed eloquence which stirred the faithful with ineffable sentiments. The Jesuits' churches were crowded when many others were empty.

In the confessional their advice was eagerly sought in all kinds of complex difficulties. They soon became the fashionable professors of the art of directing souls. 'Their purpose is not that of corrupting morals,' admits one of their most implacable opponents, Blaise Pascal. 'This is not their plan. But they do not have as sole aim that of reforming them. This would be bad politics.' They elaborated an elastic yardstick, casuistry, to measure the moral value of human actions, by which they were able to reassure, guide, persuade sinners without frightening them. 'Thus,' Pascal bitterly commented, 'they preserve all their friends and defend themselves against all their enemies.' And Fra Paolo Sarpi, who also hated the Society, wrote in one of his letters: 'The Jesuits have so many loopholes for escape, pretexts, colours of insinuation, that they are more changeful than the sophists, and, when one thinks to have caught them between thumb and finger, they wriggle out and vanish.'

There is no doubt, however, in the mind of their severest opponents and critics, that the fathers themselves allowed no casuistry to mar their own conduct. They led saintly lives. No breath of personal scandal ever touched them. At a time when most of the clergy had sunk into a moral and intellectual slough, the fathers won respect for themselves and for priests in general by their own modesty, dedication, scholarship, earnestness and the unimpeachable purity of their lives. Casuistry was only for the common people.

Pascal was right in a way. They firmly believed they were the only ones who could save the Church from disaster. They saw themselves as a body of soldiers facing overwhelming enemy forces. The comparison goes back to the military mind of the founder. The very name he gave his order, *Compagnia*, was that of the bands of soldiers following a *condottiere*. He said that the ancient monastic communities were the infantry of the Church, whose duty was to stand firm, while the Jesuits were its light horse, capable of moving swiftly and manœuvring. Like all light horse (like William T. Sherman's column, commandos, the *bersaglieri*), they were to penetrate deep behind enemy lines, explore, reconnoitre, gather information, capture hostages and prisoners, do as much damage as they could, and carry out whatever job presented itself with whatever means were available.

Ignatius' military mind also realized the unique strategic value of Italy. He knew that the decisive battles for the salvation of the Church, like most terrestrial battles for European supremacy, were to be fought south of the Alps. Elsewhere the Church could gain influence, power or authority: in Italy it could be saved or lost forever. Therefore he diligently concentrated most of his good men and his best efforts in Italy, and established his headquarters in Rome. The Society devised weapons and tactics for the particular job on hand, and adapted its approach to the local environment. It invented ingenious ways to edify, amuse, instruct, frighten, beguile and dominate Italians as it found them. It created schools everywhere, the best schools of the age, free schools for poor but clever children, expensive schools for the well-born, manned by competent scholars, so that the ruling élite of the following generation would have a Jesuit background; but, at the same time, spread culture and erudition. It made use of many Italian corrupt proclivities, but also employed the Italians' abundant intelligence, artistic talents, religious feeling, and pride in their Church.

The Society succeeded fully. Within a few years, it practically conquered the people's soul and controlled Italian society. While it never lost its stern Spanish character, it appeared so Italian to foreigners, so much the typical expression of the times and the place, that it had to face much opposition. The hostility it provoked abroad was greatly increased by the older hostility Italians had always aroused. And, vice versa, the Society made the life of the Italians more difficult, because the suspicion that had surrounded them for centuries was aggravated by the current belief that they had become the disciples of the Jesuits.

*

There are Italian writers, who, filially anxious to find outside causes for their country's many catastrophes, believe that the long Spanish domination in southern Italy and Milan, and their influence everywhere, are the origin of some of our apparently incurable ills. There is some truth in this. The Spanish, for instance, entertained a feudal contempt for useful and productive occupations. We still see, all over the south, that men of rank today consider doing nothing a sign of distinction, and idleness a status symbol. They are known as *galantuomini*. They may live on miserable pensions, or the trifling income from a few fields of broad-beans which they let: they may be definitely poorer than the baker, the owner of the petrol station or the store-keeper; but they wear a collar, a tie, a coat, a hat; they carry a cane; sit on the wicker chairs of the club on the pavement of the main street to watch people go by; they talk politics and read newspapers. They treat common people with disdain. No trade or business sullies their hands. A *galantuomo* does not go to court to defend his honour. Like a Spanish *hidalgo* he takes the law into his own hands.

As the government apparatus has been run mostly by southerners, generally coming from the *galantuomini* class, these Baroque prejudices have more or less permeated all official Italy in the last one hundred years. Common people are treated with contempt in all government offices. Taxes are as a rule still like those imposed by Spanish viceroys, haphazard, arbitrary and crushing for everybody, but especially punitive for those who show enterprise and produce things. Most officials and politicians believe that economic life is an evil which should be strictly controlled by the authorities, like a treacherous river, and the more it is regulated the better for everybody. Many of these people still dream of an orderly State in which the king owns practically everything, holds monopolies of all principal products, assures a miserable livelihood for everybody, but distributes particularly ample bounties to his friends. Often, nowadays, this Spanish Baroque dream is fashionably hidden behind Marxist formulas: the king is the Socialist or Communist state and the king's friends are the party apparatus.

The idle *galantuomini* (and, to a lesser extent, most other Italians) still like pompous titles and all sorts of honorary attributes. This foible too is definitely a Spanish importation. The oldest of all Italian nobility had no titles whatever: the Venetian aristocrats, some of whose illustrious families went back to the decline of the Roman Empire, were simply known as *Nobil Uomini*, or noble men. It was only after the Austrians annexed Venice in 1815, that they were awarded the title of counts, to give them a proper place at court. The patricians of the Republic of Genoa were officially allowed to call themselves *marchesi* only when travelling in Spain, England and France, where such things were important. The old kingdom of Naples, on the other hand, swarmed with titles. The President of the Dijon parliament, the severe Charles de Brosses, noted in 1740: 'The populace is rebellious in Naples, the bourgeoisie vain, the high nobility ostentatious, and the lower nobility greedy of titles. . . . Titles have been given to anyone who wanted one and this has given rise to the common saying: "*E' veramente duca ma non cavaliere*" (or "He is really a duke but not a gentleman"). The butcher who used to serve us personally before now serves us only through his helpers, since he has been made a duke.'

Titles wear out in the course of time, and lose value like coins. Nowadays the simplest man anywhere in Italy would consider it only natural to be called *dottore*, whether he ever went to the university or not; to be addressed as a mere lord, or *signore*, a title also introduced by the Spaniards, is practically offensive. A lowly Member of Parliament, like the author of this book, is addressed as *Onorevole* not only in his official capacity, in the Chamber of Deputies, but also by waiters and car-park attendants. The very form of address, the third person singular, which embarrasses most people learning the language, is also a Spanish left-over. It is a conventional way of talking not directly to a man but to his aura, so to speak, to a shadowy person, *la sua signoria*, his lordship. *Signoria* being feminine requires all adjectives and pronouns in the feminine gender, even in the case of males, thus engendering suspicions and confusions in foreigners. '*Come sta lei?*' for instance, usually rendered as 'How are you?', literally means 'How is she?' or 'How does this other and invisible female person fare?' With this desire for titles and empty honours went the Spanish Baroque passion for personal exhibition, ornamentation and affectation, which is still common. As a great Baroque poet, Battista Guarini (a northerner from Ferrara), complained: 'Ours is an age of appearances and one goes masquerading all the year.'

There is no doubt that some of these Spanish traits retarded or prevented progress: the disregard or contempt for the economic facts of life, the preoccupation with non-essentials and with the outward aspect of all things, the hope of bettering one's conditions not through one's efforts but through the favour of the mighty, the belief that the king (or whoever takes the king's place) must take care of all. Is it really the Spaniards' fault that these habits lingered so long after they had left? Why is it that none of the great Spanish virtues took root? And why should the Spanish domination have left such indelible traces in Italy, and more particularly in the old Kingdom of the Two Sicilies, when it made practically no mark in other European provinces ruled from Madrid at the same time? Why, to quote one example, are the Flemish and the Dutch so enterprising, modest in their appearance, industrious and thrifty? Why do most Milanese rely on their own initiative, are proud to be their own masters, and favour, as a rule, an untrammelled economy?

Obviously it is difficult to draw simple conclusions. There is no doubt that the Spanish and the Church helped shape the Italian national character during the Baroque era. There is no doubt, either, that the bent it received at the time was irremediable. But the Spanish and the Church inevitably encouraged only the characteristics which were more congenial to the Italians themselves, probably the traits the people would have developed anyway. The Spanish and the Church were not arbitrary inventions of a demigod. It was the Italians' defeat, or the fact that they could not govern themselves and satisfy the first elementary necessity of a self-respecting people, that of keeping foreign enemies out, which had created a power vacuum. The Spanish were sucked into it. The Church was not an alien machination forcing an alien way of life on a reluctant people. We now know that no domination will last and be effective if it is imposed by force alone. It must be accepted by some of the people, at least, as the genuine expression of their hopes and illusions. The Church went about its sacred, eternal and universal mission with Italian prudence, *savoir faire,* and intelligence. It was manned by Italians. It could not help embodying also some Italian ideals. It would not have had its success otherwise. The will of the people also determined the intensity and depth of the political and moral domination. The Spanish viceroys, and the local quislings, after all, were as overbearing and greedy as the Italians allowed them to be. The Church was all-pervading because it had to shoulder responsibilities which the Italians had thrust upon it. There is no final answer to the problem.

Conclusion

THE Baroque Era might have perplexed men of an earlier generation. It has unfortunately few secrets for us. We know regimentation when we see it: the suffocating oppression of economic control, the compulsion of the affluent mass society, the paralysing embrace of paternalism, the degrading influence of bloody and stupid totalitarian régimes. We now smile at what were once considered horrifying rigours. The old governments look relatively mild and ineffective to us compared to modern models; the *grands seigneurs* were rarely capable of really ignoble deeds on a vast scale; even the worst of kings wanted to be called magnanimous by posterity; man in most countries might have been defenceless before his sovereign, but the laws had man-sized holes in them, the police had no machine-guns, radio, telephone and telephone-tapping equipment. They did torture people, but we doubt if the techniques of which they were so proud were half as good as those perfected by our contemporaries. Baroque oppression, however, looked redoubtable in its day. It was new. It was frightening and stifling. And men behaved all over Europe as we have seen them behave with our own eyes, as they do in all ages in similar circumstances.

Oppressive regimentation does not come unwanted and undeserved, like floods and pestilences. Its establishment is always facilitated, sometimes provoked and often welcomed by its beneficiaries or victims after periods of anarchy and troubles. Without it, men devour each other, trade and industry decline, life itself comes to a stop. It affords familiar advantages. It imposes a truce of sorts, makes trains run on time, gives the illusion that business can go on during political alterations, keeps the lower classes in their place. Its order looks like order but it is often but a *trompe-l'oeil*. It is a smooth-polished surface covering multicoloured reality, a slab of clear glass over the stormy surface of the sea. Deep problems remain unsolved and some become gangrenous. At the end they usually provoke a catastrophe.

Oppressive regimentation begins inconspicuously with the imposition of restrictions almost everybody gladly recognizes as necessary and overdue. It proceeds with the imposition of a set of approved ideas and uniform standards of behaviour. Unless checked in time, it ends up by controlling everything. Controls are at first visible and external. Soon they grow inside men, as invisible and pernicious as cancer. Many people persuade themselves that they do what they do of their own free will, that they are living in the best of all possible worlds. Everything is decided by an Olympus of revered supermen, or by one omniscient and omnipotent supreme person. What could be better? A man learns to be grateful for every largesse or concession from above. He learns to love and admire his masters. He believes the current slogans because so many of them, after all, reflect his own prejudices. He forgets himself in the mass-spectacles and the stirring ceremonies. He is proud of serving superior purposes and obeying an historical mission. He must be careful, of course. He must keep his mouth shut. He must never do anything unusual. He must accept hypocrisy and deceit as wise rules of behaviour and teach his children the use of flattery, ambiguity, evasion and duplicity. After all, his main business is to survive. But there are men who know or vaguely feel at times that they are prisoners in an ornate concentration camp. As only a few are capable of horrifying cruelties and abject cowardice, only a few are capable of selfless abnegation and heroism. Most of the discontented, however, secretly long for the lost age of Saturn, avoid the most unpleasant spots, try to find evasions and consolations.

On the surface, Italians submitted to Baroque regimentation more easily and eagerly than other people, in order to receive benefices from above, to be entertained and dazzled. They heartily took part in the public spectacles and the private little shows. They skilfully employed flattery, ambiguity, evasion. They also had no choice. Revolt was impossible. Who could ever hope to weld all the little Italian states together in order to forge one instrument to chase out the foreigners? It was unthinkable.

Being realists, they recognized the fact that somebody had to be in command, and it was not a bad arrangement to allow foreigners and quislings to do this unpleasant job, exact taxes, levy troops, and attract the hatred of the governed. Laws were indispensable. They made life not only possible but also enjoyable. They were in a way like the hedges in a steeple-chase course. How could the clever men take the lead and win if there were no obstacles to keep the weaker men behind? How could one circumvent laws if there were none?

Under the surface the Italians invented ways to defeat oppressive regimentation. As they could not protect their national liberty in the field of battle, they fought strenuously to defend the liberty of the individual and his family, the only liberty they understood anyway. This necessity honed the single man's private virtues to an edge unsurpassed anywhere else. As Vittorio Alfieri boastfully wrote (and Stendhal and Garibaldi after him, using his very own words): 'The plant man grows in Italy second to none.' Single men, in the heart of their families, developed superior qualities. Added together, millions of them, they always amounted to no more than a weak, gullible and foolish mob. In peace-time, many achieved world fame in their fields. In war-time, many became invincible heroes, like the knights who defeated the French at Barletta, or the naval officers and sailors who, during the last war, penetrated the harbour of Alexandria underwater at night to torpedo British warships at their moorings. But the Italian nation never managed to solve its elementary problems and the Italian armed forces rarely succeeded in defeating their enemies. Italy has never been as good as the sum of all her people.

The people not only defeated their rulers but also managed to invent splendid and melodramatic ways of making each humble or ignoble hour as bearable and satisfying as possible. This is the reason why their manners, food, houses, cities, love-life are so delightful. This is also why their art, or most of it, is principally designed to give the public oblivion and bliss. They have naturally been accused of being frivolous and never going beneath the brilliant surface of things. The reproach is justified, of course. But they are not frivolous because they cannot be anything else. Many great artists left private documents showing they were deeply tormented by the tragedy of their life. Italian literature is filled with anguished cries. Dante bitterly railed: 'Ah, slave Italy, the abode of sorrow, ship without a pilot in a tempest, not the ruler of domains but a brothel!' Petrarch saw her covered with sores no words could cure but only deeds: 'Valour will take up arms again and let the fighting be short as the ancient courage is not dead in Italian hearts!' Leopardi saw ruins and mementoes of past glories about him but not 'the laurel crowns of heroes and the steel weapons' which were to make a coutry free. And Filicaja found reasons for weeping in Italy's 'fatal gift of beauty', which attracted foreigners' appetites. Even the Popes sometimes raged against the conquerors from across the Alps. *'Fuori i barbari!'* was the battle cry of Julius II.

The reason why so many great or near-great Italian artists turned themselves into superior decorators and entertainers is that, *faute de mieux*, in the absence of any possibility of solving the national problem, they thought it was their moral duty to assuage their countrymen's suffering and to make them forget their unhappy and indecorous fate.

Italians were also accused of not having a sufficient respect for truth. Of course few people have a real respect for truth. The Italians are not alone. And yet they know truth when they see it. They are no fools. Each of them tries to steer his private boat by the light of truth, because anything else would be disastrous. But collectively they seem sometimes to forget truth's unique importance. They often ignore it, embellish it, embroider around it, deny it, as the case may be. They lie to please, to round off a picture, to provoke an emotion, to prove a point. Above all, they consider lying about their unfortunate country a sacred duty, as justified morally as the humane inventions one tells a dying man, to delude him and his relatives. This is another reason why the single Italian is almost always wise while his country, directed on the basis of flattering distortions and exaggerations, has fatally made so many disastrous mistakes down the centuries.

*

That Italians have been living in the Baroque age for the last four centuries can be proved by a cursory examination of all their régimes of the recent past. The eighteenth-century monarchies swept away by Napoleon, the united kingdom established after the Risorgimento, the veiled dictatorships of liberal statesmen at the end of the last century and the beginning of this one, the Fascist un-concealed dictatorship, and the Socialist and Catholic combinations ruling today are all specimens of pure Baroque. The names and the official rhetoric change. The recipe is always the same.

This is the formula. It was good in the past and it will probably be good enough for many years to come. Take a vast, hard-working, pliable, ingenious population, worried about its daily bread, capable at times of accepting untold sacrifices, but restless and anxious for novelties. Keep the people ignorant by providing the minimum amount of schools. Keep them in want by regimenting with an iron hand or persecuting industry and trade. Keep them be-wildered and insecure by the arbitrary manipulation of vaguely worded laws. See that there never are clearly defined rights and duties, but always favours from above or abuses of power. Keep the people happy with a steady rain of miserable alms, distracted with many holidays, more holidays than any other nation in Europe, feasts, the in-auguration of splendidly decorated and sometimes useful public works. Spend most of the money on superfluous things, the armed forces and insensate wars in the past, and now on entertainments, public spectacles, games; spend as little as possible on improviing the people's moral and physical conditions. Keep them always drunk with stirring appeals to their more primitive emotions.

Then take a small oligarchy of leaders, eternally squab-bling among themselves, frightened for their position and, often enough, for their life, whose power depends pre-cariously on the favour of a few or of one man, sometimes even a foreign chief, residing abroad. Put these leaders above the law. This tends to make the best of them wary, pitiless, overbearing, unscrupulous and avaricious. In the old days such men were courtiers, landowning aristocrats, high dignitaries and generals; later they were also bankers, shipowners, industrialists; yesterday they were Fascist chieftains. Today they are the heads of mass parties, exponents of organizations turning out millions of votes, controllers of industrial empires privately- or State-owned and trades union chiefs. The *grands seigneurs* of old had better taste, were braver, more polite, and carried themselves with greater dignity; the liberal patriots of the nineteenth century often loved their country, encouraged industry and trade, and tried at times to do something to better the people's living conditions; today's leaders are more intelligent, efficient and have studied more. But such differences are as unimportant as the fashions of the clothes they wore.

When one forgets superficial variations, one can see that the Italian leaders of today behave more or less as their predecessors have always behaved. They manage Italy as if it were *cosa nostra;* carry out vast, ambitious, impressive political designs, which are described as essential to the welfare of the country but are brutally and transparently conceived mainly to reinforce their own power. They use the people as if they were extras on a Graeco-Roman film set, to be moved by remote control, to whom nobody explains the plot. Anything else would be unthinkable. To persuade their countrymen to cultivate the arts of reading and writing, to allow them to gain and enjoy a moderate prosperity, to encourage as many as possible to become soberly responsible would endanger the hold of the élite, or, as the élite prefers to say, weaken the social structure. There is, however, this to be said in the leaders' defence. They are the product of their society. The *grands seigneurs* of old as well as the contemporary cabinet ministers or controllers of State monopolies share the qualities and defects of the people, nourish the same ideals. They are, in fact, what the Italians make them.

It was always obvious to clear-thinking Italians that their country was the unfortunate victim of a vicious circle: the national character fatally generated tyrannies, tyrannies strengthened and exasperated the defects of the national character and inevitably led the country to catastrophe. If Italy was to be saved one day from her disgraceful destiny, the vicious circle had to be smashed. Patriots agreed from the earliest times that only the conquest of independence, the establishment of a national unified state (or a close confederation of Italian states), and the acceptance by the people of their civic and military duties would in the end regenerate the country. All this, however, could not be gained by luck or imposed by external agents, with little Italian collaboration, otherwise its results would be ephemeral at best, the usual dazzling show, one more spectacle behind which the old reality would have persisted practically unchanged.

All this had to be done the hard way. It had to come about through a spontaneous process of Italian history, provoked by a slow rising tide of popular indignation, and was to be purchased by blood, in victorious wars or revolts. Italian political thinkers, of course, knew that successful revolutions and victorious wars were not desirable *per se*. They were merely the ultimate proofs of the people's whole-hearted solidarity, of their belief in their common destiny, of their acceptance of a common law and common duties. They were the sign that the individual Italian had abandoned the struggle for his own private welfare and had begun to think in collective terms. But how could the Italians be brought to fight and die for their country? Clearly, if they could be persuaded to do that, there was, after all, no need for them to do so, as they would already be what the best of them hoped they would become.

This, it must be pointed out with solemnity, was in the past and still is today the crux of the Italian problem, of *all* Italian problems, the heart of the matter, the only significance in many apparently meaningless and disorderly intricacies of Italian history. It is the only explanation of many otherwise puzzling aspects of the national behaviour, the question people debated passionately down the centuries and are still debating today in cafés and Parliament, the thorn in the heart of all good Italians of all ages. Why did Italy, a land notoriously teeming with vigorous, wide-awake and intelligent people, always behave so feebly? Why was she invaded, ravaged, sacked, humiliated in every century, and yet failed to do the simple things necessary to defend herself?

The hope of achieving national unity and of conquering independence seemed to thinking Italians a dear but unattainable dream. To begin with the people never seriously felt the need to become one nation. After a survey of his country's history, Guicciardini bitterly admitted: 'This was never an easy country to reduce under one rule.' Even in the days of Imperial Rome, in fact, she successfully resisted being blanketed by uniform laws. When Gaul, Spain, Germany and Britain were, administratively speaking, compact and orderly provinces, she managed somehow to remain a vast mosaic of free cities, partially autonomous regions, rebellious mountain tribes, almost independent peoples with their dialects, gods and customs. Later, during the Middle Ages, unification of sorts could have been brought about any number of times by the Emperors of Germany. They came, in the spring, when the snows melted, to conquer, pillage and try to weld the mutable populations into a manageable system of feudal fiefs. The Germans were occasionally repulsed in bloody battles, and, when this was not possible, flattered by treacherous negotiations, deceived by fragile and ambiguous treaties, betrayed or corrupted. The results of their many military successes were inevitably short-lived. Most conquered cities put up a good show of loyalty as long as the imperial forces were around, but reverted to their customary seditiousness as soon as they turned their backs.

There were many reasons for this. Not only had the Italians always been, as Guicciardini says, generally difficult 'to reduce under one rule', but they also never felt they were a 'new' people, one of those immature and semi-barbaric nations which needed harsh laws and iron discipline in order to maintain a semblance of civilized order when the Roman Empire disappeared. The Italians felt much too old and wise to become imitation northerners. They clung to the decayed remnants of Roman ways, which, like all decayed remnants, were sweet and comfortable enough for them. Neither could they abandon the memory of their past greatness, a memory which was strong even when, in the darkest ages, it was but a dim and fabulous legend. It was not only strong enough to prevent the victory of foreign ideas and institutions, but was also a good substitute for them. The Italians felt themselves sufficiently unified, morally and culturally, anyway, to want political and military unification. They were held together by their language, ruins, arts, literature, habits, ruses, the fame of their great men and the memory of their great saints.

Later still, when other European nations were unified by powerful monarchies, the Italians still struggled to maintain their political divisions. Native princes and dynasties often tried to found unified kingdoms or confederations. The roster is a long one. It starts with Ardoin, Marquis of Ivrea, who almost managed it, and died in 1015; includes Frederick II, King of Sicily and Emperor of Germany, Italian born and educated, the 'wonder of the world'; the Visconti of Milan, the Medici of Florence, and many others. Joachim Murat, King of Naples, tried to conquer the country in 1814, taking advantage of the defeat of his brother-in-law Napoleon. Even an Englishman dabbled with the problem, Lord William Bentinck, His Britannic Majesty's Minister to the exiled court of Naples during the Napoleonic wars, who thought of setting up an independent Italy, after 1815, in opposition to the Austrians and the French. Nobody down the centuries, no prince, revolutionary chief, republic or princely family was ever allowed to become strong enough to congregate all Italians under one flag and one law, until Victor Emmanuel of Savoy, King of Sardinia, became King of Italy, in 1861, with the aid of the French army, Garibaldi's volunteers, and republican revolutionaries.

The Popes, of course, were at all times among the most powerful and influential Italian princes. The Church was at all times the most vigorous and lively of Italian institutions. All Italians whole-heartedly belonged to it and served it. A Pope could presumably have unified the country without many difficulties. Why did this never happen? The Church was the people's traditional ally against the Empire. It led coalitions against the northern invaders, time and again. But the people were never durably grateful for the help received. They were never the Church's partisans for long. They became Guelphs for no longer than the situation required and as long as it suited them, turned Ghibellines as soon as the Church's political supremacy became threatening, and went back to being Guelphs when the Germans came once again over the Alps. In fact, Italians fought to prevent either of the two great rival institutions gaining the upper hand. The people considered their country with equal pride both the Garden of the Empire and the Throne of God on Earth, but not one of these things exclusively for all times.

It must be admitted that these unconscious patterns of behaviour are still valid today. As Italy is now indirectly being governed by the Church, through the Christian Democrat Party, a growing number of Italians instinctively join the party which can be considered the contemporary equivalent of the Ghibellines, a powerful organization sustained by an alien power which is hostile to the Vatican and the temporal influence of priests in Italian and world affairs. Should the Communists eventually gain the upper hand some day, any student of Italian history knows what will happen. The people will, secretly or openly, as the case may be, go to swell the Church's organizations in ever-increasing numbers, daring persecution and death if necessary, in order to fight what they consider an alien and hateful tyranny.

Machiavelli had not quite understood this pendular mechanism of Italian history. He thought the national ills had all been caused solely by the Church. This is what he wrote in a famous passage:

'No province was ever united and prosperous unless it was under the sway of one republic or one monarch, as is the case of France and Spain. And the reason why Italy is not in this condition is none other than the Church, for the Church has never had the vigour to extend its sway over the whole country. . . . Nor, on the other hand, has it been so feeble as not to be able, when afraid of losing its temporal power, to call in a foreign potentate, as counterpoise in its defence against those powers which threatened to become supreme. The Church has kept us under sundry lords and princes. These have caused so much discord and debility that Italy has become the prey not only of powerful barbarians but also of every assailant.'

This over-simple thesis is important because it is still held by many good Italians, who cannot easily admit that the people could, at any time, if they had wanted to, have won their independence and liberty against both foreign powers and the Church. It is comforting to think that priestly intrigues were too strong for any spontaneous movement to arise and develop. And yet the thesis is not wholly wrong, not wrong all the time. The Church's power was always strong, not because the Popes were great statesmen, the Curia a farseeing body, and the Italians frightened of religious sanctions, but because the Italians never really wanted to become the actors of their own history, the arbiters of their destiny, and used the Church (as they used the Empire at different times) to prevent unification or, when unification was achieved, to undermine and weaken it.

This is illustrated by what happened in the last century and a half. It took three generations of patriots, thinkers, dreamers, soldiers, poets, musicians, statesmen, revolutionaries, and adventurers to achieve unity in 1861. And yet, in spite of the great number of people who contributed to it, it was not won by the Italians as a whole. No rising tide of popular indignation animated the movement. The people believing in the Risorgimento, or the rebirth of their country, were the liberal and progressive minorities of the aristocracy and the enlightened bourgeoisie. The great masses, the majority of the élite and the peasants, watched the events with scepticism and diffidence. As a result the national state, the new Kingdom of Italy, was a fragile and unsafe structure. The *liberali* managed to maintain themselves in power by means of subterfuges, the same subterfuges and police methods the foreign oppressors or the small and weak princes had employed before them. They were forced at all times to stir up strong patriotic emotions, to keep the people in a frenzy, as all feeble governments do, by spending a lot of money on the armed forces and waging disastrous wars. They exhausted most of their energies mainly trying to put up a show as Italy the great world power.

The Kingdom was undermined by the alliance of the popular classes with the Church, the incredulity of the majority of citizens, and the national character. It struggled for decades, trying to educate an élite, improve the state administration, encourage commerce and industry. Its achievements were many, some were unique and admirable. But it never really solved fundamental problems. Its highest moment came in November 1918, when the army triumphed over their broken-down and dispirited Austrian and Hungarian enemies. But the effort had been too much for such a brittle and recent country. The unified state practically collapsed. The Fascist dictatorship was a police superstructure which postponed the ruin of the new Italy and propped it up as wooden beams support a crumbling wall. The moment of truth came in 1945 with the defeat in the last war. With the allies' invasion, the Italians understood that what they had believed to be the final solution of their century-old problems, the regeneration of the country and the people, the formation of a modern nation, had been but a heart-rending Baroque structure, which had cost the lives of millions, had wasted a precious part of the available resources, and had deluded for a century the best Italians. At the end, Italy was left without illusions to contemplate herself as she had always been. Anarchy prevailed, the Italian anarchy of all times, sweet anarchy at times, invisibly and spontaneously regulated by secret rules and customs, always mitigated by scepticism, forbearance, indulgence for man's foibles. It is often pleasant, definitely more satisfactory, in the short run, than the rigid rule of law, but the cause, in the long run, of untold suffering, humiliations, injustice, and outrages.

Foreign visitors are fascinated. They are won over, as they have always been, by the 'charm of Italy'. Italian life is gay, effervescent, intoxicating. The *dolce vita* looks now more *dolce* than it ever was. Very few travellers see the ugliness underneath, the humiliation, the suffering. Not one in a hundred perceives the fundamental dreariness of everything under the glittering ormolu, the bitter fate of men who are condemned perennially to amuse themselves and the world, to hide their innermost feelings, to be *simpatici* at all costs in order to make a living. What do they know of the peculiar feeling of frustration and resigned discontent which paralyses the best Italians? One of Ignazio Silone's characters describes it: 'There is a sadness, a subtle sadness that's not to be mistaken for the more ordinary kind that is the result of remorse, disillusionment or suffering; there is an intimate sadness which comes to chosen souls simply from their consciousness of man's fate. . . . This sort of sadness has always prevailed among intelligent Italians, but most of them, to evade suicide or madness, have taken to every known means of escape: they feign exaggerated gaiety, awkwardness, a passion for women, for food, for their country, and, above all, for fine-sounding words; they become, as chance may have it, policemen, monks, terrorists, war heroes. I think that there has never been a race of men so fundamentally desolate and desperate as these gay Italians.'

It is not surprising that few foreigners see these things when only a tiny minority of the natives are aware of them. Foreigners are delighted also because they always find themselves, without knowing it, in a favoured position. The Italian social structure can be compared to the olive tree, that most Italian of all trees, which looks entirely different when seen from above from what it looks when seen from below. The leaves are glossy dark-green on top and powdery grey underneath. The faces of the Italians look flattering, smiling, and kindly from above but overbearing, insolent, pitiless from below. Foreigners are automatically promoted to be honorary members of the ruling class. They occupy a position of vantage. Theirs is the bird's-eye view of the olive tree.

The illusion Italy creates is a relief. Countries which believe in discipline, the meticulous administration of justice, the cultivation of unbending moral virtues, universal education, the conquest of military glory and the diligent accumulation, distribution and administration of wealth, whether they really achieve their ideals or merely pay respect to them, can be worthy of esteem but are seldom amusing. Even those countries which pursue the ideal of liberty can be stifling and oppressive, for liberty is after all assured only by the impartial enforcement of the law. The Italian way of life down the centuries attracted people who wanted to take a holiday from their national virtues. In the heart of every man, wherever he is born, whatever his education and tastes, there is one small corner which is Italian, the part which finds regimentation irksome, the dangers of war frightening, strict morality stifling, that part which loves frivolous and entertaining art, admires larger-than-life-size solitary heroes, and dreams of an impossible liberation from the strictures of a tidy existence.

The consolations which Italy afforded at all times have become infinitely more precious today than they ever were. The Western world is deeply uneasy. It is coming to doubt the utility and sanctity of some of its traditional virtues, those on which it based its moral tranquillity and its self-respect. The bourgeois' industry and thrift are considered more and more injurious to society; the soldier's undaunted heroism is no longer required; unbridled patriotism has led men and nations to tragic mistakes; morality has lost some of its shining certainty; laws have become fluid; nobody really knows any more whether one truth exists. The era of powerful nations, proud of their racial superiority, masters of their own destinies, is at an end. Everybody's life is governed by the decisions of distant and practically unknown men, as powerful and out of reach as Charles V seemed to the Italians in the sixteenth century, who can make us rich or poor, can make us live or can kill all of us in our beds while we sleep. The regimentation of an industrial mass society is becoming more and more stifling. Men are kept working like galley slaves of old by their desire to conquer more and more garish material possessions. They are fed ready-made ideas, they are supplied with art approved by the authorities, entertained by the same shows, dazzled by the same ceremonies, stirred by the same slogans, moved by the same collective emotions. Modern men get lost in a maze of larger and larger anonymous organizations. Loneliness and tedium envelop each of them whenever he can get out of the uproar long enough to think about himself.

The art of living, this disreputable art developed by the Italians to defeat regimentation, is now becoming an invaluable guide for survival for many people. *La dolce vita* is spreading to countries which despised it and feared it, or coming to the surface in countries which liked to think it did not exist. Tax-payers are trying to avoid their sacred duty everywhere. The little pleasures of life have acquired a new importance, food, wines, a day in the sun, a pretty girl, the defeat of a rival, good music. Naturally more and more people flock to Italy every year. Most of them do not exactly know why. They think it is a wonderful place for a holiday. They are attracted by the pleasant sensation of peace, the lightness in their hearts. In reality they are drawn to the place where new perplexing problems of the contemporary world are familiar monsters, problems with which the natives learned to live long ago. Other Western men are newcomers in the New Baroque age. Many are still reluctant, incredulous and unprepared newcomers, who cling to the old approved ways of doing things and are perpetually surprised to discover that they no longer have the same power to attain results. The Italians have invented ancient ruses to defeat boredom and discipline, to forget disgrace and misfortune, to lull man's *angst* to sleep and comfort him in his solitude. They still remember the age of Saturn, and reconstruct it longingly in a perennial Saturnalia. They do not make the mistakes some eager foreigners make, who rush blindly into new paths and accept indiscriminately all corrupt and cynical solutions. The Italians know the relative utility of all the tricks, know which ones are dangerous and which are deceptive. They know where to stop. In a minor way, Italy has perhaps become once again a teacher of nations.

*

The Italian way of life cannot be considered a success except by temporary visitors. It solves no problems. It makes them worse. It would be a success of sorts if at least it made Italians happy. It does not. Its effects are costly, flimsy and short-range. The people enjoy its temporary advantages, to be sure, without which they could not endure life, but are constantly tormented by discontent. They rage against their fate today as they have always done. They have been on the verge of revolution for the last one hundred and sixty odd years, against kings, foreign dominations, the Church, disunity, landowners, capitalists, centralization in turn. All these, of course, at one time or another contributed something to the national ills. Politicians eternally tinker with laws and institutions. But the fundamental cause escapes everybody. It is the Italian way of life which makes all laws and institutions function defectively. It is the illusion of a solution, lotus-eating, the resigned acceptance of the very evils man has tried to defeat, the art of decorating, ennobling them, calling them by different names and living with them.

Conclusion

The unsolved problems pile up and inevitably produce catastrophes at regular intervals. The Italians always see the next one approaching with a clear eye, but, like sleepers in a nightmare, cannot do anything to ward it off. They can only play their amusing games, try to secure their families against the coming storm, and delude themselves for a time. They console themselves with the thought that, when the smoke clears, Italy can rise again like a phoenix from its ashes. Has she not always done so? The tenacity and the eagerness with which the individual pursues his private interests and defends himself from society, his mistrust of noble ideals and motives, the splendid show, the all-pervading indulgence for man's foibles make Italian life pleasant and bearable in spite of poverty, tyranny and injustice. They also waste the efforts and the sacrifices of the best Italians and make poverty, tyranny and injustice very difficult to defeat.

INDEX

354

Index

Borromeo, Saint Charles, 204, 316, 320

Borromeo, Count Giovanni, 214

Borromeo, Countess Giulia Sanseverino, 214

Borromini, Francesco, 205, 318

Boston, 55

Boswell, James, 30

Botticelli, Sandro, 6-7

Bourbon, Constable of, 305

Boxer Rising, 303

Bragadin, Admiral, xin.

Brenner Pass, 161

Bresci (assassin), 114

Brescia, 91

Briçonnet, Cardinal, 293

Brolio, 216-17

Brosses, Charles de, 335

Browning, Elizabeth Barrett, 9

Browning, Robert, 9

Bruno, Giordano, xiii, 327

Bukharin, N. I., 115

Bülow, Prince von, 101

Buoncampagno, Giacomo, 204

Burgos, 187

Burgundy, 304

Byron, Lord, 9, 39-40, 43-4, 138, 215

Cabala, The (Wilder), 239

Cabot, John and Sebastian, xin.

Caesar, Julius, 31, 123

Cagliostro, Count Alessandro di, xin., 96, 98-104

Calabria, 327

Calcagnini, Clelio, 328

Campagna, 30, 204

Campanella, Tomaso, xin., xii

Canino, 205

Cannae, plains of, 30-1

Caporetto, xiii

Capponi, Piero, 292

Capri, 9, 11, 31, 52, 178

Capulet family, 228

Carabinieri, 224-5

Caracci family, 317

Caracciolo, Prince Francesco, xin.

Carafa, Don Fabrizio, Duke of Andria, 214

Caravaggio, Michelangelo de, xin., 317

Carnesecchi, Pietro, 327

Caroline (Bonaparte), Queen of Naples, 206

Casanova, Giacomo, xin., 96-8, 103-4

Casati, Countess Teresa Confalonieri, 211

Casatico, 86

Cassian way, 16, 30

Castelfidardo, 245

Castiglione, Baldassar, 86-7

Catania, 62, 264, 274, 282

Catarina da Siena, Saint, xin.

Catherine, Queen of Westphalia, 206

Catholic Action, 230, 342

Cavour, Count, xin., 239, 252

Cellini, Benvenuto, xin., 305, 317

Cerceau, Abbé Jean Antoine de, 138

Cesena, 291

Chaos, 250

Charlemagne, 17, 268, 308

Charles V, Emperor, 27, 168, 288, 351; and sack of Rome, 305, 306-8; crowned at Bologna, 308-9, 311, 317

Charles of Bohemia, 131

Charles VIII of France, and Fornovo, 288-302, 303

Chartreuse de Parme, La (Stendhal), 239

Chateaubriand, Vicomte de, 37-8

Chaucer, Geoffrey, 17, 81

Chesterfield, Lord, 172

Childe Harold (Byron), 138

China, 11, 54, 199, 251, 302, 303

Chitarella, Mgr., 191

Christian Democrat Party, 120, 206, 225, 230, 253, 281, 347

Church, 108, 137, 225, 308; and miracles, 45-6; and sainthood, 46, 47-8; Mussolini's peace with, 150; Guicciardini and, 169; and cult of Madonna, 212-13; influence and power of, 229-30, 314-15, 316-17, 346-8; and Spain, 314-15, 336-7; and Baroque art, 317, 318, 319-21, 325-33, 336-7; and music, 319-20; Machiavelli and, 325, 347; and Inquisition, 327, 329; and Index, 329-30; and Society of Jesus, 330-3

Cicero, 30, 123

Ciociaria, 214

Cisa pass, 295

Clemenceau, Georges, 266

Clement V, Pope, 123

Clement VI, Pope, 125, 131, 133

Clement VII, Pope, 168, 204, 305, 308

Coda di paglia, La (Piovene), 232-3

Code Napoléon, 251

Codice cavalleresco italiano (Gelli), 192-4

Cologne, 20, 55

Colonna family, 124, 126

Colonna, Giovanni, 126

Colonna, Prince Marcantonio, 214

Colonna, Prospero, 323

Colonna, Stefano, 126, 133

Columbus, Christopher, xin., 287

Comiso, 262

Commentaries on the Decades of Livy (Machiavelli), 180

Communism, Communists, 12, 112, 114-15, 116-17, 120, 173, 182, 200, 227, 230, 233, 235, 236, 347

Commynes, Philippe de, 299

Como, Lake, 162

Conjuration de Nicholas, dit de Rienzi (Cerceau), 138

Constantine, Emperor, 130, 132

Constantinople, 289, 293

Contarini, Cardinal Gaspare, 326

Copenhagen, 53, 55

Corberio, Eufrosina, 214-15

Cordoba, Consalvo de, 323

Corinne (De Staël), 53

Correggio, Antonio da, 34

Corriere della Sera, 150

Cortesi, Salvatore, 52

355

Index

357

The Italians

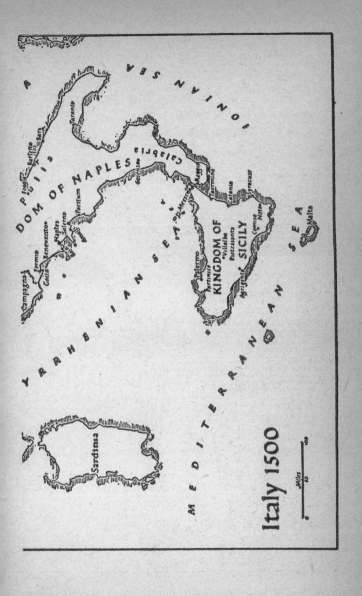

Italy 1500

Miles
0   20   40

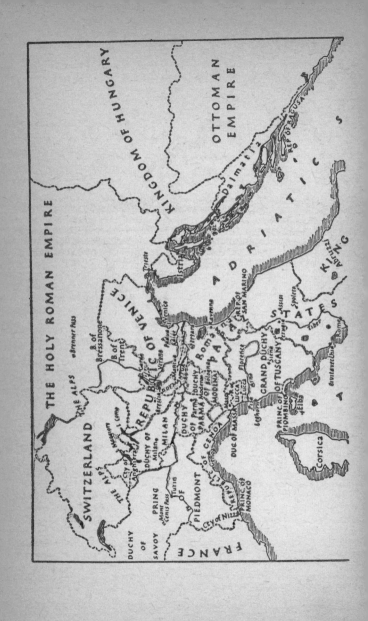

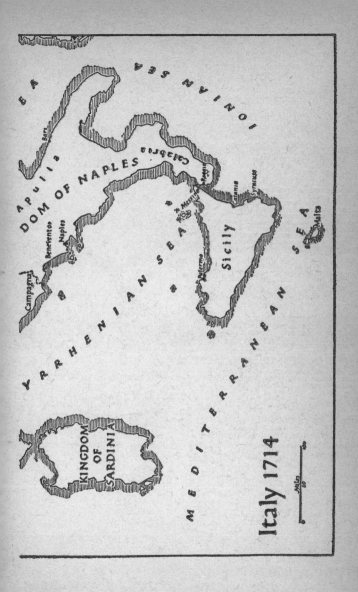

Italy 1714

Italy 1810

Italy Today

Miles
0   50   100